8.95

Introduction to Laser Physics

Introduction to Laser Physics

BELA A. LENGYEL

Professor, San Fernando Valley State College
Northridge, California

JOHN WILEY AND SONS, INC.
New York · London · Sydney

Library of Congress Catalog Card Number: 65–27659
Printed in the United States of America

SECOND PRINTING, JANUARY, 1967

Foreword

The proliferation of laser development and research into so many interest-ing ideas, so many types of lasers and devices, so many piecemeal or even erroneous reports, and so many fascinating papers has made the writing of a comprehensive book both terribly difficult and highly important. We can be grateful that Bela Lengyel has been bold enough to attempt such a book, and that he has succeeded.

There are very likely still striking inventions and developments to come in quantum electronics, or more specifically in coherent amplification of light and its use. However, many of the important ideas in this field are probably now known and the basic processes broadly understood. Furthermore, the field has developed so far that it is becoming increasingly difficult for scientists or engineers to enter it without considerable work toward familiarization with present knowledge. This makes a comprehen-sive and careful treatment especially timely.

A field in the state of roaring adolescence, such as laser research, can most comfortably be treated either by discussing well-known physical principles on which the field depends, or simply by listing all topics and literature that have appeared. The author has not been satisfied with either of these easy extremes, but undertakes the valuable task of selecting the more important publications and ideas, of developing the general theory far enough to apply it clearly in a variety of experimental directions, and of blending basic theory with current findings into a coherent and in-structive view of the whole field.

The engineer, or the scientist who is rather unfamiliar with radiation and spectroscopy, will find here the theoretical bases of lasers discussed simply and clearly, with attention to physical ideas, definitions, and the practical use of theoretical expressions. The treatment is typically carried far enough to interest more advanced students of the field. Careful selec-tions of references at the end of each topic make the text still more useful for those who wish to go deeply into the subject. This volume thus seems likely to be widely useful and to provide for a long time an important tool and stimulus for further exciting laser developments.

Although each active person in the field of quantum electronics will probably have his own selected list of most important topics and preferred emphases which will be a little different from that of anyone else, I believe each will recognize that this book covers a very broad spectrum of the field well, and represents a thoughtful choice of topics to be emphasized. The author has been assiduous in searching out pertinent references and contributions; his good coverage of the Russian literature is especially impressive.

It is probably only now that a comprehensive treatment of lasers which is also full of specific experimental information could be rather detailed and at the same time of lasting value. And only dedication and broad knowledge of the field, such as Professor Lengyel has brought to the effort, could have made it successful.

Cambridge, Mass.　　　　　　　　　　　　　　　　CHARLES H. TOWNES
October 1965

Preface

Unlike most scientific discoveries, lasers received immediate public attention; they stimulated the imagination not only of scientists but of people in many walks of life. Mankind acquired entirely new sources of light whose radiation is vastly superior in precision and intensity to light obtainable from sources known heretofore. Although the new light is not one that we may look at or see by, its remarkable properties open ways for unprecedented scientific, technical, and military applications. The creation, the study, and the application of this type of light draws on knowledge and experience from several fields: classical and quantum physics, chemistry, electronics, and engineering. The field of lasers contains science, art, and technology; the applications of lasers go hand-in-hand with new scientific discoveries. The rapid public recognition of the scientific and practical significance of lasers came to a climax with the award of the 1964 Nobel prize in physics to Townes, Basov, and Prokhorov, who opened the field of quantum electronics ten years earlier by discovering the maser, the ancestor of the laser. Their continued work contributed in large measure to the evolution of lasers, whose possibilities they clearly foresaw.

Laser research gathered momentum at an amazing rate after Maiman succeeded in constructing a laser in 1960. I was a member of the staff of the Hughes Research Laboratories when the first laser was built there, and I was attracted to the tasks of organizing and recording the expansion of this field of knowledge. My first book, *Lasers*, which was prepared in 1962, grew out of this work. At that time no books were available on the subject and the urgent need for an introductory work was strongly felt.

Soon I set to work to prepare a second edition of *Lasers*, with the aim of bringing the book up to date and eliminating the inadequacies caused by the time pressure under which the book was first written and published. Owing to the growth of laser art and my deepening interest in the subject,

vii

by the time I had finished only traces of the original book remained. As in the evolution of species mutations accumulated until gradually a new species came into being, so in my work a time came when the manuscript was so different from *Lasers* that it was misleading to call it by the same name. Not only had the amount of material trebled, but the emphasis had shifted from technical description to the exposition of physical principles. This new emphasis motivated the choice of a new title. The material in this book generally reflects the state of the laser art as it appeared in the literature published before the fall of 1964. In certain special instances advances published in early 1965 were also included.

This book is written for readers with some knowledge of modern atomic physics and electronics. My objective was to keep the book at an introductory level and to carry out the exposition of physical principles in a language not too difficult for graduate students in the physical sciences or engineering, or for advanced undergraduate students in physics and chemistry. This book is not written in the form of a college textbook, although it might be used in an advanced college course. It is intended to prepare the reader for independent study of the current research literature of lasers and for work involving applications of lasers.

The number of references to periodical literature is greater in this book than is usual in introductory books of this size. Their abundance is caused mainly by the fragmentation of laser literature. The reader concerned with the problem of information retrieval may find use for the short section on laser reference material which follows the historical introduction. On the other hand, the expert reader, who deplores the omission of certain valuable articles from the list of references, is reminded that the book is intended as an introduction to laser literature rather than a review of the entire field.

I have kept in mind that the book may be used by readers of rather diverse backgrounds and interests, and have taken special care to define the technical terms and concepts used.

Numerical and technical data are introduced primarily for illustration and orientation, and secondarily for aid to preliminary estimation and computation. The various tables serve this purpose. Their accuracy is limited, although it is entirely adequate not only for engineering purposes, but for the planning and interpretation of relevant physical experiments. These tables are not intended to be used for the critical evaluation of new scientific material.

The following organization is used: first, the physical, or engineering problem is introduced and discussed roughly and qualitatively. This step is followed by the development of the quantitative general relations. Finally, the quantitative physical and technical data and results are presented and related to the analytical results of the second step. Mathematical derivations are included only when they can be stated simply and when their length and complexity do not interrupt the trend of thought significantly. Derivations of standard relations available in advanced college textbooks are not included.

In order to avoid frequent interruptions in the discussion of lasers, the book opens with a chapter containing general background material on radiation and atomic physics. The second chapter contains a brief general description of lasers of various types followed by analytical considerations pertaining to threshold condition, modes of oscillation, and laser linewidth. In the following three chapters solid, liquid, and gas lasers are described in detail. Chapter VI on mode structure, pulsations, and giant pulse, and Chapter VII on nonlinear phenomena round out the discussion of laser physics. Time and space limitations prevent the inclusion of an adequate account of laser applications. Only a "preview" of these is given in Chapter VIII.

An explanation is in order for readers who miss an adequate discussion of applications or the description of the engineering aspects of laser construction and operation. To include all these matters, a book must be about twice the size of this one. With the rapid advances of the entire field, it is difficult enough for a single author to keep a manuscript dealing with laser physics alone up to date. Laser technology and laser applications deserve a separate book written from an industrial vantage point. In any case, I have chosen a more limited goal and have striven to attain it by concentrating my effort on factual accuracy and clarity of presentation.

Northridge, Calif.   BELA A. LENGYEL
September 1965

Acknowledgments

The author of a book is indebted to more people than he can name in a preface of moderate length. This is so because the basic factors that lead to the writing of a book and determine the quality of a book are the author's interest, motivation, knowledge, and skill. These personal attributes and abilities develop through every deep and lasting human contact; parents, teachers, friends, colleagues, wife, and critics make their contributions.

One of my old debts is to Professor Edwin C. Kemble with whom I apprenticed while he was writing his *Fundamental Principles of Quantum Mechanics*. He was my teacher in scientific bookwriting. His lasting influence on my career is gratefully acknowledged.

Numerous colleagues and friends at Hughes Research Laboratories aided me with their explanations, suggestions, and critical comments. Dr. Harvey Winston suggested many valuable improvements in the sections dealing with semiconductor and fluid lasers. Dr. Robert W. Hellwarth contributed the material on linewidth. Dr. Gisella Eckhardt provided material on the Raman effect. Dr. Ira M. Green assisted in the gathering of the data and the preparation of the first three chapters of the manuscript. I thank the management of Hughes Research Laboratories, represented by Dr. George F. Smith and Dr. Harvey Winston, for supporting a large part of this work while I was employed at the Laboratories and for permission to use several illustrations belonging to the company.

Work on this book continued at the San Fernando Valley State College; it was completed in the invigorating climate of Uppsala University. I am greatly indebted to the Director of the Institute of Quantum Chemistry, Professor Per-Olov Löwdin for his constant encouragement and for his steady support of all my scientific work. Several Swedish colleagues made direct contributions: Docent Kjell Bockasten has critically read the chapter on gas lasers and made valuable suggestions concerning all matters pertaining to spectroscopy. The eagle eyes of Fil. lic. Yngve Öhrn caught many minor errors; Mr. Sten Lunell assisted with bibliography, collection of spectroscopic data, and tabulations.

Through correspondence I received valuable information and illustrations from Drs. S. P. S. Porto, W. W. Rigrod, C. L. Tang, W. T. Ham, and W. B. Bridges. Bell Telephone Laboratories and the American Institute of Physics permitted the reproduction of a number of their illustrations. To these colleagues and institutions I express my sincere thanks for sharing their knowledge and their material.

Mrs. Birgit Lengyel not only gracefully endured a preoccupied husband over a long period, but actively participated by drawing many illustrations, typing, correcting, and proofreading.

B. A. L.

Contents

HISTORICAL INTRODUCTION   1

LASER LITERATURE AND BIBLIOGRAPHY   4

I. BACKGROUND MATERIAL ON RADIATION AND
    ATOMIC PHYSICS   8
    1. Light and the General Laws of Radiation   8
    2. Units and Physical Constants   12
    3. Observation and Measurement of Radiation   14
    4. Coherence of Light   23
    5. Emission and Absorption of Radiation by Atoms   29
    6. Interaction of Radiation with Atomic Systems   38

II. GENERAL DESCRIPTION AND THEORY OF LASERS   49
    1. The Laser   49
    2. Threshold Condition and Rate Equations   57
    3. Theory of Oscillation and Radiation Modes   67
    4. Linewidth Problems   83

III. SOLID-STATE LASERS   90
    1. The Ruby Laser of Maiman   90
    2. The Spectroscopy of Ruby   97
    3. Ruby Lasers Operating at Unconventional Frequencies   101
    4. Concentration of the Exciting Radiation   103
    5. Continuously Operating Ruby Lasers   109
    6. Four-Level Solid Lasers   112

xiii

       7. Semiconductor Lasers   136
       8. Phonon-Terminated Lasers   158

IV. FLUID-STATE LASERS   **161**
       1. Exploration of Liquids as Laser Materials   161

V.   GAS LASERS   **168**
       1. Negative Absorption of Optical Radiation in Gases:
          Qualitative Discussion   168
       2. Spectroscopy of Noble Gases   177
       3. Conditions for Laser Oscillation in Gases   183
       4. Common Helium-Neon Lasers   191
       5. Noble Gas Lasers   201
       6. Miscellaneous Gas Lasers   207

VI. VARIATION OF LASER OSCILLATIONS IN SPACE
     AND TIME   **214**
       1. Mode Structure and Radiation Pattern   214
       2. Pulsations of the Output of Solid Lasers   221
       3. Giant Pulse Techniques   228
       4. Giant Pulse Theory   235

VII. NONLINEAR PHENOMENA   **252**
       1. Theory of Nonlinear Phenomena in Light Propagation   252
       2. Frequency Conversion Experiments   261
       3. Raman Effect   266
       4. Classical Theory of Amplification and Raman Effect   272
       5. Multiple-Photon Absorption   277

VIII. LASER APPLICATIONS   **279**
       1. Applications to Measurement and Instrumentation   279
       2. Communications and Ranging Applications   284
       3. Applications to Shaping and Welding   287
       4. Biological and Medical Applications, Discussion of Health
          Hazards   289

APPENDIX   **293**

INDEX   **301**

Introduction to Laser Physics

Historical Introduction

The use of stimulated emission for microwave amplification was proposed during the early 1950's independently by Weber and by Townes in the United States and by Basov and Prokhorov in the Soviet Union. During 1954 Townes and his students at Columbia University completed the construction of the first such microwave amplifier, or maser.* Ever since this time there have been speculations concerning the possibility of extending this principle to amplification and generation in the optical region. Considerable analytical work preceded the successful construction of the first light amplifier, or laser, in 1960. Most notable were the works of Schawlow and Townes, who explored the general physical conditions necessary for the operation of a laser in either the gaseous or the solid state and who have analyzed the feasibility of several concrete systems, such as the optically excited potassium and cesium vapors, and even the optical excitation of several of the fluorescent lines of ruby which were later found suitable for laser action. Schawlow pointed out that stimulated emission in the R_1 ruby line would be difficult to produce because this line terminates on the ground state. Maiman soon afterward overcame the difficulty by the brute-force method of applying a greater intensity of excitation than was earlier thought possible.

There has been considerable speculation both in the United States and in the Soviet Union about the creation of a state of negative absorption in gases. In 1959 Javan and Sanders of the Bell Telephone Laboratories explored the effectiveness of electron excitation and exchange of excitation as a means of producing negative absorption. This work led to the development of the helium-neon laser in the fall of 1960, shortly after the ruby laser was discovered by Maiman at the Hughes Research Laboratories. Subsequently, Basov and his co-workers at the Lebedev Institute (Moscow) carried out a mathematical analysis of the conditions under which the exchange of excitation in a mixture of different gases leads to negative

---

* The word maser is an acronym from the initial letters of microwave amplification by stimulated emission of radiation.

1

absorption. This work was published in 1960, shortly after Javan's discovery. Before the end of that year Sorokin and Stevenson announced the operation of a four-level solid laser. Many such lasers were discovered during the years 1961 and 1962. Essentially all rare earth metals were found to be suitable laser materials when incorporated in certain crystals.

Intensive speculation about the use of semiconductors as laser materials began about 1959. Basov published many interesting calculations concerning the possibility of utilizing a variety of processes in semiconductors for the purpose of light amplification. Significant theoretical contributions were also made by B. Lax at Lincoln Laboratories and by several French investigators. The semiconductor laser became a reality during the fall of 1962. While the theoreticians were giving their attention mainly to pure semiconductors, the experimentalists succeeded with a rather complex material, the p-n junction of GaAs.

As soon as the five lines of the helium-neon laser in the 1.1–1.2-μ region became known, a search started for other gaseous lines. Curiously, for two years no other lines were found; even the now "obvious" 6328-Å and 3.39-μ lines of He remained undetected. During the fall of 1962 the discovery of gaseous lasers began like an avalanche. By mid-1964 over 500 lines of the noble gases alone had been observed in stimulated emission, and several new methods utilizing ions, atoms, and molecules of other elements had been discovered for exciting laser oscillations. A tabulation of published laser lines prepared in August 1962 contained fewer than 20 entries; a similar table prepared two years later would contain more than 1000.

Laser research and development proceeded at an unprecedented pace. The discovery of new lasers was only one of the achievements. The properties of the light emitted from lasers underwent precise analysis and were related to the parameters of the laser. An endless sequence of more and more powerful lasers was constructed, and new potential applications were discovered which in turn suggested the need for new types of lasers. New and spectacular scientific experiments were performed which depend either on the high degree of coherence of laser light or on its intensity, which surpasses that of all other light by many orders of magnitude. The proposed applications, scientific, technical, medical, and military, are too numerous to list here.

Efforts toward light amplification and generation by stimulated emission were regarded as extensions of the maser art. Therefore, the investigators at Bell Telephone Laboratories, who explored this subject, introduced the term *optical maser* and have for the most part continued to use it. However, this name provokes the observation that in and near the visible region we are not dealing with microwaves. The problems, techniques, and achievements in the optical region are sufficiently distinct from those in the microwave region to merit for this art a separate name. Laser stands for light amplification by stimulated emission of radiation. This word has now been accepted internationally, and we shall use it consistently, noting here that it means the same thing as optical maser.

Laser Literature and Bibliography

A special problem in the field of lasers is the extreme fragmentation of its literature and the diverse quality of publications pertaining to the subject. This situation creates unusual difficulties for the person seeking technical information. It arose as a consequence of the atmosphere in which the laser art developed. The laser was in the public eye from the time of Maiman's discovery, and its development was fostered by government support and private speculation. Workers in the laboratories were not only encouraged to make public their discoveries, they were in many instances harassed. Newspapers and trade papers constantly discussed laser developments in different laboratories, frequently announcing a discovery or a claim before a scientific or technical paper could be written and published. In this atmosphere many investigators felt impelled to submit abstracts of papers to be presented at various meetings before their work was completed. An enormous number of short papers were contributed at the many laser sessions that the scientific and technical societies arranged at their meetings. Since the abstracts were ordinarily required about four months before the meetings, the papers actually delivered often did not resemble too closely the abstracts printed in the program. Nevertheless many important discoveries in the laser field became known to other investigators either through oral presentations at meetings and conferences, or through newspaper-type coverage in the trade journals. Since the publication of an article in the ordinary scientific or technical journal takes six months to one year, most contributions were channelled into the letter-type journals, which publish short communications in about one month after the receipt of the final manuscript. Brevity and speed are the main characteristics of the "Letters," and the text is not as carefully scrutinized before publication as is the custom in regular journals.

The literature of lasers opened with a grotesque note: Maiman's original paper announcing stimulated emission in ruby was rejected by *Physical Review Letters*. It was subsequently published by another journal, whose editor obtained a copy of the manuscript privately circulated. To compensate for the blunder of rejecting Maiman's paper, the journals printed many contributions that should have been returned to the authors for further consideration. Particularly annoying is the carelessness with which spectroscopic problems were treated in the literature. Frequently it is not made clear whether wavelengths are measured in air or in vacuum, or whether the values printed as results represent the author's measurements or the previously tabulated values of a spectral line which the author believes to be identical to the one he observed. The reader is urged to read the laser literature critically, keeping in mind the pressure under which the publications were written.

Under the circumstances described it is often difficult to arrive at the correct conclusion concerning priorities in the literature. The author offers his apologies to those whose work he inadvertently overlooked. It is also difficult to include in a text all references which enable the reader to test the correctness of the conclusions presented in the book and which provide him with additional information without overwhelming him with bibliographic material in such quantity as to make his position nearly hopeless. Certain criteria had to be arrived at in selecting references for inclusion in this book. It was thought best *not* to use any of the following material:

a. Oral presentations and their abstracts.
b. Reports in newspapers and trade papers, even when they were written by the original investigator, which was rarely the case.
c. Reports and documents whose circulation is limited.

Items of the excluded type constitute the majority of entries in a "complete" bibliography of the subject. The remaining material is still too great for inclusion. An effort was made to include the first technical article announcing a new discovery, a summary or review article, if there is one, and at least the major publications appearing after the closing date of the review article.

The original titles of articles published in western languages are included. When a publication was written in Russian, the reference to an English translation, if any, comes first, followed by the original reference in parenthesis. The titles as officially translated are often stilted or cumbersome. These were retranslated and listed in a form which renders the Russian meaning in current English terminology. Thus, for example, a "molecular generator in the optical region of frequency" is a laser.

The following two articles are of fundamental historical significance:

J. P. Gordon, H. J. Zeiger, and C. H. Townes, The maser. New type of amplifier, frequency standard, and spectrometer, *Phys. Rev.* **99**, 1264–1274, 1955.
A. L. Schawlow and C. H. Townes, Infrared and optical masers, *Phys. Rev.* **112**, 1940–1949, 1958.

The first article is the original exposition of the maser principle by Townes and his students and a report of the achievement of the ammonia maser. The second article is a signpost which points the way from masers to lasers. It is devoted to the examination of stimulated emission techniques from the point of view of extending their application to the infrared and optical region.

Entry into the voluminous scientific literature of lasers is facilitated by the existence of conference reports, review articles, laser bibliographies, and abstract services.

The most notable conference reports are those of the three international conferences in quantum electronics. They were held in September 1959, March 1961, and February 1963. The papers presented at these conferences were of high quality; the texts were edited after the conference and represent an exceptionally fine collection of review articles and original scientific contributions. The complete titles of these records are:

Quantum Electronics, edited by C. H. Townes, 606 pp., Columbia University Press, New York, 1960.

Advances in Quantum Electronics, edited by J. R. Singer, 641 pp., Columbia University Press, New York, 1961.

Quantum Electronics III, edited by P. Grivet and N. Bloembergen, 1923 pp., 2 vols., Columbia University Press, New York, and Dunod Éditeur, Paris, 1964.

The journal *Applied Optics* published an *Optical Masers Supplement* in December 1962. This issue contains several review articles and reprints of some important basic papers pertaining to the laser art. It also has a short bibliography extending to about the end of 1961. A similar supplement entitled *Chemical Lasers* was published in March 1965.

Among review articles not included in the publications already mentioned the following are especially recommended:

A. Yariv and J. P. Gordon, The laser, *Proc. IEEE* **51**, 4–29, 1963.

L. F. Johnson, Optical maser characteristics of rare earths in crystals, *J. Appl. Phys.* **34**, 897–909, 1963.

P. A. Franken and J. F. Ward, Optical harmonics and nonlinear phenomena, *Rev. Mod. Phys.* **35**, 23–39, 1963.

G. Burns and M. I. Nathan, *P-n* junction lasers, *Proc. IEEE* **52**, 770–794, 1964.

A number of bibliographies were compiled by private firms and military agencies. The following two have received rather wide distribution and may be available in many libraries:

J. F. Price and A. K. Dunlap, *Masers and Lasers, A Bibliography*, Space Technology Laboratories, Redondo Beach, California. Original issue 1962. Supplements.

K. J. Spencer, *Lasers*, Ministry of Aviation United Kingdom, Central Library, St. Giles Court, London. Bibliographies covering different periods.

The above bibliographies include not only scientific and technical journal articles, but company and government reports as well as trade journal coverage. The following bibliography is restricted to articles in scientific and technical journals:

E. V. Ashburn, B. A. Lengyel, and R. W. Merry, Bibliography of the open literature on lasers I and II, *J. Opt. Soc. Am.* **53**, 647–652, 1963; **54**, 135–142, 1964.

A more complete indexed and cross-referenced work is the following bibliography written in Russian:

N. S. Volfson and E. I. Shitova, *Quantum Optical Generators—Lasers*, Science Publishers, Moscow, 1964.

Articles published in the Western languages are listed in the original language along with Russian translation.

Abstract cards on laser literature can be purchased from Lowry-Cocroft Abstracts, 516 Main Street, Evanston, Illinois. The abstracts cover not only journal articles but unclassified company and government reports as well as papers offered at scientific and engineering meetings. They are mailed to subscribers weekly.

Abstracts are also available in book form:

A. K. Kamal, *Laser Abstracts*, Plenum Press, New York, 1964.

I

Background Material on Radiation and Atomic Physics

Laser art uses material that originates in different branches of physics and engineering. Only an exceptional person is familiar with all concepts and relations that are bound to play a role in the discussion of the various phases of this art. Therefore, it is probably worthwhile to present in summary form the ideas and results needed from physics and other disciplines. Most of this material is discussed in undergraduate courses in optics, modern physics, and atomic theory; therefore the summary may be a brief reminder. A short discussion of units, conversion tables, and measurement techniques serves only to orient the reader about practical matters and point the way to literature where more adequate information may be found.

1. LIGHT AND THE GENERAL LAWS OF RADIATION

The subject of this book is the generation and amplification of light by stimulated emission of radiation. It therefore seems appropriate to commence by gathering material from classical electromagnetic theory and ordinary optics that is needed as a background for the subject to be discussed. At the risk of boring the experienced reader, we begin with some elementary definitions and statements.

Our interest is in electromagnetic radiation in or near the visible region. The wavelength in this region varies from 0.3 to 3 μ, the frequency, from 10^{14} to 10^{15} cps. The emphasis is on the fact that we are dealing with electromagnetic radiation and not that it is visible. We shall avoid all terms, so common in ordinary optics, that assess light in terms of its effects on the human eye. Consequently, we shall not speak of luminous but of *radiative* quantities, which are determined by using a detector capable of registering the transport of energy by means of electromagnetic radiation. We recapitulate the basic terms used in connection with such transport of energy.

8

The counterpart of luminous flux in ordinary optics is *radiative flux*. This is the rate at which radiant energy passes through a surface; it is measured in units of power; that is, in watts (joules per second) or in ergs per second. The intensity of radiation incident on a surface is the *radiative flux density*, whose MKS unit is watts per square meter. To indicate the directional distribution of radiation of a radiating surface, we need the concept of the *radiance in a given direction*. This is the radiant flux in a given direction per unit solid angle per unit projected area of the radiator. It is usually denoted by the symbol N, and its meaning can be clarified as follows: given a radiating surface of area A and a direction at an angle ϑ from the surface normal, the radiative flux in a small cone of $d\Omega$ steradians around the given direction is $NA \cos \vartheta \, d\Omega$. When N is independent of the direction, we say that the surface radiates or scatters according to *Lambert's law*. In this case the total radiation from the surface is πNA. Related to N is the energy density of the radiation u, which is simply the radiative energy contained in the unit volume.

We now make use of the existence of filters and monochromators, which enable us to classify radiation according to its frequency or wavelength. All quantities pertaining to radiation may be regarded as functions of the frequency v or the wavelength λ; their symbols are then provided with appropriate subscripts. The symbol u_v is defined as follows: the energy density of radiation between the frequencies v and $v + dv$ is $u_v \, dv$. The symbol u_λ refers to energy density in the wavelength interval λ to $\lambda + d\lambda$; consequently, u_v and u_λ are related but different functions of the variables. The frequency interval v, $v + dv$ and the wavelength interval λ, $\lambda - d\lambda$ are equivalent descriptions of the same spectral region when $dv/v = d\lambda/\lambda$. It is easily shown that $u_v v = u_\lambda \lambda$. Here v and λ are in arbitrary units, but their product is the velocity of light.

It is usually convenient to characterize radiation by its wavelength whenever experiments or applications are concerned, but in theoretical calculations, particularly in those involving energy, frequency is a more suitable variable. When electromagnetic radiation in a cavity is in thermal equilibrium at the absolute temperature T, the distribution of radiation density according to frequency follows *Planck's law*:

$$u_v \, dv = \frac{8\pi h v^3}{c^3} \frac{dv}{e^{hv/kT} - 1}. \tag{1.1}$$

Here h is Planck's constant, k is Boltzmann's constant, and c is the velocity of light. Their numerical values are given in Section 2.

Radiation will escape through a hole cut into the walls of such a cavity at the rate of $W = uc/4$ per unit area of the hole. This is the radiative flux density at the exit of the cavity; it is called black-body radiation, and many solids radiate like this idealized black body. Therefore the frequency distribution of the flux radiated from the surface of a solid may be approximated by means of Planck's formula.

In experimental work distribution according to wavelength is preferred, and the radiation formula takes the form

$$W(\lambda, T)\, d\lambda = \frac{C_1 \lambda^{-5}\, d\lambda}{e^{C_2/\lambda T} - 1}, \tag{1.2}$$

where $C_1 = 2\pi hc^2$ and $C_2 = hc/k$. However, rather than work with pure CGS or MKS units, it is often convenient to express W in watts per square centimeter and to measure λ and $d\lambda$ in Ångström units. With these changes the constants become

$$C_1 = 3.74 \times 10^{20} \text{ watts/cm}^2 \text{ (Å)}^4, \qquad C_2 = 1.438 \times 10^8 \text{ Å}^\circ\text{K}.$$

According to the *Stefan-Boltzmann law*, the total black-body radiation is

$$W = \int_0^\infty W(\lambda, T)\, d\lambda = \sigma T^4, \qquad \sigma = 5.679 \times 10^{-12} \text{ watt/cm}^2 \text{ deg}^4. \tag{1.3}$$

It follows from what has been said that an incandescent solid is the source of radiation whose energy is not concentrated in any frequency region. For each temperature there is naturally a wavelength at which the emitted radiation is maximum. This wavelength λ_M is calculable from *Wien's displacement law*:

$$\lambda_M T = 2.898 \times 10^7 \text{ Å}^\circ\text{K}, \tag{1.4}$$

and the peak of $W(\lambda, T)$ for a given T is

$$W_M(T) = W(\lambda_M, T) = 1.290 \times 10^{-19} T^5 \text{ watt/cm}^2 \text{ Å}. \tag{1.5}$$

Numerical calculation of the black-body radiation in a given spectral region is facilitated by the introduction of the variable $x = \lambda T$ because the functions $W(\lambda, T)/W_M(T)$ and $\int_0^\lambda W\, d\lambda / W_T$ are functions of the variable x alone. These two functions are tabulated [1, pp. 6–64]. The calculation is carried out by finding the total radiation or the peak value first by means of (1.3) or (1.5). The relative radiation density, or the integrated relative radiation density, is then found by using the tables.

A black body at the temperature of 5200°K has its radiation peak at 5575 Å, which is about the center of the visible spectrum, the part to which the human eye is most sensitive. Yet only about 40 per cent of the radiation of this body falls within the visible part of the spectrum, about 6 per cent is in the ultraviolet, and the rest is in the infrared.

Gaseous sources of light when operated at low pressures emit radiation consisting of groups of more or less sharp lines and possibly a continuous spectrum of lesser intensity. The frequencies of the spectral lines depend on the composition of the gas; their intensities and linewidths depend on a number of factors, such as the pressure and the temperature of the gas and the method of excitation. At low pressures the lines will be sharp, but the brightness of the gas as a lamp will be low. As the pressure increases, the brightness will increase and so will the linewidths, some extending over tens of Ångströms, until at last the lines overlap and the discrete character of the spectrum disappears.

Sources of greatest brightness—greatest radiative flux in the visible—are the high-pressure arcs and flashtubes. In order to obtain maximum brightness, flashtubes are operated at an extremely high power level which they can sustain for only short periods of time. This requires intermittent operation with a low duty cycle. They are energized by discharging large capacitors ranging from 100 to a few thousand microfarads charged between 1000 and 3000 volts. Xenon tubes so activated provide a flash of the order of 1 msec with a spectral distribution approximating that of a black body between 6500 and $10,000°K$ temperature. According to the unpublished measurements of V. Evtuhov, between 15 and 20 per cent of the electrical input is converted into radiation in the spectral range 3500 to 6500 Å.

Light emanating from the sources discussed will be radiated in all available directions. From the flat surface of an incandescent solid it will fill a solid angle of 2π steradians (not with uniform intensity, but according to Lambert's law!). To produce a parallel beam of radiation from the sources discussed so far, it is necessary to place the radiator in the focal plane of an optical system. Since the source is of finite size, the resulting beam will not be a parallel one, but will have an angular divergence equal to the angular size of the source viewed from one of the principal planes of the optical system. In order to get a sharp beam, only a small portion of an extended source may be utilized. In addition, not all energy radiated from this quasi point source will be utilized because the aperture of the optical system will act as an effective stop, eliminating a large part of the radiation. Therefore, it appears that only a minute fraction of the energy of an ordinary light source may be converted to a nearly parallel beam. The higher our requirements for parallelism, the smaller this fraction becomes.

A system of mirrors and lenses can be used to direct the radiation from a source onto an object. In this manner it is possible to concentrate light at a target, and we might be tempted to try to devise an optical system that would create on a surface an image brighter than the extended source from which the light originates. In the present terminology this would mean that an image of the source is formed so that the radiance at the image is higher than at the source. A famous theorem of classical optics states that this cannot be done. More precisely, it cannot be done with Lambert law radiators if the refractive indices of the object and image space are the same. [2, p. 188.]

We may sum up the principal limitations of classical sources of light as follows:

Energy radiated from an intense source is distributed over a relatively broad spectral region. Powerful monochromatic sources do not exist.

The radiated energy is generally poorly collimated and the collimation cannot be improved without sacrificing the intensity available.

Radiation from an extended source cannot be imaged with an increase in brightness.

We shall see how these limitations are overcome in the case of coherent sources.

REFERENCES

1. *American Institute of Physics Handbook*, McGraw-Hill, New York, 1957.
2. M. Born and E. Wolf, *Principles of Optics*, Pergamon Press, New York, 1959.

2. UNITS AND PHYSICAL CONSTANTS

It is, in principle, most desirable to adopt one system of units and to use it consistently and exclusively. This procedure is cumbersome to follow in all details in the laser field, which encompasses atomic quantities as well as those of power engineering. It is doubtful that anyone's preference for the rationalized MKS system extends to the point of measuring the volumes of ruby crystals in cubic meters. On the laboratory and atomic scale we shall give preference to the CGS system, thus ensuring compatibility with our sources of reference. Some deviations from the CGS system are customary in spectroscopy. The wavelength of visible radiation is most conveniently expressed in Ångström units (10^{-8} cm), whereas in the infrared the micron (10^{-6} meter) is a more convenient unit. No one measures atomic energy levels in ergs or joules. They are expressed and tabulated either in electron volts (1.602×10^{-12} erg) or in reciprocal centimeters. The use of the reciprocal centimeter as a unit of energy originates from the relationship $h\nu = E_2 - E_1$, which may be written

$$\frac{1}{\lambda} = \frac{E_2 - E_1}{hc}. \qquad (2.1)$$

The quantity E/hc has the dimension of reciprocal length. It is frequently referred to as the energy, although correctly it should be called the *wave number*. The tabulation of energy levels in reciprocal centimeters enables us to obtain by direct subtraction of two tabulated entries the reciprocal of the wavelength (*in vacuo*) corresponding to a transition between the levels.

Wavelengths in the visible and the near infrared are measured in air and usually the value in air is quoted. For this reason the reciprocals of the wave numbers obtained by subtracting tabulated entries must be corrected to secure agreement with the measured values. The correction is determined by the deviation of η, the refractive index of air, from 1. Its magnitude can be gauged by the fact that $\eta - 1$ varies from 277×10^{-6} to 274×10^{-6} as the wavelength varies from 0.6 to 1.0 μ. Conversion to wavelength in air is facilitated by the use of tables of wave numbers [1] in which wavelengths in air are listed against wave numbers. A short table of wavelength corrections appears in the Appendix (Table A.1).

As is often true, the representation convenient for the theorist is less convenient for the experimentalist. Most experimentalists working in atomic spectroscopy prefer to express their results in wavelengths measured in air. Those conditioned in the field of infrared molecular spectroscopy use wave numbers more frequently, because combinations of molecular vibrations lead to simple relations among the wave numbers and the organization of the experimental material is easier with the data displayed on a scale proportional to the frequency. Authors of articles about lasers regrettably often do not declare whether their wavelengths are measured in air or in vacuum. When the published data are not too accurate, this omission is of no consequence. Otherwise it is best to assume that a wavelength stated without qualification is a wavelength in air and that results published on the wave number scale were calculated after reduction to vacuum.

One of the useful atomic units of energy is the *electron volt*. One electron volt is equivalent to 8066 reciprocal centimeters. When the energy E of a level is expressed in cm^{-1} and it is necessary to find the energy in ergs required to raise a gram atom of the material to this state, starting from the ground level, then E must be multiplied by Nhc, where $N = 6.02 \times 10^{23}$ is Avogadro's number, and $hc = 1.986 \times 10^{-16}$ erg cm.

The following constants are frequently used in this book:

$h = 6.625 \times 10^{-27}$ erg sec, $c = 2.9979 \times 10^{10}$ cm/sec,
$k = 1.380 \times 10^{-16}$ erg/deg, $\hbar = 1.054 \times 10^{-27}$ erg sec [3].

It is sometimes desirable to relate the radiative flux density and the stored energy density of radiation to the peak values of the electric and magnetic fields. These fields are most conveniently measured in practical (MKS) units. The instantaneous power flow across a unit surface when expressed in rationalized MKS units is $W = E \times H$. The radiative flux density $\overline{W}$ is the time average of W. In a plane wave propagating in a medium with a dielectric constant ϵ and permeability μ we have

$$W = \tfrac{1}{2}\sqrt{\epsilon/\mu}\, E^2. \tag{2.2}$$

Therefore the magnitudes of the vectors concerned are related by the equation

$$E = \sqrt{2\overline{W}\sqrt{\mu/\epsilon}}.$$ (2.3)

Here E is the peak value of the electric field.

The values of ϵ and μ that relate to vacuum (or air) are denoted by the subscript 0. It is known that $\sqrt{\mu_0/\epsilon_0} = 376.7$ ohms. For a plane wave that creates a flux density of 1 MW/cm² we obtain in vacuum a peak electric field of 2.74×10^6 volts/meter. The stored-energy density is $u = \frac{1}{2}\epsilon E^2$; therefore

$$E = \sqrt{2u/\epsilon_0}\sqrt{\epsilon_0/\epsilon}.$$ (2.4)

For nonmagnetic materials, $\sqrt{\epsilon/\epsilon_0} = \eta$, the index of refraction; therefore

$$E = \frac{1}{\eta}\sqrt{2u/\epsilon_0},$$ (2.5)

where $\epsilon_0 = 8.85 \times 10^{-12}$ farad/meter. For example, for ruby, whose refractive index is 1.76, an energy density of 0.01 joule/cm³ corresponds to a peak electric field of 2.70×10^7 volts/meter. Note that these calculations are independent of the frequency. They should not be applied without further thought to situations involving other than a single plane wave. In the general case, the calculation of the energy density may involve both the electric and the magnetic vectors.

REFERENCES

1. C. D. Coleman, W. R. Bozeman, and W. F. Meggers, *Table of Wavenumbers*, National Bureau of Standards Monograph 3, U.S. Govt. Print. Off., Washington, D.C., 1960.
2. C. H. Moore, *Atomic Energy Levels*, National Bureau of Standards Circular 467, U.S. Govt. Print. Off., Washington, D.C., 1949.
3. *American Institute of Physics Handbook*, McGraw-Hill, New York, 1957.

3. OBSERVATION AND MEASUREMENT OF RADIATION

Anticipating the encounter with radiation originating from lasers, we survey some of the methods available for its observation and for quantitative measurement of its characteristics.

We expect to observe a highly collimated beam of radiation confined to a narrow spectral region. The intensity of the radiation is very high; frequently the radiation is available only in pulses of less than 1 msec duration. The frequency region of greatest interest includes the red portion of the visible and extends to about 3.5 μ in the infrared.

Direct visual observation *with a screen* may be adequate to indicate the presence and the general shape of the beam in the case of visible radiation, such as may be obtained from ruby (6943 Å) and neon (6328 Å). One must absolutely avoid looking into the laser beam directly, for severe eye damage may result from one pulse before the eyelid has time to close. Similarly, care must be taken that the laser beam does not strike a specularly reflecting object from which it may be reflected into someone's eyes. In the near infrared (up to about 1.5 μ) an image converter tube may be used to examine the laser beam visually. Farther in the infrared one may use a Liquid Crystal Viewer (Westinghouse) [1]. This device consists of a thin radiation-absorbing layer in contact with a liquid crystal layer. The color of the light scattered from the latter is a sensitive function of the temperature. The crystal layer is illuminated by white light and the color pattern is observed as the laser beam strikes the absorber.

More precise observations may be made by means of red-sensitive film or photographic plate. The laser beam may be permitted to strike the plate directly without an intervening lens. In this manner the spatial distribution of energy is recorded. One may also photograph interference patterns by interposing suitable apertures between the laser and the film.

Photographic records are convenient for recording the approximate spatial distribution of energy, but are not suitable for absolute energy or intensity measurements because the blackening of the plate has no simple relation to the radiant energy received. Energy-measuring devices in the visible and the infrared region are of either the thermal type or the photoelectric or quantum detector type.

A thermal detector absorbs the incident radiation. The energy is distributed over the receiving element as heat, and the measurement of the intensity of the incident radiation is reduced to the measurement of the temperature rise of the receiving element. Any physical property that is a known function of the temperature may serve as an indicator, and the detector may be calibrated by transferring to it a known amount of electrical energy. Thermoelectric detectors, bolometers, and calorimeters are constructed in this manner; the first two serve as indicators of intensity, the last one as an indicator of energy received during a pulse. We note that thermal detectors generally respond to incident radiation without discrimination to frequency, except that their ability to absorb may vary slowly with frequency. With moderate care, such variations may be made negligible over a wide band. Because of the finite mass of the receiving element that is heated, thermal detectors are not as sensitive as quantum detectors; moreover, the response time of thermal detectors is long compared with that of quantum detectors. For these reasons the application of thermal detectors in laser technology is limited to the measurement of the total energy of a short pulse and to the calibration of quantum detectors, which are generally useful only as indicators of relative intensity.

Calorimeters specifically constructed for the measurement of laser energy consist of an absorber of small heat capacity provided with a temperature-measuring element. The absorber may be a light carbon cone, a rat's nest of copper wire, or razor blades assembled in a parallel stack [2, 3, 4]. The temperature rise may be measured by a thermistor, or a platinum resistance thermometer. These electrical elements are built in matched pairs and operated as parts of a balanced Wheatstone bridge. The instrument is calibrated by dissipating a known amount of electrical energy in a resistance incorporated in the absorber. The lighter absorber elements operate satisfactorily in the 0.01- to 1-joule range. Heavier instruments, such as the razor blade stack, are useful for higher energies. It is essential for accurate measurement that the laser pulse should produce only small temperature changes (a few degrees). Damon and Flynn [5] designed a liquid calorimeter for the energy range 1 to 100 joules.

As an alternative to direct energy measurement the momentum of a light pulse may be measured with a torsion pendulum, but this type of instrument is rather difficult to build [6].

Quantum detectors or photodetectors depend on the action of a light quantum on a *single electron*, not on the absorption and distribution of energy over an entire macroscopic body. A photodetector counts the number of quanta of radiation absorbed, in contrast to the thermal detector which responds to the total energy.

The operation of a photodetector is based on the photoelectric effect, that is, the liberation of an electron from its bound state. Free (mobile) electrons may be created in the interior of a solid by the absorption of appropriate quanta of radiation; this is the *internal photoelectric effect*. Alternatively, electrons may be ejected from the surface of a solid; this is the *external photoelectric effect*. Both effects may be used for the detection of radiation.

In the visible region the photomultiplier is the most convenient detector. It is based on the external photoelectric effect. Since it depends on the ejection of an electron from a surface by incident quanta, these quanta must have sufficient energy to overcome the work function of the photo-surface. This requirement sets a long wavelength limit for the use of photo-detectors. The work function of clean, pure metals has a value of several electron volts; therefore quanta of ultraviolet light are required to eject electrons from such materials. Special composite surfaces have been developed with effective work functions somewhat below 1 eV. With such surfaces the long wavelength limit to which photodetectors based on external photo effect may be used is extended to about 1.2 μ. The ratio of the number of electrons emitted to the number of photons incident is the quantum efficiency of the photosurface. The variation of this parameter

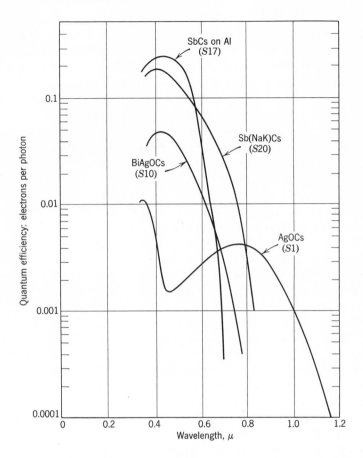

Fig. 1. Spectral response of various photocathodes in the visible and the near infrared region. (Source E.M.I. Electronics Ltd. catalog.)

with wavelength is shown in Fig. 1 for several commercially available photocathodes. The photoemissive surfaces form the cathodes of the photomultiplier tubes which conveniently amplify the current arising from electron emission. These tubes vary in size, in sensitivity, and in intrinsic noise which limits the detection of very weak signals. Technical data required for the selection and operation of photomultipliers are easily available in the literature [7, 8].

Internal photoeffect produces an increase in the conductivity of the material. The change in conductivity serves as an indicator of the incident radiation. The common materials usable as photoconductive sensors are tellurides, selenides, and sulfides of thallium, bismuth, and lead, and quite a few doped semiconductors. Photoconductors are excellent detectors of infrared radiation in the 1- to 10-μ range. Their characteristics depend strongly on the temperature.

Internal photoeffect in a semiconductor produces other effects in addition to increasing the conductivity. When an electron-hole pair is created near a *p-n* junction the charges separate and a photovoltaic effect takes place. This means that a potential difference appears across the junction; this potential difference may be used as a measure of the photon absorption that caused the charge separation. Typical photovoltaic materials suitable as radiation detectors are InSb and InAs.

The choice of a detector in laser experiments depends not only on the frequency of the radiation employed, but also on what is to be detected. When, for example, the spatial distribution of radiation is to be detected, we choose a device suitable for image formation. A variety of television pickup cameras based on either the photoemissive or the photoconductive effect are sensitive in the near infrared. These cameras as well as numerous image converters operative between 0.8 and 1.3 μ are described by Kruse, McGlauchlin, and McQuistan [9].

When the application requires the monitoring of radiation at only one or a few points in space, and quantitative data concerning intensity are required, detectors other than image conversion devices will be used. The choice then depends on the intensity and the time variability of the signal to be detected or measured, the output device to which the detector is to be coupled, and the control the experimenter can afford to exercise over the environment of the detector. In addition to differing in intrinsic noise level, detectors of different types differ greatly in their response time, that is, in their ability to respond to rapid intensity fluctuations.

The detection of weak infrared signals developed into an advanced art during and after World War II. The theory as well as the necessary equipment are now available for the design of receivers for laser-based communications systems. The excellent and exhaustive treatises recently published about infrared detection [9, 10] make a detailed discussion unnecessary here. However, it is well to note that there are a number of criteria current in infrared technology which are intended to provide answers to the following questions:

1. What is the minimum level of power incident on the detector which gives rise to a signal voltage output equal to the noise voltage of the detector?

2. What output signal will be obtained for incident radiant power of unit intensity?

3. How does the output signal vary with the frequency of the incident radiation?

4. What is the minimum response time of the detector?

The parameters that provide at least partial answers to these questions are tabulated [7, 8, 9, 10]. We note briefly that devices based on external photoeffect (photomultipliers) are highly sensitive in the proper frequency range and provide a high output signal. Moreover, their response is fast— 10^{-8} sec. They are greatly limited in their spectral response, the long wavelength cutoff being around 1.2 μ at most, and their excellent characteristics deteriorate long before this limit is reached. Photoconductive detectors have a detective sensitivity about two orders of magnitude lower than the photomultipliers at their optimal frequency. The lead selenide, telluride, and sulfide types have response times of the order of 10^{-4} sec; some of the doped semiconductors, however, have shorter response times, down to 10^{-7} sec. The virtue of the photoconductive detectors is their response for wavelengths longer than 1 μ. Their cutoff wavelengths depend on the material and on the temperature.

The 1- to 3.5-μ range can be covered adequately with detectors at room temperature, for example, photoconductive PbS or photovoltaic InAs detectors. From 2 to 6 μ, detectors at liquid nitrogen temperature (77°K) are considerably superior. Beyond 6 μ, special semiconductors are employed which must be refrigerated to a still lower temperature [9].

Photoelectric devices are eminently suitable for *relative* measurements of laser output. When absolute intensity measurements are required one must follow a tedious procedure of calibration. The integrated intensity may be measured by a calorimeter; then, *if the waveform of a pulse is known*, an intensity scale may be established. We shall see that the waveform of the laser is frequently very irregular. When that is so, the calibration may be accomplished by using a steady monochromatic beam of light derived from an ordinary light source as an intermediary reference. The mean frequency of this beam should approximate that of the laser. A complicating factor of this procedure is that we cannot get a monochromatic pulse powerful enough to register on the calorimeter from a classical source. It is therefore necessary to determine the absolute intensity of the auxiliary monochromatic beam by comparing its effect on a thermopile with that of the radiation derived from a standard lamp certified by the National Bureau of Standards and operated observing all precautions required for the use of such secondary radiation standards.

Wavelength is conveniently measured by means of a grating spectroscope. Difficulties arise if one attempts to determine the linewidth of a laser output with a spectroscope, especially if one attempts to resolve two or

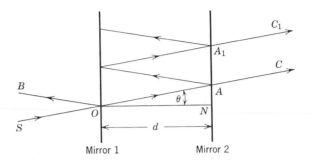

Fig. 2. Schematic diagram of the Fabry-Perot interferometer.

more components separated by minute differences in wavelength, because the resolution of the spectroscope proves to be insufficient. The necessary high resolution may be obtained by means of a Fabry-Perot interferometer. This instrument is important in the laser art for reasons other than its great resolving power in spectroscopy. It deserves detailed attention.

A Fabry-Perot interferometer consists of an airspace or transparent medium* bounded by two parallel, partially transmitting mirrors. It is shown schematically in Fig. 2. Let a plane wave be incident on Mirror 1 at a small angle θ from the normal ON of the mirrors. This plane wave is represented in Fig. 2 by the ray SO; the splitting of this wave by the first mirror is represented by the rays OA and OB. The ray OA is split again on the second mirror, and this procedure continues. The waves leaving the interferometer after a varying number of reflections finally combine into a resultant reflected and a resultant transmitted wave. The amplitude of the resultant transmitted wave is calculated by adding the amplitudes of all waves transmitted an odd number of times through the interferometer. These are represented by the rays AC, A_1C_1, and so on. Addition is performed with due regard to the phase differences resulting from passages between the mirrors. The phase difference resulting from one additional round-trip passage between mirrors separated by distance d is

$$\delta = \frac{4\pi}{\lambda} d \cos \theta. \tag{3.1}$$

Let the (intensity) reflectivity and transmissivity of the mirrors be denoted by R and T respectively. Then for lossless mirrors, which we shall assume, we have

$$R + T = 1. \tag{3.2}$$

* For the sake of simplicity we confine ourselves to the case when the index of refraction is the same between the mirrors and outside.

The intensity I_t of the light transmitted through the interferometer is then given by the equation [11, p. 324]

$$I_t = \frac{(1 - R)^2 I_i}{(1 - R)^2 + 4R \sin^2 \dfrac{\delta}{2}},$$ (3.3)

where I_i is the incident intensity.

When light incident on the Fabry-Perot interferometer originates from a point source, the transmitted intensity will be the same in directions at equal inclination to the normal. Therefore, when the radiation emerging from the interferometer is focused on a screen, a set of concentric rings centered around the image of the normal is obtained. Such a pattern is shown in Fig. 3.

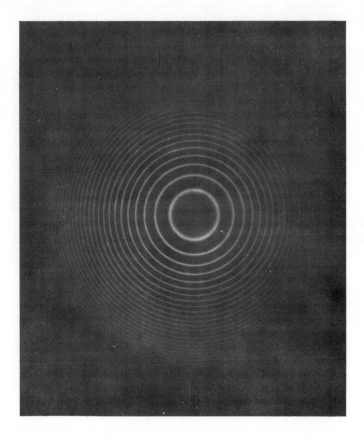

Fig. 3.   Fabry-Perot pattern obtained with red cadmium light.

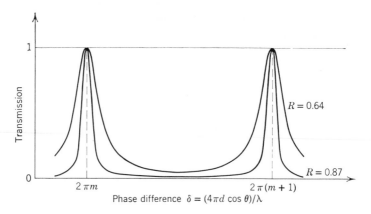

Fig. 4. Variation of intensity of light transmitted through a Fabry-Perot interferometer as a function of phase difference.

In practice $4\pi d/\lambda$ is a large number (tens of thousands); therefore,
$\sin(\delta/2)$ goes through a full cycle for a small variation of θ. Then, as
$\sin(\delta/2)$ varies from 0 to 1, the normalized transmitted intensity varies
from 1 to $(1 - R)^2/(1 + R)^2$. The variation of the intensity with δ is
shown in Fig. 4 for two values of R. Clearly the pattern associated with
$R = 0.87$ consists of much finer rings than the pattern with $R = 0.64$.
It is customary to define the fineness parameter as follows:

$$F = 4R/(1 - R)^2.$$

The curves in Fig. 4 pertain to $F = 20$ and $F = 200$ respectively. When
light containing several monochromatic components is incident on a
Fabry-Perot interferometer, sets of rings pertaining to each wavelength
will appear displaced with respect to each other. As the reflectivity of the
mirrors, and thus the fineness F, is increased, the individual rings become
sharper, and the fringes produced by different monochromatic components
are more easily separated. If the wavelength separation of two components
is sufficiently large, the displacement of the two patterns may become
greater than the distance between adjacent maxima of either pattern and
the different orders may overlap. This overlapping limits the spectral range
over which the Fabry-Perot interferometer may be used without auxiliary
apparatus for the elimination of the overlap.

The virtue of the Fabry-Perot interferometer is its extremely high
resolving power in a narrow spectral range. In the visible region lines
differing by about 0.02 cm^{-1} in wave number may be resolved. For the
complete theory of this instrument we refer to the literature [11].

REFERENCES

1. J. R. Hansen, J. L. Fergason, and A. Okaya, Display of infrared laser patterns by a liquid crystal viewer, *Appl. Optics* 3, 987–988, 1964.
2. T. Li and S. D. Simms, A calorimeter for energy measurements of optical masers, *Appl. Optics* 1, 325–328, 1962.
3. S. Koozekanani, P. P. Debye, A. Krutchkoff, and M. Ciftan, Measurements of laser output, *Proc. IRE* 50, 207, 1962.
4. J. A. Ackerman, Laser energy measuring device, *Appl. Optics* 3, 644–645, 1964.
5. E. K. Damon and J. T. Flynn, A liquid calorimeter for high-energy lasers, *Appl. Optics* 2, 163–164, 1963.
6. J. J. Cook, W. L. Flowers, and C. B. Arnold, Measurement of laser output by light pressure, *Proc. IRE* 50, 1693, 1962.
7. R. W. Engstrom, Absolute spectral response characteristics of photosensitive devices, *RCA Review* 21, 184–190, 1960.
8. W. Summer, *Photo Sensitors*, Chapman and Hall, London, 1957.
9. P. W. Kruse, L. D. McGlauchlin, and R. B. McQuistan, *Elements of Infrared Technology*, John Wiley and Sons, New York, 1962.
10. R. A. Smith, F. E. Jones, and R. P. Chasmar, *The Detection and Measurement of Infrared Radiation*, Oxford Univ. Press, London, 1957.
11. M. Born and E. Wolf, *Principles of Optics*, Pergamon Press, New York, 1959.

4. COHERENCE OF LIGHT

The classical theory of light describes optical phenomena in terms of electromagnetic oscillations. One of the basic tools of this theory is harmonic analysis. The variation of the electromagnetic field at a point is represented as the superposition of harmonic oscillations of the form

$$E = E_i \cos (2\pi\nu_i t - \varphi_i). \qquad (4.1)$$

Each oscillation has a definite amplitude E_i, frequency ν_i, and phase φ_i. The phase varies in space from point to point in a linear manner. It is useful to *think* in terms of a monochromatic radiation, which is an electromagnetic oscillation of a single frequency.

In a physical experiment one always deals with superposition of harmonic oscillations of different frequencies, but it is possible to filter radiation in such a way that for most purposes it will behave as an ideal monochromatic radiation. When this is the case we call the radiation quasi-monochromatic, or briefly monochromatic. Whether a radiation is quasi-monochromatic or not depends on the experiment for which it is used.

An ideally monochromatic wave is necessarily of infinite duration; an oscillation that has the shape described by (4.1) for the finite time interval $0 < t < T$, and is zero outside of that interval, may be represented as a superposition of harmonic oscillations whose frequencies are confined to a narrow region of width approximately $1/T$ around the center frequency ν_i.

Practically monochromatic radiation is characterized by a center frequency ν_0 and a bandwidth Δ so defined that the frequency interval from

$\nu_0 - \Delta/2$ to $\nu_0 + \Delta/2$ contains a large part of the energy of the radiation. In theoretical work one must perform a Fourier analysis in order to assign energy content to a frequency interval; in experimental studies it is necessary to employ an instrument with sufficient resolving power to analyze the spectral composition of the radiation.

In experimental optics it is possible to resolve radiation into its quasi-monochromatic components; it is possible to measure the average intensity of radiation over a period long compared with ν^{-1} and Δ^{-1}, and over an area whose diameter is large compared with the wavelength. Neither instantaneous nor sharply localized values can be measured; all relevant quantities must be determined in terms of the measured averages.

Theory, on the other hand, deals with amplitudes and phases. These are combined according to the rules of electromagnetic theory, but only the long-term average of the square of the resultant amplitude is subject to experimental test. While the phase of a monochromatic wave at one point is not observable, its variation from point to point is demonstrable. Evidence for the existence of phase comes from classical interference experiments, which demonstrate that when light emanating from a point source is split into two beams traveling to the same final destination over two different paths the amplitudes must be added according to the well-known rules of vector addition, and that the direction of the vectors to be added depends on the length of the paths traveled.

Let the amplitudes and phases of the waves arriving over paths 1 and 2 be distinguished by appropriate subscripts. The intensity observed at a given point will be equal or proportional to (depending on the choice of units)

$$I = I_1 + I_2 + 2\sqrt{I_1 I_2}\cos\Phi, \qquad (4.2)$$

where $I_1 = \frac{1}{2}E_1{}^2$ and $I_2 = \frac{1}{2}E_2{}^2$ are the (time average) intensities and $\Phi = \varphi_2 - \varphi_1$ is the phase difference. The latter is related to the path difference $s_2 - s_1$ as follows:

$$\Phi = 2\pi\nu(s_2 - s_1)/c. \qquad (4.3)$$

In those regions of the space where the phase difference is 0 or an even multiple of π, the intensity is large, namely $\frac{1}{2}(E_1 + E_2)^2$, while at those points where the phase difference is an odd multiple of π, the intensity is small, namely $\frac{1}{2}(E_1 - E_2)^2$.

A typical interference experiment is so arranged that the path difference $s_2 - s_1$ varies over a screen or over the field viewed by a telescope and the amplitudes E_1 and E_2 are adjusted to be nearly equal. Consequently, when a monochromatic point source is used, a series of alternating light and dark bands is observed. These are the interference fringes. The light band which corresponds to zero path difference is particularly important; it is common to all frequencies. The positions of the other bands are frequency dependent; therefore, light fringes of one frequency overlap with dark ones of another. This overlap depends on the frequency difference and on the order of the fringe reckoned from the central light fringe which corresponds to zero path difference.

It is clear from (4.2) and (4.3) that reinforcement occurs when $\nu(s_2 - s_1)/c$ is an integer, and cancellation when it is a half integer. Therefore the nth light fringe for wavelength λ will coincide with the nth dark fringe for wavelength $\lambda - \Delta\lambda$ when

$$s_2 - s_1 = n\lambda = (n + \tfrac{1}{2})(\lambda - \Delta\lambda).$$

Hence when

$$\frac{\Delta\lambda}{\lambda} = \left|\frac{\Delta\nu}{\nu}\right| = \frac{1}{2n + 1} \tag{4.4}$$

the interference pattern around the nth fringe will be seriously impaired when radiation of frequency ν and $\nu + \Delta\nu$ is present in approximately equal quantities.* Since actual interference experiments are performed with a quasi-monochromatic source and not an ideal monochromatic source, the number of fringes that may be clearly observed is limited by the spread of the spectrum of the source. Sometimes this fact is expressed in a different form: It is known that in a Michelson interferometer using an ordinary spectral line as a light source interference fringes are observed only when the path difference in the two branches is less than a few centimeters. When the path difference exceeds, say, 30 cm, interference is not observed. Apparently the phase of the radiation is not preserved by the source over the length of time it takes the light to travel this distance. In an ideal monochromatic wave field the amplitude of vibrations at any fixed point is constant, whereas the phase varies linearly with time. This is not the case in a wave field produced by a real source; the amplitude and phase undergo irregular fluctuations, the rapidity of which is related to the width $\Delta\nu$ of the spectrum. The time interval $\Delta t = 1/\Delta\nu$ is the coherence time. During a time interval much shorter than Δt, the radiation behaves like a truly monochromatic wave; this is not true for a longer time interval.

So far we have considered only the properties of light emanating from a *point source.* Such an ideal source may be approximately realized by a real source located so far from the observer that its physical dimensions are negligible compared to its distance. Now we turn to *light sources of finite extent.*

* The distinctness of the fringes is also affected by the finite extent of the illuminating source.

A common characteristic of all classical sources of light is the lack of coherence between light emanating from different points of the radiator. By the term coherence or spatial coherence we mean a correlation between the phases of monochromatic radiation emanating at two different points. To be precise, we ought to speak not of coherent and incoherent light but of different degrees of correlation. From a practical point of view, however, we may regard radiation emanating from two distinct sources as incoherent if we observe that the intensities of the radiation are additive. We take it as an established experimental fact that light emanating from two points of an ordinary source located well over a wavelength apart cannot be brought into interference even with extreme filtering to segregate a "monochromatic" component. We attribute this fact to a lack of correlation between the phases of distant radiators.

Related to the question of phase correlation on a light source is the question of phase correlation in a radiation field away from the source and its relation to the properties of the source as well as the geometry of the situation.

Consider more closely the electromagnetic vectors at two points P_1 and P_2 in a wave field produced by an extended monochromatic source many wavelengths removed from both P_1 and P_2. (See Fig. 5.) If P_1 and P_2 are so close to each other that the difference $SP_1 - SP_2$ between the paths from each source point S is small compared to the wavelength λ, then it may be expected that the fluctuations at P_1 and P_2 will be effectively the same. Furthermore, it may be expected that some correlation will exist even for greater separations of P_1 and P_2, provided that the path difference

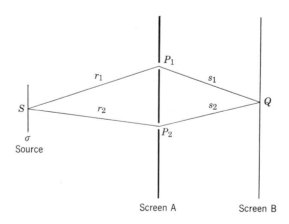

Fig. 5.   An interference experiment with light from an extended source.

does not exceed the coherence length $c \Delta t = c/\Delta \nu$. By using the correlation of the electromagnetic disturbance, we are led to define a region of coherence around any point in a wave field generated by an essentially monochromatic source.

The value of correlation can be tested experimentally by observing the illumination on the screen B as a function of position. The observation is carried out generally so that the illumination is measured in a region which is approximately equally distant from P_1 and P_2. The illumination is determined with small apertures around P_1 and P_2. In addition to measuring the intensities I_1 and I_2 at Q with the first and second apertures, respectively, opened, we may also measure interference effects arising from the superposition of radiation passing through these two apertures. Complete incoherence of the radiation field at P_1 and P_2 means that the intensity $I(Q)$ is

$$I(Q) = I_1 + I_2,$$

while in the case of complete coherence any value between $|I_1 - I_2|$ and $I_1 + I_2$ may be obtained depending on the path difference $s_1 - s_2$. In the general case an expression of the form

$$I(Q) = I_1 + I_2 + 2\sqrt{I_1 I_2} \, \mathrm{Re}\, \gamma$$

is obtained where γ is a complex number of constant modulus $|\gamma| \leqq 1$, whose phase varies linearly with the path difference. In fact, $\mathrm{Arg}\, \gamma = \varphi_0 + 2\pi(s_1 - s_2)/\lambda$. The case $\gamma = 0$ corresponds to complete incoherence and $|\gamma| = 1$ to complete coherence, while an intermediate value of $|\gamma|$ characterizes a *partially coherent field*. As the point of observation Q is moved parallel to the line $P_1 P_2$, the intensity varies between a maximum of $I_M = I_1 + I_2 + 2\sqrt{I_1 I_2}|\gamma|$ and a minimum $I_m = I_1 + I_2 - 2\sqrt{I_1 I_2}|\gamma|$. The visibility of the interference fringes on screen B is defined as

$$v = \frac{I_M - I_m}{I_M + I_m}.$$

When the intensities I_1 and I_2 are equal, v reduces to $|\gamma|$.

The extension of the correlation concept to a polychromatic (nonmonochromatic) field is quite straightforward but mathematically more demanding. The radiation must be represented in terms of Fourier integrals and cross correlation must be defined as it is in the theory of stationary random processes. This analysis is carried out in the literature [1, 2]. The result is that, given two points and a time interval τ, a degree of coherence $\gamma_{12}(\tau)$ whose absolute value varies from 0 to 1 can be calculated. With this concept at hand, the variation of the degree of coherence of a wave field generated by an extended source can be discussed. The degree of coherence

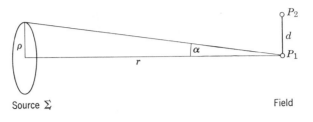

Fig. 6. Production of a partially coherent field.

of radiation between the points P_1 and P_2 can be related to the diffraction pattern of the source regarded as an aperture of specified amplitude and phase distribution. This is the substance of the van Cittert-Zernike theorem which permits the calculation of the variation of $\gamma(0)$ in a plane illuminated by an extended incoherent source.

The ideal case $\gamma(0) = 1$ represents a fully coherent plane wave with the phase front coincident with the plane of observation. This, of course, cannot be achieved with a finite incoherent source. With the point P_1 held fixed and P_2 moving away from P_1, the degree of coherence $|\gamma(0)|$ decreases. Arbitrarily, the tolerance limit $|\gamma| \geq 0.88$ is set to specify the region within which the radiation is called "almost coherent." With the aid of the van Cittert-Zernike theorem it can be shown that radiation derived from a uniform, quasi-monochromatic, noncoherent source of circular shape is almost coherent over a distance $d = 0.16\lambda/\alpha$, where $\alpha = \rho/r$ is the angular radius of the source as viewed from the point of observation, ρ being the radius of the circle and r its distance from the observer. (See Fig. 6.) Therefore, an almost coherent beam of finite cross section can be obtained from a noncoherent source but only a minute fraction of the energy radiated can be utilized in the process. In order to obtain an almost coherent beam of 1 cm diameter at 5000 Å, the source must be so far removed optically that its angular radius α is 8×10^{-6} rad. If a source of flux density w_s and surface area A radiates according to Lambert's law, the flux density at a distance R from the radiator near the normal to its surface is

$$w_p = \frac{AN}{R^2} = \frac{Aw_s}{\pi R^2}.$$

Consequently, for a circular radiator of radius ρ,

$$w_p = \frac{\rho^2 w_s}{R^2}.$$

In order to obtain coherence over 1 cm, we must have $\alpha = \rho/R = 0.16\lambda$; therefore $w_p = (0.16\lambda)^2 w_s = 0.64 \times 10^{-10} w_s$. In the present case the flux density in the almost coherent part of the beam is less than 10^{-10} times the flux density emitted by the source.

An almost coherent beam can be focused into a region whose dimensions are of the order of the wavelength. Once an almost coherent beam is obtained, it is possible to concentrate this energy, and the degree to which this concentration is successful depends on the degree of coherence of the beam.

We can now readily appreciate some of the advantages gained by having a coherent, or almost coherent, source whose radiation is already in the form of a spherical wave or a plane wave of limited cross section. Such radiation can be concentrated by lenses and mirrors to images much brighter than the original source. Moreover, radiation emitted from a source already in the approximate form of a plane wave can be directed at a distant object with only negligible losses from diffraction effects, whereas only a small part of the radiation from a noncoherent source can be converted into an approximately plane wave.

REFERENCES

1. M. Born and E. Wolf, *Principles of Optics*, Pergamon Press, New York, 1959.
2. M. J. Beran and G. B. Parrent, *Theory of Partial Coherence*, Prentice-Hall, Englewood Cliffs, New Jersey, 1964.

5. EMISSION AND ABSORPTION OF RADIATION BY ATOMS

It is well known that atomic systems such as atoms, ions, and molecules can exist in certain stationary states, each of which corresponds to a definite value of energy. The states are characterized by quantum numbers. The energy values are called the *levels* of the atomic system. When two or more states have the same energy, the level is called degenerate, and the number of states with the same energy is the *multiplicity* of the level. Frequently the word state is used to mean level; all states with the same energy are regarded as identical. Transitions between stationary states may occur with attendant emission or absorption of energy as radiation, or with the transfer of energy to or from another system. If the transition is radiative, the frequency of the radiation emitted or absorbed by the system is given by *Bohr's frequency relation*:

$$hv = E_2 - E_1, \qquad (5.1)$$

where E_1 and E_2 are the energies of the states among which transition takes place and h is Planck's constant.

The level of the system with the lowest energy is the *ground level*; every other level is an *excited level*. The terms ground state and excited state are also used. An atom in the ground level can only absorb radiation. Starting with the ground level, we number the levels in increasing order of energy. When the atomic system is not in the ground level, it may change to a lower level with the emission of radiation without any external causation. This is the phenomenon of *spontaneous emission*. The probability that an atom in level n will spontaneously change to the lower level m within a unit of time is called the *spontaneous transition probability*.* It is denoted by A_{nm}. This quantity is a characteristic of the pair of energy levels in question. In multiple levels A_{nm} is obtained by summation over all pairs of states involved. If there is a large collection of atomic systems on hand and N_n is the number of systems in the nth level, the total number of transitions from level n to level m will be approximately $N_n A_{nm}$ per second, and the power radiated at the frequency $\nu_{nm} = (E_n - E_m)/h$ will be $N_n(E_n - E_m)A_{nm}$. Spontaneous radiation will emerge from the atoms of the assembly in a random phase; therefore the assembly of independent atoms (gas) will emit this radiation as an incoherent source.

Transitions between different atomic or molecular energy levels take place not only spontaneously but also under stimulation by electromagnetic radiation of appropriate frequency. The total probability that an atomic system will change during a unit of time from a level of index n to a level of lower energy of index m is

$$P_{nm} = A_{nm} + u_\nu B_{nm}, \qquad (5.2)$$

where u_ν is the radiation density at the frequency $\nu = \nu_{nm}$; A_{nm} and B_{nm} are constants determined by the atomic system. In the presence of radiation of the proper frequency the atomic system may also pass from a lower to a higher energy level. The probability of such an event (absorption) is

$$P_{mn} = u_\nu B_{mn}. \qquad (5.3)$$

Radiation emitted from an atomic system in the presence of external radiation consists of two parts. The part whose intensity is proportional to A_{nm} is the spontaneous radiation; its phase is independent of that of the external radiation. The part whose intensity is proportional to uB_{nm} is the *stimulated radiation*; its phase is the same as that of the stimulating external radiation. The main concern in this book is this stimulated radiation.

For the sake of simplicity, we assume at this point that the spectral extent of each atomic line is so narrow that the distribution of energy with frequency within the line is not resolved and what we observe is only the total energy emitted or absorbed. We imply here also that the radiation density u does not vary significantly over the frequency range of the spectral line.

---

* Strictly speaking, we are dealing with quantities that should be called rates, not probabilities. Their dimension is reciprocal time. This matter is discussed further on p. 31.

The relations between the A's and B's are known as *Einstein's relations*. They are usually stated in the form

$$B_{nm} = B_{mn}, \qquad A_{nm} = \frac{8\pi h\nu^3}{c^3} B_{nm}. \qquad (5.4)$$

These equations are valid in vacuum for particles having only non-degenerate energy levels. When the energy levels are degenerate, Einstein's first relation takes the form [1, p. 450]

$$g_n B_{nm} = g_m B_{mn}, \qquad (5.5)$$

where g_n and g_m are the multiplicities of levels n and m, respectively. The second relation is not affected by the multiplicities. In solids in which the index of refraction η differs appreciably from unity, the second relation must be replaced by

$$A_{nm} = \frac{8\pi h\nu^3 \eta^3}{c^3} B_{nm}. \qquad (5.6)$$

The reason for the appearance of the η is that the factor in front of B_{nm} arises from the counting of the radiation modes in a volume element. The wave numbers that enter into this calculation are defined in terms of the frequency and the velocity of the radiation in the material. In fact, $k^2 = (2\pi\nu)^2/v^2$, which leads to the replacement of c in (5.4) by $v = c/\eta$.

We turn now to the concept of *lifetime*, which is frequently used in describing transitions between different states of an atom. The lifetime of a state is simply related to the probability of transition from that state. Let $p\, dt$ be the probability that an atom originally in state s will leave that state during a short time interval dt. (This interval must be so short that $p\, dt \ll 1$.) Then, for a constant p, the number of atoms in state s will decrease exponentially according to the formula $N(t) = N_0\, e^{-pt}$. Hence the number of atoms leaving the state s in the time interval from t to $t + dt$ is $pN_0\, e^{-pt}\, dt$. Therefore the average lifetime of the atom in state s is

$$T = \frac{1}{N_0} \int_0^\infty tpN_0\, e^{-pt}\, dt = \frac{1}{p}. \qquad (5.7)$$

In view of (5.7), the reciprocal of the transition probability of a process is called its lifetime. If an atomic state can be altered by several processes with lifetimes $\tau_1, \tau_2, \ldots, \tau_n$ and these processes are statistically independent, then the lifetime of the state is related to the lifetimes of the processes by means of which the state can be altered by the equation

$$\frac{1}{T} = \frac{1}{\tau_1} + \frac{1}{\tau_2} + \cdots + \frac{1}{\tau_n}. \qquad (5.8)$$

We shall now make a few statements about the nomenclature of the atomic energy levels and some of the rules governing the transitions between them. These are intended not as a brief presentation of the quantum theory of the atom, but as a recapitulation of some of the working rules of that discipline.

The electrons in an atom are characterized by three orbital quantum numbers n, l, and m, and the spin quantum number s. The orbital quantum numbers are integers; s is $\frac{1}{2}$. The first, n, governs the radial distribution of the wave function; it corresponds to the principal quantum number of Bohr's theory. In the case of atoms with relatively simple structure the value of n is the primary determinant of the energy of the electron in question. The quantum number l varies from 0 to $n - 1$; it determines the orbital angular momentum, whose largest component is $l\hbar$. For brevity we shall say that the orbital angular momentum is $l\hbar$ with apologies to the expert in quantum mechanics who knows that the *magnitude* of this vector is $\sqrt{l(l + 1)}\hbar$. The quantum number m describes the orientation of the angular momentum vector with respect to an external field; it may assume the values $-l$ to $+l$; that is, for a fixed value of l a total of $2l + 1$ values of m are possible. With different quantum numbers there are associated different wave functions, i.e., different states of the electron. When several states have the same energy, the level is said to be degenerate, as we have already noted. The degeneracy of a level may be removed by the application of an external field, or by the field of the other electrons of the same atom, or by that of neighboring atoms. This removal of degeneracy comes about most often by the appearance of a small energy difference associated with the reversal of the spin of an electron.

When an atom contains many electrons the electrons that form a closed shell may be disregarded and the energy differences associated with transitions in the atom may be calculated by considering only the electrons outside of the closed shell. Thus in the case of the alkali metals only one electron, and in the case of the alkali earths only two, need to be considered.

An electron is called an s, p, d, or f electron if its azimuthal quantum number is $l = 0$, 1, 2, or 3, respectively. For larger values of l the letters of the alphabet are used in their natural order starting with f for $l = 3$. The notation $3p$ indicates an electron with $n = 3$, $l = 1$.

In describing the state of a multielectron atom it is well to remember that the electrons within the atom are interchangeable and that no two electrons can have the same quantum numbers (including s). The ground state of Li, for example, is described by the symbol $1s^2 2s$, which means that there are two electrons (with opposing spins) in the $1s$ state, and one in the $2s$ state. The sum of the orbital angular momenta of these electrons is 0, and the sum of the spin angular momenta is $\frac{1}{2}$, giving the total angular momentum $\frac{1}{2}$. All these momenta are in the units of $\hbar = h/2\pi$.

The total angular momenta of most atoms and ions of interest to us may be obtained by first adding vectorially the orbital angular momenta of the individual electrons, and combining the spin angular momenta separately. According to the rules of quantum theory the sum of the orbital angular momenta combine into a vector characterized by the integer L; the spins combine into a vector characterized by S, which is an integer for an even number of electrons and a half integer for an odd number. The total angular momentum J of the atom may then be obtained by vector addition of L and S.[*] When the vectors L and S are constants of motion (invariants) we speak of L-S, or *Russell-Saunders, coupling*. It is shown in quantum theory that for each fixed value of S there are $2S + 1$ different possible spin configurations. Configurations with $S = 0$ are called singlets, those with $S = \frac{1}{2}$ are doublets, etc. For an atom or ion with two electrons, S is either 0 or 1; therefore such an atom will have singlet and triplet states. The collection of states with common values of J, L, and S is called a *term*. In general, a term will contain a number of states differing in the orientation of their momentum vectors. The multiplicity of a term is $2J + 1$.

The following nomenclature evolved historically for the designation of atomic terms in the Russell-Saunders momentum coupling scheme. The symbol characterizing the term is of the form $^{2S+1}X_J$, where the letter X stands for S, P, D, F, G, etc., depending on the value of the orbital angular momentum L. The letter S is used as a symbol for the terms with $L = 0$ and is not to be confused with the spin quantum number; P, D, F, etc. are used for $L = 1, 2, 3$, etc. The superscript preceding the basic symbol is determined by the spin quantum number; it indicates whether the state is a singlet, doublet, or triplet, etc. Different elements of the multiplet are distinguished by the value of J, the total angular momentum. This is added as a subscript to the right. When necessary, the configuration of the excited electron is also given; it precedes the letter symbol. Thus the ground state of Li has the symbol $2s\,^2S_{1/2}$; the symbols of some of its excited states are $3s\,^2S_{1/2}, 2p\,^2P_{3/2}, 2p\,^2P_{1/2}$. The last two states differ by the opposite orientation of the spin of the excited $2p$ electron with respect to the orbital momentum. In general J varies in integral steps from $|L - S|$ to $L + S$. Hence when $L \neq 0$ then $S = 1$ leads to three different values of J, namely, $L - 1, L,$ and $L + 1$, but when $L = 0$ then $J = 1$ is the only value possible. Nevertheless, such a state is still called a triplet state, since there are three independent wave functions that belong to the common energy of a $^3S_1$ state.

Note that the notation based on the Russell-Saunders coupling scheme is applicable only when the interaction of the orbital angular momenta l_i of the individual electrons is so strong from one electron to another that

---

[*] We are using the symbols L, S, and J to denote the angular momentum *vectors* whose maximal components are $L\hbar$, $S\hbar$, and $J\hbar$.

these momenta combine to give a resultant $\mathbf{L} = \sum \mathbf{l}_i$ which is a constant of the motion. Similarly the individual spins $\mathbf{s}_i$ must so combine to form the constant $\mathbf{S} = \sum \mathbf{s}_i$. The general laws of dynamics assure the constancy of $\mathbf{J} = \mathbf{L} + \mathbf{S}$ only; the constancy of $\mathbf{L}$ and $\mathbf{S}$ separately follows only when the spin-orbit interaction is small compared to the spin-spin and orbit-orbit interactions. This type of situation prevails for a large number of elements; its presence is recognized spectroscopically by noting that the splitting of the levels of a multiplet is small compared to the energy differences of levels having the same electron configuration but different values of L.

The reverse case of the one described above is one in which there is a considerable interaction between the orbital angular momentum $\mathbf{l}_i$ and the spin angular momentum $\mathbf{s}_i$ *of the same electron*. Then each $\mathbf{l}_i$ combines with the corresponding $\mathbf{s}_i$ to form a $\mathbf{j}_i$, the total angular momentum of an individual electron. The $\mathbf{j}_i$'s are loosely coupled to each other; they are approximate constants of motion. (Naturally $\mathbf{J} = \mathbf{j}_1 + \mathbf{j}_2 + \cdots + \mathbf{j}_n$, is always a constant.) When this is the case we speak of *j-j coupling*. Its presence is recognized by the observation of the Zeeman splitting of spectral lines which follows laws different from those applicable in the Russell-Saunders case.

Pure *j-j* coupling occurs very seldom. Instead, we find atoms like neon in which electrons in inner shells obey the rules of Russell-Saunders coupling, while the total angular momentum $\mathbf{j}$ of an additional electron with a higher quantum number n may be weakly coupled to the resultant $\mathbf{J}_C$ of the core electrons.

The discussion of atomic and ionic energy levels so far was based on an atomic system free of external influence. When an ion is located in a crystal lattice the electric and magnetic fields prevailing at the site of the ion may exert a profound influence on the energy level structure of the ion. This is the case for a chromium ion in ruby, which is of great importance for laser technology. In ruby the Cr^{3+} ion is surrounded by an approximately octahedral field of oxygen ions. The crystal field, i.e., the electrostatic field resulting from the presence of the O^{--} ions, splits the originally degenerate levels of Cr^{3+}. Not only are the levels split, the fields are so strong that the higher components of the ^4F level overtake the lower components of the ^2G level, which lies considerably above the ^4F level in the free ion. The calculation of the splitting of ionic levels in a crystal field is based on the theory of group representations. It involves the irreducible representations of the symmetry group applicable to the crystal in question. The number of components into which a multiple level may be split is determined by group theory; the split levels are designated by the appropriate symbol of group theory with the spectroscopic symbol of the original level suppressed or abbreviated. The actual shift in energy levels is determined by the crystal field parameters; their calculation is among the most complicated tasks of quantum theory. [2, 3]

The transition probabilities between atomic states are related to the wave functions associated with these states. Our interest is in radiative transitions, i.e., transitions in which an energy exchange takes place between the atom and the electromagnetic field. The principal factor in this exchange is the electric dipole radiation, which is already familiar from classical electrodynamics. Given a distribution of charges e_i with position vectors $\mathbf{r}_i$ such that the sum of the charges is 0, the vector

$$\boldsymbol{\mu} = \sum_{i=1} e_i \mathbf{r}_i \qquad (5.9)$$

is independent of the origin of the coordinate system. It is the electric dipole moment of the charge system. If the position coordinates undergo harmonic oscillations at the frequency ν, the rate at which energy is radiated according to classical electrodynamics is proportional to $\nu^4 |\boldsymbol{\mu}|^2$. Here

$$|\boldsymbol{\mu}|^2 = |\mu_x|^2 + |\mu_y|^2 + |\mu_z|^2, \qquad (5.10)$$

where

$$\mu_x = \sum_{i=1}^{n} e_i x_i. \qquad (5.11)$$

In quantum theory the intensity of electric dipole radiation is calculated essentially by means of the same formula with the dipole moment replaced by the corresponding quantum mechanical matrix element. For a transition from state q to state q' this matrix element is defined by the equations*

$$\mu_x(q, q') = e \int \psi_{q'}^* x \psi_q \, dv, \qquad (5.12)$$

$$\mu_y(q, q') = e \int \psi_{q'}^* y \psi_q \, dv, \qquad (5.13)$$

$$\mu_z(q, q') = e \int \psi_{q'}^* z \psi_q \, dv, \qquad (5.14)$$

$$|\boldsymbol{\mu}(q, q')|^2 = |\mu_x(q, q')|^2 + |\mu_y(q, q')|^2 + |\mu_z(q, q')|^2. \qquad (5.15)$$

The rate (probability) of transition from q to q' is given by [1, p. 451]:

$$A_{q, q'} = \frac{64\pi^4 \nu^3}{3hc^3} |\boldsymbol{\mu}(q, q')|^2. \qquad (5.16)$$

When multiple levels are involved and these are designated with the letters n and m, as at the beginning of this section, the probabilities are calculated

* The symbol q represents all quantum numbers required to specify the initial state; q' has similar meaning for the final state.

by summing over all terminal states and averaging over all initial states. This process leads to the expression

$$A_{nm} = \frac{64\pi^4\nu^3}{3hc^3g_n} |\mu(n, m)|^2, \qquad (5.17)$$

where

$$|\mu(n, m)|^2 = \sum_{i=1}^{g_n} \sum_{j=1}^{g_m} |\mu(q_i, q'_j)|^2. \qquad (5.18)$$

As a consequence of the symmetry properties of the integrals (5.12) to (5.14) most combinations of states lead to a zero matrix element. Such transitions are called *forbidden transitions*. The term forbidden means that a transition among the states concerned does not take place as a result of the interaction of the electric dipole moment of the atom with the radiation field. The allowed transitions are specified by the *selection rules*, which help to sort out the pairs of states capable of yielding a non-zero matrix element for electric dipole radiation.

The *parity* of a state is even or odd according to the parity of the (scalar) sum $\sum l_i$, where summation is extended over all electrons of the atom. Since the parity of a closed shell is always even, it is sufficient to sum over the orbital quantum numbers of the valence electrons.

The general selection rules are the following:

1. Transitions must change the parity.
2. $\Delta J = 0$ or ± 1, but transition from $J = 0$ to $J = 0$ is excluded.

In atoms for which Russell-Saunders coupling is applicable the following additional selection rules hold:

3. $\Delta L = 0$, or ± 1;
4. $\Delta S = 0$.

When the state of only one electron changes, the parity rule requires a change in L. In this case the third rule becomes $\Delta L = \pm 1$. Transitions in which the states of two electrons change at the same time are considerably less probable than transitions involving a single electron.

In order to facilitate the application of the selection rules terms of odd parity are usually provided with an upper index o. For the same reason it is practical to list or plot the energy levels of singlets, triplets, etc. in separate groups. Such groupings are illustrated on the example of He in Fig. 7. An abbreviated notation is employed in this figure; the symbols $n\,^1S$ and $n\,^1P^o$ stand for $ns\,^1S$ and $np\,^1P^o$ respectively.

The selection rules were derived by considering electric dipole radiation only. Other radiative mechanisms are less effective, they lead to less frequent transitions in general than electric dipole radiation. However,

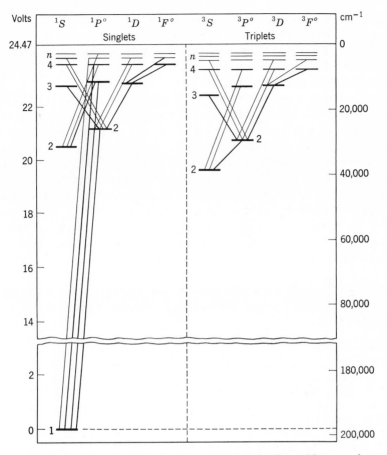

Fig. 7. Energy-level diagram for helium. Typical permitted transitions are shown by slant lines. The scale on the left is in electron volts measured from the ground state; that on the right is in wave numbers measured from the ionization level.

when the electric dipole transition is forbidden, secondary mechanisms lead to transitions rates that are generally several orders of magnitude slower than the rates of permitted dipole transitions. Thus transitions forbidden by the selection rules will occur, but they will occur relatively rarely. The selection rules are most rigidly in force for elements at the beginning of the periodic table. They lose their effectiveness in complex atoms and in a strong interaction of an atom with another as it takes place in a collision or in a crystal lattice.

As a result of the selection rules, an atom may get into an excited state from which it will have difficulty returning to the ground state. A state from which all transitions to lower energy states are forbidden is *metastable*; an atom entering such a state will generally remain in that state much longer than it would in an ordinary excited state from which an easy escape is possible. A metastable state has a long lifetime. An example of such a state is the lowest triplet state of He.

The purpose of this section was to introduce the concepts used in the discussion of the stimulated emission of radiation and to establish the basic relationships between the Einstein coefficients and the quantum mechanical matrix elements.

We reviewed some of the basic properties of atomic structure, introducing the spectroscopic nomenclature for the most common energy levels, and indicated some of the complications that arise under less usual circumstances, for example, when an atomic system is embedded in a crystal field. We stated the simplest selection rules applicable to electric dipole transitions. These concepts are constantly used in laser literature. An interested reader not already familiar with these subjects will find an elementary discussion of atomic energy levels and selection rules in Herzberg's book [4] on atomic spectra. The quantum mechanical background is available in any of the numerous books on modern physics and quantum theory.

REFERENCES

1. E. C. Kemble, *Fundamental Principles of Quantum Mechanics*, McGraw-Hill, New York, 1937.
2. D. S. McClure, Electronic spectra of molecules and ions in crystals, Part II, Spectra of ions in crystals, *Solid State Physics* Vol. 9, 399–525, Academic Press, New York, 1959.
3. J. L. Prather, *Atomic Energy Levels in Crystals*, National Bureau of Standards Monograph 19, U.S. Govt. Print. Off., Washington, D.C., 1961.
4. G. Herzberg, *Atomic Spectra and Atomic Structure*, Dover Publications, New York, 1944.

6. INTERACTION OF RADIATION WITH ATOMIC SYSTEMS

In a practical situation observations are made not on a single atom but on a collection containing billions of atoms not necessarily in the same state.

Given a large number N_0 of atoms, it is known that in thermal equilibrium at absolute temperature T the distribution of these atoms among the different states will follow *Boltzmann's law*; that is, the number of atoms in state j will be

$$N_j' = \frac{N_0\, e^{-E_j/kT}}{\sum_i e^{-E_i/kT}}, \tag{6.1}$$

where E_j is the energy in state j. All states of the same level will be equally populated; therefore the number of atoms in level n is $N_n = g_n N_n'$, where N_n' refers to the population of any of the states in level n. It follows, then, from (6.1), that the populations of the energy levels n and m are related by the formula

$$\frac{N_n}{g_n} = \frac{N_m}{g_m} e^{-(E_n - E_m)/kT}. \tag{6.2}$$

At absolute zero all atoms will be in the ground state. Thermal equilibrium at any temperature requires that a state with a lower energy be more densely populated than a state with a higher energy.

Consider now an ensemble of atoms initially at absolute zero. This ensemble will absorb only radiation whose frequency is contained in the sequence $(E_i - E_1)/h$, where $i = 2, 3, \cdots$. If the ensemble is at equilibrium at a finite temperature T, then not only the ground state will be populated; consequently, radiation whose frequency corresponds to a transition between excited states may also be absorbed. As a matter of practical fact it is well to remember that the first excited levels of most atoms and ions are at least 2×10^{-12} erg above the ground level and that for $T = 500°K$ the product kT is approximately 0.07×10^{-12} erg. Therefore, at moderate temperatures, generally, few atoms will occupy even the first excited level compared to the number present in the ground state, because the exponential factor in (6.2) is so small. The absorption of radiation requiring the transition from an excited level will be weak, for the number of transitions from the nth to the mth level is proportional to N_n.

As a consequence of the absorption of radiation, the equilibrium of the ensemble will be disturbed. Let us assume that monochromatic radiation is absorbed. Atoms that become excited above the first excited level by the absorption of radiation may return directly to the ground state by spontaneous or stimulated radiation or they may follow another path and change to a lower level other than the ground level. In this manner they may cascade down on the energy scale, emitting at each step radiation different in frequency from that which originally lifted them out of the ground state. Because of the relationship (5.1) connecting energy and frequency, the radiations emitted in the cascade process, which is called fluorescence, have lower frequencies than the exciting radiation.

Consider now an ensemble that is not necessarily in thermal equilibrium and again designate the number of atoms per unit volume in state n by N_n. Assuming $n > m$, what is the response of the ensemble to collimated radiation of frequency ν_{nm} and density u?* The number of downward

---

* Actually the density u should have the subscript ν_{nm} to indicate that we are discussing the radiation density within a spectral region surrounding the frequency ν_{nm}. To simplify notation we drop subscripts in every instance where there is no ambiguity concerning the transition to which it refers.

transitions from level n to level m will be $(A_{nm} + uB_{nm})N_n$ per second, and the number of upward transitions, $uB_{mn}N_m$. Whenever N_n is less than N_m, which is usually the case, the incident beam will suffer a net loss of $(N_m - N_n)uB_{nm}$ quanta per second. The $A_{nm}N_n$ quanta, which are radiated spontaneously, will appear as scattered radiation. Thus a beam passing through matter in which the lower energy states are more populated than those of higher energy will always lose intensity; the material will have a positive coefficient of absorption.

An ensemble can be constructed (on paper, easily) in which N_n, the number of atoms in state n, is *greater* than N_m, even though $n > m$. This ensemble is said to contain a *population inversion*. It is definitely *not* in thermodynamic equilibrium. Let us assume now that a population inversion is accomplished somehow for the pair of levels 1 and 2. This means that we have found a stationary, nonequilibrium process that leads to $N_2 > N_1$. In this situation the material will radiate spontaneously. It will also act as an amplifier of radiation at the proper frequency, $\nu = (E_2 - E_1)/h$; the spontaneous radiation of the same frequency will appear as amplifier noise.

In order to develop the quantitative relations that govern this amplification process, it is advisable to take a closer look at the process of absorption and to sacrifice the mathematical idealization we have made concerning the infinite sharpness of the levels and spectral lines. When light of constant intensity I_0 but variable frequency is incident upon an absorbent medium, it is found that at depth x within this medium the intensity of the light follows the law

$$I_\nu(x) = I_0\, e^{-k_\nu x}. \tag{6.3}$$

The observational material from which (6.3) is determined is usually the type shown in Fig. 8, which represents the intensity at a fixed depth in the absorbing material. The frequency ν_0 is the center of the absorption line. When x is measured in centimeters, k_ν is expressed in cm^{-1}. From these observations, we may obtain k_ν as a function of frequency, and when this is done we will have a curve similar to that shown in Fig. 9. The total width of the curve at the place where k_ν has fallen to one-half its peak value, k_m, is the *width of the absorption line* and is denoted by $\Delta\nu$. Frequently this quantity is called the "halfwidth." This does not mean one-half of the width of the curve, but the full width at half peak value.

An important relationship links the total area under the curve in Fig. 9 with the Einstein coefficients and the populations of the states that are responsible for the absorption centered around ν_0. This relationship was derived by Füchtbauer and Ladenburg in the early 1920's.*

---

* The present proof follows the method of Mitchell and Zemansky [1]. However, our definition of the Einstein coefficients and theirs differ by a factor of $c/4\pi$.

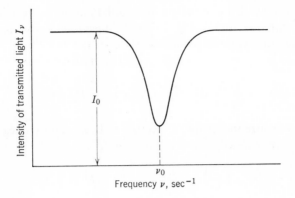

Fig. 8.   An absorption line.

Consider a parallel beam of light of frequency between ν and $\nu + d\nu$ and intensity I_ν traveling in the positive x-direction through a layer of atoms bounded by the planes x and $x + dx$. Let the velocity of light in this medium be $v = c/\eta$, where η is the index of refraction. The phase front will travel through the slab of thickness dx in the time $dt = dx/v$. Suppose there are N_1 atoms/cm³ in level 1, of which $dN_{1\nu}$ are capable of absorbing in the frequency range ν to $\nu + d\nu$, and N_2 atoms/cm³ in level 2, of which $dN_{2\nu}$ are capable of emitting in the same range. Then, as the phase front advances from x to $x + dx$, the decrease of energy in the beam is

$$-d(I_\nu \, d\nu) = h\nu(B_{12} \, dN_{1\nu} - B_{21} \, dN_{2\nu})I_\nu \frac{dx}{v}. \tag{6.4}$$

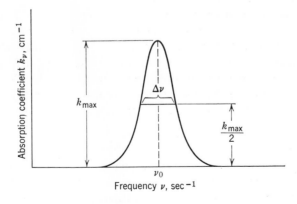

Fig. 9.   Variation of absorption coefficient with frequency in an absorption line.

Here we have made use of the fact that radiation emitted by stimulation is coherent with the stimulating radiation; therefore it will reinforce the beam. Radiation emitted spontaneously does not contribute significantly to the beam because it is not collimated. From (6.4) it follows that

$$-\frac{1}{I_\nu}\frac{dI_\nu}{dx}\,d\nu = \frac{h\nu\eta}{c}\,(B_{12}\,dN_{1\nu} - B_{21}\,dN_{2\nu}). \tag{6.5}$$

We now recognize the left-hand member as $k_\nu\,d\nu$, and by integration over the entire line centered around ν_0 we obtain

$$\int k_\nu\,d\nu = \frac{h\nu_0\eta}{c}\,(B_{12}N_1 - B_{21}N_2). \tag{6.6}$$

Here B_{12} may be eliminated by means of (5.5) and B_{21} may be expressed in terms of A_{21} by making use of (5.6). In this manner we get the *Füchtbauer-Ladenburg formula*:

$$\int k_\nu\,d\nu = \frac{c^2 A_{21} g_2}{8\pi\nu_0^2\eta^2 g_1}\left(N_1 - \frac{g_1}{g_2}N_2\right). \tag{6.7}$$

This is a basic formula, which we write as

$$\int k_\nu\,d\nu = \kappa\left(N_1 - \frac{g_1}{g_2}N_2\right). \tag{6.8}$$

The constant κ may be written in various forms, one of which is

$$\kappa = \frac{\lambda_0^2 A_{21}}{8\pi\eta^2}\frac{g_2}{g_1}, \tag{6.9}$$

where λ_0 designates wavelength in vacuum.

Consider now the case in which level 1 is the ground level. In electrically excited gases, or in a laser material excited by means of intense irradiation, the number of excited atoms N_2 may become an appreciable fraction of the total number of atoms. In this case the last term in (6.8) cannot be neglected. However, when the only agency responsible for the formation of the excited atoms is the absorption of a beam of moderate intensity, the ratio N_2/N_1 is exceedingly small. Consequently, (6.8) may be written

$$\int k_\nu\,d\nu = \kappa N_0. \tag{6.10}$$

where N_1 is identified with the total number N_0 of atoms present. It is interesting to note that under the conditions described the integral of the absorption coefficient is simply proportional to the number of atoms present and that its value is completely independent of the line shape (the curve in Fig. 9). The constant κ is the *integrated absorption cross section* per atom for the line in question; the quantity $\sigma_\nu = k_\nu/N_0$ is the *absorption cross section* per atom.

When the material is in thermal equilibrium, the distribution of atoms among the levels is described by (6.2). For any positive value of the absolute temperature we get

$$\frac{N_i}{g_i} > \frac{N_j}{g_j} \tag{6.11}$$

whenever the inequality $E_j > E_i$ holds.

The nonequilibrium situation in which the inequality (6.11) is reversed is frequently referred to in the literature as a state of *negative temperature*. A negative value of T is calculated from the distribution of atoms among the energy levels by means of Boltzmann's formula (6.2). The idea is applicable only to a pair of levels, and it arises from the use of this formula in connection with a pair of levels in a system not in thermal equilibrium. Temperature in this connection does not have its customary meanings: $kT/2$ is not the average energy of the system per degree of freedom, and nothing can be inferred from the value of T about the distribution of the population in states other than the pair from which this negative value of T was calculated. I feel that the use of the term "negative temperature" does not facilitate the understanding of nonequilibrium phenomena, and therefore will avoid the use of this term and speak of population inversion instead. The term negative temperature is introduced here merely to provide a connection with the language of the pertinent literature. The expression that "the negative temperature T is established for levels n and m" means nothing other than that $E_n > E_m$, $N_n > N_m$, and the value of T is defined by (6.2).

When population inversion takes place for levels n and m, formula (6.8) gives a negative value for the integrated absorption coefficient. We have a condition of *negative absorption*; that is, we have amplification. Negative absorption, or amplification, is the consequence of the excess of stimulated radiation over absorbed radiation. In a material that is in the condition of negative absorption for a frequency region, an incident light wave will grow according to the law (6.3), which in this case represents an exponential growth at the rate of $\alpha = -k_\nu$.[*]

[*] In complex materials, typically in semiconductors, the intensity of a light beam may be diminished by processes other than the one contemplated here. Light might be scattered, for example. When such additional loss mechanisms are present, population inversion may not always lead to amplification because the gain due to the excess of stimulated emission over absorption may be cancelled by losses of other kinds. In this case $N_2/g_2 > N_1/g_1$ is necessary but not sufficient for negative absorption.

It is desirable now to take a closer look at the shape of the absorption and emission lines observed from an assembly of atomic systems such as a gas. Figure 9 gives a general indication of what is observed; the exact shape will vary from one situation to another depending on the principal causes of line broadening.

The natural or intrinsic linewidth of an atomic line is extremely small. This is the linewidth that would be observed from atoms at rest without interaction with one another. There is a theoretical limit for linewidth under such circumstances, but this may be disregarded in most instances because it is small compared with the broadening effects of other causes which are invariably present. The two major factors of line broadening are the frequency variations resulting from the thermal motion of the atoms and those resulting from the interruption of absorption or emission of radiation by atomic collisions.

The thermal motion of the atoms is the cause of the *Doppler* (or homogeneous) *broadening* whose frequency dependence is calculated as follows: The probability that a fixed (say x) component of the velocity of an atom in a gas at absolute temperature T is between v_x and $v_x + \Delta v_x$ is proportional to $[\exp - (mv_x^2/2kT)] \Delta v_x$. The Doppler shift in frequency is related to the relative velocity v_x toward the observer according to the equation:

$$\frac{v - v_0}{v_0} = \frac{v_x}{c}, \qquad (6.12)$$

where c is the velocity of light. Therefore the Doppler effect gives rise to the following Gaussian frequency distribution

$$P(v)\, dv = P_0 e^{-\beta(v - v_0)^2/v_0^2}\, dv, \qquad (6.13)$$

where $\beta = mc^2/2kT$.

The constant P_0 is determined from the requirement that the integral of the probability distribution $P(v)$ over all frequencies must be 1; therefore

$$P_0 = \frac{c}{v_0} \sqrt{\frac{m}{2\pi kT}}. \qquad (6.14)$$

The width of the distribution (6.13) at half power is

$$\Delta v = 2\frac{v_0}{c} \sqrt{\frac{2kT \log 2}{m}}. \qquad (6.15)$$

Here m is the mass of the molecule. One may introduce the molecular weight $M = N_0 m$ and the gas constant $R = kN_0$ by multiplying the atomic quantities by Avogadro's number. Upon substitution of the proper numerical values, the following formula is obtained for the Doppler broadening of spectral lines:

$$\Delta\nu = 7.162 \times 10^{-7}\sqrt{\frac{T}{M}}\,\nu_0. \qquad (6.16)$$

It is to be noted that this linewidth, for a given line, depends only on the temperature of the gas.

The second major cause of line broadening is the collision of radiating particles (atoms or molecules) with one another and the consequent interruption of the radiative process. A finite wavetrain is never purely monochromatic; the spectrum of a wavetrain is spread in inverse proportion to the length of the train in the time domain. As an atomic collision interrupts either the emission or the absorption of radiation, the long wavetrain which otherwise would be present becomes truncated. After the collision the process is restarted without memory of the phase of the radiation prior to the collision. The result of frequent collisions is the presence of many truncated radiative or absorptive processes. The linewidth of the radiation of this aggregate is, of course, greater than that of an individual uninterrupted process. The lineshape, i.e., the distribution of frequencies, must be computed statistically.

The original classical computation of this kind was carried out around the turn of the century by H. A. Lorentz, who showed that when the frequency of collisions is small compared to the undisturbed frequency ν_0, the following expression describes the frequency distribution of the collision-broadened line:

$$g(\nu) = \frac{\Delta\nu}{2\pi}\frac{1}{(\nu - \nu_0)^2 + (\Delta\nu/2)^2}. \qquad (6.17)$$

Here ν_0 is the center frequency, and $\Delta\nu$ is the width between the half-power points of the curve. The factor $\Delta\nu/2\pi$ assures normalization according to area under the curve:

$$\int_{-\infty}^{+\infty} g(\nu)\, d\nu = 1. \qquad (6.18)$$

Actually, formula (6.17) is an approximation valid in the vicinity of $\nu = \nu_0$. The complete Lorentz formula is of the form

$$g(\nu) = \frac{\Delta\nu}{2\pi}\left[\frac{1}{(\nu - \nu_0)^2 + (\Delta\nu/2)^2} + \frac{1}{(\nu + \nu_0)^2 + (\Delta\nu/2)^2}\right], \qquad (6.19)$$

but the second term in the brackets is negligible in the optical range, where the linewidth $\Delta\nu$ is much smaller than the central frequency. The linewidth

Δv is related to the average time τ which elapses between consecutive interrupting collisions:

$$\Delta v = \frac{1}{\pi \tau}. \tag{6.20}$$

Since the frequency of collisions is proportional to the density of the gas, the Lorentz linewidth is proportional to the density.

Although the derivation of Lorentz's formula was based on the simple classical model of a radiating dipole, Van Vleck and Weisskopf [2] have shown that the final result, as embodied in (6.17), is still valid in the optical region in the vicinity of v_0, even after the requirements of quantum theory and other refinements are taken into consideration.

The Lorentz-type broadening is frequently referred to as *inhomogeneous broadening*. Although both homogeneous and inhomogeneous broadening result in bell-shaped curves for the distribution of frequencies, these curves are quite different. The difference is illustrated in Fig. 10, which shows

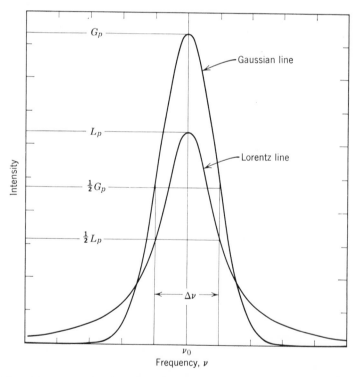

Fig. 10. Gaussian and Lorentz lines of common linewidth. (G_p and L_p denote the peak intensities.)

Gaussian and Lorentz-type curves of the same linewidth plotted on the same scale. The peak values of these curves are related to the linewidths as follows:

for the Gaussian curve

$$G_p = \frac{2}{\Delta\nu} \sqrt{\frac{\log 2}{\pi}} = \frac{0.939}{\Delta\nu}, \qquad (6.21)$$

for the Lorentz curve

$$L_p = \frac{2}{\pi\Delta\nu} = \frac{0.637}{\Delta\nu}. \qquad (6.22)$$

The peak of the Gaussian curve exceeds that of the Lorentz curve by almost 50 per cent.

In an actual situation factors producing both homogeneous and inhomogeneous broadening may be present at the same time. The combination of these factors leads to more complex lineshapes for which we refer to the literature [1, 3]. Frequently one of the factors predominates, and when that is the case, calculations based on that factor alone will lead to approximately correct results.

We return now to the process of amplification in a material with population inversion. When a beam propagates in the x-direction, its intensity varies according to the formula

$$I = I_0 e^{\alpha x}, \qquad (6.23)$$

where $\alpha = -k_\nu$ is a function of the frequency and the integral of k_ν is determined by the population inversion according to equations (6.7), or (6.8) and (6.9). The integrated value of α is related to the population distribution in the following manner:

$$\int \alpha_\nu \, d\nu = \kappa N_0 \left(\frac{g_1}{g_2} \frac{N_2}{N_0} - \frac{N_1}{N_0} \right), \qquad (6.24)$$

where κN_0 is the integrated absorption of the unexcited material which can be determined readily. The quantity

$$N = \frac{g_1}{g_2} N_2 - N_1$$

is called the population inversion. Most useful is the quantity $n = N/N_0$, the relative population inversion, which is -1 for the totally unexcited material and 0 for the material which neither absorbs nor amplifies. With the introduction of n, equation (6.24) takes the form

$$\int \alpha_\nu \, d\nu = \kappa N_0 n. \qquad (6.25)$$

The actual value of α_ν for a given frequency ν depends on the lineshape, but as long as the lineshape does not change, we have

$$\alpha_\nu = k_{\nu 0} n, \tag{6.26}$$

where $k_{\nu 0}$ is the absorption of the unexcited material at the frequency ν. The peak values are $0.939 \kappa N_0 n / \Delta\nu$ for the Gaussian line and $0.637 \kappa N_0 n / \Delta\nu$ for the Lorentz line.

REFERENCES

1. A. C. G. Mitchell and M. W. Zemansky, *Resonance Radiation and Excited Atoms*, Cambridge University Press, Cambridge, England, 1934 (1961).
2. J. H. Van Vleck and V. F. Weisskopf, On the shape of collision-broadened lines, *Rev. Mod. Phys.* **17**, 227–236, 1945.
3. G. Birnbaum, *Optical Masers*, Academic Press, New York and London, 1964.

II

General Description
and Theory of Lasers

1. THE LASER

The laser, by definition, is a device that amplifies light by means of stimulated emission of radiation. In practice, a laser is generally used as a source or generator of radiation. The generator is constructed by adding a feedback mechanism in the form of mirrors to the light amplifier. The basic physical problem is the creation of a material with a sufficient degree of negative absorption for some frequency, so that adequate amplification is available to overcome incidental losses of a device and to deliver useful power. We shall now describe the original ruby laser more or less as it was invented by Maiman [1, 2], and we shall introduce lasers of several other types.

The description will be brief and preliminary. Its purpose is to prepare the reader for the analytical discussions that follow. These in turn are necessary to provide a foundation for an adequate presentation of the current state of the art. Therefore we shall not attempt completeness or precision in this section, and we shall avoid digressions pertaining to improvements of the laser. We shall return to this subject in later chapters to provide an accurate and up-to-date picture.

The working element of the ruby laser is a cylinder of pink ruby containing 0.05 per cent chromium. The cylinder is usually between $\frac{1}{2}$ and 1 cm in diameter and 2 to 10 cm long; the end faces are plane and parallel to a high degree of accuracy. One of the end faces is provided with a completely reflecting surface; the other is partially reflecting. The ruby is irradiated on its side by light from a flashlamp operated usually for a few milliseconds at a time with an input energy of 1000 to 2000 joules. The schematic diagram of a typical configuration is shown in Fig. 11, a photograph of the essential parts in Fig. 12. Most of the input energy is dissipated as heat; a fraction of it, however, is emitted by the flashlamp as blue and green radiation, which is absorbed by the ruby. This energy provides the excitation. The ruby funnels the energy, which it absorbs over a broad spectral

49

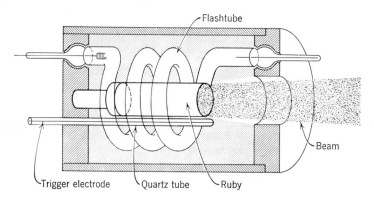

Fig. 11. Ruby laser.

region, into a narrow emission line of the trivalent chromium ion around 6943 Å. The radiation emerges coherently through the partially reflecting end of the ruby.

Actually, this coherent radiation does not appear immediately at the beginning of the excitation. At first, fluorescent radiation of about the same wavelength appears. This is broader in spectral content; it radiates in all directions, and there is no coherence between radiation arising from different points of the ruby. This radiation arises by spontaneous transitions in the chromium ions of ruby. Unless the exciting radiation is sufficiently intense, this fluorescent radiation will be the only one emitted from the ruby. When, however, the exciting radiation exceeds a certain threshold, coherent radiation appears through the end with the partially reflecting surface approximately 0.5 msec after the start of the irradiation.

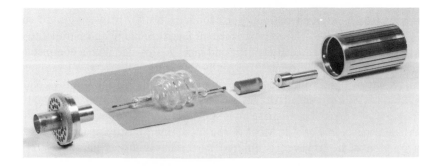

Fig. 12. Ruby laser (photograph of essential parts).

In the simplest case the partially reflecting surface is a phase front of the radiation that emerges perpendicular to the end face. The intensity of this radiation exceeds that of the spontaneous radiation by several orders of magnitude, and the spectral range of the coherent radiation is considerably narrower than that of the fluorescence. The narrowing of the linewidth is due to the effect of the resonant cavity formed by the mirrors. The exact laser linewidth depends on numerous circumstances, which are discussed in Sections II.3 and II.4.

A simple laser of the kind described may produce a radiant flux density of several kilowatts per square centimeter, and in a more elaborate laser the flux density may reach several megawatts per square centimeter. All this radiation is in the spectral interval about 0.1 Å wide.

Let us contrast this with black-body radiation, making use of the radiation laws introduced in Chapter I. By means of (1.4), we find that the black body whose peak emission is at 6943 Å has a temperature of 4174°K. The total radiation of this body in the entire spectrum is approximately 1700 watts/cm^2, as calculated from (1.3). However, we find from (1.2) that only 0.016 watt/cm^2 falls into an 0.1-Å interval around the peak of the emission.

The variation of the intensity of the laser beam described is irregular. In experiments with the early lasers it was observed that even the time delay between the start of excitation and the onset of coherent oscillations was variable, in spite of efforts to keep all experimental variables under control. Once coherent light appeared, its intensity varied greatly and irregularly, with spikes or pulsations of duration of about 1 μsec. The intensity and frequency of these pulsations depend on the temperature of the ruby. Their existence may be explained by the observation that, once stimulated emission sets in, the downward transitions proceed at a rate greater than that at which atoms are excited to the state from which the stimulated emission originates. When this occurs, the stimulated emission may drive the population of this upper state below the level at which the process first sets in, and thus the stimulated emission stops.

The coherence of the light radiated through the partially transmitted mirror can be inferred from the angular distribution of the radiation. The fluorescence of ruby with excitation below the threshold is essentially nondirectional, but with excitation above the threshold the beam is confined to a cone of the order of one degree or less in diameter.

Diffraction experiments with an aperture placed at the mirror result in the anticipated Fraunhofer diffraction pattern for an aperture illuminated by wavefronts approximately plane and coherent.

The processes of fluorescence and stimulated emission in ruby are readily comprehended with the aid of Fig. 13, which is the energy-level diagram of

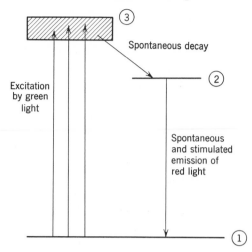

Fig. 13.   Simplified energy-level diagram of chromium ions in ruby.

a three-level fluorescent solid. The ground state is denoted by index 1. Excitation is supplied to the solid by radiation of frequencies which produce absorption into the broad band 3. Most of the absorbed energy is transferred by fast radiationless transitions into the intermediate sharp level 2. The emission of radiation associated with the spontaneous return from level 2 to ground level is ordinary fluorescence. Such fluorescence will take place even at a low level of excitation. When the exciting radiation is sufficiently intense, it is possible to obtain more atoms at level 2 than are left at ground level. The spontaneously emitted photons traveling through the crystal will stimulate additional radiation, and thus induced emission is superposed on the spontaneous emission. Stimulated emission will also take place when the population of the ground level is larger than that of level 2, but the stimulated absorption will be larger than the emission and the net result will be a loss in the number of photons.

Ordinary fluorescence acts as a drain on the population of level 2. After the exciting radiation is extinguished, level 2 is emptied by fluorescence at a rate that varies from material to material. In ruby, at room temperature, the lifetime of level 2 is 3 msec. When the ruby is excited by a light flash, no laser output is obtained for the energy invested in removing, by excitation, one-half of the atoms from the ground level. This inefficiency is an intrinsic property of every three-level solid laser. To overcome it, it is necessary to utilize a material possessing four levels capable of participating in laser action. The schematic energy-level diagram of such a material is shown in Fig. 14. In this case there is an additional normally unoccupied

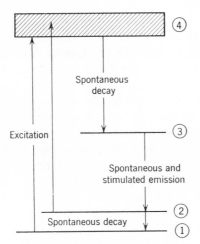

Fig. 14. Simplified energy-level diagram of a four-level laser.

level above ground level at which the relevant transitions terminate; therefore laser action can begin as soon as there is significant occupation of the initial level, which in this diagram bears index 3. A pulsed four-level laser need not operate with the energy waste of a three-level laser. Sorokin and Stevenson [3, 4, 5] constructed the first four-level laser, utilizing uranium or samarium ions embedded in a calcium fluoride crystal. These and others are described in Chapter III.

Laser action is possible only if the material can be placed in a condition of amplification (negative absorption) for some wavelength region and if, in addition, a minimum feedback is established by means of reflectors. Negative absorption takes place in a stationary, nonequilibrium state that depends on the rate at which excitation is provided and also on the rates of relaxation and transition, stimulated and spontaneous, that govern the passage of atoms through the cycles illustrated in Figs. 13 and 14.

It is necessary, in general, that the rate of radiationless transfer from the uppermost level to the level at which the laser action begins be fast compared with the other spontaneous transition rates in a three-level laser. In a four-level laser there is the additional requirement of a rapid rate of spontaneous transition from the laser terminal level to ground level; without this, a phenomenon analogous to the stopping up of a drain will occur. In a four-level laser we must also guard against overpopulation of the terminal state by electrons raised from the ground level by thermal fluctuations. Hence the separation of the terminal level from the ground level must exceed kT. If this is not the case at room temperature, the laser must be refrigerated.

The top levels in Figs. 13 and 14 are shown as broad bands in contrast with the other levels. This breadth at the top level is a practical necessity because there is not enough energy available from ordinary sources of radiation in a narrow band. If a laser were to be used to excite a second laser, a material with a narrow top level would be acceptable. Under ordinary circumstances powerful flashlamps are pushed to the limit of their capabilities to provide sufficient excitation for materials, such as ruby, that are capable of utilizing incident radiation from 3800 to about 6100 Å.

Solid-state lasers generally operate intermittently. The reasons for this are mostly technical. First, it is difficult to provide a sufficiently powerful source of exciting light capable of continuous operation; second, a great deal of heat evolves within the laser which must be dissipated. Ordinary ruby lasers are excited for periods of a few milliseconds, the length of the period being determined by the duration of the exciting flash.

In addition to chromium ions, which are the active ingredients in ruby, laser action has been observed in uranium, and in most rare-earth ions embedded in solids. These are four-level laser materials; the first continuously operating solid laser was of this type.

The lasers described so far operate by optical excitation.

Stimulated emission may also be obtained from semiconductors. Highly doped GaAs p-n junctions have been found to exhibit laser action when a large current passes through a junction refrigerated to 77°K. The radiation is due to transitions of injected electrons from low-lying levels of the conduction band to the uppermost levels of the valence band; the frequency corresponds to the band gap energy. In this case the primary source of energy is not irradiation but an electric generator which causes the injection of the electrons into the semiconductor.

Gases offer interesting possibilities as laser materials because their atoms are more accessible for excitation by a variety of means. In addition to optical excitation, which is not very effective for gases, there are at least three other processes capable of producing population inversion in a gas. Collision by electron impact in a suitable discharge will in certain gases such as pure neon, argon, krypton, and xenon produce population inversion for some energy levels. Laser operation has been obtained in this manner in the infrared region in all these gases. By far the most effective method of achieving laser action involves the use of a gaseous mixture, such as helium and neon, in which there occurs, in addition to excitation by electron impact, a transfer of excitation between colliding atoms of different kinds. The upper state of neon is populated by the transfer of excitation from helium atoms in a metastable state. Finally, collisions between atoms and molecules which lead to dissociation may leave one of the dissociated fragments in an excited state from which a radiative

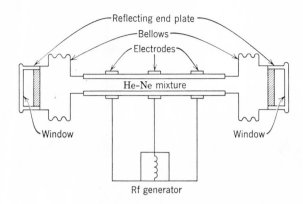

Fig. 15. A schematic of the first gaseous laser. (Built at Bell Telephone Laboratories.)

transition to a lower unpopulated level is possible. Stimulated emission has been produced in several elements in this manner.

We defer the detailed discussion of the considerable variety of gas lasers until Chapter V and confine ourselves here to the brief introduction of the helium-neon laser. The first such laser was built in 1960 by Javan, Bennett, and Herriott [6] at Bell Telephone Laboratories. It consists of a discharge tube 100 cm long with an inside diameter of 1.5 cm filled with helium at 1 torr pressure and with neon at 0.1 torr. Flat reflector plates, which must be adjusted parallel within a few seconds of arc, are included in the gas-filled section of the tube. A simplified diagram of this laser is given in Fig. 15, while Fig. 16 is the photograph of Javan's original apparatus. More complete drawings and pictures showing the adjusting mechanism have been published by Herriott and Schawlow [7, 8]. The technical complications in the fabrication of this laser arise mostly from the inclusion of the bellows for the adjustment of the mirrors. These complications may be avoided by the simple expedient of using external reflectors, but when external reflectors are used care must be taken to minimize unwanted reflections from the glass or quartz windows at the ends of the tube. This is accomplished by terminating the tube with optical flats oriented at the Brewster angle.

The radio-frequency (rf) generator shown in Fig. 15 is usually operated in the 25- to 30-Mc region. It serves to establish an electric discharge in the gas, although a d-c discharge may serve the purpose as well. In the discharge electrons acquire energy from the driving electrical source; a part of their energy is communicated to the helium and neon atoms. The relevant stimulated transitions take place in neon; the presence of helium serves to aid in the establishment of population inversion in neon.

Fig. 16.   Javan's helium-neon laser. (Courtesy Bell Telephone Laboratories.)

Javan and associates originally observed laser action at five different frequencies which correspond to wavelengths between 1.12 and 1.21 μ. The strongest stimulated emission occurs at $\lambda = 1.1523\ \mu$. Laser action was later observed in neon at many other frequencies. The most notable neon laser line has a wavelength of 6328 Å; it provides the most convenient, steady source of coherent radiation in the visible region of the spectrum. The conditions for the excitation of different neon laser lines are similar; one may change from the 1.15-μ laser to the 6328-Å laser by replacing the reflectors which have a high reflectivity in the near infrared by reflectors with high reflectivity between 6300 and 6400 Å.

The great value of helium-neon lasers is their remarkable monochromaticity and stability under carefully controlled experimental conditions. The power output of helium-neon lasers is of the order of 1 mW, but this power level remains fairly constant and may be maintained essentially indefinitely.

We began this book with the statement that the laser is a light amplifier, yet so far our discussion has pertained only to light generation. Amplification was described as a part of generation, but not independently. Those readers who recall the exceptionally fine properties of the maser as a microwave amplifier might wonder why the laser is not employed as an amplifier of an incident light of low intensity.

The reason for the unsuitability of a laser as a low-level amplifier is its extremely high noise level. The second of Einstein's relations (5.4) in Chapter I shows that the rate of spontaneous emission is proportional to ν^3 times the rate of stimulated emission. In an amplifier the spontaneous emission is the noise; the stimulated emission is the amplified signal. In the microwave region the noise is extremely low, but changing to the optical region changes the frequency by a factor of about 10^4; therefore the signal-to-noise ratio deteriorates by a factor of about 10^{12}. Under these circumstances the amplifying properties of a laser are useful only in situations in which the high noise is not objectionable. This is the case when the input signal arises from another laser and is already very intense. Further amplification can then be accomplished as demonstrated by Kisliuk and Boyle [9], who amplified the output of a ruby laser oscillator by means of a second ruby which was naturally not provided with reflecting mirrors.

REFERENCES

1. T. H. Maiman, Optical maser action in ruby, *Brit. Commun. and Electr.* 7, 674–675, 1960.
2. T. H. Maiman, Stimulated optical radiation in ruby, *Nature* 187, 493–494, 1960.
3. P. P. Sorokin and M. J. Stevenson, Stimulated infrared emission of trivalent uranium, *Phys. Rev. Lett.* 5, 557–559, 1960.
4. P. P. Sorokin and M. J. Stevenson, Stimulated emission from $CaF_2:U^{+3}$ and $CaF_2:Sm^{+2}$, *Advances in Quantum Electronics*, J. R. Singer, ed., Columbia Univ. Press, New York, 1961, 65–76.
5. P. P. Sorokin and M. J. Stevenson, Solid state optical maser using divalent samarium in calcium fluoride, *IBM J. Res. Dev.* 5, 56–58, 1961.
6. A. Javan, W. R. Bennett, Jr., and D. R. Herriott, Population inversion and continuous optical maser oscillation in a gas discharge containing a He-Ne mixture, *Phys. Rev. Lett.* 6, 106–110, 1961.
7. D. R. Herriott, Optical properties of a continuous He-Ne optical maser, *J. Opt. Soc. Am.* 52, 31–37, 1962. *Appl. Optics Suppl.* 1, 118–124, 1962.
8. A. L. Schawlow, Optical masers, *Scientific American*, June 1961, 52–61.
9. P. P. Kisliuk and W. S. Boyle, The pulsed ruby maser as a light amplifier, *Proc. IRE* 49, 1635–1639, 1961.

2. THRESHOLD CONDITION AND RATE EQUATIONS

The basic ideas concerning absorption and emission of radiation in an atomic ensemble were introduced in Section I.6. We defined an absorption coefficient k_ν, a quantity representable in the form

$$k_\nu = Kg(\nu; \nu_0), \tag{2.1}$$

where K is the integrated absorption for the entire line

$$K = \int k_\nu \, d\nu, \tag{2.2}$$

and $g(\nu; \nu_0)$ is the normalized lineshape. The quantity K is related to the distribution of atoms among the energy levels and to the lifetime of the relevant spontaneous transition. The relation is equation (6.7) of Chapter I. The peak value of the absorption coefficient is $k_m = Kg(\nu_0; \nu_0)$; it depends on the integrated absorption and the lineshape. For Lorentz lineshape we have as a consequence of equation (6.22) of Chapter I

$$k_m = \frac{2K}{\pi \, \Delta\nu}. \tag{2.3}$$

For a given integrated absorption the peak value of the absorption coefficient is inversely proportional to the linewidth. If the peak absorption k_m of the material having a certain distribution of population among the levels is compared with the peak absorption k_0 of the unexcited material $N_1 = N_0$, $N_2 = 0$, then it follows from (6.8) and (6.10) that

$$\frac{k_m}{k_0} = \frac{N_1 - (g_1/g_2)N_2}{N_0}, \tag{2.4}$$

provided that the lineshape remains the same.

Consider now an aggregate of atoms in which the natural population distribution has been inverted and which has the property of negative absorption in some frequency range. The necessary condition is

$$\frac{N_i}{g_i} < \frac{N_j}{g_j}, \tag{2.5}$$

and $E_i < E_j$ for some pair of levels i and j. In such a material k_ν is negative in the vicinity of the frequency $\nu_0 = (E_j - E_i)/h$; the intensity of a parallel beam of the proper frequency will grow according to the equation

$$I = I_0 e^{\alpha x}, \tag{2.6}$$

where $\alpha = -k_\nu$. Under certain circumstances this amplification of light may lead to light generation or laser action.

We have seen that the laser as a device consists of a pair of parallel mirrors, between which is a piece of material that is brought into a condition of negative absorption for some frequencies. This device is represented schematically in Fig. 17, where the reflectors are shown detached from the amplifying material (ruby). However, this separation is not necessary. In order to obtain a power output from the laser, at least one of the reflectors is made partially transmitting. Transmissivity t, reflectivity r, and loss q are connected by the equation $r + t + q = 1$. When good dielectric multilayer reflectors are used, q may be neglected, and we may write $t = 1 - r$.

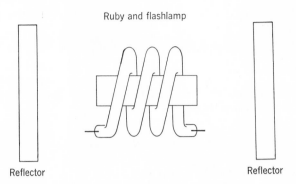

Ruby and flashlamp

Reflector $\qquad$ Reflector

Fig. 17. Schematic diagram of a laser.

As a result of spontaneous and stimulated emission, light is generated within the laser. Light that does not pass out through the sides travels the length of the laser and is reflected back and forth between the mirrors. At the time of each reflection a fraction $1 - r$ of the energy is lost. Therefore oscillations may be sustained only if the gain of the radiation passing through the full length of the crystal is sufficient to compensate for the energy loss at the end and other losses due to secondary causes. Starting at one point, the radiation will suffer two reflections before it passes the same point in the original direction. In each passage through the material the intensity gains by a factor of $\exp \alpha L$. If the reflection coefficients at the end faces are r_1 and r_2, the energy of the wave will have changed by a factor of $F = r_1 r_2 e^{2\alpha L}$.

We introduce r, the geometric mean of the reflection coefficients r_1 and r_2, and also the loss coefficient $\gamma = -\log_e r$. The gain in one complete (round trip) passage is $F = e^{2(\alpha L - \gamma)}$. When F is not less than 1, oscillations will build up, starting from a small disturbance; when F is less than 1, they will die out. Clearly, if somehow the situation $\alpha L > \gamma$ is brought about, the intensity of radiation of the proper frequency will build up rapidly until it becomes so large that the stimulated transitions will deplete the upper level and reduce the value of α. This is a dynamic situation that will be encountered again in connection with pulsations and giant pulses. In order to determine what may happen in a stationary or steady-state situation, we recall that there is a steady generation of light of the proper frequency in the laser as a result of spontaneous emission which proceeds at the rate of, say, n quanta per second. Let t denote the transmission coefficient of the partially transmitting reflector. Then on every complete two-way passage of the light through the laser the fraction t of the intensity incident on the reflector leaves the laser, and the intensity changes by the factor $\exp 2(\alpha L - \gamma)$. Therefore light will be emitted from the laser at the following rate:

$$p = nh\nu t[1 + e^{2(\alpha L - \gamma)} + \cdots] = nh\nu t[1 - e^{2(\alpha L - \gamma)}]^{-1}.$$

The output would become infinite if αL were equal to or greater than γ. A steady output may be maintained, however, if the peak value α_m of $\alpha(\nu)$ remains just below the value

$$\alpha_m = \frac{\gamma}{L}. \tag{2.7}$$

This equation is the *threshold condition.*

Since $\alpha(\nu)$ is nearly equal to α_m in a very narrow spectral range, it is clear that only in this range will the amplification be large enough to offset losses. Consequently, the output of the laser will be sharply peaked, and its linewidth will be much narrower than the atomic linewidth. We will see in Section II.4 how the linewidth of the laser output is related to the linewidth of the atomic spectrum, to the Q of the cavity formed by the reflectors of the laser, and also to the level of the power output.*

The threshold condition relates the *peak* of the amplification curve to the length of the laser and to the losses at the ends. The Füchtbauer-Ladenburg formula relates the *integral* of the amplification curve to the population inversion, or excitation. The threshold as a function of the excitation can be given if the shape of the amplification curve is known. Let P be the peak value of the amplification curve normalized so that its integral is 1. Then

$$P\kappa g_1\left(\frac{N_2}{g_2} - \frac{N_1}{g_1}\right) = \frac{\gamma}{L} \tag{2.8}$$

is the threshold condition. In special cases one may express P in terms of the linewidths and thus obtain

$$\frac{N_2}{g_2} - \frac{N_1}{g_1} = \frac{\pi \, \Delta\nu}{2} \frac{\gamma}{\kappa g_1 L} \tag{2.9}$$

for the Lorentz line, and

$$\frac{N_2}{g_2} - \frac{N_1}{g_1} = \frac{\Delta\nu}{0.939} \frac{\gamma}{\kappa g_1 L} \tag{2.9'}$$

for the Gaussian line.

It is to be noted that the linewidth $\Delta\nu$ of the Lorentz line is independent of the frequency of the radiation, but the linewidth of the Doppler-broadened line is proportional to the frequency (Chapter I, equation

* For the definition of Q see p. 80.

(6.15)). The quantity κ is proportional to ν^{-2} (Chapter I, equation (6.9)). Consequently the population inversion required for threshold is proportional to ν^2 for Lorentz lines and to ν^3 for Doppler-broadened lines. When other things are equal, it is therefore easier to fulfill the threshold condition at lower frequencies.

Equation (2.8) can be used to determine the minimum value of N_2 when κ is known. When k_0 is known, we may turn to (2.4) and write the threshold condition in the form

$$\frac{g_1}{g_2} N_2 - N_1 = \frac{N_0 \gamma}{k_0 L} = \frac{\gamma}{\sigma_0 L}, \tag{2.10}$$

where ratio k_0/N_0 is σ_0, the peak absorption cross section per atom. According to the measurements of Maiman [1], the value of σ_0 for the ruby R_1 line is 2.5×10^{-20} cm^2.

A general conclusion may be drawn from equation (2.10). Since the intensity of the excitation determines the population inversion, and this in turn has to exceed the minimal value $\gamma/k_0 L$, a certain tradeoff is possible between the reflection coefficient that determines γ and the active length L of the laser. Any deterioration of the reflector must be compensated by increased length or a penalty is paid in the form of increased threshold of excitation. It is also significant that the onset of oscillations can be prevented by lowering r and thereby increasing γ.

If the negatively absorbing material is kept in a stationary state by means of *steadily supplied* excitation, the left-hand side of (2.9) or (2.10) may be related to the rate at which excitation is provided. We shall show how this calculation can be carried out in the case of the ruby. For the relevant levels in ruby $g_1 = g_2$;* therefore the statistical weights may be canceled out. The reader is warned against the indiscriminate dropping of the factor g_1/g_2 in (2.9) or (2.10). Neglect of this factor where needed has led to erroneous conclusions in the literature.

The occupation of levels in a three-level system with a total of N_0 atoms is governed by the *rate equations*

$$\frac{dN_3}{dt} = W_{13}N_1 - (W_{31} + A_{31} + S_{32})N_3,$$

$$\frac{dN_2}{dt} = W_{12}N_1 - (W_{21} + A_{21})N_2 + S_{32}N_3, \tag{2.11}$$

$$N_0 = N_1 + N_2 + N_3.$$

Reference is made to Fig. 18, which shows such a system.

* Strictly speaking, it is not true that $g_1 = g_2$ for the ruby R_1 line. Practically, however, this is a good assumption because of the close coupling of the two levels, each of multiplicity 2, at which the R_1 and R_2 lines originate. The ground state of ruby has a multiplicity of 4.

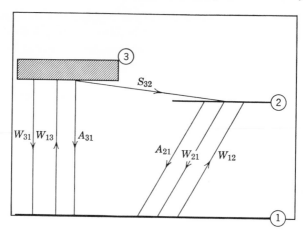

Fig. 18. Energy-level diagram for a three-level fluorescent solid. (Stimulated transitions are indicated by W, spontaneous radiative transitions by A, and spontaneous nonradiative ones by S.)

Here the W's denote probabilities of stimulated transitions which involve the radiation density; the A's indicate probabilities of spontaneous transitions, S_{32} the probability of radiationless transition from level 3 to level 2, and N_0 the constant total number of active atoms per unit volume. In a steady state the derivatives in (2.11) are 0, and we can solve for the ratio N_2/N_1. A simple solution is obtained under the assumption that A_{31}, the rate of spontaneous return from the top level, is low compared to all other processes. In this case

$$\frac{N_2}{N_1} = \left(\frac{W_{13}S_{32}}{W_{31} + S_{32}} + W_{12}\right)(A_{21} + W_{21})^{-1}. \qquad (2.12)$$

Further simplification is possible by noting that $W_{13} = W_{31}$ and $W_{21} = W_{12}$, as a consequence of one of Einstein's relations (5.4), and by restricting ourselves to materials in which the radiationless relaxation between levels 3 and 2 is fast. The last condition means that $S_{32} \gg W_{13}$. With this restriction,

$$\frac{N_2 - N_1}{N_0} = \frac{W_{13} - A_{21}}{W_{13} + A_{21} + 2W_{12}} \qquad (2.13)$$

follows. The quantity W_{13} is proportional to the incident exciting light, and W_{12} is proportional to the laser action in progress. (At the threshold of oscillations $W_{12} = 0$.) Given k_0, r, and L, we may calculate the fraction $(N_2 - N_1)/N_0$ from (2.10). The minimum value of W_{13} necessary to achieve this fraction is then computed from (2.13).

Clearly W_{13} must be larger than A_{21}; equality is insufficient because of the unavoidable losses at the reflectors. Yet the condition $W_{13} = A_{21}$ is frequently used in estimating the threshold power required for oscillations. Actually, this is only the condition for the attainment of negative absorption in the material.

Let us estimate the exciting radiation required to produce negative absorption. If the excitation is accomplished by a monochromatic plane wave at the frequency ν_p and n photons per second are incident on the unit surface area of the crystal, the following relations hold:

$$P = nh\nu_p \quad \text{and} \quad W_{13} = u_p B_{13} = \frac{1}{c}(nB_{13}h\nu_p\eta) = n\sigma_p, \quad (2.14)$$

where the quantity

$$\sigma_p = \frac{1}{c}(B_{13}h\nu_p\eta) \quad (2.15)$$

is the integrated absorption cross section for the pumping radiation. Then, in order to achieve the condition $W_{13} \geqq A_{21}$, the incident radiative flux density P must be at least

$$P_{\min} = \frac{A_{21}h\nu_p}{\sigma_p}. \quad (2.16)$$

Equation (2.16) shows the relevant factors that determine the required level of irradiation. The power required increases proportionally with the spontaneous transition probability; hence it varies inversely with the lifetime of the excited state.

Illumination by means of a plane wave is a mathematical artifice. A configuration more likely to be realized in practice is one in which the material is isotropically illuminated over most of its surface. Moreover, the illuminating source is likely to be a high-pressure discharge with a more or less continuous spectral output resembling the spectral distribution of the black-body radiator. It is therefore realistic to consider the laser crystal to be immersed in an isotropic black-body radiation and determine the minimum temperature of the black-body source which may produce population inversion in a three-level fluorescent solid. In view of (5.5) of Chapter I we may write

$$W_{13} = \frac{g_3}{g_1} B_{31}u(\nu_{13}), \quad (2.17)$$

where $u(\nu_{13})$ is the energy density of black-body radiation. The expression for $u(\nu)$ valid in vacuum is (1.1) of Chapter I. In a solid this has to be modified by replacing c with the appropriate velocity in the solid, namely

c/η. Combining the correct equation for $u(\nu)$ with (5.6) of Chapter I, we obtain

$$u(\nu)B_{31} = \frac{A_{31}}{e^{h\nu/kT} - 1} \qquad (2.18)$$

for $\nu = \nu_{13}$. The condition for population inversion is $W_{13} > A_{21}$; it requires that

$$\frac{g_3}{g_1}\frac{A_{31}}{A_{21}} > e^{h\nu/kT} - 1 \qquad (2.19)$$

for $\nu = \nu_{13}$. Thus the minimum source temperature, T_s, is given by

$$T_s = \frac{E_3 - E_1}{k \log (1 + g_3 A_{31}/g_1 A_{21})}. \qquad (2.20)$$

We note that these calculations are independent of the shape and width of the absorption curve as long as the absorption band is narrow enough so that the variation of the intensity of black-body radiation over the band may be neglected.

We may now make a rough estimate of the source temperature required for producing negative absorption in ruby, neglecting the known fact that what we designated as level 2 is actually a double level, and that only the lower one of these levels produces the 6943 Å radiation. According to the measurements of Maiman [1, 2],

$$E_3 - E_1 \sim 18{,}200 \text{ cm}^{-1} = 3.6 \times 10^{-12} \text{ erg,}$$
$$A_{31} = 3 \times 10^5 \text{ sec}^{-1},$$
$$A_{21} = 232 \text{ sec}^{-1}.$$

The multiplicities of the relevant levels are $g_1 = 4$ and $g_3 = 12$. (See Section III.1.) Therefore

$$\frac{g_3}{g_1}\frac{A_{31}}{A_{21}} = 3880.$$

With these numerical values we obtain from (2.20) the temperature $T_s = 3160°K$. The actual temperature required for laser operation is higher than this because several complicating factors were neglected in the computation. Nevertheless this computation, which follows the line of reasoning employed by Maiman [1, 3], provides an indication of the magnitudes involved.

The preceding calculation is in principle applicable to any three-level solid laser excited by irradiation (optical pumping). The analysis of the kinetics of a similarly excited four-level solid laser requires equations involving the populations of all four levels and transitions of several types from every level to every other level. Approximate equations may be

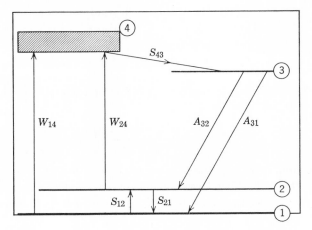

Fig. 19. Principal transitions in a four-level solid laser.

obtained, however, by concentrating on the few dominant transitions shown in Fig. 19. The notation is similar to that for three-level lasers; W's denote stimulated transitions, A's spontaneous transitions, S's non-radiative transitions. A few physical assumptions simplify the mathematical problem: It is assumed that the transition from level 4 to level 3 is very fast, which is equivalent to saying that level 4 is always practically empty and that the pumping takes place directly into level 3. Moreover, it is also assumed that transitions between levels 1 and 2 take place so fast that up to the time the stimulated emission begins, the occupancy of level 2 can be calculated by Boltzmann's formula

$$N_2 = N_1 \, e^{(E_1 - E_2)/kT}. \tag{2.21}$$

The essential variables of the problem are then N_2 and N_3, and the threshold condition is

$$\frac{g_2}{g_3} N_3 - N_2 = \frac{\gamma}{\sigma_{32} L}, \tag{2.22}$$

where σ_{32} is an absorption cross section that is not easy to determine experimentally.

It must be remembered that the pumping radiation covers a broad spectral band; therefore it will cause transitions not only from the ground level but also from level 2 to level 4. The transitions take place into a band (level 4) which arises from the ionic levels under the influence of the crystal field. This structure of level 4 prevents the application of the selection rules, which in the case of a free atom forbid either the 1 to 4 or the 2 to 4 transition. The approximate rate equation is (before the onset of stimulated emission)

$$\frac{dN_3}{dt} = W_{14}N_1 + W_{24}N_2 - (A_{31} + A_{32})N_3. \tag{2.23}$$

We may eliminate N_1 by means of (2.21). A stationary state is reached when $\dot{N}_3 = 0$, i.e., when

$$\frac{N_3}{N_2} = \frac{W_{14}\,e^{(E_2 - E_1)/kT} + W_{24}}{A_{31} + A_{32}}. \tag{2.24}$$

It is customary to introduce $A_3 = A_{31} + A_{32}$, the total spontaneous decay rate of level 3. When levels 1 and 2 are separated by a very small gap it is also permissible to assume that W_{24} is equal to W_{14}. In this case

$$\frac{N_3}{N_2} = \frac{W_{14}(1 + e^{(E_2 - E_1)/kT})}{A_3}. \tag{2.25}$$

To obtain an equation of the type of (2.13) we introduce the total number of available active ions

$$N_0 = N_1 + N_2 + N_3 = N_2[1 + e^{(E_2 - E_1)/kT}] + N_3. \tag{2.26}$$

From (2.25) and (2.26) it follows that in the steady state

$$\frac{N_3 - N_2}{N_0} = \frac{W_{14} - A_3[1 + e^{(E_2 - E_1)/kT}]^{-1}}{W_{14} + A_3}. \tag{2.27}$$

This formula, as well as (2.13), was obtained by Maiman [4]. It is convenient for threshold calculations when the *multiplicities of levels 2 and 3 are equal*. In the general case one must fall back on equations (2.22), (2.25), and (2.26).

We emphasize that the above simplified calculations are applicable only when the population of the terminal level is determined by thermal processes and the transition rate between the ground level and the terminal level is high. This is definitely not the case in gaseous lasers whose terminal levels are generally very high above the ground level compared to kT and where the transition rate between the terminal level and the ground level is often the limiting factor of laser operation. The kinetics of such lasers is discussed in Chapter V. Moreover, the "stationary" distribution of population calculated according to (2.24) is applicable only *before* the onset of stimulated emission. In the case when laser operation is possible this distribution will not be stationary because stimulated emission will begin with a depletion of $N_3 - N_2$. Therefore, equations (2.24) to (2.27) are useful only in that they help to decide whether or not laser operation is possible. Once such operation is possible the population of the levels involved in a steady-state laser operation must be calculated from equations which take into account the stimulated transitions between levels 2 and 3.

It is relatively easy to make input and output calculations for a ruby laser in a hypothetical steady radiating state. Such calculations are of little value, however, because of the large intensity fluctuations which seem inherent in the situation.

The power generated at frequency v_{21} in a uniformly excited ruby laser of volume V is

$$P_0 = W_{21}(N_2 - N_1)Vhv_{21}. \tag{2.28}$$

Here W_{21} is proportional to the radiation density, and $N_2 - N_1$ depends on the radiation density as well as on the intensity of excitation. Starting with zero radiation density at frequency v_{21} when the threshold is first reached, the radiation density builds up and depletes $N_2 - N_1$ until either a steady state is arrived at or the radiation density starts to fall again and an oscillation of intensity ensues. This oscillation of intensity is called pulsation. It has already been mentioned in Section II.1. Further material on pulsations is included in Chapter VI.

REFERENCES

1. T. H. Maiman, R. H. Hoskins, I. J. D'Haenens, C. K. Asawa, and V. Evtuhov, Stimulated optical emission in fluorescent solids II, *Phys. Rev.* **123**, 1151–1157, 1961.
2. T. H. Maiman, Optical and microwave optical experiments in ruby, *Phys. Rev. Lett.* **4**, 564–565, 1960.
3. T. H. Maiman, Optical maser action in ruby, *Brit. Commun. and Electr.* **7**, 674–675, 1960.
4. T. H. Maiman, Stimulated optical emission in fluorescent solids I, *Phys. Rev.* **123**, 1145–1150, 1961.

3. THEORY OF OSCILLATION AND RADIATION MODES

Standing Waves

The laser consists of a vast number of atomic amplifiers placed between two partially reflecting mirrors which cause radiation to travel back and forth through the amplifying medium. Our concern at present is the structure of the electromagnetic field built up within the laser and the properties of the electromagnetic field radiated from the laser. The electromagnetic field within the laser may be regarded as a field in a cavity which is weakly coupled to the outside. The different types of electromagnetic oscillations of the laser regarded as an isolated cavity are called *modes of oscillation* or briefly *modes*. Simple optical theory tolerates the existence of uniform plane waves of finite extent. The field between the mirrors may be regarded as the superposition of plane waves traveling back and forth. The plane waves that travel longitudinally, that is, perpendicular to the mirrors, form a standing wave pattern which leads to reinforcement when the distance of the mirrors is an integral multiple of the half-wavelength. Reinforcement takes place when

$$n\lambda = 2L, \tag{3.1}$$

where n is an integer, λ is the wavelength in the laser material, and L is the distance between the mirrors.* Similar relations are known for waves traveling in other directions.

For a ruby laser a few centimeters long, the integer n is of the order of 100,000. Each value of n corresponds to a frequency at which oscillations may occur provided that sufficient amplification is available at that frequency. A fixed value of n characterizes a resonance or a mode. Strictly speaking, two modes of radiation must be considered for each permissible frequency because of the possible variation of polarization.

From the equation

$$\frac{1}{\lambda_0} = \frac{n}{2L\eta}, \tag{3.2}$$

we find that two consecutive resonances (or modes) are separated by the wave number

$$\varDelta\left(\frac{1}{\lambda_0}\right) = \frac{1}{2L\eta}, \tag{3.3}$$

and that the fractional change in wavelength from one axial mode to the next is

$$\frac{\varDelta\lambda_0}{\lambda_0} = \frac{1}{n}. \tag{3.4}$$

Consecutive modes of this type are so closely spaced that many lie within one atomic linewidth. In other words, the band width of the atomic amplifiers generally encompasses a number of laser modes.

The uniform plane wave theory correctly predicts the frequency separation of the principal resonances. However, other resonances may also occur. Moreover the assumption of uniform plane waves of finite extent is inconsistent with the principles of electromagnetic radiation. Finally observations of the radiation emerging from the laser offer a positive proof that the surface of the mirrors is not a uniform phase and amplitude surface. Consequently, a refinement of the theory is in order.

Cavity Theory

A solid-state laser, such as the ruby laser, in many ways resembles a metallic cavity in which a hole is cut so that some of the radiation may

---

* The symbol λ_0 is used for wavelength in vacuum; hence $\lambda_0 = \lambda\eta$, where η is the index of refraction.

escape. The principal interest in the laser field is in the radiation which propagates nearly, or exactly, along the longitudinal direction. It is useful, although somewhat inexact, to think in terms of the ray theory and to note that radiation directed at large angles away from the longitudinal axis of the laser encounters the surface of the laser before the amplification within the laser can offset the inevitable loss at the surface. Therefore, at large angles away from the axial direction one will encounter negligible stimulated radiation. Nearly axial rays suffer total reflection at the polished side surfaces; therefore their fate is the same as it would be if the side surfaces were metalized. One of the end surfaces is generally completely reflecting and the other almost completely so. Therefore, for the purpose of describing the modes of the stimulated radiation, we may in a first approximation assume a conductive cavity and take the output into account as a perturbation of the cavity field.

It is easily shown that the vector potential in a rectangular cavity is the sum of terms of the form

$$A_{k_1, k_2, k_3} \, e^{i(k_1 x + k_2 y + k_3 z)}, \tag{3.5}$$

where

$$k^2 = k_1{}^2 + k_2{}^2 + k_3{}^2 = \omega^2 \eta^2 / c^2. \tag{3.6}$$

The boundary conditions are $k_1 a = l\pi$, $k_2 b = m\pi$, and $k_2 L = n\pi$, where a, b, and L are the dimensions of the rectangular box and l, m, and n are integers. The resonant frequencies are then determined from the equation

$$\left(\frac{l\pi}{a}\right)^2 + \left(\frac{m\pi}{b}\right)^2 + \left(\frac{n\pi}{L}\right)^2 = k^2 = \left(\frac{2\pi\nu\eta}{c}\right)^2. \tag{3.7}$$

For a cylindrical laser of radius r, expression (3.5) is replaced by the cylinder functions, and (3.7) is replaced by

$$\left(\frac{\chi_{lm}}{r}\right)^2 + \left(\frac{\pi n}{L}\right)^2 = k^2, \tag{3.8}$$

where χ_{lm} is the mth zero of the Bessel function of order l or its derivative. The *longitudinal or axial modes* in either case are obtained by setting $l = 0$ and $m = 0$ and defining χ_{00} as 0. Then we obtain equation (3.2). In other words, the cavity theory produces all the modes of the simpler theory plus additional, *transverse modes*, the latter being the modes for which $l^2 + m^2 \neq 0$. The first transverse mode in the cylindrical case corresponds to $l = 0, m = 1$. Let us calculate the separation of the first transverse mode from the axial mode for a large value of n using k_1 and k_0 to indicate the

wave numbers of the transverse and axial modes, respectively. Then from
(3.8) it follows that

$$k_1^2 - k_0^2 = \frac{\chi_{01}^2}{r^2},$$ (3.9)

and the corresponding relative frequency difference is

$$\frac{\nu_1 - \nu_0}{\nu_0} = \frac{\chi_{01}^2 \lambda^2}{8\pi^2 r^2}.$$ (3.10)

Here λ is the average wavelength and $\chi_{01} = 2.405$ is the first zero of the
Bessel function J_0. For a ruby rod 1 cm in diameter the quantity on the
right of (3.10) is 4.56×10^{-10}.

Actually, the solid laser is not a metallic box but a dielectric resonator,
and the exact theory of the latter leads to more complicated field configurations within the cylinder than are obtained for a resonator enclosed
by metal [1]. It is found, for example, that transverse electric and transverse
magnetic fields exist only in the axially symmetric modes. However, the
equation which determines the resonant frequencies is always of the form

$$\kappa_{lm}^2 + \left(\frac{\pi n}{L}\right)^2 = k^2.$$ (3.11)

While in the cylindrical resonator bounded by metal the quantities κ_{lm} are
determined by the solutions of $J_l(\kappa r) = 0$ and $J_l'(\kappa r) = 0$, the equations
determining the κ's in the dielectric case are more complicated and lead to
κ's that are only approximately equal to those obtained in the simpler case.
However, for the nearly axial modes of the laser the number n is very large,
the second term predominates in (3.11), and a moderate error in κ does not
significantly alter the value of the frequency. Where frequency differences
of modes are involved one must be careful to use the correct values.

It is shown in electromagnetic theory that the cavity modes discussed
above are orthogonal to each other. Physically this means that oscillations
of a single mode may be excited without exciting others. This isolation of
modes, however, is true only in the ideal case when the cavity walls are
infinitely conducting and have the exact geometrical shape postulated.
Deviations from these idealized conditions or inclusion of polarizable
material in the cavity may result in the coupling of modes, i.e., the transfer
of energy from one mode of oscillation to another.

The number of possible modes of oscillation in a laser is very large.
In general, different modes have different frequencies, and it is of some
interest to inquire concerning the distribution of the modes in frequency.
It is easy to determine the density function $p(\nu)$ which is defined as follows:
$p(\nu)\, d\nu$ is the number of modes per volume element in the frequency interval
ν to $\nu + d\nu$.

Let us return to equation (3.7) and apply it to a cube of side a. When a triplet of integers (l, m, n) satisfies the relation

$$l^2 + m^2 + n^2 = k^2 a^2 / \pi^2, \qquad (3.12)$$

there is a pair of modes (two polarizations!) with a wave number k that have the frequency $\nu = ck/2\pi\eta$. Reflection on one of the sides changes k_1 into $-k_1$, or k_2 into $-k_2$, or k_3 into $-k_3$. Therefore a single mode in a reflecting cube consists of a combination of eight terms differing only in the signs of their k's. When counting modes one should count only triplets with positive integers l, m, and n. The number of such triplets that satisfy the inequality

$$l^2 + m^2 + n^2 \leq \left(\frac{2\nu a \eta}{c}\right)^2 \qquad (3.13)$$

is one-half the number of modes whose frequency does not exceed ν. But the number of points with integral coordinates located in one octant of the sphere

$$l^2 + m^2 + n^2 \leq R^2$$

is $\pi R^3 / 6$; therefore the number of modes with frequencies not exceeding ν is

$$P(\nu) = \frac{8\pi\nu^3 a^3 \eta^3}{3c^3}. \qquad (3.14)$$

Hence

$$p(\nu) = \frac{1}{a^3}\frac{dP}{d\nu} = \frac{8\pi\nu^2\eta^3}{c^3} = \frac{8\pi}{\lambda^3 \nu}. \qquad (3.15)$$

The expression for the mode density just derived plays an important role in connecting the spontaneous and the induced transition probabilities. See equation (5.6) of Chapter I.

We note that for ruby $\lambda = 4 \times 10^{-5}$ cm, $\nu = 4.3 \times 10^{14}$ sec; therefore (3.15) gives a mode density in the relevant frequency region as approximately 1 per cycle per cubic centimeter volume. Only a very small fraction of these modes, however, lies in a narrow cone around the longitudinal axis, and the laser acts as a generator only in these axial or nearly axial modes. The principal problem in laser cavity design is to create a structure which has only a few high-Q resonances within the linewidth of the atomic transition. This selectivity must be accomplished in spite of the large volume of active material required for amplification and for the attainment of adequate power levels.

Diffraction Theory of the Fabry-Perot Interferometer

The cavity theory serves as a basis for orientation and provides adequate solutions for solid-state lasers with reasonably high refractive indices. It is not applicable to gas lasers which are open structures consisting of a pair of plane or curved mirrors at the ends of an amplifying column. In a typical case a pair of plane circular mirrors 2 cm in diameter may be located at a distance of 1 meter from each other. In a situation of this type diffraction loss may not be negligible, in fact it may be an important factor determining the distribution of energy in the interferometer during oscillation. For laser oscillations to occur the total loss in power from scattering, diffractive spillover, and incomplete reflection on the mirrors must be balanced with power gained by travel through the active medium. In the presence of decoupled or orthogonal modes of oscillation, the threshold condition must be satisfied for each mode in which oscillations are to occur.

The parallel, partially transparent mirrors of the laser form a Fabry-Perot interferometer. When such an instrument is operated as a passive device with uniform plane waves continuously supplied from the outside, the internal fields may also be essentially uniform plane waves. In a laser, however, where power is supplied only from within the interferometer, the loss of power from the "edges" of the wave by diffraction will cause a marked departure from uniformity.

What, then, are the modes of the Fabry-Perot interferometer? These modes may be defined and discussed in terms of *self-reproducing field configurations* over the surfaces of the reflectors. A field configuration is called self-reproducing or a *transverse mode* if, after propagation from one reflector to the other and back, the field returns in the same phase and amplitude pattern; i.e., the function representing the complex amplitude over the reflector is multiplied by a fixed complex number which gives the total phase shift and the loss of the round trip. For every such transverse mode, there is a sequence of longitudinal modes, for which the round-trip phase shift is an integral multiple of 2π. The nomenclature and the general appearance of the simplest transverse modes of plane circular and rectangular reflectors are illustrated in Fig. 20. The modes of the Fabry-Perot interferometer are called TEM modes, presumably to indicate that the electric and magnetic fields are mostly perpendicular to the longitudinal axis of the interferometer. They resemble uniform plane waves which are truly transverse electromagnetic waves.

Fox and Li [2] calculated the most important self-reproducing field configurations for a variety of mirrors. Their calculations are based on the standard diffraction formula of physical optics, which gives field distribution at a point of observation in terms of the phase and amplitude distribution at a given aperture [3]. Starting with a uniform amplitude and phase distribution on one reflector, they computed the amplitude and phase distribution on the other numerically. The functions obtained served as a

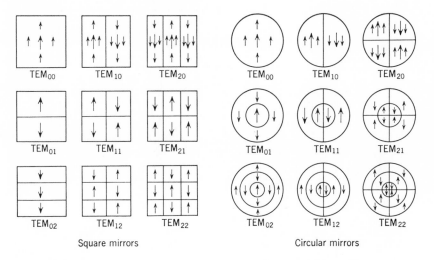

Fig. 20. Electric field configurations for interferometers with plane mirrors.

starting point for the next calculation. In this manner a sequence of pairs of amplitude and phase distributions was generated which eventually converged toward a self-reproducing pair of amplitude and phase distributions. (A uniform decrease of the amplitude by a constant factor must be permitted in this calculation to allow for the inevitable losses.)

This self-reproducing pair of phase and relative amplitude distributions over the aperture may be regarded as the dominant resonant mode of the interferometer. The phase and amplitude configuration is a function of the parameter (Fresnel number) $N = a^2/\lambda L$, where a is the radius of the circular apertures and L the distance between them. Figure 21 shows the amplitude and phase distribution in the dominant (TEM_{00}) mode for a pair of circular plane mirrors for Fresnel numbers $N = 2$, 5, and 10. The undulations on the curves are related to the number of Fresnel zones. Fox and Li also obtained interesting nonsymmetric distributions, and for several geometries calculated the diffraction losses associated with their modes as functions of the number N. In Fig. 22 we reproduce their diffraction-loss data pertaining to the interferometer with plane circular mirrors. From this figure it appears that the loss due to diffraction in a single passage in the TEM_{00} mode is about 0.9 per cent for $N = 10$, a value comparable to the usual loss caused by incomplete reflection in a gas laser. The Fresnel number $N = 10$ is applicable to a laser 1 meter long and 7 mm in diameter, with a wavelength of 1.15 μ. It is interesting to note that the adjustment of phase and amplitude distribution over the

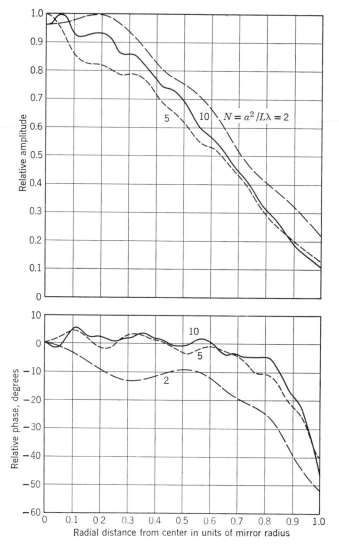

Fig. 21. Relative amplitude and phase distributions of the dominant (TEM_{00}) mode for circular plane mirrors. (Reproduced from the *Bell System Technical Journal* with the permission of the American Telephone and Telegraph Company.)

reflectors causes the diffraction loss to decrease in comparison to its value for a uniformly illuminated aperture.

The variation of diffraction loss from mode to mode is of interest because if there is not much difference in loss between the modes, a laser excited

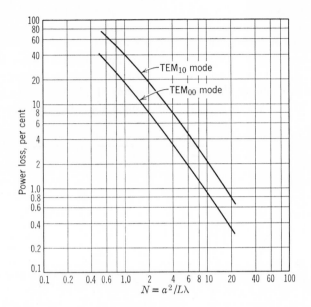

Fig. 22. Diffraction loss per transit versus $N = a^2/L$ for circular plane mirrors. (Reproduced from the *Bell System Technical Journal* with the permission of the American Telephone and Telegraph Company.)

well above threshold will oscillate in several modes simultaneously. Although losses associated with incomplete reflection at the mirrors may be larger than the diffraction losses, the former are constant for all modes; therefore the differences from mode to mode in the sum of all losses arise mainly from differences in diffraction losses. The threshold condition, as we know, involves the total gain along the path and the sum of all losses in a two-way passage. Kotik and Newstein [4] pointed out that in a laterally extended active Fabry-Perot interferometer an oblique mode may be excited before an axial one because the oblique ray passes through a longer amplifying path than an axial ray, and the losses of the modes are nearly identical. The maximum transverse dimension of the mirrors must be limited in terms of the mirror distance, mirror reflectivity, and wavelength in order that the axial mode be favored.

Although the original self-reproducing configurations were obtained by a long series of numerical computations involving about 300 iterations, the problem may be formulated as an integral equation whose eigenvalue is the fractional (diffraction) loss per transit, and whose solution is the self-reproducing complex amplitude distribution. Tang [5] obtained a variational solution for this formulation for the case of infinite plane strip mirrors; Bergstein and Schachter [6] completely solved the physically more important case of flat circular mirrors by analytic techniques.

The frequency separation of different modes is of interest in connection with gas lasers, since they possess an extremely high resolution. In calculating the mode separations, we must proceed with the self-reproducing configurations, and not the cavity calculations which led to (3.9) and (3.10). Waveguide theory warns us not to assume that the velocity of phase

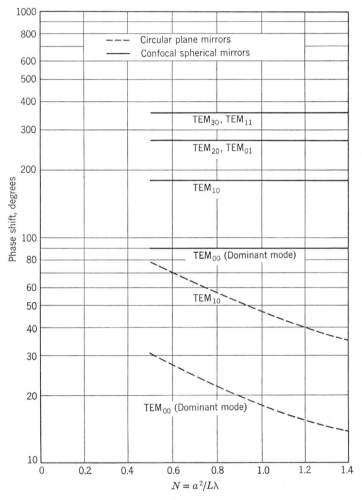

Fig. 23. Phase shift per transit (leading relative to geometrical phase shift) versus $N = a^2/L\lambda$ for confocal spherical mirrors. (Dashed curves for circular plane mirrors are shown for comparison.)

propagation of the interferometer modes is equal to the velocity of light. Rather, it is to be expected that this velocity approaches that of light for large values of $N = a^2/\lambda L$. Fox and Li calculated the phase shift in one passage relative to the geometrical phase shift, that is, $2\pi L/\lambda$. Their results are shown in Fig. 23. The resonance condition for the nth mode of any kind is then

$$\frac{2\pi L}{\lambda_n} + \varphi = \pi n, \qquad (3.16)$$

where $\lambda_n = c/\nu_n$ and φ is the phase shift appropriate for the transverse configuration. From (3.16) it follows that

$$\nu_n = \frac{cn}{2L} - \frac{c\varphi}{2\pi L}; \qquad (3.17)$$

therefore the frequency difference of consecutive modes of the same type is

$$\nu_{n+1} - \nu_n = \frac{c}{2L}, \qquad (3.18)$$

which is the same as in the plane wave case. However, the frequencies of the TEM_{00n} and TEM_{10n} modes, which belong to different transverse configurations, namely TEM_{00} and TEM_{10}, will be shifted relative to each other, and the shift is calculable from the phase shift data such as those shown in Fig. 23.

The radiation pattern of the laser is calculable from the phase and amplitude distributions of the self-reproducing configurations.

Confocal Spherical Interferometers

A plane parallel interferometer formed by two parallel plane mirrors is not the best multimode resonator. Considerable improvement may be obtained when two concave spherical reflectors are used in a confocal arrangement, that is, with the center of one sphere on the other reflector. Such spherical interferometers were proposed by Connes [7], who recognized that the spherical system has a greater resolving power than a plane system of similar dimensions. A schematic representation of the confocal interferometer is shown in Fig. 24.

Fox and Li [2] calculated the first few modes of a confocal spherical interferometer, using the technique already described. They observed the remarkable properties of the confocal system as contrasted with the plain one: In the confocal system the field is much more concentrated near the axis of the reflector and falls to a lower value at the edge than in the plane system. The amplitude distribution is smooth; the ripples of Fig. 21 are absent. The surface of the reflector is a phase front of the wave. The losses

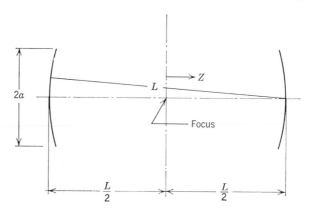

Fig. 24.   Confocal spherical interferometer.

are orders of magnitude lower in confocal systems than in comparable plane systems. The phase shifts per transit for each configuration are independent of N and are multiples of $\pi/2$. This is shown in Fig. 23. The frequency relations (3.17) and (3.18) are applicable to the confocal interferometer.

Boyd and Gordon [8] solved the integral equation pertaining to the confocal case. Their calculations show that the distribution of amplitude in the central part of the reflector is nearly Gaussian and that the surface of the reflector is an equiphase surface, which is not so in the case of plane reflectors. On the reflectors the amplitude falls to $1/e$ of its peak value at the center at a distance

$$w_s = \sqrt{L\lambda/\pi}, \tag{3.19}$$

where L is the radius of curvature of the mirrors (Fig. 24). In the space between the reflectors near the symmetry axis (z-axis) the transverse distribution of the amplitude follows the Gaussian curve with a spread that varies with the axial position. This is illustrated in Fig. 25. The variation of amplitude is approximately proportional to e^{-u}, where $u = (x^2 + y^2)/w^2$, and

$$w^2 = \frac{L\lambda}{2\pi}(1 + \xi^2). \tag{3.20}$$

Here $\xi = 2z/L$ is the displacement from the focus measured in units of the focal length. At the reflector we have $\xi = 1$ and $w = w_s$; at the focus we have $\xi = 0$ and $w = w_s/\sqrt{2}$. Thus the beam at the focus narrows down to one-half its cross section at the reflectors.

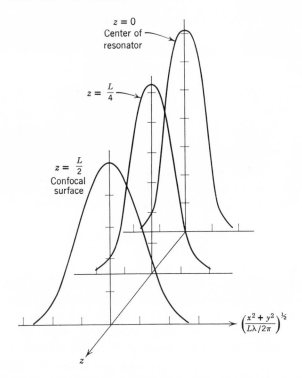

Fig. 25. Field strength distribution within the confocal resonator for the TEM_{00q} mode.

To obtain the angular beam width of the radiation pattern, we take the ratio of the spot diameter obtained from (3.20), as ξ tends to infinity, to the distance from the center of the resonator. The beam width between half-power points is given by

$$\theta = 2\sqrt{ln2/\pi}\sqrt{\lambda/L} = 0.939\sqrt{\lambda/L} \text{ radian.} \tag{3.21}$$

The numerical factor arises from the half-power width of the Gaussian curve. It is interesting to note that a, the radius of the reflectors, does not enter into these formulas which govern the spread of the beam. However, (3.19), (3.20), and (3.21) are applicable only when $a > 3w_s$. It must also be emphasized that the Gaussian approximation is not valid near the edges of the reflector and that the diameter of the reflector is an important parameter for diffraction losses. According to Boyd and Gordon [8], the diffraction loss per transit of the fundamental mode of the confocal interferometer is $10.9 \times 10^{-4.94N}$, where $N = a^2/\lambda L$, as in the case of the plane interferometer. For the sake of simplicity we shall use 11×10^{-5N}.

The following comparison may then be made between the diffraction loss of the plane and spherical interferometers of similar size.

$N = \dfrac{a^2}{\lambda L}$	1	2	4
Loss: plane	0.18	0.08	0.03
spherical	11×10^{-5}	11×10^{-10}	11×10^{-20}

All losses refer to the fundamental modes; the values for the plane interferometer are taken from the curves of Fox and Li reproduced in Fig. 22. Clearly the diffraction losses of the spherical system are orders of magnitude lower than those of the plane system. The confocal spherical system possesses several other significant advantages over the plane one. Not the least of these for the experimentalist is the noncritical nature of the adjustment of the reflectors.

Confocal resonators of equal size represent a special case of two spherically curved reflectors facing each other. Deviations either in size or in curvature of the mirrors as well as an axial displacement of one of the mirrors result in structures with rather complicated properties. These were analyzed in detail by Boyd and Kogelnik [9], who concluded that the true confocal system is an optimal one with respect to diffraction losses. A small deviation from equal curvature will, however, produce a disproportionate increase in loss in the confocal case; therefore in order to allow for manufacturing tolerances it may be advisable to deviate from the true confocal arrangement, or to imitate it by means of a spherical and a plane mirror.

It may be well to state that the incomplete reflectivity of the mirrors does not affect the mode structure of the plane or the confocal interferometer as long as the reflectivity is uniform over the mirror [10].

The Competition of Modes

The different modes of a resonant cavity may be regarded as almost independent oscillators. It is known that an oscillator is characterized by its resonant frequency and its dissipation. The dissipation is usually described in terms of the quality factor Q, which is defined by the formula

$$Q = \frac{2\pi v_0 E}{P_d}, \tag{3.22}$$

where v_0 is the resonant frequency, E the energy, and P_d the rate at which energy is dissipated in the oscillator. When the oscillator is excited by a periodic force of frequency v, the power absorbed by the oscillator varies with ν in the manner described by the function $g(\nu, \nu_0)$ of Section I.6, with the full linewidth $\Delta\nu$ replaced by ν_0/Q. Therefore we shall refer to ν_0/Q as the linewidth of the oscillator or the linewidth of the cavity mode. A high Q represents low dissipation and narrow linewidth.

In a laser a complicated interaction takes place between an ensemble of atoms on the one hand and a resonant cavity with many available resonant frequencies on the other. The atomic system is characterized by a center frequency ν_a and a linewidth $\Delta\nu$, and the resonant cavity is characterized by the resonances centered at $\nu_1, \nu_2, \ldots, \nu_n$, with quality factors $Q_1, Q_2, \ldots, Q_n$, respectively. Before entering into a discussion of the general interaction problem it would be well to contemplate the interaction of the atomic system with a cavity possessing only one available mode in the frequency range of the atomic system. This is the standard problem encountered in connection with masers.

In this case the atoms and the cavity are equivalent to two coupled resonant circuits. The classical analysis of these systems shows that if the center frequencies of the coupled circuits are slightly different, the frequency of free coupled oscillations will be determined primarily by the circuit with the higher Q. Let this be system 1, whose resonant frequency and linewidth are ν_1 and $\Delta\nu_1$, respectively. The oscillation of the coupled circuit will not take place at the frequency ν_1 but approximately at

$$\nu_0 = \nu_1 + (\nu_2 - \nu_1)\frac{\Delta\nu_1}{\Delta\nu_2}, \tag{3.23}$$

or in terms of the Q's, at

$$\nu_0 = \nu_1 + (\nu_2 - \nu_1)\frac{Q_2}{Q_1}. \tag{3.24}$$

In an ammonia maser there is a cavity with a single resonance frequency and a low Q coupled to an atomic line with a high Q. Consequently, the frequency of the system is very nearly that of the atomic line. In a laser there are many competing cavity modes. In the first approximation, coupling between them may be neglected. All derive their excitation from the same pool of atomic systems and all dissipate energy partly through incomplete reflection and partly through diffraction or escape of radiation to the sides that may occur when the modes are not axial. Axial modes have the least dissipation, the highest Q.

As the excitation progresses to the point at which the excess $N_2 - N_1$ is large enough to cause a net stimulated emission, energy begins to rise in the various resonator modes. The driving force acting on these modes is the largest for frequencies near the center of the atomic resonance ν_a. As the excitation increases, the dominant fraction of the energy goes to a small number of modes which have the highest Q's and whose frequencies are near the peak of the atomic resonance. The mathematical theory of this process in a multimode cavity has been developed by Wagner and Birnbaum [11, 12], who calculated the frequency distribution of the output in terms of the atomic linewidth and the degree of excitation. Sidestepping the intricate mathematical analysis of Wagner and Birnbaum, we may state qualitatively that modes with more energy than others tend to grow faster and their growth rate increases with increasing Q. All feed on the same supply of excited atoms; therefore the rich modes get richer, the poor poorer, until almost all of the radiative energy is concentrated "in the hands of a privileged few." The two privileges are, of course, being near the center ν_a, where the supply of quanta is the greatest, and having the highest Q, which enables the mode to grow faster than its competitors.

The significance of the relationships pertaining to diffraction losses introduced at the beginning of this section now becomes apparent. The Q of each mode is determined according to formula (3.22), in which the denominator P_d consists of the sum of all losses from that mode. The loss caused by incomplete reflection does not vary from mode to mode; it is determined by the nature of the reflecting layer. The diffraction loss, as we have seen, is variable. The effect this variation will have on the Q depends on the ratio of the diffraction loss to the reflection loss. Once the diffraction loss of a mode is less than one-half the reflection loss, further reduction of the diffraction loss is of little consequence. Certainly this is the case for the dominant modes of the confocal spherical resonators. However, the diffraction losses of plane resonators may contribute significantly to the determination of Q when the reflectors are small. The large loss of off-axis modes usually lowers their Q's to the point at which their excitation becomes negligible and the laser may be correctly described entirely in terms of the axial modes.

The losses of the axial modes are about equal. We have already noted that these modes are located so close to each other in the frequency domain that the width of an atomic line will stretch over dozens or hundreds of these lines. Ordinarily quite a few of them lie so close to the top of the atomic line that they are excited simultaneously. However, even a small difference in the diffraction losses among modes of different types may provide a great discrimination in the excitation of these modes, and if the laser is operated sufficiently close to threshold, oscillations will occur only in modes of lowest loss.

Relation of Mode Theory to Experiments

The theory of the laser as a resonant structure was developed in this section on the basis of certain idealizations. The most important of these is the assumption that the laser material is homogeneous and isotropic. Crystalline lasers are certainly not isotropic, and even if they are practically homogeneous in their unexcited state, the excitation necessary for laser action is not uniform over the material. Hence the assumption of an isotropic material with a uniform amplification and with no internal scattering leads to conclusions that are only partially verifiable with experiments on less perfect materials. These experiments will be discussed in Chapter VI. The discussion of this section serves as a guide to that material.

REFERENCES

1. J. P. Carlson, S. P. Mead, and S. A. Schelkunoff, Hyper-frequency waveguides, *Bell Syst. Tech. J.* **15**, 310–333, 1936.
2. A. G. Fox and T. Li, Resonant modes in a maser interferometer, *Bell Syst. Tech. J.* **40**, 453–488, 1961.
3. S. Silver, *Microwave Antenna Theory and Design*, McGraw-Hill, New York, 1949, p. 167.
4. J. Kotik and M. C. Newstein, Theory of laser oscillations in a Fabry-Perot resonator, *J. Appl. Phys.* **32**, 178–186, 1961.
5. C. L. Tang, On diffraction losses in laser interferometers, *Appl. Optics* **1**, 768–770, 1962.
6. L. Bergstein and H. Schachter, Resonant modes of optic interferometer cavities I, *J. Opt. Soc. Am.* **54**, 887–903, 1964.
7. P. Connes, L'étalon de Fabry-Perot sphérique, *J. Phys. Radium* **19**, 262–269, 1958.
8. G. D. Boyd and J. P. Gordon, Confocal multimode resonator for millimeter through optical wavelength masers, *Bell Syst. Tech. J.* **40**, 489–508, 1961.
9. G. D. Boyd and H. Kogelnik, Generalized confocal resonator theory, *Bell Syst. Tech. J.* **41**, 1347–1369, 1962.
10. A. G. Fox, T. Li, D. A. Kleinman, and P. P. Kisliuk, Comment on discrimination against unwanted orders in the Fabry-Perot interferometer, *Bell Syst. Tech. J.* **41**, 1475–1476, 1962.
11. W. G. Wagner and G. Birnbaum, Theory of quantum oscillators in a multimode cavity, *J. Appl. Phys.* **32**, 1185–1193, 1961.
12. G. Birnbaum, *Optical Masers*, Academic Press, New York and London, 1964.

4. LINEWIDTH PROBLEMS*

The output of the laser oscillator, like that of many electronic oscillators, is essentially amplified noise. In an electronic oscillator the noise is thermal; its energy is uniformly distributed over a wide band of frequencies, which includes the amplification band of the amplifier, whereas in the laser the noise is the spontaneous emission of radiation characterized by a center frequency and linewidth. In either case amplification is regenerative; a part of the output is returned as input. Consequently, the frequency corresponding to the peak of the amplifier gain predominates in the output. Under certain circumstances there may be several such peaks.

* The material in this section was contributed by R. W. Hellwarth.

Let us now consider a photon packet emitted spontaneously within the laser. This packet will have the frequency distribution characteristic of the natural atomic line: a center frequency ν_a and a linewidth Δ_a. It was explained in Section II.2 that after m passes through the laser the packet is amplified by the factor $r^m e^{m\alpha(\nu)L}$. As m becomes large, the exponential factor tends to cause the spectral distribution to narrow around one frequency, which corresponds to the peak value of the amplification. If it were possible to add intensities, and if r did not depend on the frequency, matters would be simple indeed. The fact that light amplitudes must be added has the consequence that reinforcement of light will take place only if light arrives back at its point of origin in a proper phase. Whether this takes place depends on the dimensions of the laser in terms of the wavelength. Clearly, we are dealing here with the problem of oscillations in a cavity combined with selective amplification.

In a moderately loss-free medium the different modes of a resonant cavity may be regarded as independent oscillators, each characterized by its resonant frequency and by its linewidth, or Q. The general problem encountered in lasers is the interaction of the atomic generators and amplifiers with all relevant modes of the cavity at the same time. We shall not attempt to solve that general problem here, but we shall find it instructive to discuss the interaction with one resonator mode chosen so that its resonant frequency approximately coincides with the peak of the atomic line. In lasers, the atomic line is wide compared with the closely spaced cavity lines, so that there are many cavity resonances near the peak of the atomic line. The calculation that follows pertains to the linewidth of any one of these modes. The analysis of the spectral distribution of radiation in a given mode is based on the assumption that the oscillations in one mode are independent of the oscillations in another mode in the following sense: The presence of electric oscillations at one frequency does not produce a polarization of laser atoms at another frequency. This assumption is unimportant in the case of single-mode operation, which has been obtained in both solid and gas lasers. In usual operation, which involves simultaneous oscillations in many modes, it is difficult to assess the accuracy of the results that are calculated on the basis of this assumption; some experiments indicate that there are instances when the assumption is incorrect. However, even in these cases the estimate of spectral purity based on the above assumption of independence, or linear amplification, is probably still reasonably accurate.

The expression we shall derive for linewidth was first stated by Schawlow and Townes [1] in 1958 as a modification of a corresponding calculation for the ammonia maser; it suggested extremely pure spectral output and spurred efforts at experimental realization of a maser in the optical region. The modification of the original ammonia analysis consisted of reversing the inequalities: $h\nu \ll kT$ and $\Delta_{cav} \gg \Delta_{mat}$, where the last two symbols represent the linewidths of cavity and material, respectively.

The discussion of linewidth is invariably tied to the concepts of noise theory and power spectrum, since what we seek to determine is a distribution of the output energy over frequencies. The source of the original signal is the spontaneous emission of radiation, about which we have statistical knowledge: we know its energy distribution in frequency. In the mathematical treatment of such problems it is necessary to make transformations from time domain to frequency domain and back. It is convenient in this connection to use the angular frequency $\omega = 2\pi\nu$ as a variable. Thus the chosen oscillator which represents the cavity has resonant frequency ω_0 and linewidth Δ_0. These quantities and the Q of the oscillation are connected by the relation $\omega_0 = Q\Delta_0$. Let the peak angular frequency of the atomic line also be ω_0 and let the atomic linewidth Δ_a be much larger than Δ_0.* The particular oscillation of the cavity is described by a coordinate X, which may be the instantaneous electric field. It satisfies the differential equation

$$\ddot{X} + \Delta_0\dot{X} + \omega_0^2 X = F(t), \tag{4.1}$$

where $F(t)$ is the driving force. The second term on the left is the dissipative term. For a harmonic driving force $F(t) = F_0 e^{i\omega t}$, the excitation of the oscillator depends on the amplitude F_0 and the frequency of the exciting force. The energy E stored in the oscillator and the rate P at which energy is dissipated by the oscillator are related by the equation

$$P = \frac{\omega_0 E}{Q} = \Delta_0 E. \tag{4.2}$$

This last relation is independent of the exciting force. In a cavity oscillation there may be several dissipative processes. One may be dissipation in the material within the cavity; others may permit energy to escape to the outside through various ports. When several independent processes of energy dissipation act simultaneously, there is associated with each of them a power P_i and a linewidth, so that

$$P = \sum P_i, \qquad \Delta_0 = \sum \Delta_i. \tag{4.3}$$

The power dissipated through the ith port is then

$$P_i = \Delta_i E. \tag{4.4}$$

The energy in a steady state is determined by the linewidth Δ_0 and by the power spectrum of the exciting force. Physically it is quite plausible that

---

* This linewidth is $2\pi\Delta\nu$.

the energy stored in the oscillator should be proportional to the integral of $|f(\nu)|^2$ over the frequency region that is capable of exciting the oscillation to a significant degree. In fact, when the power spectrum of the exciting force is essentially uniform over the linewidth of the oscillator, calculation gives the following approximate result for the *average* energy of the oscillator

$$\langle E \rangle = \frac{\langle |f(\nu_0)|^2 \rangle}{2\Delta_0}. \tag{4.5}$$

Here $f(\nu)$ is the Fourier transform of $F(t)$ and the brackets designate statistical averages. This result is obtained in the following way. Equation (4.1) is solved by Fourier transform techniques. One readily obtains the Fourier transform $x(\nu)$ of $X(t)$:

$$x(\nu) = \frac{f(\nu)}{\omega_0^2 - \omega^2 - i\omega \Delta_0}, \tag{4.6}$$

where $\omega = 2\pi\nu$. The frequency range varies from $-\infty$ to $+\infty$ with $f(-\nu) = f(\nu)^*$. The average energy is found by integration $\omega_0^2 \langle |f(\nu)|^2 \rangle$ over all frequencies. (A constant factor, which depends on the units, can be ignored at this point.) In practice, only the vicinity of those frequencies where the denominator of (4.6) is small needs to be considered, so integration may be confined to a region R_1 around $\nu = \nu_0$ and to a region R_2 around $\nu = -\nu_0$. In R_1 we set $\omega \approx \omega_0$, except in the difference term; therefore

$$\omega_0^2 |x(\nu)|^2 = \frac{\omega_0^2 |f(\nu)|^2}{(\omega + \omega_0)^2 (\omega - \omega_0)^2 + \omega^2 \Delta_0^2} \approx \frac{\frac{1}{4} |f(\nu_0)|^2}{(\omega - \omega_0)^2 + (\Delta_0/2)^2}.$$

Integrating according to $\nu = \omega/2\pi$, we obtain $|f(\nu_0)|^2 / 4\Delta_0$. The integral over the region R_2 provides an equal contribution; therefore

$$\omega_0^2 \int_{-\infty}^{+\infty} |x(\nu)|^2 \, d\nu \approx \frac{|f(\nu_0)|^2}{2\Delta_0}.$$

Our problem is to determine the statistical average of $|f(\omega_0)|^2$ when the driving force is supplied by the spontaneous emission of atoms acting independently. Consider for a moment oscillations in a cavity with absorbing material at a temperature T. It is known that the average energy of a high-Q lossy oscillator in equilibrium at temperature T is given by the Planck function

$$E = \frac{\hbar\omega_0}{e^{\hbar\omega_0/kT} - 1}. \tag{4.7}$$

Suppose that the absorbing material consists of two-level quantum systems whose energy separations $\hbar\omega$ are broadly distributed in the neighborhood of $\hbar\omega_0$. In equilibrium the populations of these levels obey Boltzmann's equation. Therefore in the simplest case of equal multiplicities we have

$$e^{\hbar\omega_0/kT} = \frac{N_1}{N_2}. \tag{4.8}$$

Consequently, for an oscillator in equilibrium with an ensemble of two-level systems, (4.7) reduces to

$$\langle E \rangle \approx \frac{N_2 \hbar\omega_0}{N_1 - N_2}. \tag{4.9}$$

Therefore from (4.5) and (4.9) the noisy driving force associated with the two-level system is given by

$$\langle |f(\omega_0)|^2 \rangle = \frac{2\Delta_1 N_2 \hbar\omega_0}{N_1 - N_2}, \tag{4.10}$$

where Δ_1 is the net contribution to the cavity linewidth arising from absorption and stimulated emission by the two-level systems. In the case of nondegenerate levels the loss rate is proportional to the number of atoms N_1 that are available for absorption minus the number of atoms N_2 available for emission. Therefore, equation (4.10) indicates that the noise power $\langle |f(\omega_0)|^2 \rangle$ is proportional to the number of atoms in the upper level N_2. This conclusion agrees with our introductory statement that the noise arises from spontaneous emission. The constant of proportionality, $2\Delta_1 \hbar\omega_0/(N_1 - N_2)$, is independent of N_1 and N_2; it remains the same when N_2 exceeds N_1, and the contribution to linewidth Δ_1 is negative.

Let us now return to the oscillation of the laser. Here real damping is provided by the radiation to the outside. The descriptive quantities are P_L, the power output of the laser, and the corresponding damping term Δ_2. The atomic ensemble provides the negative term Δ_1, so that the total damping term or linewidth is

$$\Delta = \Delta_1 + \Delta_2. \tag{4.11}$$

Then, according to (4.4) and (4.5), the average power radiated is

$$\langle P_L \rangle = \Delta_2 \langle E \rangle = \frac{\Delta_2 \langle |f(\omega_0)|^2 \rangle}{2\Delta_0}. \tag{4.12}$$

In view of (4.10), this becomes

$$\langle P_L \rangle = \frac{\Delta_1 \Delta_2}{\Delta} \frac{N_2 \hbar\omega_0}{N_1 - N_2}. \tag{4.13}$$

We drop the brackets around the power output P_L, and we note that Δ is the sum of a positive and a negative term which are nearly equal at threshold because the losses balance the gains. In approximation, we write in the numerator $-\Delta_1 \approx \Delta_2$ and replace Δ_2 by the symbol Δ_c to indicate that it is the linewidth of the cavity determined solely by the rate of escape of radiation from the cavity. Then

$$P = \frac{\Delta_c{}^2}{\Delta} \frac{N_2 \hbar \omega_0}{N_2 - N_1}. \tag{4.14}$$

Hence the final formula for the linewidth in angular frequency is

$$\Delta = \frac{\Delta_c{}^2}{P} \frac{N_2}{N_2 - N_1} \hbar \omega_0. \tag{4.15}$$

Schawlow and Townes [1] derived this relationship for the special case $N_1 = 0$ in terms of half-widths of the lines at half maximum power. The corresponding variables are related to ours as follows: $\delta \nu = \Delta/4\pi$, $\delta \nu_c = \Delta_c/4\pi$. Consequently, in their notation

$$\delta \nu = \frac{4\pi(\delta \nu_c)^2}{P} \frac{N_2 \hbar \nu_0}{N_2 - N_1}. \tag{4.16}$$

It has been stated that the calculations starting with (4.4) are applicable in the case of equal multiplicities. In the general case, N_1 and N_2 are to be replaced by N_1/g_1 and N_2/g_2 respectively wherever they occur in equations (4.8) to (4.16).

We repeat, we have treated the special case in which the center of the cavity resonance coincides with the center of the broader atomic line. When this condition is not strictly true, (4.15) and (4.16) are still approximately valid; the oscillation frequency of the cavity mode is pulled toward the center of the atomic line as described in Section II.3. [Cf. (3.23), (3.24).] The competition of different cavity modes near the peak of the atomic line is also described qualitatively in Section II.3; for a more detailed discussion we refer to Wagner and Birnbaum [2].

What is observed in anything but the most refined experiments is not the linewidth given by (4.15) or (4.16) but an empirical linewidth that results from the simultaneous unresolved observation of many lines. This is one of the reasons that the early experiments with ruby lasers showed a measured linewidth of the order of 0.1 Å, which is strictly an engineering variable with little physical meaning. The real linewidth is much narrower and depends on the level of the power output. Even the measured linewidth of the most stable He-Ne laser is orders of magnitude larger than the intrinsic linewidth calculated from the equations derived here. This discrepancy indicates that the measured linewidth represents the effects of fluctuations in the laser structure.

The calculation for a typical He-Ne laser operating at 1.15 μ wavelength may run as follows: Assuming a length of 100 cm and a reflector loss of 2 per cent gives

$$\Delta_c = c(1 - r)/L = 6 \times 10^6 \text{ rad/sec.}$$

For the laser in question $h\nu = 1.72 \times 10^{-12}$ erg. Hence, for an assumed output of $P = 1$ mW $= 10^4$ erg/sec, we obtain from (4.15)

$$\Delta = 36 \times 10^{12} \times 10^{-4} \times 1.72 \times 10^{-12} N_2/(N_2 - N_1)$$
$$= 0.0062 \, N_2/(N_2 - N_y).$$

The factor $N_2/(N_2 - N_1)$ depends on the operating conditions. From measurements of the decay times of the relevant levels we can conclude that $N_2/N_1 < 8$; therefore the factor $N_2/(N_2 - N_1)$ is at least 8/7. Assuming $N_2/(N_2 - N_1) = 2$, we obtain

$$\Delta = 0.0124 \text{ rad/sec} = 0.002 \text{ cps.}$$

Actual measurements indicate linewidths of tens of cycles per second for the most stable He-Ne laser. (Cf. Section V.4.)

REFERENCES

1. A. L. Schawlow and C. H. Townes, Infrared and optical masers, *Phys. Rev.* **112**, 1940–1949, 1958.
2. W. G. Wagner and G. Birnbaum, Theory of quantum oscillators in a multimode cavity, *J. Appl. Phys.* **32**, 1185–1193, 1961.

III

Solid-State Lasers

1. THE RUBY LASER OF MAIMAN

Construction

It has already been stated that the first laser built was a ruby operating at a wavelength of 6943 Å. Many other materials capable of laser action have been developed since Maiman's discovery, and the ruby itself has been used as a laser operating at other frequencies. Nevertheless, with minor modifications, the original ruby laser is still the most powerful source of coherent light.

In the preceding sections the technical description of the laser was rather sketchy; the material introduced was only that necessary to support the analytical discourse. The technical and descriptive details are given now.

The heart of Maiman's laser is the pink ruby crystal, whose chemical composition is Al_2O_3 with 0.05 per cent (by weight) Cr_2O_3. The aluminum and oxygen are inert; only the chromium ions participate in the phenomena of interest here. At the concentration stated, the density of chromium ions is $N_0 = 1.62 \times 10^{19}/cm^3$. The crystal has almost cubic symmetry, with a distortion along one of the body diagonals. As a result of this distortion, the true symmetry of the ruby is rhombohedral. Its symmetry element is a threefold axis of rotation which naturally coincides with the optic axis of the ruby (c-axis). The spectroscopy of this crystal is a separate topic and will be discussed in the next section. This section is confined to the description of the ruby laser and the properties of the radiation emitted by it.

In the commonly used laser configuration a cylindrical sample of ruby is surrounded by the coils of a helical flashlamp, as shown in Figs. 11 and 12, but other geometries that provide intensive irradiation may be employed. The large variety of flashlamps used successfully includes the following: GE FT-506 and 524, EGG FX-1 and 38, and a number of other lamps specially designed. The lamps are flashed by discharging a condenser bank of 50 μF or larger through the lamp. Capacitors up to 2000 μF have been used. The discharge is initiated by a pulse transformer which provides the peak voltage for the breakdown after the supply voltage has been placed across the discharge tube. Supply voltages are generally in the range of 1 to 2 kV, but occasionally voltages of more than 4 kV have been used. Higher voltages permit the dissipation of the same energy in the lamp with a smaller capacitance, but they can be used only with lamps that do not break down under the higher voltage in the absence of the starting pulse or with a hold-off switch, such as an ignitron, in series with the lamp.

The ruby rods vary in size from approximately 0.1 to 2 cm in diameter and from 2 to 23 cm in length. The ends of the cylinders are polished flat and parallel within 1 min of arc. The performance of the laser improves with the degree of precision achieved in flatness and parallelism. Silver coating is applied to make one end fully reflective; the other end is partially silvered to provide transmission from 5 to as high as 80 per cent. Ten to 25 per cent transmission is typical, except for very long rubies. In some instances partial transmission is obtained by leaving a hole in a fully silvered surface. Partially transmitting silver surfaces are not loss free; therefore the reflectivities of the partially transmitting silver coatings on the rubies seldom exceed 85 or 90 per cent. When a higher reflectivity is necessary, multilayer dielectric films must be employed. The reflectivity enters into the threshold condition and into the rate at which the oscillations build up in the ruby. High reflectivity results in a low threshold and in a high radiation density within the ruby. The latter will increase the losses of the laser and lessen the total output obtainable. The optimum reflectivity of the partially transmitting end depends on the length of the laser and on the intended application as well as on the rate at which excitation is supplied to the laser.

It is essential for the operation of the ruby as an oscillator (a source of radiation) that a part of the radiation propagating axially be returned after passing through the ruby. This "feedback" process need not be accomplished by mirrors coincident with the terminal surfaces of the ruby. One may shape one end of the ruby into a 90-degree roof prism which returns the radiation because of total reflection on its sides, or one may use an external 90-degree prism [1] or an external plane mirror. When an external reflector is used the maintenance of alignment becomes a critical factor [2], and reflections on the ruby faces have to be reduced by anti-reflection coatings or by cutting the ends at the Brewster angle. If this is not done, complicating multireflection effects will take place.

Pulsations of Output

Figure 26 shows a trace of the laser output with a trace of the exciting radiation. Fluorescence begins immediately after the irradiation starts, but

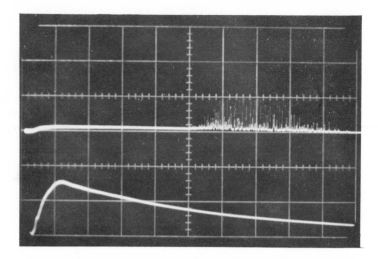

Fig. 26. Intensity of radiation from ruby versus time. Light emitted from ruby: upper trace. Light emitted from flashlamp: lower trace. Time scale: 0.1 msec/cm.

stimulated emission starts in this case about 0.5 msec later. The sharp spikes correspond to the rapid pulsations of the intensity of stimulated emission. They are shown on an enlarged time scale in Fig. 27.

The irregularity of these pulsations and their apparent lack of reproducibility indicate that they are caused or influenced by a number of factors. These pulsations and methods for controlling them are discussed in detail in Chapter VI.

Spectrum

The wavelength of the ruby R_1 laser radiation is 6934 Å at 77°K and 6943 Å at room temperature [3].* The variation of wavelength with

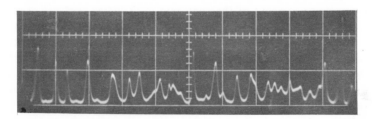

Fig. 27. Pulsations of ruby on an expanded time scale. Time scale 5 μsec/cm.

* Additional information on the thermal variation of the ruby spectrum is included in the next section.

temperature accounts for some of the uncertainty concerning the linewidth of the laser. Although the duration of the ordinary laser flash is only of the order of 1 msec, considerable warming of the crystal takes place during this period. The 0.1-Å linewidth observed in relatively crude measurements is in part the result of a frequency shift during the period of observation, and is in part caused by the presence of several unresolved modes of oscillation with slightly differing frequencies [4]. The number of modes excited and the linewidths of the individual modes depend on the power level at which the laser is operated and on the geometrical configuration employed. Unless special precautions are taken, the output of the ruby laser consists of oscillations in many modes and the different oscillations attain their peaks at different times. The presence of a series of axial modes in one ruby flash was demonstrated spectroscopically by resolving the modes with a Fabry-Perot etalon [5, 6]. The conclusions of the spectroscopic analysis were confirmed and extended by the observation of the beat frequencies between the modes. These were obtained by mixing in a photodetector the outputs of the different oscillatory modes which appear simultaneously [7, 8]. Using a ruby rod 5.66 cm long, McMurtry observed a number of axial modes 1.5 Gc apart. The spectral width of the individual modes varies with temperature and with the excitation of the ruby between 3 and 20 Mc, while the entire spectrum excited during a flash extends over a frequency region of over 5 Gc.[*] The coverage of this frequency region is in the form of a fine-toothed comb covering an area containing many teeth. The comb does not remain stationary, however; it shifts back and forth from one spike of the laser to the next. Such displacement of the entire spectrum of the ruby is not demonstrated by experiments in which different modes of the output of the same laser are mixed because the difference frequencies are not changed by the shifting process. It was, however, demonstrated by means of a fast time-resolution interferometric technique [4, 9, 10]. During a single flash which consists of a very large number of spikes there is a gradual frequency drift attributable to the change of the length and of the refractive index of the ruby with temperature, and in addition there is a variation of the oscillatory mode pattern from one spike to the next, so that one particular pattern persists only for the fraction of a microsecond. The rapid shifting of the mode patterns has the consequence that time (phase) coherence of the radiation is not maintained from one spike to the next. This fact has been demonstrated by Berkley and Wolga [11], who have observed the interference patterns produced by a split beam obtained from a ruby laser. When the path difference exceeded 3000 cm, fringes could no longer be obtained,

---

[*] A large number of experiments were reported using different rubies. The numerical values appear here for orientation only.

indicating that the phase memory of the laser was of the order of 0.1 μsec.

Polarization

The polarization of the laser output depends on the orientation of the optic axis of the ruby with respect to the cylinder axis. According to the measurements of Nelson and Collins [12], the output is completely unpolarized when these axes are parallel. Ruby rods with their optic axes at a 60- or 90-degree angle with the cylinder axis give a 100 per cent linearly polarized output with the electric vector perpendicular to the plane containing the optic axis. The measurements were extended over the temperature range from 100 to 300°K and confirmed what was to be expected from the polarization properties of the fluorescence of ruby.

Radiation Pattern

Coherence of the light emerging from different areas of the partial reflector and sharp directionality of the beam are related phenomena; directional characteristics of the beam are determined in a well-known manner by the phase and amplitude distribution over the radiating aperture. In fact, the most conspicuous proof of the appearance of stimulated radiation in ruby is the sudden change in the directional distribution of light emitted when the threshold of excitation is exceeded. Collins and others [13] observed this change in directionality with a carefully prepared ruby rod 0.5 cm in diameter, whose ends were parallel within 1 min. The fluorescent radiation was essentially nondirectional until the threshold was reached; at this point a beam appeared, which was confined to an angle of 0.3 to 1 degree from the axis of the sample. In general, the collimation of the beam varies greatly from one ruby laser to another; it depends on the qualities of the crystal, on the geometry, on the reflectivity and the alignment of the mirrors, as well as on the degree of excitation. A 10-mrad beam is easy to obtain, and a 1-mrad beam can be achieved with considerable care. These beamwidths are considerably larger than we would expect from diffraction theory, assuming radiation from a circular aperture of diameter d radiating in phase and with uniform amplitude. The theory leads to the value

$$\theta_0 = \frac{1.22\lambda}{d}$$

for the angular distance of the first zero from the center of the diffraction pattern. For $d = 1$ cm and $\lambda = 6943 \times 10^{-8}$ cm, the value of θ_0 is 0.085 mrad. The explanation of the much larger observed beamwidths lies in the fact that the entire surface area does not participate in radiation in the manner assumed, namely in uniform phase and amplitude.

Examination of the ruby surface by photography shows that light distribution is not at all uniform over the surface. Isolated luminous spots appear on the surface of the ruby, and stimulated radiation emanates from these spots [13]. Evtuhov and Neeland [14] made a detailed study of the patterns of these spots as they appear under various experimental conditions with the rubies excited barely above threshold. On rubies 2 and 3 mm in diameter the individual spots were of the order of 100 μ; the patterns or clusters they formed extended up to 850 μ. The divergences of the beams radiated from these rubies appear to have the correct magnitude when related to the pattern size. Evtuhov and Neeland measured the polarization of the light emanating from different patterns and attempted to correlate the appearance of the patterns with various other variables, such as the time dependence of the output pulse and the frequency of the radiation. A tentative identification was made of several patterns with a variety of cavity modes. Modes other than axial may enter into the picture, especially when the length-to-diameter ratio of the laser is not large. This is surmised from the fact that, other things being equal, lasers with longer reflector separation give sharper beams.

Coherence of the laser output was also studied by means of interference experiments with radiation emanating from different parts of the ruby surface. Direct examination of coherence by means of interference experiments has confirmed expectations. Collins and his associates [13, 15] have obtained diffraction patterns from a rectangular aperture of 50 by 150 μ on one of the reflectors and interference patterns from a pair of long parallel slits 7.5 μ wide separated by 54.1 μ, also on one of the reflectors. Examination of these patterns discloses that the areas of the reflector that undergo simultaneous laser action are of the order of at least 0.005 cm in diameter. The narrowest beamwidths obtained from these lasers indicate that the area of coherence is at least an order of magnitude larger than this. Further experiments of Galanin, Leontovich, and Chizhikova [16] show that coherence in fact extends over the entire end surface of the crystal notwithstanding the broadness of the beam which suggests a more restricted region of coherence. The divergence of the beam results from the fact that the phase is not uniform over the crystal surface.

Power Output and Efficiency

The peak power radiated from a laser without control of the pulsations in intensity is a somewhat indefinite quantity, since the peaks of intensity, as shown in Figs. 26 and 27, are irregular. Under favorable circumstances, peaks of 20 to 30 kW were obtained from lasers 1 cm in diameter and 4 cm long. The average during a flash of a millisecond or two is considerably lower. More meaningful and easier to measure is the total energy radiated in one flash. This depends on the excitation and on the size of the ruby; values between 0.1 and 1.5 joule may be typical for lasers about 1 cm in diameter and 4 cm long. Much depends, of course, on the excitation, on the quality of the ruby, and on the quality and alignment of the reflectors. Larger lasers which deliver hundreds of joules in a single flash are commercially available and the records of energy output per flash are superseded almost every month.

The over-all efficiency of the laser expressed in coherent energy output per input electrical energy in the flashlamp is a function of many variables. Among the most significant are the spectral characteristics of the flashlamp, which in turn depend on the composition and pressure of the gas in the lamp. A xenon lamp at a pressure of 150 mm Hg seems to be most efficient. With ordinary ruby lasers of 1 cm diameter and 4 cm length it is customary to use an exciting flash of 500 to 1000 joules energy. The output under favorable circumstances is about 1 to 1.5 joules. The over-all efficiency of energy conversion is between 0.1 and 1 per cent.

Extremely high peak values of radiated power can be obtained by preventing the irregular pulsations and causing all the stored energy to be radiated in one burst. This technique leads to the so-called "giant pulse," a phenomenon discussed in Chapter VI.

It should be kept in mind that in order to produce laser action a certain minimum energy has to be supplied per unit volume of the ruby and that it must be supplied above a minimum rate sufficient to overcome spontaneous decay. This "minimum" rate, as we have noted, is so high that it can be provided only by the most powerful lamps. The energy absorbed in the ruby is, of course, only a small part of the radiative output of the flashlamp, since a significant part of this radiation will not reach the ruby and only radiation in the proper absorption region of the ruby is effective in providing excitation.

The most serious engineering problems encountered in connection with laser design pertain to the concentration of the available radiation on the ruby and the efficient removal of that overwhelming portion of the input energy which is converted into heat.

REFERENCES*

1. M. Bertolotti, L. Muzii, and D. Sette, On cavity termination of ruby laser, *Nuovo Cimento* **26**, 401–402, 1962.
2. J. F. Ready and D. L. Hardwick, Effect of mirror alignment in laser operation, *Proc. IRE* **50**, 2483–2484, 1962.

   * The basic references to the ruby laser are to be found at the end of Section II.1.

3. I. D. Abella and H. Z. Cummins, Thermal tuning of ruby optical maser, *J. Appl. Phys.* **32**, 1177, 1961.

4. G. R. Hanes and B. P. Stoicheff, Time dependence of the frequency and linewidth of the optical emission from a pulsed ruby maser, *Nature* **195**, 587–588, 1962.

5. M. Ciftan, A. Krutchkoff, and S. Koozekanani, On the resonant frequency modes of ruby optical masers, *Proc. IRE* **50**, 84–85, 1962.

6. I. D. Abella and C. H. Townes, Mode characteristics and coherence in optical masers, *Nature* **192**, 957, 1961.

7. B. J. McMurtry, Investigation of a ruby-optical-maser characteristic using microwave phototubes, *Appl. Optics* **2**, 767–786, 1963.

8. M. Di Domenico, R. H. Pantell, O. Svelto, and J. N. Weaver, Optical frequency mixing in bulk semiconductors, *Appl. Phys. Lett.* **1**, 77–79, 1962.

9. T. P. Hughes, Time resolved interferometry of ruby laser emission, *Nature* **195**, 325, 1962.

10. T. P. Hughes and K. M. Young, Mode sequences in ruby laser emission, *Nature* **196**, 332, 1962.

11. D. A. Berkley and G. J. Wolga, Coherence studies of emission from a pulsed ruby laser, *Phys. Rev. Lett.* **9**, 479–482, 1962.

12. D. F. Nelson and R. J. Collins, The polarization of the output from a ruby optical maser, *Advances in Quantum Electronics*, Columbia Univ. Press, New York, 1961, pp. 79–82.

13. R. J. Collins, D. F. Nelson, A. L. Schawlow, et al., Coherence, narrowing, directionality, and relaxation oscillations in the light emission from ruby, *Phys. Rev. Lett.* **5**, 303–305, 1960.

14. V. Evtuhov and J. K. Neeland, Observations relating to the transverse and longitudinal modes of a ruby laser, *Appl. Optics* **1**, 517–520, 1962.

15. D. F. Nelson and R. J. Collins, Spatial coherence in the output of an optical maser, *J. Appl. Phys.* **32**, 739–740, 1961.

16. M. D. Galanin, A. M. Leontovich, and Z. A. Chizhikova, Coherence and directionality of ruby laser radiation, *Soviet Phys. JETP* **16**, 249–251, 1963 (**43**, 347–349, 1962).

2. THE SPECTROSCOPY OF RUBY

Fluorescence and stimulated emission of radiation in ruby have heretofore been described in terms of a three-level scheme illustrated in Fig. 13. Although such a description serves a didactic purpose, it represents an oversimplification. The finer details of the optical processes that take place in ruby must be comprehended in the light of a more accurate picture of the relevant energy levels.

It has already been stated that the active material in ruby is the Cr^{3+} ion. This ion has three d electrons in its unfilled shell; the ground state of the free ion is described by the spectroscopic symbol ^4F, which indicates that the orbital angular momentum is $L = 3$; the spin is $S = \frac{3}{2}$. The ^4F term is a quartet as indicated by the superscript 4 preceding the letter symbol; its total multiplicity is $(2S + 1)(2L + 1) = 28$. The next lowest group of states of the free Cr^{3+} ion is characterized by the quantum numbers $L = 4$, $S = \frac{1}{2}$; their term symbol is ^2G. The multiplicity of this group is 18.

In ruby the chromium ion is surrounded by a crystal field of nearly octahedral symmetry. This field causes a splitting of the degenerate levels of the free ion. The number of ways in which the levels are split and the remaining degeneracy of the split levels are determined by the symmetry of the crystal field; the extent of the shift of the split levels with respect to the levels of the free ion is determined by the strength of the crystal field, which in turn depends on the lattice constant, i.e., on the separation of the adjacent like atoms in the crystal.

By applying group theory, we can show that in an octahedral field the ground level of the free Cr^{3+} ion splits into three levels. It is customary to denote these levels by the symbols $^4F_1$, $^4F_2$, and $^4A_2$; their multiplicities are 12, 12, and 4, respectively. The symbols F_1, F_2, and A_2 arise from group theory; they refer to matrix representations of the octahedral group and are not to be related to values of the orbital angular momentum. In this shorthand notation the upper index 4 is the only reminder that the three levels in question arise from the ground level of the free Cr^{3+} ion, namely ^4F. The next level, ^2G, splits into four sublevels, which are designated by the symbols $^2A_1$, $^2F_1$, $^2F_2$, and ^2E, with multiplicities 2, 6, 6, and 4, respectively. Here again the symbols A_1, F_1, F_2, and E are borrowed from group theory and the only symbol retained from the spectroscopy of the free ion is the prefix 2 indicating the doublet (G) level.

Some of the levels described are outside of the range of interest for stimulated emission in ruby. The relevant levels are shown in Fig. 28. It is to be noted that the ^2E level is shown not as one but as two closely spaced levels. This subdivision is caused by the fact that the symmetry of the crystal is not completely octahedral, but rhombohedric. As a result of the lower symmetry the ^2E level splits into two levels of multiplicities 2 each.

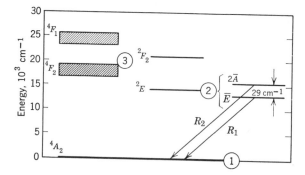

Fig. 28. Energy-level diagram for chromium ion in ruby. (Reprinted from *The Physical Review.*)

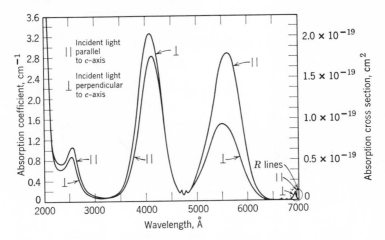

Fig. 29. Absorption spectrum of pink ruby. (After Maiman [1].)

These are only 29 cm^{-1} apart; therefore, in equilibrium at room temperature their populations are nearly equal.

The absorptive properties of pink ruby shown in Fig. 29 are dependent on the direction of the light propagation with respect to the optic axis. The peaks of the absorption curves clearly correspond to centers of the bands shown in Fig. 28. Fluorescence of ruby consists of the R_1 and R_2 lines (Fig. 28), but ordinarily laser action will take place only at the R_1 line (6943 Å), because the transition probability for this line is greater than that for the R_2 line. Once the level $^2E(\bar{E})$ is depleted by stimulated emission, a rapid transfer of electrons takes place from the level $^2E(\bar{A})$ to the level $^2E(\bar{E})$, and in this manner the population of the upper level never quite reaches the threshold value for laser operation. The ratio of transition probabilities corresponding to the R_1 and R_2 lines is 7 to 5 [2]. The relaxation between the components of the ^2E level occurs with the assistance of lattice vibrations, which are plentiful in the required energy region; therefore the relaxation time will be short ($\approx 10^{-9}$ sec). The levels $^4F_1$ and $^4F_2$ jointly constitute level 3 of the simplified scheme used in Fig. 13, while the ^2E levels constitute level 2.

The following quantitative data are applicable at room temperature:

The peak absorption coefficient for the R_1 line is $k_0 = 0.4$ cm^{-1}, and the absorption cross section is $\sigma_0 = 2.5 \times 10^{-20}$ cm^2. The lifetime of the R_1 transition is 3.0 msec.

As the temperature is decreased to 77°K the lifetime of the R_1 transition increases to 4.3 msec, indicating that the transition rate observed at 300°K is not the true spontaneous radiative transition rate given by Einstein's

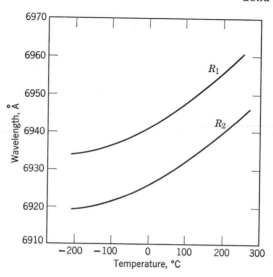

Fig. 30. Wavelengths of the R_1 and R_2 fluorescent lines of ruby as functions of temperature.

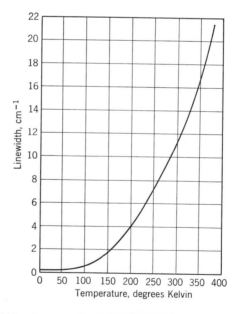

Fig. 31. Linewidth of the R_1 line of ruby as a function of temperature. (After Schawlow [5].)

formula; it is the sum of this rate plus the rate of thermal transitions [1]. The correct (Einstein) transition rate is approximately the reciprocal of 4.3×10^{-3} sec; i.e., $A_{21} = 232$ sec^{-1}. The other relevant transition rates in ruby are $A_{31} = 3 \times 10^5$ sec^{-1} and $S_{32} = 2 \times 10^7$ sec^{-1} [3]. Variation of temperature causes a variation in the wavelength of the fluorescent lines and in their linewidths. Figure 30 illustrates the variation of the wavelength of the R_1 and R_2 lines as compiled by Wittke [4] from the data of many investigators. Figure 31 illustrates the variation of the width of the R_1 line as a function of temperature. Since the width of the line is simply related to the peak k_m of the absorption line (Section II.2), it is clear that k_m varies with temperature, and this variation in turn shows up in a variation of the excitation required for reading the threshold of oscillations. Narrowing of the linewidth results in the lowering of the threshold.

The output of the ruby laser at 77°K has a wavelength of 6934 Å. In the temperature region from -80°C to $+20$°C the wavelength of the ruby laser is given approximately by the formula

$$\lambda(T) = 6943.25 + 0.068 \, (T - 20),$$

where T is the temperature in degrees centigrade.

REFERENCES

1. T. H. Maiman, R. H. Hoskins, I. J. D'Haenens, C. K. Asawa, and V. Evtuhov, Stimulated optical emission in fluorescent solids II, *Phys. Rev.* **123**, 1151–1157, 1961.
2. F. J. McClung, S. E. Schwarz, and F. J. Meyers, R_2 line optical maser action in ruby, *J. Appl. Phys.* **33**, 3139–3140, 1962.
3. T. H. Maiman, Optical and microwave optical experiments in ruby, *Phys. Rev. Lett.* **4**, 564–565, 1960.
4. J. P. Wittke, Effects of elevated temperatures on the fluorescence and optical maser action of ruby, *J. Appl. Phys.* **33**, 2333–2335, 1962.
5. A. L. Schawlow, Fine structure and properties of chromium fluorescence in aluminum and magnesium oxide, *Advances in Quantum Electronics*, Columbia Univ. Press, New York, 1961, pp. 50–62.

3. RUBY LASERS OPERATING AT UNCONVENTIONAL FREQUENCIES

The energy-level diagram of the ruby (Fig. 28) discloses two closely spaced ^2E levels. We have been concerned so far only with laser action resulting from a transition from the lower one of these to the ground state, the R_1 transition. McClung, Schwarz, and Meyers [1] demonstrated that the R_2 transition can be used for the construction of a laser operating at $\lambda = 6929$ Å at room temperature. The two levels from which the R_1 and R_2 transitions originate are separated by an energy difference corresponding to about 29 cm^{-1}. The relaxation time between these nearby levels is short compared with the lifetimes and relaxation times involved in laser action. Under ordinary circumstances laser action will occur only in the R_1 transition because the threshold condition for this line is met at a lower level of excitation than that for the R_2 line. Once laser action commences in the R_1 line, the level from which the R_1 line originates becomes depleted and population transfer from the other nearby level proceeds at such a fast rate that the threshold population is never reached for the R_2 line. Quantitatively, the situation is as follows: The threshold condition is given by equation (2.7) of Chapter II. The coefficient α is proportional to the excitation, but it is greater for the R_1 transition than for the R_2 transition by a factor 1.4. Thus, in the case of constant r and increasing α's, the threshold is first reached for the R_1 line. Laser action in the R_2 line was obtained by employing interference filters as reflectors. The filters were chosen to be highly reflective for the R_2 line ($\gamma = -\log_e r = 0.18$) and considerably less reflective for the R_1 line ($\gamma = 1.25$). In all respects, other than wavelength, the R_2 laser is similar to the R_1 laser.

Still another type of laser action is observed in red ruby. This material has a chromium concentration of about 0.5 per cent, about 10 times that of pink ruby. It is known that the energy-level structure of chromium in the red ruby is different from that of the pink ruby because of the exchange interaction between the strongly magnetic chromium ions. Fluorescence in red ruby is known to have peaks at 7009 and 7041 Å, and it is also known that these lines, which terminate above the ground state, must be attributed to interaction between chromium ions.

Wieder and Sarles [2] at Varian Associates and Schawlow and Devlin [3] at Bell Telephone Laboratories demonstrated simultaneously that laser action can be obtained at these wavelengths. These are called the satellite N_1 (7041 Å) and N_2 (7009 Å) lines. In contrast to the R_1 and R_2 lines, laser action in the N_1 and N_2 lines may appear simultaneously, indicating that their initial levels are not so closely coupled as those of the R_1 and R_2 lines.

Laser action in the satellite lines is observed at liquid nitrogen temperature. Cooling is desirable to depopulate the terminal levels which are about 100 cm^{-1} above ground state. Although the red ruby laser is the four-level type, the pump power required for its operation is not less than that required for the R_1 laser. The reason for this is not yet understood, and much about the red ruby still needs to be clarified.

REFERENCES

1. F. J. McClung, S. E. Schwarz, and F. J. Meyers, R_2 line optical maser action in ruby. *J. Appl. Phys.* **33**, 3139–3140, 1962.
2. I. Wieder and L. R. Sarles, Stimulated optical emission from exchange-coupled ions of Cr^{3+} in Al_2O_3, *Phys. Rev. Lett.* **6**, 95, 1961.

3. A. L. Schawlow and G. E. Devlin, Simultaneous optical maser action in two ruby satellite lines, *Phys. Rev. Lett.* **6**, 96, 1961.

4. CONCENTRATION OF THE EXCITING RADIATION

One of the limiting factors in laser technology is the large radiation density required to produce population inversion by means of optical excitation. It is important to use light available from exciting sources with high efficiency partly because these sources are frequently pushed to the limit of their capacity and partly because the unused radiation is converted into heat which must be removed from the system. With ordinary ruby lasers 1 cm in diameter and 4 cm long it is customary to use an exciting flash with an electrical input energy of 500 to 1000 joules; larger rubies frequently require input energies of several thousand joules.

Elliptic Cylinders

Although the original arrangement for ruby involves a helical flashtube surrounding the ruby cylinder as shown in Figs. 11 and 12, other geometries are also available. A configuration based on an elliptic cylinder consists of a straight discharge tube placed in one focal line of the cylinder, and the laser rod in the other. The elliptic cylinder is made of highly reflective material and is provided with reflective end plates. The first such laser was described by Ciftan and co-workers [1], who operated a ruby laser 6 cm long and 0.6 cm in diameter, with an input energy of only 150 joules, which was only a small fraction of the energy required for the same ruby in the helical configuration. An objective scale is not available for direct comparison of laser performance because the excitation energy required for reaching threshold varies with the efficiency of the lamp, the quality of the ruby, and the reflective coating, as well as with the size of the ruby.

The elliptic configuration is based on the geometrical theorem which assures that rays originating from one focus of an ellipse are reflected into the other focus. The application of this simple theorem leads to a number of complications when the objects to which it is applied are no longer mathematical points and lines but physical bodies of finite dimensions.

In order to concentrate a large amount of power in a small volume we would like to make the laser rod thin and the source lamp thick because its power-handling capability increases with its diameter. We shall see, however, that the efficiency of radiative power transfer is greater in the reverse case, namely when the laser is thick and the source is thin. Moreover, we shall find that this efficiency depends on the eccentricity of the ellipse as well as on the radius of the source and that of the laser expressed in terms of the length of the major axis of the ellipse.

There are two principal reasons why radiation emanating from a source of a finite size will not all reach the laser. First, rays that leave the source at an angle to the surface normal will be imperfectly focused. Second, some rays will be blocked by the source itself; they will be intercepted after reflection before they can reach the laser. It is sufficient to examine this problem in two dimensions because all rays may be replaced by their projections in the plane perpendicular to the cylinder axis. The complication caused by defocusing is illustrated in Fig. 32. A cylindrical source of radius R_1 is placed at the focal line F_1, while the laser whose radius is R_2 is at the focal line F_2. We contemplate the rays reflected at a fixed point P on the ellipse; this point may be characterized by the angle θ included between F_1P and the major axis of the ellipse. The lines PA_2 and PB_2 are drawn tangent to the laser and the corresponding rays are extended back to the source to points A_1 and B_1. It is clear that A_1PA_2 and B_1PB_2 represent limiting rays for the point P. Any ray arriving at P which originates outside of the arc A_1B_1 will miss the laser. Such a ray is illustrated by C_1P. One could argue that such a ray would eventually reach the laser after many reflections, or would be returned to the source. The many reflections, however, are not immaterial because the reflection coefficient of the best reflector usable in this case is considerably less than 1. The loss of energy transfer by source blocking may be demonstrated by following the path of the ray emanating from C_1 and directed toward the nearest vertex of the ellipse. A ray returned to the source does not represent energy completely lost; nevertheless it is not communicated to the laser on the first leg of its journey and it suffers a certain loss by reflection. Similarly, it should not

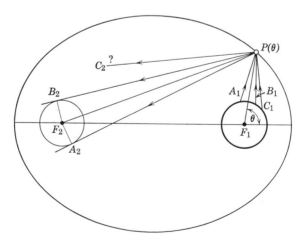

Fig. 32. Defocusing as a source of loss in an elliptic configuration.

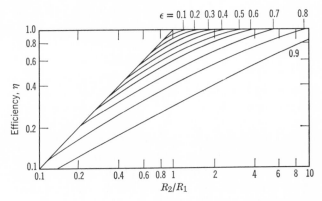

Fig. 33. Efficiencies calculated for a Lambertian source distribution and negligible source-blocking. (After Schuldt and Aagard [2].) Notation: R_1 source radius, R_2 laser radius, ϵ eccentricity.

be assumed that any ray reaching the laser thereby delivers the full energy associated with it to the laser. Nevertheless, there is merit in defining the efficiency of the system in terms of the relative percentage of rays which travel from the source to the laser and reach there suffering no more than one reflection on the elliptic cylinder. In counting the rays it is satisfactory to assume that the source radiates according to Lambert's law. Such efficiencies were calculated by Schuldt and Aagard [2] who obtained the

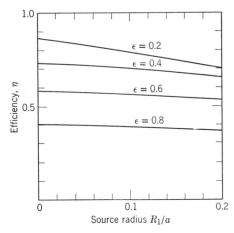

Fig. 34. Efficiency of elliptic configuration as a function of the relative source radius. Source and laser have equal radii; a is the semimajor axis of the ellipse. (Data of Schuldt and Aagard [2].)

curves of Fig. 33 for ellipses of varying eccentricities. The values of the efficiency η shown in Fig. 33 were obtained neglecting source blocking. Clearly, largest efficiencies are obtained for nearly circular ellipses which require close arrangement of the source and the laser. Source blocking is relatively unimportant; it is a function of the parameter R_1/a, where a is the semimajor axis of the ellipse. In Fig. 34 we illustrate the dependence of η on this parameter for the case of $R_1 = R_2$ for several values of the eccentricity ϵ.

The elliptical configuration is especially suitable for work at low temperatures. Its use is illustrated in Fig. 47 (p. 126) in connection with the neodymium laser. Lasers with multiple elliptical cavities were constructed for high-power applications [3, 4]. These cavities contain the ruby in a focal line common to several incomplete elliptical cylinders; the other focal lines contain the exciting sources. There is considerable disagreement about the extent of the advantages obtainable with compound elliptical configurations [5, 6].

Composite Lasers

Uniform and powerful irradiation of the laser does not in itself ensure uniform excitation or efficient distribution and utilization of the incident radiative energy in the laser. When a dielectric rod is irradiated by isotropic radiation from the outside, not every portion of the rod is subjected to illumination of the same intensity. The reason for this variation is the refraction of the rays at the surface, which is illustrated in Fig. 35. Light incident at any point will be confined to a cone within the dielectric, whose aperture is determined by the angle of total reflection $\theta_{max} = \sin^{-1} 1/n$, n being the index of refraction. For sapphire and ruby n is equal to 1.76, so that $\theta_{max} = 35$ degrees. A ray refracted at this angle passes the axis of the cylinder with a minimum distance $r = R/n$, where R is the radius of the cylinder; that is, all the light that penetrates the surface of the cylinder of radius R eventually passes through a smaller internal cylinder of radius R/n. The calculation of the energy density u in a dielectric cylinder is complicated by the fact that the light entering the cylinder is partially reflected internally every time it strikes the cylinder surface; the reflection coefficient depends on the angle of incidence as well as on the direction of polarization. Only under simplifying assumptions do we obtain tractable expressions.

Assuming that all light is incident in a plane perpendicular to the laser axis with the electric vector polarized along the axis, Devlin, McKenna, May, and Schawlow [7] calculated the variation of u/u_0 with the distance ρ from the axis of the cylinder. Here u_0 denotes the energy density of the isotropic illumination on the outside of the cylinder. In a nonabsorbing

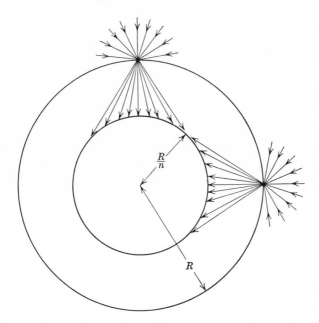

Fig. 35. Rays of light incident on the side walls of a dielectric cylinder. (Reprinted from *Applied Optics*.)

cylinder with index of refraction $n = 1.76$ the relative energy density varies as shown in Fig. 36. The variation of u/u_0 with ρ is described by the equations

$$\frac{u}{u_0} = n^2 \qquad \text{for } 0 \leqq \rho \leqq \frac{R}{n}$$

and

$$\frac{u}{u_0} = \frac{2n^2}{\pi} \sin^{-1} \frac{R}{n\rho} \qquad \text{for } \frac{R}{n} \leqq \rho \leqq R.$$

A complicated integral formula describes the situation for an absorbing cylinder or for a cylinder containing an absorbing core. However, for moderately absorbing materials the general characteristics of the situation are still adequately illustrated by Fig. 36.

Therefore in a solid rod of ruby the threshold of oscillations will be reached in the central region before it can be reached near the periphery. Light absorbed near the periphery may be completely wasted because the threshold level may not be reached before the center part is discharged.

A superior light economy is achieved by means of the composite rod shown in Fig. 37. The rod is constructed of sapphire (pure Al_2O_3), with

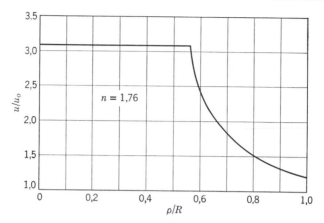

Fig. 36. Energy density of light, as a function of radius ρ inside a nonabsorbent dielectric cylinder of radius R. The cylinder is illuminated by rays from all directions in a plane perpendicular to the cylinder axis. Energy density on the outside is u_0. (Reprinted from *Applied Optics*.)

chromium ions added to the central region, so that the index of refraction n is the same in the entire rod. The radius of the core and the radius of the entire rod are in the proportion $1:n$. A composite rod can be made by first preparing a core rod of a single crystal ruby and then using it as a seed onto which sapphire is deposited. With a composite rod of this sort, the light intensity at the ruby core is greater than it is without the sapphire sheath.

Removal of heat is also facilitated by the composite rod structure. Sapphire is a good conductor of heat, especially at low temperatures. The worst barrier to heat flow is at the surface of the crystal, and the surface area of the composite rod is considerably larger than that of the core.

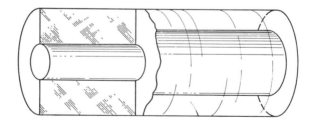

Fig. 37. Composite laser of Devlin. The core section is doped, as for ruby, whereas the outer sheath is clear (e.g., sapphire).

Composite rods of 2-mm inner and 5-mm outer diameter and 2.5-cm length were excited to laser action below 100°K by input energies that ranged from 460 to 490 joules, whereas ruby rods of the size of the core required 750 joules or more when no sheath was provided. These data refer to excitation by helical flashlamps. With a straight lamp and rod at the two foci of an elliptic cylinder, laser action was achieved with input energies as low as 44 joules per flash at 77°K.

Further calculations concerning composite rod lasers removed some of the restrictive assumptions underlying the calculations of Devlin and co-workers; it is not essential to require incidence in the plane perpendicular to the laser axis. The effects of a sheath with an index of refraction different from that of the core have also been calculated. In order to obtain a true measure of efficiency of a composite rod laser one must take into account the effect of sheathing on the entire geometry including that of the exciting source. Assuming that the active core of the laser is unchanged, the introduction of the sheathing requires that the inner radius of the helical flashtube be enlarged. Alternatively, if an elliptic configuration is used the sheathed rod will occupy a larger volume surrounding the focal line of the elliptic cylinder and will by this fact affect the efficiency of the elliptic reflector system [8, 9, 10].

REFERENCES

1. M. Ciftan, C. F. Luck, C. G. Shafer, and H. Statz, A ruby laser with an elliptic configuration, Proc. IRE 49, 960–961, 1961.
2. S. B. Schuldt and R. L. Aagard, An analysis of radiation transfer by means of elliptical cylinder reflectors, Appl. Optics 2, 509–513, 1963.
3. C. Bowness, D. Missio, and T. Rogala, A high-energy laser using a multi-elliptical cavity, Proc. IRE 50, 1704–1705, 1962.
4. J. L. Wentz, Eight-inch ruby amplifier, Proc. IRE 50, 1528–1529, 1962.
5. T. Li and S. D. Simms, Observations on the pump-light intensity distribution of a ruby optical maser with different pumping schemes, Proc. IRE 50, 464–465, 1962.
6. D. L. Fried and P. Eltgroth, Efficiency of a multiple ellipses confocal laser pumping configuration, Proc. IRE 50, 2489, 1962.
7. G. E. Devlin, J. McKenna, A. D. May, and A. L. Schawlow, Composite rod optical masers, Appl. Optics 1, 11–15, 1962.
8. O. Svelto, Pumping power considerations in an optical maser, Appl. Optics 1, 745–751, 1962. (Also Appl. Optics Suppl. 1, 107–113, 1962.)
9. O. Svelto and M. Di Domenico, High-index-of-refraction spherical sheath composite-rod optical masers, Appl. Optics 2, 431–439, 1963.
10. R. L. Aagard, D. L. Hardwick, and J. F. Ready, Emission pattern of ruby laser output, Appl. Optics 1, 537–538, 1962.

5. CONTINUOUSLY OPERATING RUBY LASERS

The operation of the ruby lasers described so far is intermittent, with exciting flashes of 1 to 5 msec duration, repeatable, at most, a few times per minute. The attainment of continuous (cw) laser operation in ruby hinges on the construction of a powerful light source capable of continuous operation combined with suitable optics to concentrate irradiation on the ruby and with adequate cooling mechanism to remove the heat generated within the ruby as a result of radiationless transitions. This was first achieved in 1961 by Nelson and Boyle [1]. Their cw ruby laser consists of a tiny trumpet-shaped combination of sapphire and ruby whose cross section is shown in Fig. 38 with the longitudinal dimension shortened. The cone is made of sapphire; it serves to collect and concentrate the exciting light on the shank made of ruby. The cone is designed so that any ray entering the large end from the solid angle subtended by a spherical collecting mirror is totally reflected at every encounter with the polished conical surface until it passes into the ruby at the small end of the cone. Furthermore, the cone is terminated at a certain point so that all the rays leaving the small end of the cone are totally internally reflected at every encounter with the sides of the ruby shank until they strike the mirror at the end face of the ruby.

Radiation from a short mercury arc lamp is directed at the cone end of the trumpet by means of two spherical mirrors as shown in Fig. 39. The coherent radiation emerges through the central portion of the cone, which is covered with a reflecting coating of transmissivity 0.05. It is calculated that a mercury arc of 400 watts/cm² steradian brightness is needed in the wavelength region of 3500 to 6000 Å for the operation of this laser.

The attainment of a critical intensity of exciting radiation guarantees

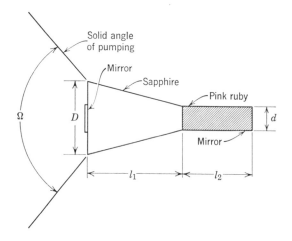

Fig. 38. The cw ruby laser of Nelson and Boyle [1]. (The dimensions used by Nelson and Boyle: $d = 0.061$ cm, $D = 0.150$ cm, $l_1 = 1.05$ cm, $l_2 = 1.15$ cm, $\Omega = 0.73$ steradian.)

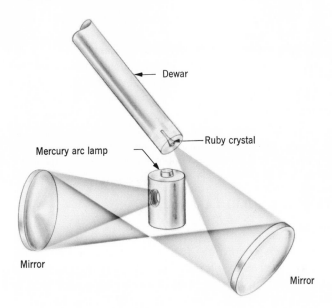

Dewar

Ruby crystal

Mercury arc lamp

Mirror

Mirror

Fig. 39. Concentration of pumping light on the cw ruby laser. (Courtesy Bell Telephone Laboratories.)

sufficient absorption in the ruby to attain an inverted population adequate for laser action at a given temperature. The temperature dependence, as we have already seen, enters through the variation of k_0 with temperature. In order to maintain the proper temperature, it is necessary to design the laser so that the trumpet surface is capable of transferring the heat evolved in the ruby to a coolant. The entire laser is operated in a Dewar filled with liquid nitrogen, and thus temperature is maintained at 77°K. The operation of this cw laser required a minimum input (electrical) power of 850 watts which was used to feed a Hanovia 941 B mercury-xenon lamp. Exciting radiation was absorbed at the rate of about 0.3 watt, and the laser beam had a measured output of about 4 mW.

Evtuhov and Neeland [2] constructed a rather simple water-cooled ruby laser capable of continuous operation at room temperature. The cooling water circulates directly through the elliptic cavity which contains the ruby and the mercury arc used for excitation. The following dimensions were used: ruby diameter 2 mm, ruby (and cavity) length 25 mm, eccentricity 0.4, cavity major axis 25 mm. The successful operation of this cw ruby laser was reported early in 1965. With an output reflector of 1 per cent transmission threshold was reached for 840 watts input to the arc. A continuous output radiation of 70-mW intensity was obtained when the input was raised to 2000 watts.

The cw ruby laser does not provide constant intensity output; it is subject to essentially the same high-frequency relaxation oscillations (pulsations) that are observed in pulsed ruby lasers.

REFERENCES

1. D. F. Nelson and W. S. Boyle, A continuously operating ruby optical maser, *Appl. Optics* **1**, 181–183, 1962. (Also *Appl. Optics Suppl.* **1**, 99–101, 1962.)
2. V. Evtuhov and J. K. Neeland, Continuous operation of a ruby laser at room temperature, *Appl. Phys. Lett.* **6**, 75–76, 1965.

6. FOUR-LEVEL SOLID LASERS

Introduction

Four-level lasers are distinguished by the fact that their excitation and emission cycle involves four levels in place of the three characteristic of the ruby. Stimulated transitions terminate not on the ground level but on an intermediate level which has a relatively short lifetime. Since this terminal level is generally empty, it is possible to obtain population inversion with a relatively moderate expenditure of energy in a four-level laser, while in ruby one-half the active atoms must be excited before stimulated emission prevails over absorption.

Excitation and emission in a four-level solid laser are comprehended in terms of the energy-level scheme illustrated in Fig. 14. The levels are those of an ion in a host crystal. The crystal field splits the degeneracy of multiple levels of the active ion, thus creating a relatively broad absorption band (level 4), and it facilitates the transition from level 4 to level 3, the starting level of stimulated emission.

The energy gap between level 2, the terminal level, and level 1, the ground level, varies from ion to ion but it is generally smaller than the energy difference of levels 2 and 3. The lifetime of level 2 must be short, or a phenomenon analogous to the stopping up of a sink will occur. Until stimulated emission begins, the occupancy of level 2 is determined by the conditions of thermal equilibrium applicable to levels 1 and 2.* In order that the terminal level 2 remain essentially unoccupied it is necessary that $E_2 - E_1$ be greater than kT. Therefore frequently the temperature of the crystal determines whether or not population inversion can be established at a certain pumping rate; the threshold pumping rate is a function of temperature.

---

* A brief mathematical discussion of the population exchange in a four-level system was given in Section II.2.

Most four-level lasers are operated intermittently; they are excited by a flashlamp. It has been customary to publish threshold pumping energy figures for a given line in a crystal. These values refer to the lowest energy input to an FT 524 xenon flashlamp with which stimulated emission is observed. The figures are for orientation only; they have no genuine physical significance. Threshold figures determined under pulse illumination conditions depend greatly on the pulse duration relative to fluorescence lifetime. For materials with lifetimes small in comparison with the pulse duration, lower threshold will be measured with shorter pulses. Moreover, the threshold figures depend also on the efficiency of conversion of electrical energy to radiation suitable for pumping and on the efficiency with which the available pumping radiation is utilized.

Systematic and exhaustive description of four-level lasers is a difficult task because of the large number of combinations possible with a variety of active ions embedded in a variety of host lattices. The compilation of information in this field is further hindered by investigators whose aim is to maximize the number of their publications. The four-level laser field is notorious for the fact that separate papers were written about stimulated emission in several ion-host-lattice combinations even when the same apparatus was used for making the measurements and when the papers had to appear in the same issue of a journal. It is not feasible to give adequate references here to the fragmented literature. In what follows we shall concentrate on the exposition of the physical principles and minimize our involvement in technical operational details.

The best-known four-level laser materials are crystals that incorporate a small percentage of uranium or a rare earth element. Sorokin and Stevenson [1, 2] observed stimulated emission from U^{3+} and Sm^{2+} ions incorporated in CaF_2 crystals shortly after the discovery of the ruby laser. Since then, many crystal and ion combinations have been investigated; approximately one hundred four-level lasers were known in 1964. The most useful ion seems to be Nd^{3+}, which is capable of stimulated emission at a number of frequencies and in a number of host lattices. It may also be incorporated in certain glasses and performs there as a laser material. Neodymium laser is the only four-level laser that competes with ruby in power output. The technical characteristics of neodymium and other four-level lasers will be summarized after the physical mechanisms are discussed. To facilitate this discussion we now review the energy-level structure of rare earth ions.

Spectroscopy of the Rare Earths

The rare earth elements fit into the periodic table following the period ending with the fifty-fourth element, xenon. In this element the shells for which the principal quantum number n has values 1, 2, and 3 are completely filled. The shell $n = 4$ has its s, p, and d subshells filled; the $4f$ subshell capable of accommodating 14 electrons is completely empty. Nevertheless the $n = 5$ shell has acquired its first 8 electrons which fill the $5s$ and $5p$ orbits. Thus in the customary notation the electron configuration of xenon is written as follows:

$$1s^2\, 2s^2\, 2p^6\, 3s^2\, 3p^6\, 3d^{10}\, 4s^2\, 4p^6\, 4d^{10}\, 5s^2\, 5p^6.$$

All elements beyond xenon have this electronic structure and in addition have electrons in the $4f$, $5d$, $6s$, etc. orbits. The first addition takes place not in the inner $4f$ orbits, but in the outer $6s$ orbits. Cesium and barium, the elements following xenon, have one and two $6s$ electrons respectively. Rare earth elements begin after barium with the building of the inner vacant $4f$ orbits. The electronic structure of the first few rare earth atoms is illustrated in Table III.1 with only the $5s$ and $5p$ electrons shown of the completed xenon structure.

TABLE III.1. ELECTRONIC STRUCTURE OF ELEMENTS 57 TO 62
IN THEIR GROUND STATE

Inner electrons of completed shells omitted [3].

N	Element	$4f$	$5s$	$5p$	$5d$	$5f$	$5g$	$6s$
57	La	0	2	6	1	0	0	2
58	Ce	1	2	6	1	0	0	2
59	Pr	3	2	6	0	0	0	2
60	Nd	4	2	6	0	0	0	2
61	Pm	5	2	6	0	0	0	2
62	Sm	6	2	6	0	0	0	2

The energy differences between the $4f$ and $5d$ orbits are generally small, and in the case of some rare earth elements the distribution of the electrons between these orbits in the ground state of the atom is not known.

A divalent rare earth ion is formed when the atom gives up its outermost $6s$ electrons. When a trivalent ion is formed the atom also loses its $5d$ electron if it has one; otherwise, one of the $4f$ electrons is lost. Thus divalent and trivalent ions of rare earths are simpler than the corresponding atoms. In their ground state they contain only $4f$ electrons in addition to the basic common xenon shell. Table III.2 contains the number of $4f$ electrons of these ions together with the standard spectroscopic symbol describing the ground state of the ion. The Russell-Saunders coupling scheme is applicable to these ions.

The great complexity of the rare earth spectra arises from the large number of states that have nearly the same energy. The excited ion con-

TABLE III.2. $4f$ ELECTRONS AND LEVELS
OF RARE EARTH IONS

After Dieke and Crosswhite [4].

R^{2+}	R^{3+}	$4f$	Ground Level
—	La	0	$^1S_0$
La	Ce	1	$^2F_{5/2}$
Ce	Pr	2	$^3H_4$
Pr	Nd	3	$^4I_{9/2}$
Nd	Pm	4	$^5I_4$
Pm	Sm	5	$^6H_{5/2}$
Sm	Eu	6	$^7F_0$
Eu	Gd	7	$^8S_{7/2}$
Gd	Tb	8	$^7F_6$
Tb	Dy	9	$^6H_{15/2}$
Dy	Ho	10	$^5I_8$
Ho	Er	11	$^4I_{15/2}$
Er	Tm	12	$^3H_6$
Tm	Yb	13	$^2F_{7/2}$
Yb	Lu	14	$^1S_0$

figurations of the lowest energy are obtained when one of the $4f$ electrons is promoted into an empty $4f$ or $5d$ orbit. Dieke and Crosswhite [4] calculated that for the Nd^{3+} ion one obtains in this manner 241 configurations with 5393 allowed transitions. For Sm^{3+} these numbers are 1994 and 306,604, respectively. The lowest energy levels of the trivalent rare earths are shown in Fig. 40. This figure contains all levels up to 20,000 cm^{-1} above ground; they all correspond to $4f^n$ configurations.

The nomenclature of the energy levels may be illustrated by the discussion of the Nd^{3+} ion. This ion has 3 electrons in the $4f$ subshell. In the ground state their orbits are so aligned that the orbital angular momentum adds up to $3 + 2 + 1 = 6$ atomic units. The symbol I in the last column of Table 2 expresses the fact that $L = 6$, since I is the sixth term of the conventional spectroscopic series: $P, D, F, G, H, I, K, \ldots$. (See p. 33.)

The spins of the three electrons are aligned parallel to each other, providing an additional $\frac{3}{2}$ units of angular momentum, which, when added antiparallel to the orbital angular momentum, give a total angular momentum of $6 - \frac{3}{2} = \frac{9}{2}$ units. According to the quantum rules for the addition of angular momenta, the vector sum of an orbital angular momentum of $6\hbar$ and a spin angular momentum of $\frac{3}{2}\hbar$ may result in the following four values of the total angular momentum: $\frac{9}{2}\hbar$, $\frac{11}{2}\hbar$, $\frac{13}{2}\hbar$, and $\frac{15}{2}\hbar$. The levels corresponding to these values are $^4I_{9/2}$, $^4I_{11/2}$, $^4I_{13/2}$, and $^4I_{15/2}$. The first of these, which has the lowest energy, is the ground state; the others are among the first few excited levels of Nd^{3+}. These levels are

Solid-State Lasers

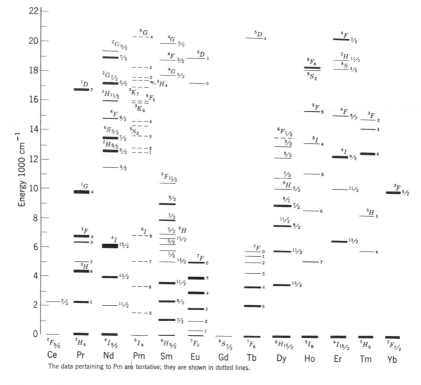

Fig. 40. Lowest energy levels of trivalent rare earth ions. (After Dieke and Crosswhite [4].)

distinguished by the orientation of the spins with respect to the resultant orbital angular momentum. Other excited levels are obtained when another combination of the orbital angular momenta is chosen. It should be noted that all these levels are multiple; they are split in electric and magnetic fields.

Isoelectronic ions, such as Sm^{2+} and Eu^{3+}, appear on the same line in Table III.2; their ground states are identical. It does not follow, however, that their excited states appear in the same order. In the case of trivalent ions (with the exception of Tb^{3+}) all levels below 50,000 cm^{-1} belong to $4f^n$ configurations [4]. Transitions between these levels are forbidden by the normal selection rules. The sharp-lined visible spectra observed on trivalent and divalent rare earths in crystals are attributed to these normally forbidden transitions, which are made possible through the action of the crystal field on the ion. These $4f \rightarrow 4f$ transitions are much weaker than the allowed $5d \rightarrow 4f$ transitions. In the case of dipositive rare earth ions the $4f^{n-1}5d$ levels lie considerably lower than in their isoelectronic tri-positive counterparts. In Sm^{2+}, for example, the $4f^{n-1}5d$ levels extend down to 20,000 cm^{-1} in Dy^{2+} to 16,000 cm^{-1}. The presence of $4f^{n-1}5d$ levels provides dipositive rare earth ions with broad and strong absorption lines in the region where these are particularly useful for optical pumping. When the excitation is transferred to an excited $4f^n$ state the conditions are favorable for laser action because the return to the ground state may then occur in a sequence of $4f \rightarrow 4f$ transitions whose narrow lines facilitate the attainment of the threshold.

The aforementioned advantages of dipositive rare earth ions are some-what offset by the fact the divalent form is usually not the most stable form of these ions, and therefore without special precautions only a small fraction of the rare earth material incorporated in a crystal will be in the divalent form.

The construction of the elements in the actinide series is similar to the rare earths; therefore the above discussion applies *mutatis mutandis* to the spectrum of uranium and related elements.

Rare Earth Lasers

We next summarize the results on rare earth and uranium lasers pub-lished before March 1964. The material is arranged in the order of atomic numbers and the principal numerical data are displayed in Table III.3.

TABLE III.3.   RARE EARTH AND ACTINIDE LASERS

Atomic Number	Ion	Host Material	Wave-length, μ	Highest Oper. Temp.	Principal References	Notes (Typical Threshold Values)
59	Pr^{3+}	$Ca(NbO_3)_2$	1.04	77°K	[7]	
		$CaWO_4$	1.0468	90°K	[6]	(20 J)
		LaF_3	0.5985	77°K	[8]	(60 J)
60	Nd^{3+}	BaF_2	1.060	77°K	[5]	(1600 J)
		CaF_2	1.0457	77°K	[5, 50]	(60 J)
		$CaMoO_4$	1.067	295°K	[5]	(100–360 J)
		$Ca(NbO_3)_2$	1.060	77°K	[7]	(2 J)
		$CaWO_4$	1.06*	295°K	[10, 22, 51]	(1 J and up)
		$CaWO_4$	0.9142	77°K	[9]	(4.6 J)
		$CaWO_4$	1.35*	295°K	[9]	3 lines (1.6 J and up)
		Gd_2O_3	1.0789	295°K	[12]	(9 J) Weaker line at 1.0741 μ
		LaF_3	1.0633	295°K	[5]	(93 J at 77°K)

* Approximate wavelength for a cluster of lines.

TABLE III.3.—(*continued*)

Atomic Number	Ion	Host Material	Wave-length, μ	Highest Oper. Temp.	Principal References	Notes (Typical Threshold Values)
60	Nd^{3+}	LaF_3	1.0399	77°K	[5]	(75 J)
		LaF_3	1.05*	20°K	[5]	
		$PbMoO_4$	1.0586	295°K	[5]	(60 J)
		SrF_2	1.0437	77°K	[5, 20]	A 1.0370-μ line at 295°K
		$SrMoO_4$	1.06*	295°K	[5, 52]	(17 J and up)
		$SrWO_4$	1.06*	295°K	[5]	(~5 J at 77°K)
		Y_2O_3	1.073	77°K	[11]	(260 J)
		Y_2O_3	1.078	77°K	[11]	(>600 J)
		Glass	0.9180	80°K	[17]	(700 J)
		Glass	1.06	295°K	[13, 19]	Pulsed and cw
		Glass	1.37	295°K	[18]	(460 J)
62	Sm^{2+}	CaF_2	0.7085	4.2°K	[24, 26]	
		SrF_2	0.6969	4.2°K	[25]	
63	Eu^{3+}	Y_2O_3	0.6113	220°K	[28]	(128 J)
64	Gd^{3+}	Glass	0.3125	78°K	[29]	(4700 J)
66	Dy^{2+}	CaF_2	2.36	77°K	[30, 31, 32, 33]	Pulsed (1 J) and cw
67	Ho^{3+}	$Ca(NbO_3)_2$	2.047	77°K	[7]	
		CaF_2	2.092	77°K	[5]	(260 J)
		$CaWO_4$	2.046	77°K	[34]	(80 J)
		$CaWO_4$	2.059	77°K	[5]	(250 J)
		Glass	2.046	78°K	[35]	(3600 J)
68	Er^{3+}	CaF_2	1.617	77°K	[36]	(1000 J)
		$Ca(NbO_3)_2$	1.61	77°K	[7]	
		$CaWO_4$	1.612	77°K	[37]	(800 J)
69	Tm^{3+}	$Ca(NbO_3)_2$	1.91	77°K	[7]	
		$CaWO_4$	1.911	77°K	[5, 38]	(60 J)
		SrF_2	1.972	77°K	[5]	(1600 J)
69	Tm^{2+}	CaF_2	1.116	27°K	[39, 40, 41]	Pulsed and cw
70	Yb^{3+}	Glass	1.015	78°K	[42]	(3400 J)
92	U^{3+}	BaF_2	2.556	20°K	[49]	(12 J)
		CaF_2	2.24	77°K	[43, 45]	
		CaF_2	2.51	295°K	[45, 46]	
		CaF_2	2.57	78°K	[45, 46]	
		CaF_2	2.613	300°K	[47]	(1200 J at 300°K, 2 J at 20°K)
		SrF_2	2.407	90°K	[48]	(38 J at 90°K, 8 J at 20°K)

The tabulated values are those found in the printed references. Frequently the published values were exceeded shortly after publication. Several of the lasers reported here as having a highest operating temperature of 77°K may be operated at room temperature.

* Approximate wavelength for a cluster of lines.

Considerable additional information may be found in Johnson's review article [5].

Praseodymium. The lowest energy levels of Pr^{3+} are shown in Fig. 41, which also shows the transitions assigned to the laser oscillations observed at 1.0468 μ and 5985 Å. Excitation is accomplished by pumping with blue and violet light to the ^3P levels located 20,000 to 22,000 cm^{-1} above ground level. The infrared laser light observed from Pr^{3+} in divalent host crystals arises from $^1G_4 \rightarrow {}^3H_4$ transitions; the terminal level of these transitions is a sublevel of the ground state [6, 7]. Stimulated emission at 5985 Å observed only in the trivalent host crystal LaF_3 is attributed to $^3P_0 \rightarrow {}^3H_6$ transitions [8]. These terminate about 4000 cm^{-1} above ground level; therefore one would expect laser action to take place at room temperature as well. It was observed, however, only at liquid nitrogen temperature.

Neodymium. Neodymium is the most important four-level laser ion. Stimulated emission has been obtained with this ion incorporated in many host lattices, and higher power level has been obtained from Nd lasers than from any other four-level material. The principal host crystals are $CaWO_4$, $SrWO_4$, $SrMoO_4$, and $Ca(NbO_3)_2$. In these crystals stimulated emission is usually observed at a variety of wavelengths around 1.060 μ.

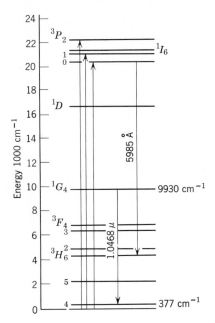

Fig. 41. Energy levels of Pr^{3+} showing laser transitions.

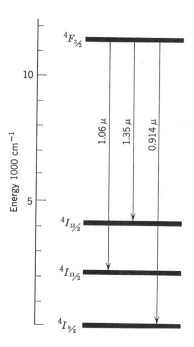

Fig. 42. Levels and groups of Nd laser lines in crystals. Each level shown represents a group of closely spaced levels.

It arises from a $^4F_{3/2} \rightarrow {}^4I_{11/2}$ transition. (See Fig. 42.) Shorter wavelengths corresponding to the same type of transition are observed in CaF_2 and SrF_2 (1.044 μ); longer wavelengths are observed in Y_2O_3 and Gd_2O_3 (1.078 μ). Stimulated emission of Nd is also obtained at 1.35 μ and at 0.914 μ. Radiation at these wavelengths results from $^4F_{3/2} \rightarrow {}^4I_{13/2}$ and $^4F_{3/2} \rightarrow {}^4I_{9/2}$ transitions, respectively.

The fluorescence spectrum of Nd incorporated in a crystal lattice consists of a multiplicity of lines corresponding to transitions between different sublevels into which these levels are resolved in the crystal field; under suitable circumstances a number of these transitions may be employed in a laser. The splitting of the $^4F_{3/2}$ and $^4I_{11/2}$ levels varies with the environment of the Nd ion. This environment may vary not only from one host crystal to another, but even within the same host crystal; the resulting ensemble of ionic levels presents a rather complex picture. Part of the complexity arises from the presence of a trivalent ion in a divalent lattice. The local imbalance of charge at the site of a given Nd ion can be neutralized in a variety of ways—calcium (strontium) vacancies, interstitial oxygen, pairing of Nd ions, etc. Each Nd ion then gives rise to a spectrum characteristic of the particular local crystal field in which it finds itself. The charge compensation problem is partially relieved by the addition of monovalent alkali metal ions to the crystal. It is customary to incorporate an alkali metal, usually sodium, into the host crystal to simplify the level structure of the Nd ion and thus to reduce the number of possible transitions that compete with each other. Different methods of charge compensation lead to somewhat different spectra; variations of this type account in part for the large number of Nd laser lines reported.

Analysis of Nd spectra in crystals requires the examination of a number of factors in addition to the charge compensation mechanism. The variation of linewidths and lineshapes with temperature and Nd^{3+} concentration affects the thresholds of oscillations of all lines. Considerable information on these matters may be found in the works of L. F. Johnson [5, 9, 10], who studied the spectra of Nd in a number of host crystals, giving particular attention to $CaWO_4$, which seems to be the most promising crystalline host for a Nd laser.

The rather extensive experience with $CaWO_4:Nd^{3+}$ lasers may be summarized as follows: Lowest threshold energies are invariably obtained in Na-compensated crystals. At 77°K the wavelength requiring lowest excitation is 1.065 μ. This line may also be excited at room temperature, but the line with the lowest threshold at room temperature has a wavelength of 1.058 μ. At 77°K we find at least two more wavelengths (1.064 and 1.066 μ) arising from $^4F_{3/2} \rightarrow {}^4I_{11/2}$ transitions. Threshold energies are 1 to 7 joules. The above data are applicable to Na-compensated crystals; in other crystals the wavelengths are slightly different and threshold energies are considerably higher.

In addition to the $^4F_{3/2} \rightarrow {}^4I_{11/2}$ transitions, stimulated emission of $CaWO_4:Nd^{3+}$ can also be obtained in $^4F_{3/2} \rightarrow {}^4I_{13/2}$ transitions and in a transition from a $^4F_{3/2}$ to a $^4I_{9/2}$ sublevel [9]. The transitions to the $^4I_{13/2}$ levels yield three laser lines when operated at 77°K; their wavelengths are 1.337, 1.345, and 1.387 μ. The thresholds of the first two lines are low; that of the last one is very high. The terminal levels of these transitions are approximately 4000 cm^{-1} above ground level. The $^4F_{3/2} \rightarrow {}^4I_{9/2}$ transition radiating at 9142 Å (10,935 cm^{-1}) has as its terminal level a sublevel of the ionic ground level, $^4I_{9/2}$, which is only 471 cm^{-1} above the true ground level in the crystal field. This terminal level is partially populated at room temperature; therefore, it is easier to produce laser action at 9142 Å in a refrigerated crystal. The splitting of the $^4I_{9/2}$ level is in general more a help than a hindrance for Nd laser technology because it broadens the absorption bands, so that the neodymium laser can be pumped more effectively at room temperature than at 77°K.

The charge compensation difficulty is avoided when the Nd^{3+} ion is located in LaF_3. This crystal is the first trivalent lattice in which stimulated emission of a trivalent ion was observed. The relevant details of the $^3F_{3/2}$ and $^4I_{11/2}$ energy levels of Nd^{3+} in LaF_3 are shown in Fig. 43 with the transitions observed at 20°K designated by solid arrows. Additional lines are observed at 77°K. These originate at the upper $^4F_{3/2}$ sublevel and are shown in dotted lines. The energy difference of the two upper sublevels is 42 cm^{-1}. On equating this energy difference to kT, we obtain $T = 60°K$; hence when the two levels are in thermal equilibrium with each other at 20°K, the lower of these levels holds almost the entire population and the upper one is almost empty. This fact explains the absence of lines originating from the upper (empty) level at 20°K. When the temperature is 77°K and the interchange between these sublevels is rapid enough to establish a condition resembling thermal equilibrium, a substantial portion of the ion population will be at the upper level and fluorescent transitions from this level may also appear. The situation described here provides an explanation for the threshold anomalies observed in $CaWO_4$ as well: some lines are hard to excite at low temperatures because their starting levels are poorly populated in comparison with other levels. Laser operation in $LaF_3:Nd^{3+}$ was achieved at the following wavelengths: 1.040 μ, 1.050 μ, and 1.063 μ. The charge compensation problem is also avoided in Y_2O_3 and Gd_2O_3, since Nd^{3+} enters as a substitute for a trivalent ion. Hoskins and Soffer [11, 12] obtained stimulated emission from $Y_2O_3:Nd^{3+}$ at 1.073 μ and at 1.078 μ, and from $Gd_2O_3:Nd^{3+}$ at 1.0741 μ and at 1.0789 μ. The excitation

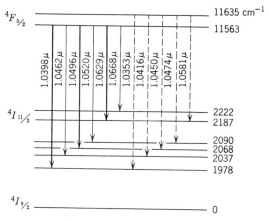

Fig. 43. Fluorescence and laser lines of $LaF_3:Nd^{3+}$. Laser lines are heavy solid lines. Additional fluorescent lines are solid if they appear at 20°K, dotted when observed only at higher temperatures [5].

thresholds in these materials are much higher than in $CaWO_4$. The observed radiation corresponds to $^4F_{3/2} \rightarrow {}^4I_{11/2}$ transitions.

The neodymium ion is known for its stimulated emission in glass as well. In fact, the powerful neodymium lasers are all of the glass type. Snitzer [13] obtained stimulated emission with Nd^{3+} incorporated in a number of glasses, barium crown glass being the most favorable medium. Early successes were obtained with thin, Nd-doped glass fibers 0.03 cm and less in diameter. The length of the fibers varied from 1 to 7.5 cm; they were coated with an ordinary glass of similar index of refraction containing no Nd. Subsequently glass rods up to 45 cm in length were used with a 6-mm-diameter core covered with a clear glass cladding, yielding an outside diameter of 9 mm. Over 100 joules of energy were obtained from such rods in a single pulse [14]. The Nd content of these glass lasers varied from 2 to 6 weight per cent of Nd_2O_3.

The output of the high-power glass lasers is very different from the output of the Nd-doped crystals operated at low power level. The spectrum of the radiation emitted extends over a broad region, the width of which increases with the power level. Figure 44 illustrates the variation of the spectral width of the laser with the input power. The center of the band is around 1.061 μ.

The power output of a Nd-glass laser may show irregular spiking, damped oscillations, or limit cycle behavior. Lasers whose output consists of random spikes produce an aggregate of sharp lines spread over the wavelength interval illustrated in Fig. 44. For a laser that gives damped oscillations the spectral output just above threshold consists of a single band a few Ångströms wide. As the laser is driven harder, this band increases in intensity but not in width. For a continued increase in pump

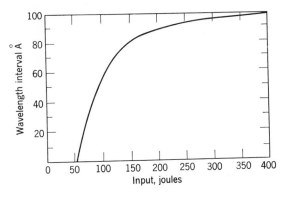

Fig. 44. Spectral width of a Nd-glass laser as a function of pump power. (Measurements of Snitzer [14] on a barium crown glass laser with 6 wt per cent Nd_2O_3.)

power, side bands appear on each side of the central band displaced about 8 Å. As the pump power is increased further, the side bands move farther away from the central band. For still higher pumping, additional sets of side bands occur and move out with increased power. The spectral character of lasers showing limit cycle behavior is rather complicated [14].

The interpretation of the spectra of power lasers is complicated by the fact that the photographic record obtained by ordinary spectroscopy registers the total energy available in different frequency regions during the entire flash; it does not record time variation during the flash. Snitzer [14] and several Russian investigators [15, 16] have shown by means of time resolution spectroscopy that the spectral composition of the Nd-glass laser varies within a single flash. In the case of a laser with random spiking the output spectrum varies from spike to spike. Whenever bands occur, as they do for a laser with damped oscillations, adjacent bands do not emit simultaneously. The time sequence indicates that a hole is burned in one part of the spectrum and the emission shifts to an adjacent part. The total power output available from a single pulse of a Nd-glass laser may be gauged from the curves of Snitzer [14] reproduced in Fig. 45. These were obtained with a short flash of 200 μsec duration (left curve) and with a flash of 1 msec duration (right curve). The exciting source was a Kemlite 4HL-18 flashtube; the total volume of the Nd-glass was 13.5 cm^3.

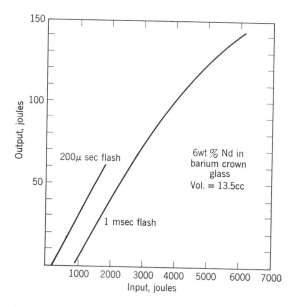

Fig. 45. Neodymium laser output versus input. (After Snitzer [14].)

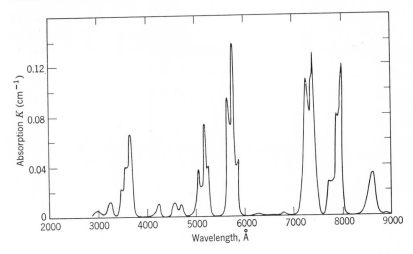

Fig. 46. Absorption of $SrF_2:Nd^{3+}$ in and near the visible region; $T = 300°K$. (Measurements of Kariss and Feofilov [20].)

Operation of the Nd-glass laser has also been achieved in the $^4F_{3/2} \rightarrow {}^4I_{9/2}$ transition [17], yielding radiation of 9180 Å, and in the $^4F_{3/2} \rightarrow {}^4I_{13/2}$ transition [18], which yields radiation at 1.37 μ. Continuous operation of a Nd-glass laser has also been demonstrated at 1.06 μ [19].

The absorption of the Nd^{3+} ion in and near the visible is represented in Fig. 46, which shows the data of Kariss and Feofilov [20]. The curves shown were obtained with Nd^{3+} in SrF_2; they do not differ significantly from the absorption curves obtained by Johnson [5] in $CaWO_4$. There are two major absorption regions in the visible part of the spectrum. The largest of these, around 5800 Å, corresponds to transitions from the ground state to the $^2G_{7/2}$ and $^4G_{5/2}$ levels. These multiple levels are split in the crystal field therefore they are capable of absorption over a reasonably wide range. Excitation into either one of these levels leads eventually to ions whose $^4F_{3/2}$ level is populated; these are required for laser action. The presence of absorption regions between 5000 and 6000 Å is fortunate because a substantial amount of the radiant energy received from the sun is located in this spectral region. It is therefore conceivable to excite a Nd laser with sunlight concentrated by means of mirrors. Such sun-powered lasers have been proposed, and calculations have shown them to be feasible [21].

The first solid-state laser operated continuously (for a few seconds) was a $CaWO_4:Nd^{3+}$ laser [22]. Originally continuous operation was achieved only at 77°K, but when the problem of charge compensation was understood and the number of available levels was reduced by the addition of Na to the crystal, continuous operation became possible at room temperature. Eventually efficient methods of excitation and cooling were developed,

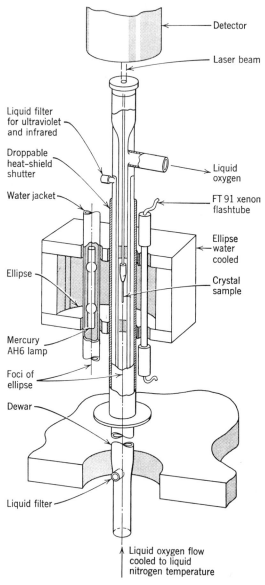

Fig. 47. Apparatus for rare earth laser studies constructed at Bell Telephone Laboratories.

so that $CaWO_4:Nd^{3+}$ lasers may be operated at room temperature continuously for periods up to an hour [23].

A schematic diagram of the apparatus used by Johnson [22] and associates for the study of stimulated emission in rare earths and uranium is shown in Fig. 47. It consists of an elliptic cylinder whose walls are well-polished reflecting surfaces. At the two foci of the ellipse are mounted, respectively, a General Electric AH6 linear high-pressure mercury lamp and the laser crystal. A flashtube (GE FT91) is incorporated within the ellipse for auxiliary measurements involving pulsed operation. The Dewar containing the laser is cooled with liquid oxygen kept below its boiling point by thermal contact with liquid nitrogen.

It is interesting to note that cw neodymium ($CaWO_4$) lasers operate at a wavelength of 1.0650μ at liquid oxygen temperature, and at a wavelength of 1.0582μ at room temperature. These lines correspond to different transitions and the shift from one transition to another is understandable in the light of what has been said about the effect of temperature on the population of several possible starting sublevels.

Samarium. The samarium ion is historically interesting because the first rare earth laser constructed was $CaF_2:Sm^{2+}$. The original discovery was made in 1960 by Sorokin and Stevenson [24], who subsequently demonstrated laser action of Sm^{2+} in SrF_2 crystals as well [25]. Stimulated emission of Sm^{2+} takes place at 7083 Å in CaF_2 and at 6969 Å in SrF_2 [25]. Excitation is accomplished in a broad band ranging from 3000 to 6000 Å.

Figure 48 shows the energy-level scheme of Sm^{2+} in CaF_2 according to the measurements of Kaiser, Garrett, and Wood [26]. The transition that leads to laser action is shown in a heavy line. It terminates 263 cm^{-1} above ground level, which is empty at low temperatures; therefore the laser is capable of operating at a relatively low level of excitation. The energy-level structure of Sm^{2+} in SrF_2 is very similar to the one shown in Fig. 48. The basic difference between lasers constructed with these two host crystals is in the lifetimes of the relevant fluorescent transitions. The relaxation time τ is 1.5×10^{-6} sec in CaF_2, and 15×10^{-3} sec in SrF_2. The large difference in relaxation times results in a corresponding difference between the rates of pulsations in the outputs of these otherwise similar lasers.

Analysis of the rate equations of laser kinetics leads to the conclusion that the rate of pulsations and the rate at which the pulsations are damped depend on the relaxation time. Pulsations of the output intensity were not observed in $CaF_2:Sm^{2+}$. Kaiser, Garrett, and Wood calculated that damped oscillations of a frequency of 4×10^7/sec should occur. These were beyond the frequency response of the measuring instruments employed. In $SrF_2:Sm^{2+}$ the calculated pulsation frequency is lower by a factor of about 100 and pulsations were indeed observed in this material [25].

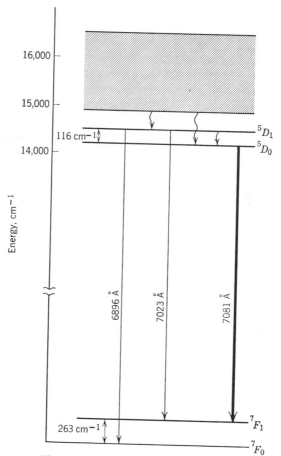

Fig. 48. Energy levels of Sm^{2+} in CaF_2.

Experiments with Sm lasers were carried out in a Dewar in thermal contact with a liquid helium bath. Excitation was accomplished by means of flashes from a Hanovia xenon flashlamp or an EGG FX-12 flashlamp with the light focused on the crystal by spherical mirrors. The flashes were of 10 to 1000 μsec duration. Attempts to approach cw operation by lengthening pulse duration failed because the temperature of the sample increased above the range in which laser operation is possible.

In estimating the number of Sm^{2+} in a CaF_2 crystal particular care must be exercised, for samarium may enter the lattice both in the divalent and the trivalent state. In the experiments of Kaiser, Garrett, and Wood about 80 per cent of the samarium was in a trivalent state and the concentration of Sm^{2+} was only 0.01 mole per cent, or 2.6×10^{18} ions/cm^3. For most experiments cylindrical crystals 2 cm long and 3 to 4 mm in diameter were used. Stimulated emission was also observed from spheres of CaF_2:Sm^{2+}. These experiments were performed with spheres between 1 and 2 mm in diameter resting at the bottom of a Dewar containing liquid hydrogen. The electromagnetic cavity necessary for laser action is the CaF_2 sphere itself, which is located in a surrounding with a lower dielectric constant. Garrett, Kaiser, and Bond [27], who performed this experiment, did not test the coherence of the emitted radiation but inferred the presence of laser action from the rapid increase in the brightness of fluorescence in time when the excitation reached a certain threshold.

Europium. Chang [28] achieved stimulated emission in Y_2O_3 containing 5 mole per cent Eu^{3+}. The radiation of wavelength 6113 Å is attributed to a $^5D_0 \rightarrow {}^7F_2$ transition with the terminal level 859 cm^{-1} above the ground state $^7F_0$. The absorption region of Eu^{3+} suitable for optical pumping of this laser is about 500 Å wide centered around 2500 Å; the peak of quantum efficiency is reached around 2400 Å. Excitation in this spectral region is attributed to transitions of f-electrons to d-electron levels. Although the physics of fluorescence in Eu^{3+} is reasonably well understood, and europium is an important liquid-laser material (see Chapter IV), the crystalline europium laser is relatively undeveloped.

Gadolinium. The tripositive ion of gadolinium has a large energy gap; the lowest level $^6P_{7/2}$ is located 32,000 cm^{-1} above the ground state $^8S_{7/2}$, above the range of Fig. 40. Stimulated emission from this ion in a glass has been reported by Gandy and Ginther [29] at a wavelength of 3125 Å, which corresponds to the $^6P_{7/2} \rightarrow {}^8S_{7/2}$ transition. The Gd laser has a very high threshold energy (4700 joules); it is most likely a three-level laser. The processes in this material have not been sufficiently investigated.

Dysprosium. The $4f \rightarrow 5d$ absorption bands of Dy^{2+} are especially favorable for optical pumping. They start no higher than 16,000 cm^{-1} above the $^5I_8$ ground level. Absorption extends throughout the visible region and the excitation is readily transferred to a $^5I_7$ level located 4325 cm^{-1} above ground [30]. Stimulated emission is obtained in a CaF_2 host crystal on a transition from this level to a level 90 cm^{-1} above ground level. This terminal state is created by the crystal field splitting of the $^5I_8$ level. The crystal must be refrigerated to 77°K, but the threshold is easily attained and continuous operation has been achieved with a mercury lamp of less than 600 watts input [31]. At liquid neon temperature (27°K) continuous operation of a CaF_2:Dy^{2+} laser has been achieved by exciting the crystal with sunlight concentrated with a spherical mirror [32]. The radiation has a wavelength of 2.36 μ. A power output of 2.5 mW has been reported from a CaF_2:Dy^{2+} laser excited by an AH6 mercury lamp with the laser operating continuously at 20°K [33].

Holmium. Stimulated emission in Ho^{3+} is similar to that in Dy^{2+}. It is attributed to a $^5I_7 \rightarrow {}^5I_8$ transition, the terminal level being one of the components of the ground level of the free ion. However, absorption in Ho^{3+} is not similar to absorption in Dy^{2+} because of the unavailability of the $4f^{n-1}5d$ levels. Nevertheless excitation may be accomplished by visible light, radiation in the vicinity of 4500 Å being most effective. Stimulated emission has been observed in $CaWO_4$ at 2.046 and at 2.059 μ [5, 34], in CaF_2 at 2.092 μ [5], and in $Ca(NbO_3)_2$ at 2.047 μ [7]. A Ho^{3+} laser operating in a $LiMgAlSiO_3$ glass has also been reported [35]. All these lasers are operated at liquid nitrogen temperature, because their terminal level is only about 250 cm^{-1} the ground level. In comparison with other rare earth ions holmium requires a rather large expenditure of energy for excitation.

Erbium. Stimulated emission in Er^{3+} has been reported in CaF_2 [36], $CaWO_4$ [37], and $Ca(NbO_3)_2$ [7]. The relevant transition $^4I_{13/2} \rightarrow {}^4I_{15/2}$ terminates on a component of the ground level of the free ion, as is the case in many other rare earth lasers. The terminal level in Er^{3+} is about 400 cm^{-1} above ground. The laser wavelength is 1.612 μ in $CaWO_4$ and 1.617 μ in CaF_2. Excitation takes place in several separated bands from 2550 Å to 9600 Å, the bands centered at 2550 Å and at 3750 Å being the most effective.

Thulium. Stimulated emission of Tm^{3+} has been observed in $CaWO_4$ [38] and in $Ca(NbO_3)_2$ [7] crystals. The wavelength of the emitted radiation is 1.911 μ. It is attributed to a transition from a $^3H_5$ level to a component of the ground level $^3H_6$. The transition terminates 325 cm^{-1} above ground. Excitation is accomplished mostly by blue light corresponding to an energy gap of about 21,000 cm^{-1}. A threshold energy of 125 joules was reported at 77°K.

Stimulated emission of Tm^{2+} has been observed in CaF_2 crystals [39, 40]. The wavelength of the emitted radiation is 1.116 μ. This radiation is emitted on a transition from a component of a $^2F_{5/2}$ level *to the ground level* over an energy gap of 8966 cm^{-1}. Thus the Tm^{2+} laser is a three-level laser; logically it does not belong in this section. The Tm^{2+} ion has strong absorption bands in the visible region, which correspond to $4f \rightarrow 5d$ transitions. Their presence makes this otherwise improbable three-level laser possible. The spectroscopy of divalent thulium is rather complicated; the reader is referred to the papers of Kiss and Duncan [39, 40, 41]. At 4.2 and at 27°K, $CaF_2:Tm^{2+}$ lasers have been operated in continuous as well as in pulsed manner.

Ytterbium. Etzel, Gandy, and Ginther [42] reported laser emission from an ytterbium-activated silicate glass. The radiation has a wavelength of 1.015 μ, which corresponds to a $^2F_{5/2} \rightarrow {}^2F_{7/2}$ transition of the Yb^{3+}

ion. This ion has a $4f$ shell with just one electron short of the maximum of fourteen characteristic of the completed $4f$ shell. Consequently Yb^{3+} has only two $4f^n$ levels, just as the Ce^{3+} ion, which has one $4f$ electron, has two such levels.

According to the observations of Etzel, Gandy, and Ginther the excitation of the ytterbium-glass laser is accomplished primarily by radiation absorbed by bands centered at 9140, 9460, and 9760 Å. These can be attributed only to components of the $^2F_{5/2}$ level split by environmental fields, because no other levels are available until one reaches the $4f^n d$ levels which lie above 50,000 cm^{-1} [4]. Thus it would seem that excitation of Yb^{3+} is accomplished by pumping into the same line that is used for stimulated emission. This unusual situation certainly deserves further investigation.

Uranium. Stimulated emission of uranium has been observed in CaF_2, SrF_2, and BaF_2. Although uranium is one of the first ions whose stimulated emission was demonstrated, there are still a number of unresolved questions about the energy-level structure of the U^{3+} ion and the transitions responsible for the lines observed. Different investigators have proposed different explanations for the complexities of the luminescent spectra of uranium-doped CaF_2, which is the best explored among the host crystals of uranium. The reason for the conflicting hypotheses is that the properties of these crystals vary considerably even when they are prepared in the same laboratory. First, it is almost impossible to ensure that all the uranium incorporated in the CaF_2 crystal will enter as a trivalent ion. Generally some uranium will be incorporated in the tetravalent form together with some oxygen, which has a role in charge compensation for the U^{4+} ion. The U^{3+} ions also call for charge compensation, since they are replacing divalent Ca^{2+} ions. This compensation is accomplished by an extra F^- ion, which may be located in different sites in the lattice. The location of this compensating F^- ion determines the symmetry of the crystal field at the site of the U^{3+} ion. Paramagnetic resonance experiments have shown that the U^{4+} ions are located in sites of trigonal symmetry, while U^{3+} ions are located in sites of tetragonal or orthorhombic symmetry depending on the position of the compensating F^- ion [43, 44, 45]. All these ions may be present in a given uranium-doped CaF_2 crystal, and the proportion of each ion may vary greatly from one crystal to another.

Sorokin and Stevenson [1] observed stimulated emission from U^{3+} in 1960. The original observations were made with a CaF_2 crystal containing uranium in 0.05 and 0.10 per cent molar concentration.* Subsequently

* The concentrations were nominal, indicating proportions used in synthesis. Analysis of the 0.1 per cent crystal indicated the presence of 0.06 mole per cent of uranium. This figure corresponds to 1.50 × 10^{19} atoms/cm^3.

other investigators [43, 45–47] obtained stimulated emission from similar crystals at 2.24, 2.44, 2.51, 2.57, and 2.61 μ with great variation in the intensity of the lines depending on uranium concentration and temperature.

Excitation of the 2.61-μ laser is most effectively accomplished by radiation around 0.9 μ, which corresponds to the energy of the $^4I_{15/2}$ level shown in Fig. 49. The absorption band, which lies above 16,000 cm^{-1}, participates in the pumping of this laser to a lesser extent. It is essential for the pumping of the 2.51-μ line, however. The multiplicity of the laser lines and their variation from crystal to crystal is explained by the presence of U^{3+} ions in crystal sites of tetragonal and orthorhombic symmetry with different splitting of the ionic levels. Some of these levels are illustrated in Fig. 50. Evidence for such energy-level structure comes from paramagnetic

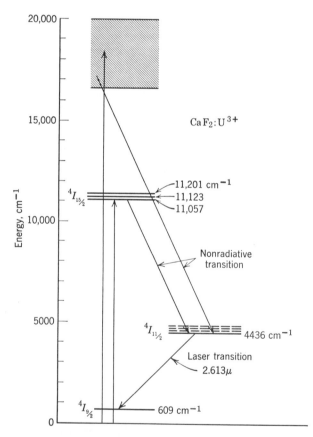

Fig. 49. The absorption-fluorescence cycle of the 2.613-μ transition in $CaF_2:U^{3+}$. (Reprinted from *Physical Review Letters.*)

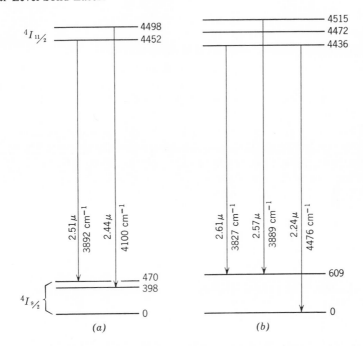

Fig. 50. Partial energy-level diagrams of U^{3+} ions in a CaF_2 lattice showing observed laser lines. (*a*) Ion compensated with tetragonal symmetry. (*b*) Ion compensated with orthorhombic symmetry. (After Porto and Yariv [45].)

resonance studies [44] as well as from the variation of fluorescence with temperature. We find, for example, that at 77°K the 2.61-μ radiation dominates; the 2.57-μ and 2.24-μ lines are either absent or weak. At room temperature these lines are greatly intensified at the expense of the 2.61-μ line, indicating that these three transitions originate at closely coupled energy levels. At a low temperature only the lowest one of these (4436 cm^{-1} above ground) is appreciably populated, while at a higher temperature the population of these levels is nearly equal.

It is impossible to obtain the accurate temperature dependence of the laser frequencies from fluorescence spectroscopic studies because the linewidths are so broad. It is known, however, that the center wavelength of the 2.51-μ transition increases by 23 Å as the crystal is cooled from 77°K to 4°K. The threshold excitation energies show a puzzling variation. For the same line the threshold drops sharply as the crystal is cooled from room temperature to 77°K. However, as the crystal is further cooled to near 4°K, the threshold energy again rises. On the other hand, the threshold energy of the 2.61-μ line rises monotonically [46].

Porto and Yariv observed stimulated emission from U^{3+} in SrF_3 and BaF_2 [48, 49]. The wavelengths are: 2.407 μ for SrF_2, and 2.556 μ for BaF_2. In both materials the starting level is the lowest component of the $^4I_{11/2}$ level. In SrF_2 the transition terminates 334 cm^{-1} above ground level; laser action was observed from 20°K to 90°K. In BaF_2 the transition terminates probably only 109 cm^{-1} above ground level. In this material laser action was observed only at 20°K. The selective excitation process mentioned in connection with $CaF_2:U^{3+}$ lasers is applicable to BaF_2 and SrF_2 lasers as well; i.e., U^{3+} ions at tetragonal sites are most effectively pumped with green light, while those at orthorhombic sites are pumped with radiation in the near infrared.

REFERENCES

1. P. P. Sorokin and M. J. Stevenson, Stimulated infrared emission of trivalent uranium, *Phys. Rev. Lett.* **5**, 557–559, 1960.
2. P. P. Sorokin and M. J. Stevenson, Stimulated emission from $CaF_2:U^{3+}$ and $CaF_2:Sm^{2+}$, *Advances in Quantum Electronics*, Columbia Univ. Press, New York, 1961, pp. 65–76.
3. *American Institute of Physics Handbook*, 2nd ed. McGraw-Hill, New York, 1963, pp. 7–15.
4. G. H. Dieke and H. M. Crosswhite, The spectra of the doubly and triply ionized rare-earths, *Appl. Optics* **2**, 675–686, 1963.
5. L. F. Johnson, Optical maser characteristics of rare-earth ions in crystals, *J. Appl. Phys.* **34**, 897–909, 1963.
6. A. Yariv, S. P. S. Porto, and K. Nassau, Optical maser emission from Pr^{3+} in $CaWO_4$, *J. Appl. Phys.* **33**, 2519–2521, 1962.
7. A. A. Ballman, S. P. S. Porto, and A. Yariv, Calcium niobate—a new laser host material, *J. Appl. Phys.* **34**, 3155–3156, 1963.
8. R. Solomon and L. Mueller, Stimulated emission at 5985 Å from Pr^{3+} in LaF_3, *Appl. Phys. Lett.* **3**, 133–137, 1963.
9. L. F. Johnson and R. A. Thomas, Maser oscillations at 0.9 and 1.35 microns in $CaWO_4:Nd^{3+}$, *Phys. Rev.* **131**, 2038–2040, 1963.
10. L. F. Johnson, Characteristics of the $CaWO_4:Nd^{3+}$ optical maser, *Quantum Electronics III*, Columbia Univ. Press, New York, 1964, pp. 1021–1035.
11. R. H. Hoskins and B. H. Soffer, Stimulated emission from $Y_2O_3:Nd^{3+}$, *Appl. Phys. Lett.* **4**, 22–23, 1964.
12. B. H. Soffer and R. H. Hoskins, Stimulated emission from $Gd_2O_3:Nd^{3+}$ at room temperature and 77°K, *Appl. Phys. Lett.* **4**, 113–114, 1964.
13. E. Snitzer, Optical maser action of Nd^{3+} in a barium crown glass, *Phys. Rev. Lett.* **7**, 444–446, 1961.
14. E. Snitzer, Neodymium glass laser, *Quantum Electronics III*, Columbia Univ. Press, New York, 1964, pp, 999–1019.
15. M. P. Vanyukov, V. I. Isaenko, and V. V. Lyubimov, Time variation of the spectral composition of the radiation from an Nd-activated glass laser, *Soviet Phys. JETP* **17**, 778–779, 1963 (**44**, 1151–1152, 1963).
16. A. M. Bonch-Bruevich, Ya. E. Kariss, and P. P. Feofilov, Pulsations in the spectrum of stimulated emission of Nd in glass, *Opt. Spectroscopy* **14**, 438–439, 1963 (**14**, 824–825, 1963).

17. R. D. Maurer, Operation of a Nd^{3+} glass optical maser at 9180 Å, *Appl. Optics* **2**, 87–88, 1963.

18. P. B. Mauer, Laser action in neodymium-doped glass at 1.37 microns, *Appl. Opt.* **3**, 153, 1964.

19. C. G. Young, Continuous glass laser, *Appl. Phys. Lett.* **2**, 151–152, 1963.

20. Ya. E. Kariss and P. P. Feofilov, Absorption, luminescence and laser action of neodymium in SrF_2 crystals, *Opt. Spectroscopy* **14**, 89–90, 1963 (**14**, 169–172, 1963).

21. P. H. Keck, J. J. Redmann, C. E. White, and R. E. DeKinder, Jr., A new condenser for a sun-powered continuous laser, *Appl. Optics* **2**, 827–831, 1963.

22. L. F. Johnson, G. D. Boyd, K. Nassau, and R. R. Soden, Continuous operation of a solid state optical maser, *Phys. Rev.* **126**, 1406–1409, 1962.

23. P. H. Keck, J. J. Redmann, C. E. White, and D. E. Bowen, Performance of a continuous-wave neodymium laser, *Appl. Optics* **2**, 833–837, 1963.

24. P. P. Sorokin and M. J. Stevenson, Solid state optical maser using Sm^{2+} in CaF_2, *IBM J. Res. Dev.* **5**, 56–58, 1961.

25. P. P. Sorokin, M. J. Stevenson, J. R. Lankard, and G. D. Pettit, Spectroscopy and optical maser action in $SrF_2:Sm^{2+}$, *Phys. Rev.* **127**, 503–508, 1962.

26. W. Kaiser, C. G. B. Garrett, and D. L. Wood, Fluorescence and optical maser effects in $CaF_2:Sm^{2+}$, *Phys. Rev.* **123**, 766–776, 1961.

27. C. G. Garrett, W. Kaiser, and W. L. Bond, Stimulated emission into optical whispering modes of spheres, *Phys. Rev.* **124**, 1807–1809, 1961.

28. N. C. Chang, Fluorescence and stimulated emission from Eu^{3+} in Y_2O_3, *J. Appl. Phys.* **34**, 3500–3504, 1963.

29. H. W. Gandy and R. J. Ginther, Stimulated emission of ultraviolet radiation from gadolinium activated glass, *Appl. Phys. Lett.* **1**, 25–27, 1962.

30. Z. J. Kiss and R. C. Duncan, Pulsed and continuous optical maser action in $CaF_2:Dy^{2+}$, *Proc. IRE* **50**, 1531–1532, 1962.

31. A. Yariv, Continuous operation of a $CaF_2:Dy^{2+}$ optical maser, *Proc. IRE* **50**, 1699–1700, 1962.

32. Z. J. Kiss, H. R. Lewis, and R. C. Duncan, Sun-pumped continuous optical maser, *Appl. Phys. Lett.* **2**, 93–94, 1963.

33. L. F. Johnson, Continuous operation of the $CaF_2:Dy^{2+}$ optical maser, *Proc. IRE* **50**, 1691–1692, 1962.

34. L. F. Johnson, G. D. Boyd, and K. Nassau, Optical maser characteristics of Ho^{3+} in $CaWO_4$, *Proc. IRE* **50**, 87–88, 1962.

35. H. W. Gandy and R. J. Ginther, Stimulated emission from holmium-activated silicate glass, *Proc. IRE* **50**, 2113–2114, 1962.

36. S. A. Pollack, Stimulated emission in $CaF_2:Er^{3+}$, *Proc. IEEE* **51**, 1793–1794, 1963.

37. Z. J. Kiss and R. C. Duncan, Optical maser action in $CaWO_4:Er^{3+}$, *Proc. IRE* **50**, 1531–1532, 1962.

38. L. F. Johnson, G. D. Boyd, and K. Nassau, Optical maser characteristics of Tm^{3+} in $CaWO_4$, *Proc. IRE* **50**, 87–88, 1962.

39. Z. J. Kiss and R. C. Duncan, Optical maser action in $CaF_2:Tm^{2+}$, *Proc. IRE* **50**, 1532–1533, 1962.

40. R. C. Duncan and Z. J. Kiss, Continuously operating $CaF_2:Tm^{2+}$ optical maser, *Appl. Phys. Lett.* **3**, 23–24, 1963.

41. Z. J. Kiss, Energy levels of divalent thulium in CaF_2, *Phys. Rev.* **127**, 718–724, 1962.

42. H. W. Etzel, H. W. Gandy, and R. J. Ginther, Stimulated emission of infrared radiation from ytterbium activated silicate glass, *Appl. Optics* **1**, 534–536, 1962.

43. S. P. S. Porto and A. Yariv, Trigonal sites and 2.24 micron coherent emission of U^{3+} in CaF_2, *J. Appl. Phys.* **33**, 1620–1621, 1962.

44. R. S. Title et al., Optical spectra and paramagnetic resonance of U^{4+} ions in alkaline earth fluoride lattices, *Phys. Rev.* **128**, 62–66, 1962.

45. S. P. S. Porto and A. Yariv, Low lying energy levels and comparison of laser action of U^{3+} in CaF_2, *Quantum Electronics III*, Columbia Univ. Press, New York, 1964, pp. 717–723.

46. J. P. Wittke, Z. J. Kiss, R. C. Duncan, and J. J. McCormick, Uranium-doped CaF_2 as a laser material, *Proc. IEEE* **51**, 56–62, 1962.

47. G. D. Boyd et al., Excitation, relaxation and continuous maser action in the 2.613 micron transition of $CaF_2:U^{3+}$, *Phys. Rev. Lett.* **8**, 269–272, 1962.

48. S. P. S. Porto and A. Yariv, Excitation, relaxation and optical maser action at 2.407 microns in $SrF_2:U^{3+}$, *Proc. IRE* **50**, 1543–1544, 1962.

49. S. P. S. Porto and A. Yariv, Optical maser characteristics $BaF_2:U^{3+}$, *Proc. IRE* **50**, 1542–1543, 1962.

50. L. F. Johnson, Optical maser characteristics of Nd^{3+} in CaF_2, *J. Appl. Phys.* **33**, 756, 1962.

51. L. F. Johnson and K. Nassau, Infrared fluorescence and stimulated emission of Nd^{3+} in $CaWO_4$, *Proc. IRE* **49**, 1704–1706, 1961.

52. L. F. Johnson and R. R. Soden, Optical maser characteristics of Nd^{3+} in $SrMoO_4$, *J. Appl. Phys.* **33**, 757, 1962.

7. SEMICONDUCTOR LASERS

Population Inversion in Semiconductors

Even before the first ruby laser was constructed, several speculative papers appeared on the subject of population inversion in semiconductors and the possible application of semiconductors for the direct and efficient conversion of electrical energy into light. This preliminary theoretical work originated primarily from two centers, the Lincoln Laboratory of the Massachusetts Institute of Technology where B. Lax led this effort and the Lebedev Institute in Moscow where N. G. Basov provided the leadership for all laser projects. Although the schemes proposed by Lax, Basov, and their associates have not resulted in an operating semiconductor laser up to the time of this writing, their calculations have contributed to the understanding of the conditions relevant for the attainment of population inversion in semiconductors. We shall return to this matter after reviewing the basic properties of semiconductors and describing the operating semiconductor lasers.

We note at the outset that semiconductors differ from ionic crystals in their energy-level structure. Moreover, although we have previously been concerned with the energy levels of individual foreign ions embedded in a crystal, we must now be concerned with the energy levels of a crystal as a whole.

The energy-level scheme of an ideal (pure) semiconductor crystal is illustrated in Fig. 51. The energy spectrum consists of broad bands of

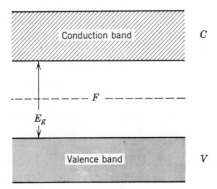

Fig. 51. Energy levels of an ideal semiconductor.

permitted levels: the *valence band* V and the *conduction band* C separated by a forbidden band (gap) of width E_g. The density of states in the valence and conduction bands is a function of the energy. Each state may be occupied by at most one electron; the probability that a given state is occupied is given by the *Fermi-Dirac distribution function*

$$f = [1 + e^{(E-F)/kT}]^{-1}, \qquad (7.1)$$

where F is the *Fermi level* shown in Fig. 51, E is the energy of the electron in the given state, and T is the absolute temperature.* At $0°$K the valence band of an ideal semiconductor is completely filled and the conduction band is empty. In this situation the semiconductor cannot conduct current; it becomes an insulator. Above $0°$K some electrons are always present in the conduction band; consequently electric current may flow both as a result of the motion of electrons in the conduction band and as a result of the motion of vacancies (holes) in the valence band created by the promotion of electrons to the conduction band. These holes in the valence band are completely equivalent to particles with a positive charge provided with a mass which is in general different from the mass of a free electron. In an ideal semiconductor the number of electrons in the conduction band is exactly equal to the number of holes in the valence band.

In a real crystal additional energy levels may arise, such as those designated by D and A in Fig. 52. They are created by the presence of crystal imperfections: impurities, vacancies, and dislocations. Usually these levels are localized in the neighborhoods of the corresponding

* For an exposition of the results stated see, e.g., C. Kittel: *Introduction to Solid State Physics*, 2nd ed., John Wiley and Sons, Inc., New York, 1956, esp. Chapters 10 and 13.

imperfections, in contradistinction to the permitted zones which belong to the crystal as a whole.

In a real crystal the number of particles that serve as current carriers is determined primarily by the presence of impurities which may be classified in the following three categories: donor impurities, whose energy levels generally lie near the conduction band, acceptor impurities, whose levels normally lie near the valence band, and finally impurities whose levels lie deep in the forbidden zone. The first two kinds are most important; they are deliberately introduced in many instances to produce an n-type or a p-type semiconductor. An *n-type semiconductor* is obtained when one introduces into the crystal lattice an element that has more valence electrons than the lattice site ordinarily calls for. Such an atom or ion becomes an electron donor; it provides an electron that can move about relatively freely. When an element with a lower than appropriate valence is incorporated into the lattice it becomes an electron acceptor; it robs the valence band of one of the electrons that belong there in the ideal crystal. In this manner a hole is created in the material, which is then called a *p-type semiconductor*. For many applications semiconductors are doped with impurities of both kinds, the donor atoms prevailing in one part of the semiconductor, the acceptors in the other. The transition region separating these parts is called the *p-n junction*.

As a result of the action of impurities described, the conduction band of the n-type semiconductor will contain electrons and the valence band of the p-type semiconductor will be partially empty. We can show by thermodynamic considerations that for materials in contact in thermal equilibrium the Fermi levels must be equal. As a consequence of the equality of the Fermi levels the distribution of the electrons in a p-n junction will take the

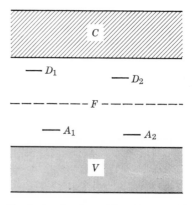

Fig. 52.   Energy levels of a semiconductor with impurities.

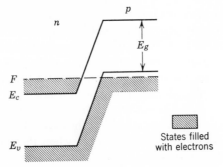

Fig. 53. Energy-level diagram of a *p-n* junction.

form shown in Fig. 53. The Fermi level is shown as separating the filled from the unfilled states; actually the probability of a state's being filled is given by (7.1), and there will always be some electrons above the Fermi level. When a forward voltage is applied to a *p-n* junction by connecting the *p* and *n* regions to the positive and negative terminals of a battery, electrons will be driven from the *n* region to the *p* region and holes from the *p* region to the *n* region. Electrons and holes are then present in the same region; their recombination results in emission of radiation. The energy-level structure of a *p-n* junction with a forward bias is shown in Fig. 54. The impressed electromotive force V displaces the Fermi levels from their equilibrium position by eV, making $eV = F_u - F_l$. The situation represented in Fig. 54, corresponds to a semiconductor doped with impurities to such high level of concentration ($> 10^{18}$ atoms per cm^3) that the donor levels merge with the conduction band and the acceptor levels with the valence band. The separate Fermi levels drawn in the *n* and *p* regions, which are not in thermal equilibrium with each other, have the following meaning: Within each band thermal equilibrium is rapidly established and the distribution of the electrons within the band may be described by a Fermi-Dirac function with a parameter F characteristic of that band.

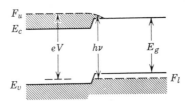

Fig. 54. Energy-level diagram of a *p-n* junction with a forward bias.

In examining conditions for population inversion in a semiconductor a variety of transitions must be considered. The transitions may take place between levels of the same band, from the conduction band to the valence band, between impurity levels, or between a band and an impurity level. The variety of these possibilities is responsible for the number of methods proposed for the creation of a semiconductor laser.

It is possible to state a general necessary condition for negative absorption which is applicable independently of the particular transition involved. Negative absorption can take place only when the number of photons emitted by stimulated transitions exceeds the number of photons absorbed by the inverse transition. Both of these processes are proportional to n, the density of photons of the proper energy, and to the same constant (Einstein's B). Emission is proportional to the probability that the upper state is full and the lower empty, while absorption is proportional to the probability that the lower state is full and the upper empty. Let f_u and f_i be the probabilities that the upper and lower states, respectively, are occupied; then negative absorption can occur only when

$$Bn[f_u(1 - f_i) - f_i(1 - f_u)] > 0. \qquad (7.2)$$

This inequality simplifies to

$$f_u > f_i. \qquad (7.3)$$

An interesting conclusion can be drawn from (7.3) in the case when the transition occurs from the conduction band to the valence band, and when the electrons in both bands have reached thermal equilibrium with the crystal lattice. Such a condition of equilibrium may be reached in a time short compared with the carrier lifetime. Then, when electrons are injected into the conduction band or holes in the valence band, the probability that a level in either band is occupied can be written in the form (7.1); namely,

$$f_u^{-1} = 1 + e^{(E_2 - F_c)/kT}; \qquad f_i^{-1} = 1 + e^{(E_1 - F_v)/kT},$$

where F_c and F_v are the parameters of the distribution in the two bands. They are called the *quasi-Fermi levels* of the conduction and valence bands, respectively; E_2 and E_1 are the energies of the initial and final states. From (7.3) it follows that

$$e^{(E_1 - F_v)/kT} > e^{(E_2 - F_c)/kT},$$

and hence

$$F_c - F_v > E_2 - E_1 = h\nu, \qquad (7.4)$$

where ν is the frequency of the emitted photon. Since $E_2 - E_1$ is not less that E_g, it also follows that

$$F_c - F_v > E_g. \qquad (7.5)$$

This condition was derived independently by Basov, Krokhin, and Popov [1], and by Bernard and Duraffourg [2]. It implies that the forward bias V must exceed E_g/e. It should be observed that the inequality (7.5) is applicable only to the so-called *direct transitions*. These are characterized by the conservation of the momentum of the electron; the entire energy difference of the states is carried away by the photon.

To understand what may happen in a more general situation one should recall that the distribution of electrons in a semiconductor is more complicated than Fig. 51 suggests. Actually the energy of an electron is a function of its momentum $\mathbf{p}$, or the related quantum-mechanical wave vector $\mathbf{k} = \mathbf{p}/h$. In a one-dimensional representation, the electron energy E as a function of $\mathbf{k}$ may be such as represented in Fig. 55a and b. The conduction band is represented by curve 1, the valence band by curve 2, and the band gap by the energy difference measured from the maximum M of curve 2 to the minimum m of curve 1. When these points belong to the same value of the momentum, an electron may be transferred from the lower "edge" of the conduction band to the top "edge" of the valence band without a change in momentum. This is the situation illustrated in Fig. 55a, which represents, for example, the energy structure of GaAs. In Ge and Si, on the other hand, the situation illustrated in Fig. 55b prevails. These latter are called *indirect semiconductors*. We note that according to solid-state theory the region of variability of a momentum component, say p_x, is from $-h/2a$ to $+h/2a$, where a is the lattice constant in the appropriate direction.

When an electron is transferred from the bottom of the conduction band to the top of the valence band with the emission of a photon and no other change takes place, the law of conservation of momentum demands that

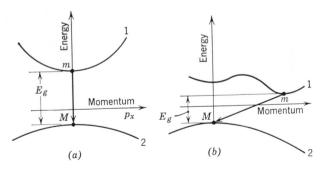

Fig. 55. Energy structure of direct (*a*) and indirect (*b*) semiconductors; line 1 conduction band, line 2 valence band.

p_1 equal $p_2 + P$, where $P = h\nu/c = h/\lambda$ is the momentum of the emitted photon. Since $p_{x,\max} = h/2a$, we have

$$\frac{P}{p_{x,\max}} = \frac{h/\lambda}{h/2a} = \frac{2a}{\lambda}.$$

Since a is only a few Ångströms, the momentum of a photon in the optical range is orders of magnitude smaller than the limits of the electronic momentum. Consequently p_1 is approximately equal to p_2, and the transition must be represented by a vertical line on the energy-momentum diagram (Fig. 55a). It must be a *direct* transition. When the extrema of the valence band and the conduction band correspond to different values of the momentum of the electron, the law of conservation of momentum requires that the electron transition be accompanied by the simultaneous emission or absorption of a phonon; i.e., a quantum of lattice vibration. This process compensates for the change of momentum the electron suffers in transition. Such a transition is illustrated in Fig. 55b; it is called an *indirect* transition. The phonon carries away not only momentum, but a part of the available energy as well.

The calculation of the transition probability of an indirect transition is a little more complicated than that of a direct transition, because we must take into account the statistics of the phonons. At very low crystal temperatures, we may neglect the process which requires the absorption of a phonon, and in this case we obtain in place of (7.5) the inequality

$$F_c - F_v > E_g - E_p$$

as the condition for population inversion, where E_p is the energy of the phonon created by the transition.

p-n Junction Lasers

While much of the theoretical speculation centered around the examination of schemes for coherent generation of light in homogeneous semiconductors, in the fall of 1962 three groups working independently succeeded almost simultaneously in obtaining stimulated emission from p-n junctions of GaAs [3, 4, 5], and another group succeeded with GaAs-GaP alloy [6]. These achievements did not come entirely as a surprise; the recombination radiation of carriers injected into GaAs had been a subject of study both in the United States [7] and in the Soviet Union [8] and the possibilities of obtaining a population inversion sufficient for light amplification by the injection of current carriers across a p-n junction had been discussed in publications of the Lebedev Institute [1, 9]. Dumke's theoretical analysis [10] indicated that stimulated emission is more likely to be achieved in direct semiconductors such as GaAs than in indirect ones such as Si and Ge. In addition to GaAs the compounds InP, GaSb, InAs, and InSb show capabilities as junction laser materials.

The semiconductor junction laser is illustrated in Fig. 56. It consists of a single crystal wafer with linear dimensions of the order of 1 mm. The *p-n* junction is plane; it passes near the center of the sample and lies perpendicular to the front and back surfaces which are cleaved or cut parallel and are highly polished. These planes form the terminating mirrors of a resonant cavity; the index of refraction of the materials used is so high that it is not necessary to increase the reflectivity of these end surfaces by coating. In the simplest configurations the side surfaces are offset by a small angle or they are roughly finished to avoid the generation of radiation in an undesired direction. The *p* and *n* regions are doped to a degree sufficient to ensure what is known as a *degenerate* distribution of charge carriers. This term means that there are so many electrons in the conduction band that at the temperature of the system the distribution of the electrons is essentially independent of the temperature, or, in other words, that the transition region of energy which separates the filled states from the unfilled ones, and which is of the order of kT, is narrow compared with the energy which separates the Fermi level from the bottom of the band. The lasers usually operate at 77°K, or lower, and the density of donors varies between 3×10^{17} and 2×10^{18} per cm³. The *p-n* junction is usually made by diffusing Zn (acceptor) in one side of a Te (donor)-doped GaAs crystal. The entire area of the junctions is of the order of 10^{-4} cm².

An electric field is impressed in the form of a pulse lasting about 1 μsec; the electromotive force required is of the order of the band gap, that is, 1.5 V. The current through the junction is a highly nonlinear function of

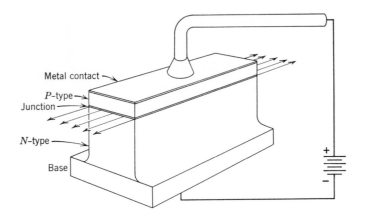

Fig. 56. Structure of a semiconductor junction laser.

the impressed voltage; it increases rapidly as the voltage approaches the band gap. The emission of light (infrared) is noticeable even at low current levels. The radiation emitted under such circumstances is called recombination radiation because it arises when electrons and holes recombine with the emission of energy in the form of photons. In studying the emitted radiation we are usually interested in observing the spectral and spatial distribution of radiant energy as a function of the current density through the junction. The original observations of Hall, Fenner, Kingsley, Soltys, and Carlson [3] are typical of what can be seen with a detector located along the beam axis, i.e., in the direction perpendicular to the polished surfaces: "Below 5000 A/cm² the light intensity varied linearly with

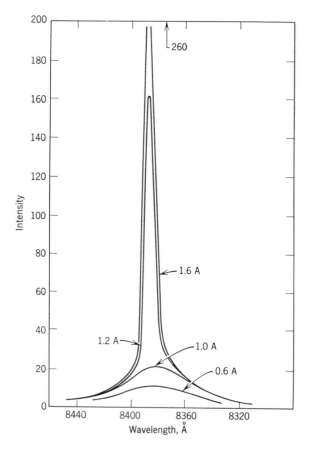

Fig. 57. Spectrum of radiation from a GaAs *p-n* junction for four values of the current. (After Burns and Nathan [11].)

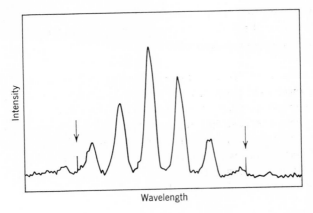

Fig. 58. Mode structure observed in the spectrum of a GaAs laser. At lower current more modes of approximately equal intensity are observed and as the current is increased the central mode becomes dominant. (The markers—arrows—are separated by 11.26 Å.)

current density. Near 8500 A/cm² the intensity increased very rapidly with current, reaching a value about ten times the extrapolated low-current intensity at 20,000 A/cm². Such a current threshold is characteristic of the onset of stimulated light emission and it is significant that the azimuthal maxima of the radiation patterns make their appearance at this threshold."

We must stress that the rapid rise of the detector current in a preferred direction is in large part due to the narrowing of the emitted beam. The actual increase in detector response depends on the solid angle intercepted by the detector.

Hall and associates observed the spectral distribution of the emitted radiation with a relatively low resolution spectrometer. "Below threshold the spectral width at half maximum is 125 Å .... As the current is increased through threshold, the spectral width decreases suddenly to 15 Å in a manner which is again characteristic of the onset of stimulated emission."

As Hall already suspected, the 15-Å width was not an intrinsic property of the GaAs laser. Subsequent investigations revealed that the spectral characteristics of the output continue to change with increasing current above threshold. The general features of the variation of the spectrum with current at the fixed temperature of 77°K are shown in Fig. 57. Additional information on the fine structure of the spectrum and its variation with temperature comes from the high resolution measurements of Burns and Nathan [11, 12] as well as those of Sorokin, Axe, and Lankard [13]. Figure 58 shows a typical record of some of the Fabry-Perot cavity modes of a GaAs laser.

As is the case with other lasers, the center of the emission spectrum is approximately at the peak of the fluorescent line, and the fine structure of the emitted radiation is determined by the resonator modes available in the spectral region where the intensity of the fluorescent line is significant. The spectrum of the fluorescent line is a property of the material, while the resonator modes are dependent on the construction of the device.

In a semiconductor laser the separation of the simplest types of cavity modes is uneven because the laser is operated in a wavelength region where the index of refraction varies rapidly, while in other solid lasers the variation of the refractive index with frequency may be neglected. In the plane wave approximation the longitudinal modes of a Fabry-Perot interferometer satisfy equation (3.2) of Chapter II:

$$\frac{1}{\lambda_0} = \frac{n}{2L\eta},$$

where λ_0 is the wavelength in vacuum and η the index of refraction. In terms of the frequency ν, this relation becomes

$$\eta\nu = nc/2L. \tag{7.6}$$

Consequently the frequency difference $\Delta\nu$ of consecutive modes must satisfy the equation

$$\left(\eta + \nu\frac{\partial\eta}{\partial\nu}\right)\Delta\nu = \frac{c}{2L}. \tag{7.7}$$

Let us introduce

$$\eta_0 = \eta + \nu\frac{\partial\eta}{\partial\nu}. \tag{7.8}$$

Then

$$\eta_0\,\Delta\nu = c/2L \tag{7.9}$$

takes the place of $\eta\,\Delta\nu = c/2L$ valid for a constant η.

The frequency of recombination radiation is determined by the energy that becomes free upon the recombination of a hole with an electron. This energy is approximately equal to the band gap energy E_g, which is uniquely determined for a pure semiconductor at a given temperature and pressure. Sturge [14] determined E_g of *pure* GaAs at 1 atm. pressure in the temperature range of 10 to 294°K. In this region a rough approximation of the experimental values is given by

$$E_g(T) = E_g(0) - \beta T^2, \tag{7.10}$$

where $E_g(0) = 1.521$ eV, and $\beta = 1.21 \times 10^{-6}$ eV/°K^2. Experimental studies of recombination radiation in doped GaAs crystals show that the peak of the emission spectrum depends on the concentration of the carriers (doping) and on the current passing through the crystal [12]. Currents well below threshold produce a broad emission band which shifts to higher energy and becomes narrower as the current is increased. This shift is illustrated in Fig. 59. A plausible (but not unique) explanation of this phenomenon is that recombination occurs directly from the valence band to the conduction band and that the shift to higher energy represents the progressive raising of the quasi-Fermi energy of the injected carriers as the current is increased [15].

In discussing the temperature dependence of coherent radiation it is practical to specify the situation by requiring that the spectrum is to be measured just above threshold. When this is done a curve of the type shown in Fig. 60 is obtained for the peak of the coherent radiation versus temperature. The center of the spectrum of this radiation shifts with the temperature at a rate calculable from the variation of the band gap energy with temperature, since $h\nu \approx E_g$. The spectrum shifts to lower frequencies as the temperature increases. It was observed that the individual peaks in the resolved mode structure of the stimulated radiation shift only about one-third as fast as the entire group; the modes at higher energies fall

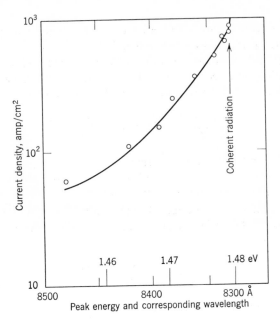

Fig. 59. Peak of the incoherent luminescence of a GaAs diode at 4.2°K as a function of the current density. (After Engeler and Garfinkel [15].)

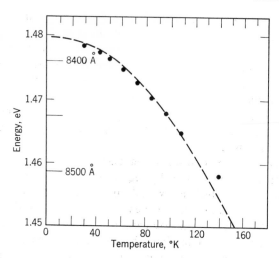

Fig. 60. Spectral variation of the coherent output of a GaAs laser with temperature. The dots represent measured photon energies with the laser excited just above threshold; the curve represents the variation of the band gap of pure GaAs with temperature as determined by optical experiments. (After Engeler and Garfinkel [15].)

behind as the temperature increases. They drop out and may be replaced by new modes at the long wavelength end [11].

The temperature dependence of the mode can be deduced from equation (7.6) by taking into account that the refractive index depends on the temperature as well as the frequency. By differentiation of (7.6) we obtain

$$-\frac{d(\log \nu)}{dT} = \frac{d(\log L)}{dT} + \frac{d(\log \eta)}{dT}. \tag{7.11}$$

The first term on the right is the thermal expansion coefficient whose value does not exceed 6×10^{-6} per °K, while the observed temperature variation of cavity modes is around 5×10^{-5} per °K. The effects of thermal expansion are therefore neglected; the major contribution to the frequency shift arises from the variation of η with the temperature. Then (7.11) is replaced by

$$-\frac{1}{\nu}\frac{d\nu}{dT} = \frac{1}{\eta}\left(\frac{\partial \eta}{\partial T} + \frac{\partial \eta}{\partial \nu}\frac{d\nu}{dT}\right), \tag{7.12}$$

which combined with (7.8) results in

$$\frac{d\nu}{dT} = -\frac{\nu}{\eta_0}\frac{\partial \eta}{\partial T}. \tag{7.13}$$

There remains only to evaluate $\partial\eta/\partial T$. The three variables η, ν, and T are connected by an "equation of state" (7.6); therefore

$$-\left(\frac{\partial\eta}{\partial T}\right)_\nu = \left(\frac{\partial\eta}{\partial\nu}\right)_T\left(\frac{\partial\nu}{\partial T}\right)_\eta. \tag{7.14}$$

Equations (7.8), (7.13), and (7.14) may now be combined:

$$\frac{d\nu}{dT} = \frac{\eta_0 - \eta}{\eta_0}\frac{\partial\nu}{\partial T}. \tag{7.15}$$

Finally, relating ν to the band gap E_g, we obtain

$$\frac{dh\nu}{dT} = \frac{\eta_0 - \eta}{\eta_0}\frac{\partial E_g}{\partial T}. \tag{7.16}$$

This relation was derived by Engeler and Garfinkel [15]. Using the available measured value of η and calculating η_0 from the spacing of adjacent modes according to (7.9), they obtained

$$\frac{\eta_0 - \eta}{\eta_0} \approx 0.35$$

when T varies in the vicinity of 50°K. The mode variation calculated from the band gap variation by means of (7.16) is in excellent agreement with the experimental observations.

The temperature dependence of the threshold current density of a GaAs laser is shown in Fig. 61. In the vicinity of liquid nitrogen temperature the threshold current density varies approximately as T^3. The total light output decreases rapidly as the temperature increases. These facts explain why experimentation with GaAs is seldom conducted above liquid nitrogen temperature.

Heat is generated in GaAs and similar lasers mostly by the absorption of the light originating in the junction in other parts of the crystal, and by joule heating at the contacts. In order to prevent the characteristics of the laser from shifting too far during a pulse, provision must be made for adequate cooling.

High conversion efficiency (from electrical energy to light) is one of the most important properties of junction lasers. The figure of merit used to describe such a laser is the *external efficiency*, defined as the number of photons emitted from the laser divided by the number of carriers injected into the crystal. This external efficiency is 4 to 11 per cent for diodes below threshold. At threshold the efficiency increases abruptly; values up to 70 per cent have been reported with GaAs lasers operating at 77°K [16]. The sudden increase of efficiency is related to the change in the directional characteristics of the radiation: Below threshold the radiation is emitted

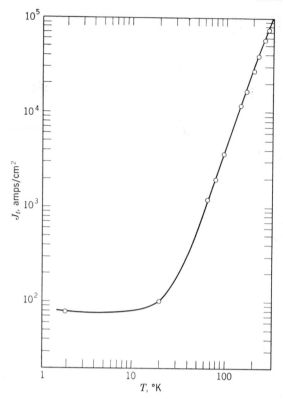

Fig. 61. Threshold current density of GaAs versus temperature. (After Burns and Nathan [12].)*

isotropically. Only a fraction of the generated radiation can leave the crystal because of the high index refraction. The radiation is reflected back and forth; a large part of it is absorbed, mostly in the p-type material where the absorption constant is large. Above threshold the coherent radiation is concentrated in the plane of the junction; it does not pass through the p-region. It should be added that for a given current above threshold, considerably more light can be obtained from one end of a laser if the other end is made completely reflective.

The significant radiation loss mechanisms in semiconductors are somewhat different from those encountered in three- and four-level lasers. In the latter types the principal losses occur at the terminating surfaces; therefore the threshold condition can be found by equating the end losses with

---

* The curve in this figure should not be taken too seriously for the temperature region below 50°K because only two observed points are available.

the amplification calculated from the value of the (negative) absorption coefficient appropriate to the population inversion. (See Section II.2). In semiconductor materials the volume losses dominate; they are caused by the absorption of coherent radiation in the semiconductor without a corresponding increase in the capability of the semiconductor to re-emit radiation of the same frequency. Such events do not take place in ruby and similar crystals because the relevant emission and absorption phenomena take place in connection with transitions between two sharply defined levels in an essentially homogeneous material. As we have already stated, the semiconductor contains energy bands and—as long as there are vacancies below—an electron may drift to a lower level within a band without the emission of radiation. It is therefore possible for an electron in either band to absorb radiation by transferring from a low-energy state to an empty high-energy state within that band. This phenomenon is called *free carrier absorption*. The electron may then return to a lower state by the release of the excess energy in the form of heat.

Free carrier absorption is a very serious limiting factor in semiconductor laser operation because it not only causes a diminution of the effective amplification but it causes the crystal to heat up with consequent further deterioration of its properties as an amplifier. Other phenomena, such as impurity absorption and scattering, also reduce the effective amplification. The combined effect of these phenomena is so large that in the first approximation we can neglect the effect of the terminations entirely and calculate the threshold current from the condition that the rate of carrier injection must be large enough to make the effective amplification at least zero. For further information of threshold calculations we refer to the literature [12].

Light emitted from a semiconductor junction is polarized with the E-vector parallel to the plane of the junction. The spatial distribution of the radiated energy has the general appearance of the diffraction pattern from a rectangular aperture complicated by distortions which may be attributed to the simultaneous presence of different modes of oscillation. The measurements of Fenner and Kingsley [17] indicate that the major beam in the plane of the junction is of the order of 1 degree wide, while in the vertical plane the beamwidth is around 10 degrees. These data were obtained on junctions of thickness 1 μ with a horizontal width 300 to 500 μ. The beam structure varies with the injection current and varies from one device to another, probably as a result of the variation of the quality and orientation of the terminating mirrors.

The device characteristics of semiconductor lasers vary rapidly with the rapid advance of technology. A typical device configuration favored in 1963 is shown in Fig. 62. The GaAs diodes are typically operated at

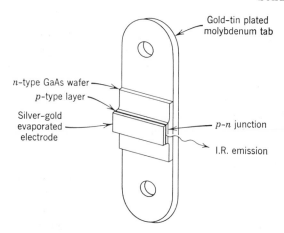

Fig. 62. Typical GaAs diode.

liquid nitrogen temperature with current pulses varying in duration from 50 to 1000 nsec at repetition rates of 100 to 1000 pulses per second. Peak power outputs of a few hundred watts at 77°K and 14 watts at room temperature were reported [18]. Specially designed GaAs junction lasers operate continuously at liquid hydrogen temperature [19]. The reported cw power output of 3.2 watts will probably have been exceeded many times by the time this book is published.

One of the technically interesting characteristics of semiconductor lasers is that their output can be modulated by varying the injection current. Modulation at gigacycle rate has been achieved in this manner [20].

Semiconductor junction lasers cover a large wavelength range because a number of III-V compounds similar to GaAs can be used as basic materials. The energy gaps of such materials with laser capabilities are known to vary from about 0.16 to about 1.5 eV with a corresponding variation in the frequency of the emitted radiation.

Gallium arsenide has the highest band gap energy of the simple III-V compounds in which stimulated emission was demonstrated. Ordinarily the light emitted from a GaAs diode has a wavelength around 0.84 μ, but special diodes have been constructed which emit light at 0.88 μ also [21]. Gallium phosphide has a higher energy gap than GaAs. The p-n junctions of the mixed semiconductor $GaAs_xP_{1-x}$ operate as lasers when x exceeds 0.6. By varying the composition, lasers can be constructed from this material covering the wavelength range from 0.84 μ (pure GaAs) to about 0.66 μ, which corresponds to approximately 40 per cent GaP [22].

The behavior of InP is very similar to that of GaAs. The band gap in InP is slightly lower than in GaAs; consequently the spectrum of the emitted radiation is shifted to longer wavelengths [23]. Still farther in the infrared lie the outputs of InAs and InSb lasers. Their wavelengths are 3.11 μ and 5.18 μ, respectively. Such lasers must be operated at very low temperatures [24, 25]. By using mixtures or alloys of these semiconductor materials, lasers can be constructed whose emission lies in the wavelength range between the pure materials. Further "tuning" of the laser frequency is possible by varying the concentration of the carriers as well as by varying the temperature and pressure, or by impressing on the semiconductor an external magnetic field.

It should be stressed that even at a fixed temperature and pressure one cannot attribute a very precise wavelength to a semiconductor laser of a given type. Variations in the preparation of *p-n* junctions lead to different distributions of donors and acceptors within the same basic material. Such variations are reflected in the spectrum of the laser. GaAs lasers with varying impurity concentrations have been shown to emit coherent radiation at 77°K over the entire wavelength region from 8380 to 8650 Å [26].

Speculations Concerning Semiconductor Lasers

Sometime during 1963 it came to light that speculations about the possible use of semiconductor junctions for the amplification or generation of light had begun before the first maser was built. In a set of unpublished notes sent to E. Teller in September 1953, John von Neumann calculated that if electrons and holes are injected into a *p-n* junction, it is possible to upset the equilibrium distribution of current carriers to such an extent that one may obtain a light amplifier based on the stimulated recombination of the carriers.* The success of this scheme was amply demonstrated nine years later. There are, however, other, better-publicized speculations concerning semiconductors which merit discussion even though they have not led to a practical laser.

Several interesting schemes were proposed for obtaining population inversion in bulk semiconductors as distinct from semiconductor junctions. Should some such scheme prove to be successful it could lead to a laser of much larger active volume and hence potentially of larger output than the junction lasers. We shall confine our attention to two schemes, the cyclotron resonance scheme of Lax [27] and the electric impulse scheme of Basov [1, 28].

The cyclotron resonance scheme is not one of direct conversion of electrical energy to coherent radiation. It is a proposed method for converting intense monochromatic radiation—say from another laser—into coherent monochromatic radiation of much longer wavelength. The basis

---

* The contents of these rather rough notes were reviewed by J. Bardeen in von Neumann's *Collected Works* (Vol. 5, p. 420).

of the proposal is the cyclotron resonance phenomenon, which indicates that in the presence of an external magnetic field the conduction band and the valence band of a semiconductor break up into a series of nearly, *but not exactly*, equidistant levels, and that certain simple selection rules govern the transitions among these levels when the transitions are associated with the emission and absorption of radiation. It follows by classical electromagnetic calculations that charges of mass m moving in a magnetic field B revolve around the direction of B with an angular frequency ω_c which in CGS (Gaussian) units is given by

$$\omega_c = \frac{eB}{mc}. \tag{7.17}$$

This frequency, which is independent of the velocity of the particles (in the nonrelativistic case), is the cyclotron frequency in the given magnetic field. Clearly an electromagnetic field of this frequency is expected to interact strongly with a material containing such particles. Cyclotron resonance absorption is experimentally observed in semiconductors; it leads to the determination of the effective mass of electrons and holes within the semiconductor. The quantum mechanical theory of this phenomenon leads to the existence of discrete energy levels with spacings of $\hbar\omega_c$, for these are required for interaction with radiation of angular frequency ω_c. Neglecting certain complications which do not affect the argument, we may write the levels in the valence band in the approximate form

$$-(n + \tfrac{1}{2})\hbar\omega_c'.$$

Those in the conduction band may be written in the form

$$E_g + (n + \tfrac{1}{2})\hbar\omega_c'',$$

where E_g is the band gap, n is an integer; ω_c' and ω_c'' are cyclotron frequencies calculated from (7.17) allowing for a different effective mass in the two bands. Most important is the quantum-mechanical selection rule: $\Delta n = 0$. As a consequence of the selection rule, photons of frequency ν for which

$$h\nu = E_g + (n + \tfrac{1}{2})\hbar(\omega_c' + \omega_c'') \tag{7.18}$$

induce transitions from the nth level below the top of the valence band to the nth level above the bottom of the conduction band, as illustrated in Fig. 63. With an appropriate optical source it should then be possible to raise a sufficient number of electrons from a given magnetic level in the valence band to the corresponding level in the conduction band to produce population inversion with respect to a lower magnetic level in the conduction band. In the illustration the population of level 3 may be inverted

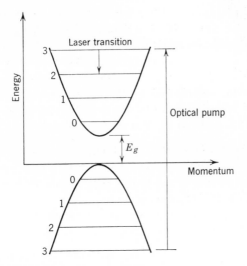

Fig. 63. Energy diagram illustrating possible transitions for a cyclotron resonance laser.

relative to that of level 2. In principle it is then a simple matter to induce a cyclotron resonance transition down to level 2 either by adjusting the magnetic field to give an energy spacing corresponding to one of the resonant modes of the interferometer which contains the semiconductor, or by tuning the interferometer to the fixed cyclotron resonance frequency. It is necessary, however, that the level spacing between 2 and 3 be unique, i.e., different from that between other adjacent states; otherwise the radiation would be absorbed. Fortunately the magnetic level spacing is sufficiently uneven in many semiconductors to ensure that this difficulty can be avoided.

Numerous calculations were made for germanium and several III-V semiconductors which indicate that with a strong spectral source in the visible, or in the near infrared, one might generate coherent radiation in the 200-μ to 1-mm region by this scheme. No experimental success was reported until mid-1964, although this matter has been actively pursued by very able investigators.

The electric impulse scheme is a proposed method for direct conversion of electrical energy to coherent radiation. It requires the application of a high electric field to a sample of pure semiconductor. The field must be high enough to produce an electric breakdown in the semiconductor, forcing electrons into the conduction band and creating holes in the valence band. Calculations show that under such conditions the mean energy of the electrons in the conduction band is about equal to the ionization energy. The electrons are distributed over a wide region within the conduction band; the distribution prevailing during the presence of the external field does not give rise to population inversion. In fact, the presence of such a field tends to increase the temperature of the carriers; i.e., it tends to broaden the energy band they occupy. After rapid removal of the external field the carriers (electrons in the conduction band, holes in the valence band) undergo the following processes:

1. Energy exchange with the crystal lattice, resulting in a slowing down of the carriers and the establishment within each band of a Fermi-Dirac distribution at the lattice temperature T. This process takes place with a time constant t_s.
2. Recombination with opposite carriers (across the band gap) with a time constant t_c.

Population inversion is possible only when t_s is much less than t_c. In addition, the density of nonequilibrium carriers must be large enough so that the quasi-Fermi levels satisfy the inequality (7.5). Krokhin and Popov [29] have shown that t_s depends on two parameters of the semiconductor: the mobility and the velocity of sound. For pure Ge and Si they estimated that the time required to cool the carriers to room temperature is 5×10^{-10} sec and 5×10^{-11} sec, respectively. These values are, of course, much shorter than the lifetime t_c. Thus population inversion over the band gap is possible in principle for the usual semiconductors, e.g., Ge and Si. There are nevertheless great difficulties owing to the requirements of large density of excited carriers, low crystal temperature, and rapid removal of the electric field. The electric field required for the production of a sufficient concentration of electrons in the conduction band by direct ionization of the valence band sharply increases with increase of the band gap. Therefore semiconductors with wide band gaps require high voltages; the carrier concentrations necessary for degeneracy require large currents. These requirements lead to a large power dissipation in the crystal with attendant difficulties of cooling. Consequently population inversion by the impulse method should be easier to establish in a semiconductor with a narrow band gap such as InSb, provided that the recombination lifetime in such a material is not too short.

The impulse excitation method described has not led to population inversion in semiconductors to the time of the writing of this book. Another related method that utilizes excitation by fast electrons incident upon the semiconductor has proved to be successful, however. This method was originally also proposed by Basov and his co-workers [30]. Its success was announced simultaneously by Russian and French investigators in

July 1964 at the Symposium on Radiative Recombination in Semiconductors held in Paris. Laser effect in GaSb obtained in this manner is described by Guillaume and Debever [31], that in GaAs by Hurwitz and Keyes [32]. The accomplishments of the Soviet scientists are reported in Basov's Nobel lecture [33], which contains in addition a preliminary report on the success of an optical excitation scheme in GaAs.

REFERENCES

1. N. G. Basov, O. N. Krokhin, and Yu. M. Popov, Generation, amplification and detection of infrared and optical radiation by quantum mechanical systems, *Soviet Phys. Uspekhi.* **3**, 702–728, 1961 (**72**, 161–209, 1960).
2. M. Bernard and G. Duraffourg, Possibilités de lasers à semiconducteurs, *J. Phys. Radium* **22**, 836–837, 1961.
3. R. N. Hall *et al.*, Coherent light emission from GaAs junctions, *Phys. Rev. Lett.* **9**, 366–368, 1962.
4. M. I. Nathan *et al.*, Stimulated emission of radiation from GaAs *p-n* junctions, *Appl. Phys. Lett.* **1**, 62–64, 1962.
5. T. M. Quist *et al.*, Semiconductor maser of GaAs, *Appl. Phys. Lett.* **1**, 91–92, 1962.
6. N. Holonyak and S. F. Bevacqua, Coherent (visible) light emission from $Ga(As_{1-x}P_x)$ junctions, *Appl. Phys. Lett.* **1**, 82–83, 1962.
7. R. J. Keyes and T. M. Quist, Recombination radiation emitted by GaAs, *Proc. IRE.* **50**, 1822–1823, 1962.
8. D. N. Nasledov, A. A. Rogachev, S. M. Ryvkin, and B. V. Tsarenkov, Recombination radiation of GaAs, *Soviet Phys. PTT* **4**, 782–784, 1962 (**4**, 1062–1065, 1962).
9. N. G. Basov, O. N. Krokhin, and Yu. M. Popov, Production of negative temperature states in *p-n* junctions of degenerate semiconductors, *Soviet Phys. JETP* **13**, 1320–1321, 1961 (**40**, 1879–1880, 1961).
10. W. P. Dumke, Interband transitions and maser action, *Phys. Rev.* **127**, 1559–1563, 1962.
11. G. Burns and M. I. Nathan, Line shape in GaAs injection lasers, *Proc. IEEE* **51**, 471–472, 1963.
12. G. Burns and M. I. Nathan, *P-n* junction lasers, *Proc. IEEE* **52**, 770–794, 1964.
13. P. P. Sorokin, J. D. Axe, and J. R. Lankard, Spectral characteristics of GaAs lasers operating in Fabry-Perot modes, *J. Appl. Phys.* **34**, 2553–2556, 1963.
14. M. D. Sturge, Optical absorption of GaAs between 0.6 and 2.75 eV, *Phys. Rev.* **127**, 768–773, 1962.
15. W. E. Engeler and M. Garfinkel, Temperature effects in coherent GaAs diodes, *J. Appl. Phys.* **34**, 2746–2750, 1963.
16. G. Cheroff, F. Stern, and S. Triebwasser, Quantum efficiency of GaAs injection lasers, *Appl. Phys. Lett.* **2**, 173–174, 1963.
17. G. E. Fenner and J. D. Kingsley, Spatial distribution of radiation from GaAs lasers, *J. Appl. Phys.* **34**, 3204–3208, 1963.
18. C. C. Gallagher, P. C. Tandy, B. S. Goldstein, and J. D. Welch, Output power from GaAs lasers at room temperature, *Proc. IEEE* **52**, 717, 1964.
19. W. E. Engeler and M. Garfinkel, Characteristics of a continuous high-power GaAs junction laser, *J. Appl. Phys.* **35**, 1734–1741, 1964.

20. B. S. Goldstein and J. D. Welch, Microwave modulation of a GaAs injection laser, *Proc. IEEE* **52**, 715, 1964.

21. H. Nelson and G. C. Dousmanis, Simultaneous laser action in GaAs at 0.84 and 0.88 μ, *Appl. Phys. Lett.* **4**, 192–194, 1964.

22. N. Ainsley, M. Pilkuhn, and H. Rupprecht, High-energy light emission from junctions in $GaAs_xP_{1-x}$ diodes, *J. Appl. Phys.* **35**, 105–107, 1964.

23. G. Burns, R. S. Levitt, M. I. Nathan, and K. Weiser, Some properties of InP lasers, *Proc. IEEE* **51**, 1148–1149, 1963.

24. I. Melngailis and R. H. Rediker, Magnetically tunable cw InAs diode maser, *Appl. Phys. Lett.* **2**, 202–204, 1963.

25. R. J. Phelan et al., Infrared InSb laser diode in high magnetic fields, *Appl. Phys. Lett.* **3**, 143–145, 1963.

26. G. C. Dousmanis, C. W. Mueller, and H. Nelson, Effect of doping on frequency of stimulated and incoherent emission in GaAs diodes, *Appl. Phys. Lett.* **3**, 133–135, 1963.

27. B. Lax, Cyclotron resonance maser, *Advances in Quantum Electronics*, Columbia Univ Press, New York, 1961, pp. 465–469.

28. N. G. Basov, Inverted populations in semiconductors, *Quantum Electronics III*, Columbia Univ. Press, New York, 1964, pp. 1769–1785.

29. O. N. Krokhin and Yu. M. Popov, Slowing-down time of non-equilibrium current carriers in semiconductors, *Soviet Phys. JETP* **11**, 1144–1146 (**38**, 1589–1593, 1960).

30. N. G. Basov and O. V. Bogdankevich, Recombination radiation of GaAs and Ge on excitation with fast electrons, *Soviet Phys. JETP* **17**, 751–752, 1963 (**44**, 1115–1116, 1963).

31. C. B. a la Guillaume and J. M. Debever, Effect laser dans l'antimoniure de gallium par bombardement électronique, *Compt. Rend.* **259**, 2200–2202, 1964.

32. C. E. Hurwitz and R. J. Keyes, Electron-beam-pumped GaAs laser, *Appl. Phys. Lett.* **5**, 139–141, 1964.

33. N. G. Basov, Semiconductor lasers, *Uspekhi Fiz. Nauk* **85**, 585–598, 1965.

8. PHONON-TERMINATED LASERS

Transition-metal and rare earth impurities incorporated in a crystal exhibit spectra whose gross features can be described by means of a *static crystal field theory*. In other words, one may regard the energy levels of the impurity ion as arising from those of the free ion when this ion is subjected to static electric and magnetic fields which would prevail if the atoms and ions of the crystal remained at rest in their positions of equilibrium. This point of view was adopted in the earlier sections of this chapter. The detailed properties of the impurity spectra, however, depend on the *dynamic interaction* of the impurity with its environment. Lattice vibrations (phonons) interact with the spectra of impurities; they give rise to emission and absorption lines, some of which correspond to electronic transitions accompanied by the emission or the absorption of a phonon. Phonon-accompanied emission and absorption can be recognized in the fluorescence spectra of many materials. The spectra contain, in addition to strong, sharp "no phonon," or electric lines, an adjacent vibrational structure. At low temperatures, when only phonon emission is possible, the vibrational structure extends in emission toward the low-energy side of the electronic line, and in absorption toward the high-energy side. In some special cases the absorption spectrum may be the mirror image of the emission spectrum, but in general these spectra will be different. Nevertheless, absorption, stimulated emission, and fluorescence spectra are connected by relations that are generalizations of the relations valid for Einstein's A and B coefficients.

Figure 64 illustrates the fluorescence spectrum of Ni^{2+} in MgF_2. The sharp peak of 6500 cm^{-1} (1.54 μ) arises from a no-photon transition; the lower, rounder maxima to its left derive from transitions in which lattice vibrations are excited simultaneously with the photon emission. The intensity distribution shown in the figure is typical of impurity spectra; the no-phonon (electronic) line is sharper than the others, and its peak intensity is conspicuously higher. Consequently one would expect that if a population inversion is somehow produced, laser oscillations will occur only at a frequency which corresponds to this sharp intense line. However, under certain circumstances the gain may be larger for one of the phonon-accompanied lines than in the no-phonon line and in that case laser oscillations can be obtained in a "phonon-terminated" transition.

Such an effect was observed by Johnson and associates [1, 2], who obtained phonon-terminated laser oscillations from Ni^{2+} in MgF_2 and from Co^{2+} in MgF_2 and ZnF_2. Population inversion was accomplished in both cases by optical pumping with a xenon lamp. The experiments were performed at 20°K and at 77°K.

At 20°K a significant portion of the fluorescence spectrum of Ni^{2+} in MgF_2 consists of three closely spaced intense lines with wave numbers 6500, 6505, and 6506 cm^{-1}. These represent electronic transitions from a common excited level to a ground level split into three closely spaced

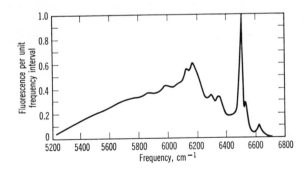

Fig. 64.   Fluorescence of $MgF_2:Ni^{2+}$ (1 per cent) at 77°K. (After McCumber [3].)

components. Stimulated emission was observed with a frequency which corresponds to 6164 cm^{-1} (1.622 μ); hence energy corresponding to about 340 cm^{-1} was carried away by phonons.

In Co^{2+}, phonon-terminated laser oscillations were obtained in two regions centered at 5020 and 4870 cm^{-1} (1.992 and 2.053 μ). With the aid of multiple-layer dielectric mirrors which favor the 1.7- to 1.8-μ region, the no-phonon oscillations were also obtained at 5714 and 5545 cm^{-1} (1.750 and 1.803 μ). It is surprising that the phonon-terminated transition should be the preferred regions of laser oscillation and that wavelength-selective reflectors are required to obtain laser oscillations on the more intense electronic lines. One must conclude that the gain, or amplification, in these materials is larger for the phonon-terminated transitions than for the electronic ones. Such a situation may come about either because the gain for the electronic lines is counteracted by larger absorption and scattering in the host crystal, or because the gain for the phonon-terminated line is intrinsically greater than for the electronic line notwithstanding the fact that in fluorescent emission the electronic line dominates. McCumber [3] has shown that when phonon-assisted transitions are taken into account the gain in a state of population inversion is not simply proportional to the intensity of the emission spectrum; therefore the maximum of gain need not occur at the peak of the no-phonon line. Nevertheless it is not certain that this theory alone can account for the strong preference observed experimentally. The properties of the host crystal may also discriminate in favor of phonon-terminated oscillations.

REFERENCES

1. L. F. Johnson, R. E. Dietz, and H. J. Guggenheim, Optical maser oscillation from Ni^{2+} in MgF$_2$ involving simultaneous emission of phonons, *Phys. Rev. Lett.* **11**, 318–320, 1963.
2. L. F. Johnson, R. E. Dietz, and H. J. Guggenheim, Spontaneous and stimulated emission from Co^{2+} ions in MgF$_2$ and ZnF$_2$, *Appl. Phys. Lett.* **5**, 21–22, 1964.
3. D. E. McCumber, Theory of phonon-terminated optical masers, *Phys. Rev.* **134**, A299–306, 1964.

IV

Fluid-State Lasers

1. EXPLORATION OF LIQUIDS AS LASER MATERIALS

Although the initial successes in the laser field were achieved with solids and gases, liquids appear to have interesting possibilities as laser materials. It has not been stressed sufficiently that when laser action is based on ions imbedded in a crystal lattice only single crystals unusually free of imperfections can serve as solid laser materials. Crystal imperfections, strains, and inhomogeneities impair coherent amplification. The crystals must be cut and polished accurately, and often attention must be paid to the orientation of the crystal axes.

Liquids and gases allow complete freedom from the problems of single-crystal growth and shaping. They permit a reasonable concentration of active material in a given volume, and large, usable samples of convenient sizes are easily obtained. Solution of the difficult cooling problem would be greatly facilitated by the use of a working fluid that could be circulated between the laser and a heat exchanger. Although liquids currently utilized in laser research are too viscous for such a system, it is hoped that sufficiently mobile liquids will be found eventually. The exploration of liquid materials for their suitability is simplified by the fact that, within limits, the concentration of the ingredients can be changed quickly and easily.

There are a number of obstacles to the construction of a laser based on the use of liquids and solutions. These were overcome, in some cases, by careful selection of the materials following an extensive analysis of the relevant spectroscopic properties.

On comparing fluorescence in liquids to fluorescence in solids it becomes apparent that the following circumstances prevail:

1. Spectral lines are broader in liquids (solutions) because of perturbing effects of the constantly changing environment.
2. Collisions may lead to nonradiative deactivation of excited atoms or molecules, causing the quantum efficiency to decrease.

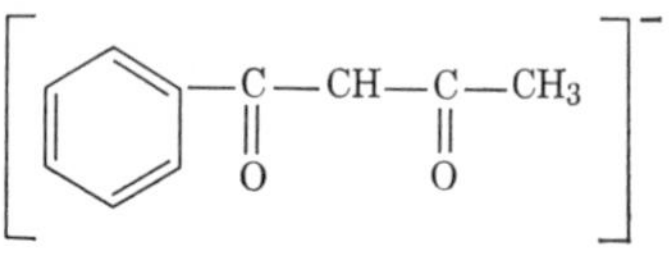

Fig. 65. Benzoylacetonate ion.

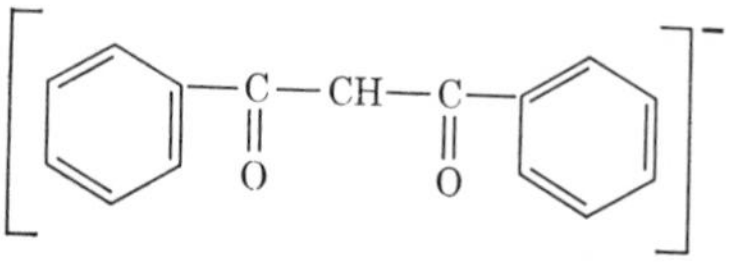

Fig. 66. Dibenzoylmethide ion.

In the light of these circumstances the search for liquid laser materials focused on materials possessing energy levels well shielded from external perturbations. The rare earth chelates form a particularly favorable class of such materials. In these the fluorescence of a central metallic ion may be excited by the absorption of radiation in the complex organic groups which surround it and shield it from the environment. A typical chelate is formed when benzoylacetonate ions enter into a combination with a trivalent metal ion. Benzoylacetonate (B) arises by the removal of a proton from the benzoylacetone molecule; the excess negative charge is distributed between the two oxygen atoms which are not essentially different. The structure of benzoylacetonate is shown in Fig. 65, and that of the similar dibenzoyl-methide (D) in Fig. 66. When three benzoylacetonate ions combine with a tri-positive metal ion the six oxygen atoms form a regular octahedron around the metal as illustrated in Fig. 67. A similar configuration may be constructed with three dibenzoylmethide (D) ions.

The ions B and D are of a class of organic molecules noted for their interesting luminescent behavior. The ground state of the radical is a singlet state, $S = 0$. Absorption of ultraviolet radiation causes excitation from the ground state S_0 to one of the lower singlet excited states S_1, S_2, etc. By dissipating energy through vibrations the molecule may change without the emission of radiation from the states S_2, S_3, etc., to the lowest singlet excited state S_1, or to one of the low triplet states T_1 or T_2. The transition $S_1 \rightarrow S_0$ is permitted by the selection rules; it takes place rapidly—the lifetimes vary between 10^{-6} and 10^{-9} sec—and it manifests itself as fluorescence. Radiative transitions from the triplet states to the ground state are forbidden by the selection rules; therefore molecules may be trapped in a triplet state with a lifetime of the order of 10^{-3} sec. Rare earth chelates differ from the radicals in that the chelate possesses, in addition to the above energy levels, a fairly isolated set of low-lying energy states derived from the $4f$ electronic configuration of the metal ion. The excited electronic states of a chelate are shown schematically in Fig. 68. Under favorable circumstances the luminescence cycle may be completed by a transfer of excitation from level T_1 (or T_2) to one of the levels of the metal ion and a subsequent return to the ground with accompanying emission of lines characteristic of the ion. In this manner the broad

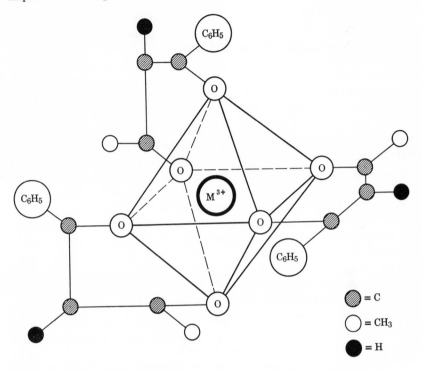

Fig. 67. Perspective drawing of a rare earth trisbenzoylacetonate chelate (MB₃). (The lines outlining the octahedron do not represent bonds. The sizes of the circles do not indicate atomic dimensions.)

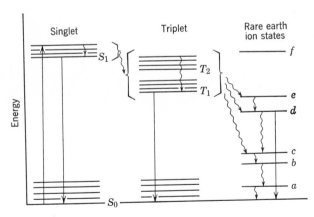

Fig. 68. Schematic energy-level diagram for a rare earth chelate possessing low-lying $4f$ electronic states. → radiative transitions; ⤳ radiationless transitions.

absorption characteristics of the organic radical combine with the narrow emission lines of the rare earth ion to form a situation favorable for the construction of an optically pumped laser.

The potential value of the chelates as laser materials was noted shortly after stimulated emission was first accomplished in ruby, and the systematic investigation of the luminescence of chelates was intensified. Crosby and co-workers [1, 2] confirmed that the absorption of a chelate is independent of the rare earth ion. Typical absorption curves are shown in Fig. 69. Crosby and Whan classified a large number of organic ligand and rare earth combinations according to the presence of ionic and molecular lines in their fluorescence spectra. The spectra of chelates with Eu^{3+}, Tb^{3+}, and Dy^{3+} exhibit principally the bright, fine lines characteristic of the ions. Similar chelates with another rare earth ion may not show ion spectra at all, or may show them in conjunction with one organic ligand and not with another. For ion-line emission the energy of the lowest triplet state must be nearly equal to, or lie above, a resonance level of the rare earth ion.

Recognition of the essential features of the fluorescence mechanism pointed to europium as the rare earth ion most likely to be a suitable laser material and caused an intensive investigation of europium in benzoyl-acetonate [3] and thenoyltrifluoroacetonate (TTA) [4] combined with estimation of the pumping energies and concentrations required to produce laser action in solutions of such molecules [4, 5]. The results of these investigations were published early in 1963 about the same time as success-

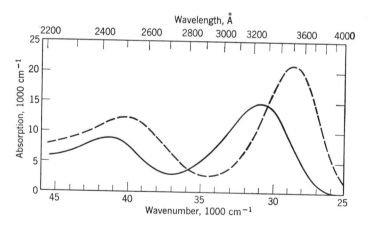

Fig. 69. Typical absorption spectra of rare earth chelates measured at 10^{-5} molar concentration in ethanol at 20°C. Solid line: benzoylacetonates; dotted line: dibenzoylmethides. Ordinate: absorption calculated for 1 mole ligand per liter. (After Whan and Crosby [2].)

ful operation of europium chelate lasers was reported simultaneously from two laboratories. Wolff and Pressley [6] at RCA obtained stimulated emission from a long coil of methylmethacrylate fiber containing Eu(TTA)$_3$, while Lempicki and Samelson [7, 8] at General Telephone and Electronics obtained the same in solutions of EuB$_3$ and EuD$_3$ in a mixture of ethyl and methyl alcohols. Both groups of experiments were carried out at low temperatures in order to work with as narrow lines as possible and thus reduce the energy required for excitation. At these temperatures the solutions resemble solids more than they resemble ordinary liquids; they flow like tar or thick honey. Later Schimitschek [9] constructed a EuB$_3$ laser using a low-temperature alcohol as a solvent which remained a mobile liquid at the operating temperature of about 120°K.

The europium laser operates at a wavelength around 6130 Å; the radiation corresponds to a transition from the $^5D_0$ level to one of the $^7F_2$ sublevels located about 950 cm^{-1} above ground. The complexities of the chelate spectrum may be surmised from Fig. 70, which illustrates the splitting of the ^7F levels of europium in EuB$_3$ and in a solution of EuB$_3$ [10]. The number of levels in Fig. 70 demonstrates a complete removal of degeneracy of the ^7F levels of Eu^{3+}, indicating that the ion is located in a

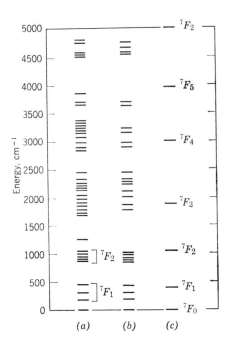

Fig. 70. Energy-level diagram: (a) solid EuB, (b) solution of EuB, (c) free Eu^{3+} ion.

field less symmetric than what one would expect by looking simply at the six oxygen atoms surrounding the ion in the form of a regular octahedron.

There is additional evidence indicating that the actual situation is considerably less symmetrical than one would expect on the basis of Fig. 67. Chemical analysis has shown an excess of the chelating agent over what one would expect from a formula of the type MB_3, and it appears likely that the lack of octahedral symmetry is to be attributed to the excess B ion [10].

Excitation of the europium chelate laser is accomplished with a powerful ultraviolet source with an output in the absorption band of the radical. This is generally in the 3000- to 4000-Å range; for EuB_3 the peak is at 3900 Å. Europium ions are present in concentrations varying between 10^{18} and 2×10^{19} per cm^3. The lower limit is set by the threshold condition, which requires a minimum gain to offset the losses at the ends of the laser; the upper limit is set by the solubility of EuB_3. It is interesting to note that the absorption constant of a EuB_3 solution containing 1.2×10^{19} ions per cm^3 is about 250 times greater than that of pink ruby of similar ion concentration. As a result of the intense absorption the excitation of EuB_3 will be extremely nonuniform and the threshold may be expected to depend strongly on cell geometry. Further quantitative information on the properties of EuB_3 may be found in the work of Samelson, Lempicki, and Brecher [11], who published considerable material pertaining to the calculation of the parameters of optical pumping of EuB_3.

Transfer mechanisms other than those operating in rare earth chelates may also produce a laser. In fact, at one time it was believed that stimulated emission at 4700 Å was obtained from a mixture of benzophenone and naphthalene, and the phenomenon was attributed to a transfer of excitation from a triplet level of benzophenone to a triplet level of naphthalene [12]. The reported observations could not be reconciled with theoretical calculations, and subsequent attempts of other experimenters [8] to reproduce the reported phenomena led to negative results.

The review article of Lempicki, Samelson, and Brecher [13], appearing when this book goes to press, contains an excellent description of the chemical and physical problems related to laser action in rare earth chelates. It is recommended both as a source of further study and as a source of references.

REFERENCES

1. G. A. Crosby, R. E. Whan, and R. M. Alire, Intramolecular energy transfer in rare-earth chelates. Role of the triplet state, *J. Chem. Phys.* **34**, 743–748, 1961.
2. R. E. Whan and G. A. Crosby, Luminescence studies of rare-earth complexes: Benzoylacetonate and dibenzoylmethide chelates, *J. Mol. Spectry.* **8**, 315–327, 1962.

3. V. A. Voloshin, A. G. Goryushko, and V. A. Kulchitskii, Spectral study of polymethylmethacrylate activated by europium benzoylacetonate, *Opt. Spectry.* (*U.S.S.R.*) **15**, 154–155, 1963 (**15**, 286–287, 1963).

4. H. Winston, O. J. Marsh, C. K. Suzuki, and C. L. Telk, Fluorescence of europium thenoyltrifluoroacetonate. Evaluation of laser threshold parameters, *J. Chem. Phys.* **39**, 267–271, 1963.

5. H. Lyons and M. L. Bhaumik, Rare-earth chelates and the molecular approach to lasers, *Quantum Electronics III*, Columbia Univ. Press, New York, 1964, pp. 699–708.

6. N. E. Wolff and R. J. Pressley, Optical maser action in an Eu^{3+} containing organic matrix, *Appl. Phys. Lett.* **2**, 152–154, 1963.

7. A. Lempicki and H. Samelson, Optical maser action in europium benzoyl-acetonate, *Phys. Lett.* **4**, 133–135, 1963.

8. A. Lempicki and H. Samelson, Stimulated processes in organic compounds, *Appl. Phys. Lett.* **2**, 159–161, 1963.

9. E. J. Schimitschek, Stimulated emission in rare-earth chelate (EuB_3) in a capillary tube, *Appl. Phys. Lett.* **3**, 117–118, 1963.

10. H. Samelson, A. Lempicki, V. A. Brophy, and C. Brecher, Laser phenomena in europium chelates, I. Spectroscopic properties of europium, *J. Chem. Phys.* **40**, 2547–2553, 1964.

11. H. Samelson, A. Lempicki, and C. Brecher, Laser phenomena in europium chelates, II. Kinetics and optical pumping in europium benzoylacetonate, *J. Chem. Phys.* **40**, 2553–2558, 1964.

12. D. J. Morantz, B. G. White, and A. J. C. Wright, Stimulated light emission by optical pumping and by energy transfer in organic molecules, *Phys. Rev. Lett.* **8**, 23–25, 1962.

13. A. Lempicki, H. Samelson, and C. Brecher, Laser action in rare earth chelates, *Appl. Optics Suppl. on Chemical Lasers*, 205–213, 1965.

V

Gas Lasers

1. NEGATIVE ABSORPTION OF OPTICAL RADIATION IN GASES: QUALITATIVE DISCUSSION

In gases, as in solids, a net stimulated emission of radiation occurs only in a condition that is variously referred to as population inversion, temperature inversion, or a state of negative absorption or negative temperature. This is a nonequilibrium condition characterized by the existence of a pair of energy levels of which the higher is more densely populated than the lower. The discussion in Chapter II is equally applicable to solids and gases; therefore, without repeating what was said there, we shall proceed to discuss the phenomena that are specifically important in gases and to contrast the properties of gases that are relevant in connection with negative absorption with similar properties of solids.

The simple appearance of the helium-neon laser is misleading. The physical phenomena that take place in a gaseous laser are complicated, and laser oscillations are achieved only if these phenomena interact in a rather sophisticated manner calculated to produce population inversion. The reproduction of a gas laser requires only a moderate skill in optics and in vacuum technology; the difficult problem is to discover what transitions among the energy levels of a gas may be used for laser oscillations and what the optimum conditions for the excitation of these oscillations are.

First we note that the spectroscopic aspects of the problem are simpler in gases than in solids. The energy-level schemes of the free atoms involved are simple compared with those of the atoms embedded in a crystal lattice. The selection rules are generally observed; nonradiative transitions are less prevalent than in solids and, in fact, in gases they consist of energy conversion in collisions. The absence of absorption bands is a simplification for the theorist, but it is no help to the experimentalist bent on producing a condition of negative absorption. It means that he cannot use an ordinary black-body type of source for excitation because the gas absorbs only in isolated lines. This limits optical excitation to irradiation by high-intensity spectral sources, one of whose emission lines coincides with an absorption

168

line of the gas. Fortunately, there are other means of excitation in a gas that are absent in a solid: excitation by electron impact and transfer of excitation between colliding atoms. Naturally one must consider not only the processes that lead to an increase of atomic energy but also the processes by means of which an excited atom may lower its energy, since the removal of electrons from the terminal level is important for the success of the fluorescence cycle.

As the atoms excited by one means or another cascade down the energy scale, a certain stationary nonequilibrium situation will be established in which the number of atoms in each energy state remains constant. This situation requires that the rate at which the atoms arrive in a state due to all causes be equal to the rate at which they leave that state. The equations governing this process are similar to those already introduced in Section II.2. The number of atoms in each state adjusts itself to establish a balance. Those states from which escape is slow will accumulate a large number of atoms. In particular, crowding will occur in the so-called metastable states, which are higher in energy than the ground state but from which radiative transitions to lower levels are forbidden by the selection rules of quantum mechanics.

Whether population inversion is achieved depends on the rate of excitation and on the decay rates of all levels involved in the cascade process. Several processes contribute to decay of a single level: radiative processes, collisions with electrons, and collisions with other atoms including those which constitute the walls of the vessel containing the gas. In addition to these phenomena one must consider the possibility of the resonance trapping of radiation, i.e., excitation of an atom to an occupied state by radiation emitted from another atom of the gas. This phenomenon is clearly dependent on the pressure of the gas and on the geometrical configuration. It slows down the rate at which the atoms return to the ground state at the end of their cascade process.

In principle the simplest method of making a gas laser is that of optical excitation. It can be accomplished by making use of the fortuitous coincidence of the emission line of one element with a suitable absorption line of another.

The classical and best-known example of the coincidence of an absorption line of an element with a strong emission line of another is the 3888-Å line common to helium and cesium. In 1930 Boeckner demonstrated that the fluorescence of cesium can be excited by irradiation with the 3888-Å helium line, and one of the early attempts made at extending the maser art to the optical region involved the optical pumping of cesium by means of this radiation. In a series of experiments performed in 1957 Butayeva and Fabrikant [1] searched for population inversions of cesium connected with transitions in the visible region. The results were inconclusive. The rather complicated structure of the fluorescence of cesium was studied in detail by Townes and his students at Columbia University [2]. They concluded that conditions were correct for obtaining laser oscillations at 3.20 and 7.18 μ. After overcoming serious technical difficulties connected with the confinement of the highly reactive Cs vapor at a temperature of 175°C, the irradiation with a powerful He discharge, and the alignment of the optical system, Rabinowitz, Jacobs, and Gould [3] observed laser action at the predicted frequencies. The energy levels and transitions involved in this laser action are shown in Fig. 71.

Excitation by electron collision can be most conveniently accomplished in an electric discharge. When an electric discharge takes place in a gas, ions and free electrons are formed. These current carriers are accelerated by the field that creates the discharge and they acquire a kinetic energy at the expense of the power fed into it. The motion of the ions is of little consequence; the electrons are the agents that acquire energy from the

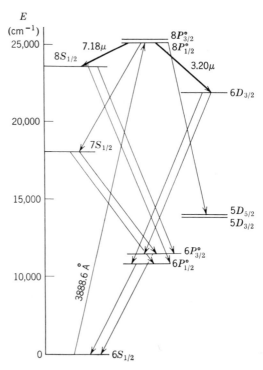

Fig. 71. Energy levels and transitions of cesium participating in the fluorescence cycle of the optically excited lasers.

power source and distribute it in their encounters with atoms. In discharges that take place well below atmospheric pressure—a few millimeters of mercury or below—the average kinetic energy of the electrons usually greatly exceeds that of the atoms and ions present in the discharge. In a steady discharge within a short time of the order of a millisecond the electrons establish an equilibrium distribution among themselves. This is essentially a Maxwell-Boltzmann distribution characterized by an electron temperature T_e that is proportional to the mean kinetic energy of the electrons. The average kinetic energy of the atoms is considerably lower; its value corresponds in equilibrium to a much lower temperature.

Inelastic collision in which the atom either gains or loses energy may occur between atoms and electrons, but only the amounts of energy consistent with its energy-level scheme can be transferred to or from the atom. If no other processes were present, these collisions would cause the atoms to distribute themselves among the energy levels according to Boltzmann's law with the temperature T_e. Then N_i would be $N_1 e^{-E_i/kT_e}$. Actually the number of excited atoms in state i will be much smaller for two reasons. (1) As a consequence of atomic collisions, some excitation energy will be transformed into kinetic energy. This process will "pull" the atoms toward a distribution, according to the lower temperature T_a. (2) Emission of radiation will take place, and as a result atoms will pass from high-energy states to lower-energy ones. As a rule, this process is more significant, since the transitions are more probable.

When more than one gas is present in a discharge, excitation may be exchanged between colliding atoms of different kinds, provided that they possess a pair of energy levels near one another. The probability of such an exchange is proportional to $e^{-\Delta/kT}$, where Δ is the energy difference of the participating levels and T is the temperature of the gas mixture. This exchange process is called *resonant transfer of energy*. It is particularly interesting when it involves a metastable level of one atomic species and an ordinary level of the other. The second species provides a path of escape from the crowded metastable level. Also the transfer of excitation to atoms of the second kind may create such a distortion of their distribution that population inversion may occur.

Population inversion can be established in a *single* gas by means of electronic excitation, but it is easier to succeed if one makes use of two gases and exploits the energy-transfer phenomenon. The operation of the helium-neon laser described in Chapter II is based on energy transfer from helium atoms to neon atoms. The functioning of this laser in the original range around 1.1μ is explained with the aid of the partial energy-level diagram of Fig. 72, which shows some of the lowest energy levels of helium and of neon. The $2\,{}^3S$ state of He is metastable; a direct radiative

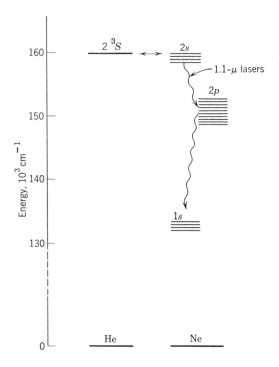

Fig. 72. Energy levels of He and Ne involved in the cycle of the 1.1-μ laser.

transition to singlet ground state is forbidden, but a helium atom can arrive in this state by way of an electron collision process. When helium atoms in the $2\,{}^3S$ state collide with neon atoms in the ground state, the excitation may be transferred to the neon atoms, which then end up in one of the 2s states, the highest of which lies only about 300 cm^{-1} below the $2\,{}^3S$ level of helium. Radiative transitions may then take place from the four 2s levels to the ten 2p levels. The 2p levels may be less populated than the 2s levels because there is no direct transfer to them from a helium level. Whether an inversion will actually take place depends on the relative abundance of the He and Ne atoms in the mixture and on the electron temperature. The 2p levels fortunately do not get overcrowded because they are readily drained by transitions to the lower 1s levels. The success of this scheme naturally depends on the achievement of the correct ratios of excitation and decay rates, which are determined by the gas pressures, the power expended in the discharge, and the radius of the discharge tube which enters into the matter because of the collision of excited atoms with the walls.

Another fortuitous near coincidence of a metastable helium level with a group of neon levels is responsible for the visible, 6328-Å laser. The cycle involved is similar to that of the infrared 1.1-μ lasers. (See Section V.4.)

The selective transfer of excitation from helium to neon atoms makes the achievement of negative absorption in neon easier, but it is not absolutely necessary. Negative absorption can be achieved in pure neon as well as in other pure noble gases provided that the electron density in the discharge is maintained at a proper level and provided gas pressure and tube dimensions are chosen so as to prevent the overpopulation of the terminal levels. The addition of helium may aid the process even in noble gases that have no common energy levels with helium. The reason for this beneficial effect of helium is believed to be that the presence of helium increases the electron density in the discharge through ionizing collisions between metastable atoms. One must not draw the conclusion that the addition of helium is *universally* beneficial for the functioning of *any* neon laser. Figures 73 and 74 illustrate the dependence of two stimulated emission lines of neon on gas composition and pressure [4]. The 1.96-μ line is most intense in a mixture containing approximately 5 per cent neon, with the maximum radiative output attained at a total pressure of 0.35 torr. In contrast to this the 2.10-μ line reaches its maximum in pure neon at 0.11 torr pressure.* Figures 73 and 74 should be viewed for the sake of comparison only, since laser outputs vary with the geometry of the discharge (tube radius) and also with the power level of the discharge. There is generally a power level at which the laser output is maximal; further increase of r.f. power decreases the laser output. The gain, or negative absorption coefficient, in neon is approximately inversely proportional to the diameter of the discharge tube. This relationship was found experimentally to hold for tube diameters ranging from a few millimeters to at least 1.5 cm. The explanation for an increase of gain with a decrease in tube diameter involves the role of the 1s levels to which the terminal levels of laser transitions decay. The 1s levels have long lifetimes, but they can be destroyed by collisions with the walls. When the rate of their destruction is too slow the overcrowding at this level will eventually create an overcrowding at the parent 2p levels and population inversion becomes more difficult to attain.

In summary, we may say that the noble gas lasers work by excitation through electron collision; this process is greatly enhanced in certain special cases by the transfer of excitation from metastable helium atoms. Lasers based on noble gas atoms generally work in continuous operation; the radiation emitted is in the infrared. The majority of lines observed so far lies between 1 and 3.5 μ. A notable exception is the popular 6328-Å

* The relatively new unit 1 torr is the pressure of 1 mm Hg.

helium-neon laser, which is visible. The construction and operation of some of these lasers are discussed in Sections V.4 and V.5.

Ions of the noble gases have also been observed to emit stimulated radiation. Their laser emission was noted in the wavelength region 2600 to 8000 Å. The ionic lasers are excited by electron collisions; it probably takes two consecutive collisions to produce an excited Ne^+ ion and three to produce an excited Ne^{++}. Although the atomic laser lines of the noble

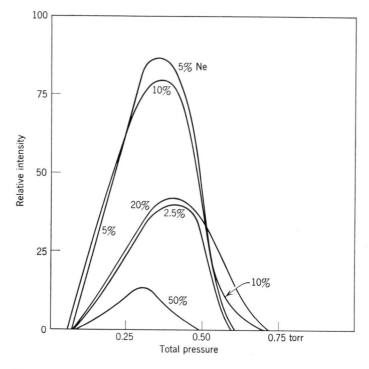

Fig. 73. Variation of the intensity of the 1.9574-μ ($3p_4 \rightarrow 2s_5$) neon line with gas pressure for various percentages of neon in the He-Ne mixture.

gases are conveniently excited with low power (20 to 80 watts), the ionic lines require a dense discharge which dissipates several thousand watts. Consequently it is much easier to obtain ionic lines in pulsed discharges with a relatively low duty cycle than in continuous discharges which require heavy current sources and well-designed heat sinks. Some laser lines require pulse excitation because the relevant population inversion cannot be established as a stationary process, the lifetimes of the decay processes being such that eventually an accumulation of population occurs at the lower laser level.

Charge transfer between colliding ions and atoms or molecules may also serve as a source of population inversion. It is possible that some of the observed laser lines may be explained by a charge transfer process [5].

Transfer of excitation between colliding atoms has already been mentioned as a process that is instrumental in producing population inversion

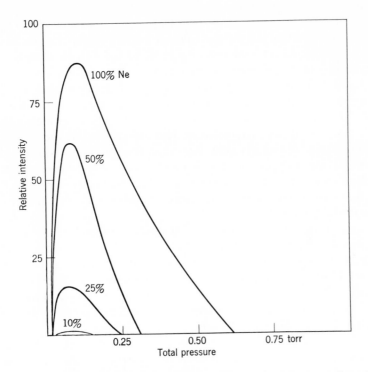

Fig. 74. Variation of the intensity of the 2.1041-μ ($3p_1 \to 2s_2$) neon line with gas pressure for various percentages of neon in the He-Ne mixture.

among some neon levels. It is interesting that a similar collision between excited atoms and diatomic or polyatomic molecules may lead to population inversion in one of the atoms of the molecule by first causing the dissociation of the molecule. Such a process has produced laser action in oxygen, nitrogen, carbon, sulfur, and bromine. The atoms of helium, neon, or argon were used as carriers of the energy. They in turn were excited in an electric discharge of the same type that is used with the noble gas lasers.

When an excited atom collides with a molecule a dissociation of the molecule may take place. The dissociation products may end in their respective ground states or in excited levels. In certain cases dissociation of this kind leads to selective excitation of atoms to particular levels of the dissociation products, which may then serve as starting levels for laser transitions. The selective excitation on dissociation of a diatomic or polyatomic molecule requires that the discrepancy between the energy of the incident excited atom and that of the dissociation products be small. However, the energy coincidence requirement is not nearly as stringent as that prevailing in the case of energy transfer in atom-atom collisions of the type encountered in the He-Ne laser. The excitation-transfer cross sections in an atom-molecule collision are comparable to those in an atom-atom collision with much smaller energy discrepancy. There are two reasons for this greater flexibility of energy transfer over a larger gap. First, in the molecular case there is a greater freedom open to each particle. Usually a number of repulsive molecular states of diverse energy terminate on the same levels of the dissociated molecule. This itself makes the energy coincidence requirement less stringent. Second, when a molecule is involved, the chance of the reaction's being reversed when the particles are separating is much smaller than in the case of two atoms because the larger number of paths available to the particles decreases the probability that they will retrace the original path.

The first successful application of dissociative excitation for laser action led to the Ne-O and the Ar-O lasers [7, 8]. In the first of these the initial laser level is reached directly on dissociation of O_2, while in the Ar-O laser this level is reached in two steps. Dissociation of O_2 by energy exchange with excited argon atoms results in the excitation of O to a metastable state from which the initial laser level is reached by further excitation through electron collision.

The dissociative excitation process described is an example of a chemical process used to produce population inversion. Currently chemical processes are systematically investigated as possible vehicles for the creation of population inversion and stimulated emission. The status in 1964 of this rapidly developing field is reviewed in the articles contained in a special issue of the journal *Applied Optics* published in March 1965 [6].

A number of the spectral lines of Cl, I, and Hg, as well as some of their ions, can be observed in stimulated emission in pulsed discharges. These discharges usually contain noble gases as well as the gas whose spectrum is being observed. The exact mechanism responsible for the excitation of these lines is still being investigated.

Many spectral lines of N_2, CO, and CO_2 molecules can also be produced in stimulated emission. They were discovered in 1963 in pulsed high-power discharges and they are known to depend on nonstationary population inversions [6]. Some of these newer lasers are discussed briefly in Section V.6.

REFERENCES

1. F. A. Butayeva and V. A. Fabrikant, A medium with negative absorption, *Investigations in Experimental and Theoretical Physics. A Memorial to G. S. Landsberg*, U.S.S.R. Acad. Sc. Publ., Moscow, 1959. (In Russian.)
2. H. Z. Cummins, I. Abella, O. S. Heavens, N. Knable, and C. H. Townes, Alkali vapor infrared masers, *Advances in Quantum Electronics*, Columbia University Press, New York, 1961, pp. 12–17.
3. P. Rabinowitz, S. Jacobs, and G. Gould, Continuous optically pumped Cs laser, *Appl. Optics* **1**, 513–516, 1962.
4. R. der Agobian, J.-L. Otto, R. Echard, and R. Cagnard, Emission stimulée de nouvelle transitions infrarouges de néon, *Compt. Rend.* **257**, 3844–3847, 1963.
5. J. W. McGowan and R. F. Stebbings, Charge transfer as a possible laser pumping mechanism, *Appl. Optics Suppl. on Chemical Lasers*, 68–72, 1965.
6. Proceedings of the San Diego Conference on Chemical Lasers, *Appl. Optics Suppl. on Chemical Lasers*, 1965.
7. W. R. Bennett, Jr., W. L. Faust, R. A. McFarlane, and C. K. N. Patel, Dissociative excitation transfer and optical maser oscillation in Ne-O_2 and Ar-O_2 rf discharges, *Phys. Rev. Lett.* **8**, 470–473, 1962.
8. C. K. N. Patel, R. A. McFarlane, and W. L. Faust, Optical maser action in C, N, O, S and Br on dissociation of diatomic and polyatomic molecules, *Phys. Rev.* **133**, A1244–1248, 1964.

2. SPECTROSCOPY OF NOBLE GASES

The common characteristic of the electronic structure of the noble gases neon, argon, krypton, and xenon is that the highest p-shells are filled and there are no electrons outside of these shells when the atom is in its ground state. Since the p-shells hold six electrons, the symbols of the electron configurations of these elements end with $2p^6$, $3p^6$, $4p^6$, and $5p^6$, respectively. The total angular momentum J, the orbital angular momentum L, and the spin angular momentum of such a closed shell configuration are all zero. When excitation takes place one of the electrons moves out of this closed shell, leaving a core of five p-electrons behind. Thus, in the case of Ne excited configurations of the type $2p^53s$, $2p^53p$, $2p^53d$, $2p^54s$, etc. arise. The symbols of the completed shells $1s^22s^2$, which logically precede the $2p^5$ symbol, were omitted.

The outer electron of an excited noble gas atom is not coupled to the core electrons according to the rules of the L-S, or Russell-Saunders, coupling discussed in Section I.6. The interactions are such that in good approximation the orbital angular momentum l of the outer electron is coupled to the total angular momentum J_c of the core.* The resultant

---

* Bold face letters are used to distinguish a vector (l) from its absolute value (l).

vector $\mathbf{K} = \mathbf{J}_c + \mathbf{l}$ is then coupled to the spin of the outer electron to give a total angular momentum whose absolute value is $K \pm \frac{1}{2}$. Such coupling is called *pair coupling*. The terms of an atom in which pair coupling prevails are designated by Racah's symbols, which consist of the symbol of the outer electron configuration followed by $[K]$. These symbols are exemplified by the first excited states of neon: $3s[\frac{3}{2}]$ and $3s'[\frac{1}{2}]$. They are arrived at as follows: The orbital angular momentum of the core must be 1 and the spin $\frac{1}{2}$; they combine either parallel or antiparallel, giving a $J_c = \frac{3}{2}$ or $\frac{1}{2}$.

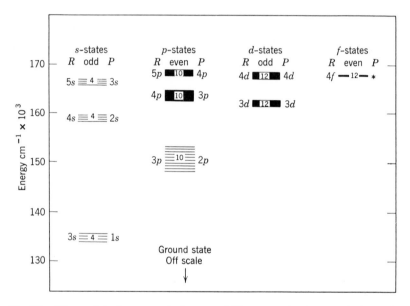

Fig. 75. Chart of the lowest excited states of Ne atoms. Paschen symbols on right, electron configuration of the Racah symbols on left, number of terms in center. (* indicates that some terms in this group have special Paschen symbols.)

Antiparallel combination of core orbital momentum and spin is indicated by the prime. Since the angular momentum of the $3s$ electron is 0, we must have $K = \frac{3}{2}$ in the first case and $K = \frac{1}{2}$ in the second. The total angular momentum $\mathbf{J}$ of the atom is obtained by adding (vectorially) the spin of the $3s$ electron to $\mathbf{K}$. Thus for $3s[\frac{3}{2}]$ the possibilities are $J = 2$ or 1; for $K = \frac{1}{2}$, on the other hand, $J = 1$ or 0. These values of J are frequently written as subscripts; thus the symbols of the four lowest excited states of neon are $3s[\frac{3}{2}]_2$, $3s[\frac{3}{2}]_1$, $3s'[\frac{1}{2}]_0$, and $3s'[\frac{1}{2}]_1$. The reader can convince himself that the $3p[K]$ configurations ($J_c = \frac{3}{2}$) of Ne are possible with $K = \frac{1}{2}, \frac{3}{2}$, and $\frac{5}{2}$, whereas the $3p'[K]$ configurations ($J_c = \frac{1}{2}$) permit only $K = \frac{1}{2}$ and $\frac{3}{2}$.

Since the spin of the outer electron permits two orientations for each orbit, we obtain a total of ten states of the $3p$ type.

Racah's notation is admittedly complicated, but it describes the physical situation or at least it provides a model. Unfortunately, the most commonly used notation, at least for Ne, is the Paschen notation, which is simply a system of shorthand symbols. Although the letters s, p, and d are used, we cannot safely infer that a Paschen symbol with the letter s always refers to an outer electron in an s orbit. Paschen's symbols must be treated as

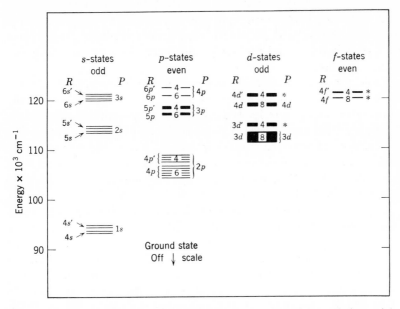

Fig. 76. Chart of the lowest excited states of Ar atoms. Paschen symbols on right, electron configuration of the Racah symbols on left, number of states in center. (* indicates miscellaneous or improvised symbols.)

arbitrary names given to levels. To find out what quantum-mechanical model represents the level, we must consult a list of these symbols which relates these to the model. Moore's atomic-energy-level tables [1] contain the necessary information.

For the sake of orientation we include a chart of the lowest excited levels of Ne (Fig. 75) and a similar chart for Ar which is representative of the heavier noble gases (Fig. 76). The change in the angular momentum of the core from $J_c = \frac{1}{2}$ to $\frac{3}{2}$ affects the energy of the neon levels by only relatively small amounts. For this reason the levels which differ by only the value of J_c are not shown separately on the chart of neon, and the primes of the Racah symbols are also omitted. The separation of the energy levels with differing values of J_c progressively increases with increasing atomic number. It is already conspicuous in the case of argon, and the grouping of the levels according to the value of J_c is shown on the argon chart.

Each column of the charts contains infinitely many energy levels; their Racah configuration numbers are ns, ns', np, np', etc. All unprimed sequences tend to the same limit, the ionization energy required to produce a singly ionized noble gas atom in the $^2P_{3/2}^o$ state; all primed sequences tend to another limit, which represents the ionization energy required to produce an ion in the $^2P_{1/2}^o$ state.* The latter energy is greater (in accordance with Hund's rules), and the energy difference increases with increasing atomic number.

Table V.1 at the end of this section contains the numerical values of 44 levels of Ne including the groups 3s, 4s, 5s, 3p, 4p, and 3d (Racah). Transitions among these levels account for the majority of observed Ne laser lines. The ground level is assigned the energy 0. Frequently tables are constructed from the ionization level E_∞ down. The entries of such tables are $E_\infty - E_n$; they are called *term values*. For Ne, the value of E_∞ is 173,931.7 cm^{-1}. Neon levels included in our short table represent but a fraction of the Ne levels contained in Moore's tables [1]. It is interesting to note that the lowest excited level of Ne is over 134,000 cm^{-1} above ground level and to compare this value with the first excited levels of ions which play a role in solid-state lasers.

Some conclusions can be drawn about the probabilities of radiative transitions between the levels listed in the tables from the selection rules (p. 36) and the quantum numbers listed in the tables. The actual calculation of the transition rates of permitted transitions is a very complicated task. It requires an approximate knowledge of the wave functions characterizing the states. The calculation of the transition rates, line strengths, and related properties of noble gases is described in the literature [2, 3]. Closely related to the transition rates are the decay rates of the states. These rates can be determined experimentally under conditions similar to those found in the laser. Although they represent engineering-type data, they have a certain physical meaning. The decay rate of any one state represents the sum of transition rates, radiative and otherwise, to all lower levels. Bennett [4] measured and compiled decay rates of the lowest Ne states. These are quite useful in laser calculations; therefore they were included in the table whose last column is the lifetime τ in nanoseconds. The decay rate is τ^{-1}. (See p. 31.)

* The superscript o indicates an odd term. See p. 36.

The spectrum of an ion is quite different from the spectrum of the neutral atom from which the ion derives. Similarities exist however among the spectra of atoms and ions which contain the same number of electrons; such structures are called *isoelectronic*. Oxygen atom, singly ionized fluorine, and doubly ionized neon, for example, form an *isoelectronic sequence*. It is customary in spectroscopy to distinguish between the spectra of an atom and its various ions in the following manner: The spectrum of the neutral atom is provided with a Roman numeral I, that of the singly ionized atom by II, and so on. Thus we have so far discussed the energy-level structures of Ne I, Ar I, etc.

The principal features of the energy-level structure of singly ionized noble gases are illustrated on the example of Ne II. The ground state configuration of Ne II is $1s^2 2s^2 2p^5$. Excited configurations are formed by promoting one of the $2p$ electrons to a higher orbit, say $3s$, $3p$, $3d$, etc., or, exceptionally, by promoting one of the $2s$ electrons to obtain the configuration $1s^2 2s 2p^6$. Leaving aside the exceptional situation, Ne II will consists of a core with a $1s^2 2s^2 2p^4$ configuration and an external electron which may be located in a variety of orbits with a principal quantum number at least 3. In the case of Ar II, the core has a $1s^2 2s^2 2p^6 3s^2 3p^4$ configuration and the external electron may be on either a $3d$ orbit or any orbit whose principal quantum number is at least 4. The halogens are isoelectronic with the singly ionized noble gases; therefore what was said about Ne II and Ar II also applies to F I and Cl I, respectively.

In these atoms two electrons are missing from the core, so that the spin of the core is 0 or 1. When this spin is combined with the spin of the outer electron, the resultant spin coordinate S has the value $\frac{1}{2}$ or $\frac{3}{2}$. The energy-level scheme will therefore consist of doublets $S = \frac{1}{2}$, and of quartets $S = \frac{3}{2}$. (Transitions between terms of different spin are not completely absent because the Russell-Saunders scheme is not completely applicable.) Removal of one of the p electrons may leave the core itself in several different states which are either singlets or triplets. Application of Pauli's principle leads to the conclusion that the possible terms are ^3P, ^1D, and ^1S. The lowest energy is associated with the ^3P core. A term of Ne II with a lowest-energy core and with the outside electron in the lowest s orbit is $3s\,^4P$, another with spin of the outside electron reversed is $3s\,^2P$. The first term permits the J values $\frac{5}{2}$, $\frac{3}{2}$, and $\frac{1}{2}$; the second only $\frac{3}{2}$ and $\frac{1}{2}$. When the core is in its next lowest state (^1D) the electronic symbol is provided with a prime; thus a term designated by $3s'\,^2D$ may be obtained. Double primes indicate a ^1S core.

In attempting to organize the energy levels of atoms we must keep in mind that the Russell-Saunders coupling scheme, as well as other coupling schemes, represents only approximations which do not have universal

TABLE V.1. ENERGY LEVELS OF NEON (Ne I)
(From Moore's Atomic Energy Levels)

Paschen	Racah	J	Energy Level, cm^{-1}	Lifetime, Nanoseconds
Ground	$2p^6\,{}^1S$	0	0	
$1s_5$	$3s[\frac{3}{2}]^o$	2	134 043.8	
$1s_4$	$3s[\frac{3}{2}]^o$	1	134 461.2	
$1s_3$	$3s'[\frac{1}{2}]^o$	0	134 820.6	
$1s_2$	$3s'[\frac{1}{2}]^o$	1	135 890.7	
$2p_{10}$	$3p[\frac{1}{2}]$	1	148 259.7	< 20
$2p_9$	$3p[\frac{5}{2}]$	3	149 659.0	17
$2p_8$	$3p[\frac{5}{2}]$	2	149 826.2	16
$2p_7$	$3p[\frac{3}{2}]$	1	150 123.6	< 13
$2p_6$	$3p[\frac{3}{2}]$	2	150 317.8	13
$2p_5$	$3p'[\frac{3}{2}]$	1	150 774.1	< 11
$2p_4$	$3p'[\frac{3}{2}]$	2	150 860.5	12
$2p_3$	$3p[\frac{1}{2}]$	0	150 919.4	< 13
$2p_2$	$3p'[\frac{1}{2}]$	1	151 040.4	< 12
$2p_1$	$3p'[\frac{1}{2}]$	0	152 972.7	< 8
$2s_5$	$4s[\frac{3}{2}]^o$	2	158 603.1	110
$2s_4$	$4s[\frac{3}{2}]^o$	1	158 798.0	98
$2s_3$	$4s'[\frac{1}{2}]^o$	0	159 381.9	160
$2s_2$	$4s'[\frac{1}{2}]^o$	1	159 536.6	96
$3d_6$	$3d[\frac{1}{2}]^o$	0	161 511.6	
$3d_5$	$3d[\frac{1}{2}]^o$	1	161 526.1	
$3d_4'$	$3d[\frac{7}{2}]^o$	4	161 592.3	
$3d_4$	$3d[\frac{7}{2}]^o$	3	161 594.1	
$3d_3$	$3d[\frac{3}{2}]^o$	2	161 609.2	
$3d_2$	$3d[\frac{3}{2}]^o$	1	161 638.6	
$3d_1''$	$3d[\frac{5}{2}]^o$	2	161 701.6	
$3d_1'$	$3d[\frac{5}{2}]^o$	3	161 703.4	
$3s_1''''$	$3d'[\frac{5}{2}]^o$	2	162 410.6	
$3s_1'''$	$3d'[\frac{5}{2}]^o$	3	162 412.1	
$3s_1''$	$3d'[\frac{3}{2}]^o$	2	162 421.9	
$3s_1'$	$3d'[\frac{3}{2}]^o$	1	162 437.6	
$3p_{10}$	$4p[\frac{1}{2}]$	1	162 519.9	
$3p_9$	$4p[\frac{5}{2}]$	3	162 832.7	
$3p_8$	$4p[\frac{5}{2}]$	2	162 901.1	
$3p_7$	$4p[\frac{3}{2}]$	1	163 014.6	
$3p_6$	$4p[\frac{3}{2}]$	2	163 040.3	
$3p_3$	$4p[\frac{1}{2}]$	0	163 403.3	
$3p_5$	$4p'[\frac{3}{2}]$	1	163 659.2	
$3p_2$	$4p'[\frac{1}{2}]$	1	163 709.7	
$3p_4$	$4p'[\frac{3}{2}]$	2	163 710.6	
$3p_1$	$4p'[\frac{1}{2}]$	0	164 287.9	
$3s_5$	$5s[\frac{3}{2}]^o$	2	165 830.1	
$3s_4$	$5s[\frac{3}{2}]^o$	1	165 914.8	
$3s_3$	$5s'[\frac{1}{2}]^o$	0	166 608.3	
$3s_2$	$5s'[\frac{1}{2}]^o$	1	166 658.5	

validity. As we progress through the elements He, Ne, Ar, Kr, Xe, we find that the forces responsible for Russell-Saunders coupling decrease in comparison with other forces. Even within one element the ratios of these forces are different for electrons that pass near the nucleus and for those whose orbits are farther removed. For heavier elements and for large quantum numbers n and l of the outer electron, the coupling approaches pair coupling.

Spectral lines, whether derived from spontaneous or from stimulated emission, can be given a transition assignment among the terms tabulated in the atomic energy tables insofar as the tables are complete. With the extension of stimulated emission spectroscopy into the infrared, lines are occasionally observed which result from transitions among levels not yet tabulated.

REFERENCES

1. C. H. Moore, *Atomic Energy Levels*, U.S. Nat. Bur. Stds., Circular 467, U.S. Govt. Print. Off., Washington, D.C., 1949.
2. G. F. Koster and H. Statz, Probabilities for the neon laser transitions, *J. Appl. Phys.* **32**, 2054–2055, 1961.
3. W. L. Faust and R. A. McFarlane, Line strengths for noble-gas maser transitions, *J. Appl. Phys.* **35**, 2010–2015, 1964.
4. W. R. Bennett, Radiative lifetimes and collision transfer cross sections of excited atomic states, *Advances in Quantum Electronics*, Columbia Univ. Press, New York, 1961, pp. 28–43.

3. CONDITIONS FOR LASER OSCILLATION IN GASES

The complete fluorescence cycle in a gas laser usually involves at least four energy levels. Let us denote the ground level by 1, and the levels of laser transition by indices 2 and 3, realizing that there may be levels above 3 and below 2 participating in the cycle. As before, let N_i designate the number of atoms per unit volume at level i, and g_i the multiplicity $(2J + 1)$ of that level.

Population inversion (negative absorption) will be achieved when

$$\frac{N_3}{g_3} - \frac{N_2}{g_2} > 0. \tag{3.1}$$

A necessary, but by no means sufficient, condition for population inversion in a stationary state may be obtained from (3.1). The population of state 2 is increased by radiative transitions from state 3 and by other processes. It is diminished by a variety of processes, resulting in a total effective decay rate of R_2. Then

$$\frac{dN_2}{dt} \geq N_3 A_{32} - N_2 R_2. \tag{3.2}$$

Therefore in a stationary state $N_3 A_{32} \leqq N_2 R_2$; hence

$$\frac{N_3}{N_2} \frac{g_2}{g_3} \leqq \frac{R_2}{A_{32}} \frac{g_2}{g_3}. \tag{3.3}$$

Population inversion takes place when the left side of (3.3) exceeds 1. This can occur only when

$$A_{32} \frac{g_3}{g_2} < R_2. \tag{3.4}$$

The left side of this inequality contains atomic constants only; the right side is under the control of the experimenter to some extent. He must arrange circumstances so that the total rate of decay from the terminal level 2 exceeds the minimum set by (3.4).

The threshold of oscillation will be reached when the left side of (3.1) is not only positive, but large enough to compensate for the losses of the instrument. According to equation (2.8) of Chapter II this will occur when

$$\frac{N_3}{g_3} - \frac{N_2}{g_2} = \frac{\gamma}{L} \frac{1}{P g_2 \kappa}, \tag{3.5}$$

where γ is the loss coefficient, L is the length of the laser, and κ is the integrated absorption coefficient of the line given by (6.9) of Chapter I. The shape of the absorption line in gases under low pressure is determined by the Doppler effect; the peak value, P, of the curve is given by (6.14) of Chapter I. Combining these equations, we obtain the *threshold condition* for a gas laser:

$$\frac{N_3}{g_3} - \frac{N_2}{g_2} = \frac{8\pi}{A_{32} g_3 \lambda^3} \sqrt{\frac{2\pi R T_g}{M}} \frac{\gamma}{L}. \tag{3.6}$$

Here M is the molecular weight of the gas $R = Nk = 8.317 \times 10^7$ erg/mole deg., and T_g is the temperature of the gas. The formula shows that, other things being equal, it is easier to fulfill the threshold condition for longer wavelengths.

We have already noted that several processes of excitation and de-excitation are operative in gases. All processes are subject to the *principle of detailed balance*, which relates the probability of a process to that of the inverse process. Let us consider a large reservoir R of interacting particles in thermal equilibrium with each other at a temperature T, and an experimental system E capable of interaction with the particles of R by means of a variety of physical processes. The principle of detailed balance asserts that *each process acting separately will ultimately produce the same statistical distribution of energy in E*, namely a Boltzmann distribution with a temperature T. In the situation of interest here, R may be represented by the electrons in the discharge, whose energy distribution is at least approximately that required for the validity of the argument. A similar result is obtained if we consider the interaction of the atomic system with a radiation field whose energy distribution is given by Planck's radiation law.

Since all such processes tend to produce thermal equilibrium if acting alone, the question arises of how one can ever obtain a steady-state population inversion. The answer is that the rates at which these processes proceed toward equilibrium are all different. Consequently, we may play one of the mechanisms against the others and operate the system in an intermediate steady-state condition where no one process dominates and where no single temperature characterizes the population of all atomic levels. The situation is helped in multilevel systems if strong departures can be obtained from a Maxwellian (equilibrium) distribution of the interacting particles or if a highly monochromatic radiation field is employed in place of black-body radiation. There is, however, for each excitation process an inverse process which tends to produce thermal equilibrium, and the production of population inversion involves minimizing the effects of the inverse process at some stage. This may be accomplished, for example, by allowing light from some levels to escape through the walls, or by allowing metastable atoms to diffuse out of the discharge. Like the thermodynamic engines, the lasers must have a sink. This sink however may be one or more steps removed from the lower laser level.

The following energy exchange processes are important in a discharge that takes place in a single gas:

1. Electron collision of the first kind in which an atom gains energy from an electron.
2. Electron collision of the second kind in which an excited atom loses energy to an electron.
3. Spontaneous emission of radiation from an excited atom.
4. Absorption of radiation by an atom.
5. Stimulated emission of radiation by an atom.

The rates at which these processes take place are determined by the numbers of atoms available in the proper states and by the probabilities that these phenomena will occur in the unit time for an individual particle. These probabilities are stated as reciprocal lifetimes and they relate to atoms in given states.

Let θ_{ij} denote the lifetime of the transition of an atom from level i to level j when the atom is subjected only to collisions with electrons of a given density in equilibrium among themselves at the absolute temperature T.* If no other processes than these collisions were to take place, the rate of change of the number of atoms at level i would be given by

$$\frac{dN_i}{dt} = \sum_j \left(\frac{N_j}{\theta_{ji}} - \frac{N_i}{\theta_{ij}} \right). \tag{3.7}$$

We shall now show that θ_{ij} and θ_{ji} are simply related. Let us assume that a thermodynamic equilibrium is established at temperature T; the number of atoms in each level will then be stationary. Let these stationary, or equilibrium, values be denoted by N_i^*. Then

$$\sum_j \left(\frac{N_j^*}{\theta_{ji}} - \frac{N_i^*}{\theta_{ij}} \right) = 0 \tag{3.8}$$

for every value i. Moreover, the *principle of detailed balance* requires that the exchanges between each pair of energy levels balance out. This means not only that the sum in (3.8) must vanish but that

$$\frac{N_j^*}{\theta_{ji}} - \frac{N_i^*}{\theta_{ij}} = 0 \tag{3.9}$$

must hold for every i and j. Therefore

$$\frac{\theta_{ij}}{\theta_{ji}} = \frac{N_i^*}{N_j^*}. \tag{3.10}$$

Since N_i^* and N_j^* are occupation numbers of the levels in thermal equilibrium at temperature T, it follows from Boltzmann's law that

$$\frac{\theta_{ij}}{\theta_{ji}} = \frac{g_i}{g_j} e^{-(E_i - E_j)/kT}. \tag{3.11}$$

When atomic transitions are the result not only of electron collisions but of other processes as well, the distribution will *not* be given by

$$\frac{N_i}{N_j} = \frac{g_i}{g_j} e^{-(E_i - E_j)/kT}. \tag{3.12}$$

This fact, however, does not affect the validity of (3.11), which is a relation between probabilities. The stationary distribution can be obtained by analysis of the change due to all causes in the population of a given level. In the simplest case of two levels, with a spontaneous radiative transition with lifetime τ_2 from levels 2 to 1, the rate equation is

$$\frac{dN_2}{dt} = \frac{N_1}{\theta_{12}} - \frac{N_2}{\theta_{21}} - \frac{N_2}{\tau_2}. \tag{3.13}$$

---

* Actually, the symbol T_e would be preferable to indicate "electron temperature," but we omit the e in view of the overabundance of subscripts.

In the stationary state

$$\frac{N_2}{N_1} = \frac{1/\theta_{12}}{1/\theta_{21} + 1/\tau_2}.$$ (3.14)

When the radiative process is comparatively fast, so that $\tau_2 \ll \theta_{21}$, we have

$$\frac{N_2}{N_1} \approx \frac{\tau_2}{\theta_{12}} = \frac{g_2\tau_2}{g_1\theta_{21}} e^{-(E_2-E_1)/kT}.$$ (3.15)

The ratio τ_2/θ_{21} is a measure of the departure from the Boltzmann equilibrium distribution. To an extent, this factor is under the control of the experimenter, since τ_2 is fixed, but $1/\theta_{21}$ is proportional to the electron density in the discharge. However, N_2/N_1 cannot be increased arbitrarily by increasing the electron density because the validity of (3.15) is based on the assumption that τ_2/θ_{21} is much less than 1.

Let us now introduce an additional level above level 2, and let us assume no direct interaction between these levels (2 and 3). Under similar assumptions, we find

$$\frac{N_3}{N_1} \approx \frac{g_3}{g_1} \frac{\tau_3}{\theta_{31}} e^{-(E_3-E_1)/kT}.$$ (3.16)

From (3.15) and (3.16) it follows that

$$\frac{g_2}{g_3} \frac{N_3}{N_2} \approx \frac{\tau_3}{\tau_2} \frac{\theta_{21}}{\theta_{31}} e^{-(E_3-E_2)/kT}.$$ (3.17)

Even though the exponential factor is always less than 1, the factor in front of the exponential may be sufficiently greater than 1 for certain values of the parameters to cause N_3g_2 to exceed g_3N_2. This is the condition of population inversion or negative absorption. In order to achieve this condition by electron excitation alone, we must select materials and states so that τ_3/τ_2 is large without an adversely large ratio of θ_{31}/θ_{21}. Actually, there are many complicating factors not yet considered. One is that levels other than those already listed become populated by electron collisions. If in their radiative decay they populate the lower level 2 in preference to level 3, they may spoil the narrow margin otherwise available for population inversion.

In order to satisfy the threshold condition for oscillation, not only must N_3 exceed N_2 but the difference $N_3 - N_2$ must exceed a certain minimum. Therefore, other conditions being equal, it is desirable to have a discharge of high density. At high densities the absorption of the photons produced by spontaneous emission in other atoms becomes important. Reabsorption of the spontaneously emitted radiation increases the lifetime in the excited level. This effect is useful when it increases the lifetime of the atom in the upper level 3. It will take place when the optical transition between levels 1 and 3 is permitted by the selection rules. Under these conditions the system can operate at relatively high densities. However, when the ground level is connected to level 2 by a permitted transition, a high density is undesirable because it increases the relative population of level 2. This unfavorable situation prevails for the levels of helium already mentioned.

The quantum theory of transitions indicates that in the case of transitions allowed by the selection rules the ratio τ_i/θ_{i1} is essentially the same for all levels. It can be seen from (3.17) that negative absorption cannot be obtained in such a case. At least one of the two levels in the system must therefore be such that optical transition between it and the ground state is forbidden. This level is excited by electron collisions; the excitation cross section for this process is generally smaller than for optically allowed transitions. In a favorable case the transition between the ground level and the lower state is forbidden, and the small excitation of this level favors the production of negative temperature. Such a situation was found for many transitions in noble gases but population inversion could be achieved by electron excitation alone only when provision was made to relieve the overpopulation of the terminal laser level resulting from transitions from higher levels to that level.

The first gaseous lasers contained a mixture of He and Ne in the proportion about 10 to 1. Population inversion was established between the $2s$ and $2p$ (Paschen) levels of neon with the assistance of resonant transfer of excitation from helium atoms to neon atoms. This transfer is not absolutely necessary, as experiments with pure neon and other noble gases have shown, but it is a process which under certain circumstances aids significantly the attainment of population inversion. The circumstances are described by the rates of the various energy exchange processes which take place between the electron gas in the discharge and the two components of the gaseous mixture.

The kinetics of this process has been developed by Basov and Krokhin [1, 2], whose work is reproduced here briefly. The two gases are distinguished by the letters a and b. The atoms of the working gas a have three relevant levels: $E_1 = 0$, the ground level, E_2, and E_3. The atoms of the auxiliary gas b have two relevant levels, $E_1 = 0$ and E_3. The coincidence, or near coincidence, of level 3 is essential for the operation of the scheme because it is a condition for significant transfer of excitation between the two atomic species.

The rate of change of the number of atoms of gas a in level E_3 is

$$\frac{dN_3{}^a}{dt} = N_1{}^a\left(\frac{1}{\theta_{13}} + \frac{1}{t_{ba}}\right) - N_3{}^a\left(\frac{1}{\theta_3} + \frac{1}{t_{ab}} + \frac{1}{\tau_3}\right). \tag{3.18}$$

Here $1/t_{ba}$ is the rate per ground state atom of gas a of resonant transfer of energy in collision with atoms of gas b on level 3, and $1/t_{ab}$ is the rate per excited atom of gas a for the inverse process; $1/\theta_3$ is the total transition rate for gas a from level 3 resulting from collisions of the second kind with electrons; that is,

$$\frac{1}{\theta_3} = \frac{1}{\theta_{31}} + \frac{1}{\theta_{32}}. \tag{3.19}$$

The parameter τ_3 is the radiative lifetime of level 3, including radiative transitions to both lower levels. Excitation from level 2 to level 3 is neglected in this analysis because a term describing the process is proportional to $N_2{}^a$, hence much smaller than the leading terms in (3.18).

The rate of change of the number of atoms $N_2{}^a$ on level E_2 is given by

$$\frac{dN_2{}^a}{dt} = \frac{N_1{}^a}{\theta_{12}} + N_3{}^a\left(\frac{1}{\tau_{32}} + \frac{1}{\theta_{32}}\right) - N_2{}^a\left(\frac{1}{\theta_{21}} + \frac{1}{\tau_{21}}\right), \tag{3.20}$$

where the τ's indicate radiative lifetimes.

In the stationary case the derivatives vanish. The condition of negative absorption between the levels E_3 and E_2 of gas a is given by

$$N_3{}^a > N_2{}^a. \tag{3.21}$$

When the left sides of (3.18) and (3.20) are set equal to zero, the ratio $N_3{}^a/N_2{}^a$ can be calculated in terms of the lifetimes occurring in these equations. The condition (3.21) becomes an inequality involving the combinations of these lifetimes. We then make use of (3.11) as well as of the fact that according to collision theory

$$\frac{t_{ba}}{t_{ab}} = \frac{N_1{}^b}{N_3{}^b}. \tag{3.22}$$

This ratio is determined by the effective excitation temperature for the atoms of gas b. It may be considered an external parameter as far as the distribution of the atoms of gas a is concerned. The condition (3.21) then becomes

$$\frac{\theta_{13}}{t_{ba}}\left[1 - \frac{N_1{}^b}{N_3{}^b}e^{-E_2/kT} + \theta_{21}\left(\frac{1}{\tau_{21}} - \frac{1}{\tau_{32}} - \frac{1}{\theta_{32}}\right)\right]$$
$$> \theta_{31}\left(\frac{1}{\theta_3} + \frac{1}{\tau_3}\right)e^{(E_3 - E_2)/kT} - 1 + \theta_{21}\left(\frac{1}{\tau_{32}} + \frac{1}{\theta_{32}} - \frac{1}{\tau_{21}}\right). \tag{3.23}$$

The quantities θ_{31}/θ_3 and θ_{21}/θ_{32} do not depend on the density of the electrons in the discharge but are determined by the cross sections of the corresponding processes and by the temperature of the electrons.

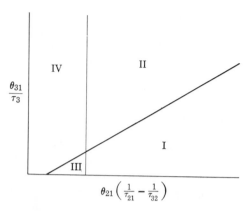

Fig. 77. The diagram of Basov and Krokhin.

Inequality (3.23) has a different meaning in different regions of the variables $\theta_{21}(1/\tau_{21} - 1/\tau_{32})$ and θ_{31}/τ_3. The range of these variables is divided by two curves into four regions. The equations of the curves are obtained by setting the expression in brackets and the right side equal to zero. To the first order of approximation the rate $1/\theta_{32}$ may be neglected in comparison with $1/\tau_{32}$ and the assumption may be made that $\theta_{31}/\theta_3 \approx 1$; the curves mentioned above then become straight lines described by the equations

$$\theta_{21}\left(\frac{1}{\tau_{21}} - \frac{1}{\tau_{32}}\right) = \frac{N_1{}^b}{N_3{}^b} e^{-E_2/kT} - 1, \qquad (3.24)$$

$$\frac{\theta_{31}}{\tau_3} = \frac{\theta_{21}(1/\tau_{21} - 1/\tau_{32}) + 1 - F(T)}{F(T)}, \qquad (3.25)$$

where $F(T) = e^{(E_3 - E_2)/kT}$.

Clearly, to the right of the vertical line in Fig. 77, whose equation is (3.24), the condition (3.23) is satisfied for any value of t_{ba} when the right side is negative. This situation corresponds to region I in the figure. In this case $t_{ba} = \infty$ also leads to population inversion, and gas b is unnecessary. In region II population inversion occurs because of the presence of gas b. In region III gas b impedes the formation of a population inversion. The occurrence of population inversion in region IV is impossible.

Unfortunately the variables involved in equations (3.24) and (3.25) are generally not known to a degree of precision necessary to make predictions from this theory in specific cases. The value of the theory lies mostly in disclosing the possibilities and in specifying the variables which affect the phenomena.

REFERENCES

1. N. G. Basov and O. N. Krokhin, Condition for electron excitation of negative temperature states in a gas mixture, *Soviet Phys. JETP* **12**, 1240–1242, 1960 (**39**, 1777–1780, 1960).
2. N. G. Basov and O. N. Krokhin, Population inversion in a discharge in a mixture of two gases, *Appl. Optics* **1**, 213–216, 1962.

4. COMMON HELIUM-NEON LASERS

The neon lasers whose operation is based on the transfer of excitation from helium to neon atoms form the most important group of gaseous lasers. They were the first to be discovered and studied and are the easiest to construct and to operate. Most of the knowledge and experience available in 1964 on gaseous lasers was obtained on such He-Ne lasers. Spectroscopic data pertaining to these lasers are summarized in Table V.2. Laser oscillations in other lines of neon are discussed in Section V.5 together with lasers of other noble gases.

Javan, Bennett, and Herriott [1] made the original discovery in 1960, observing stimulated emission on five nearby lines in the near infrared, lines 2 to 6 in Table V.2. The strongest oscillation occurs in line 3 at 1.1523 μ. The radiation arises from stimulated transitions from the $2s$ to the $2p$ levels of Ne; the population of the former group is enhanced by transfer from the $2\,^3S$ level of He. These transitions are shown on the energy-level diagram of Fig. 78; many other transitions have subsequently been observed in stimulated emission.

TABLE V.2. SELECTED LASER LINES OF NEON*

Line Number	λ_{air}, Microns	σ, cm^{-1}	Transition Paschen	Transition Racah	Gain, cm^{-1}
1	0.6328	15798.0	$3s_2$–$2p_4$	$5s'[\tfrac{1}{2}]_1{}^\circ$–$3p'[\tfrac{3}{2}]_2$	5×10^{-4}
2	1.1177	8944.07	$2s_5$–$2p_9$	$4s[\tfrac{3}{2}]_2{}^\circ$–$3p[\tfrac{3}{2}]_3$	—
3	1.1523	8676.10	$2s_2$–$2p_4$	$4s'[\tfrac{1}{2}]_1{}^\circ$–$3p'[\tfrac{3}{2}]_2$	12×10^{-4}
4	1.1614	8607.87	$2s_3$–$2p_5$	$4s'[\tfrac{1}{2}]_0{}^\circ$–$3p'[\tfrac{3}{2}]_1$	—
5	1.1985	8341.53	$2s_3$–$2p_2$	$4s'[\tfrac{1}{2}]_1{}^\circ$–$3p'[\tfrac{1}{2}]_1$	—
6	1.2066	8285.25	$2s_5$–$2p_6$	$4s[\tfrac{3}{2}]_2{}^\circ$–$3p[\tfrac{3}{2}]_2$	—
7	1.5231	6563.87	$2s_2$–$2p_1$	$4s'[\tfrac{1}{2}]_1{}^\circ$–$3p'[\tfrac{1}{2}]_0$	—
8	3.3913	2947.90	$3s_2$–$3p_4$	$5s'[\tfrac{1}{2}]_1{}^\circ$–$4p'[\tfrac{3}{2}]_2$	$>4 \times 10^{-2}$

* For a complete table of Ne lines observed in stimulated emission see Table A.2 in the Appendix.

White and Rigden [2] discovered the visible He-Ne laser (line 1) in 1962. The radiation arises from the $3s_2$–$2p_4$ transition; the population of the upper level is enhanced by the transfer of excitation from the $2\,^1S$ state

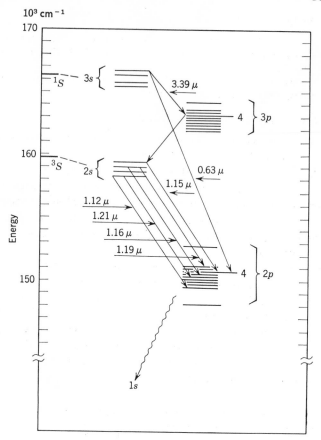

Fig. 78. Helium-neon energy levels and strongest laser transitions.

of He. This laser is the most convenient one to use for demonstration and alignment purposes; several companies market such lasers for general use.

It is somewhat inaccurate to refer to the 6328-Å laser as *the* visible Ne laser, since laser oscillations can be produced in other visible Ne lines. Once the $3s_2$ level of Ne is heavily populated, one can force laser transitions into a number of the $2p$ levels other than $2p_4$. The gain in these transitions is less than that in the $3s_2$–$2p_4$ transition; therefore longer discharge tubes are used with dispersive prisms incorporated into the path of the beam within the mirrors to separate the desired wavelength and enhance its oscillations, suppressing all others [3]. These unusual visible Ne laser lines are included in Table A.2 in the Appendix.

Shortly after the discovery of the visible He-Ne laser Bloom, Bell, and Rempel [4] observed that infrared radiation of over 3-μ wavelength frequently accompanies the emission of the visible line and that the emission of this infrared radiation interferes with the operation of the visible laser. The transition responsible for the infrared radiation originates at the $3s_2$ level, the starting level of the visible radiation. It terminates at the $3p_4$ level, yielding a radiation of 3.3913 μ in wavelength (line 8). The operation of this 3.39-μ laser not only depletes the $3s_2$ level—to the detriment of the population inversion required for the visible laser—it overpopulates the $3p_4$ level and thereby offers the possibility of enhancing laser action originating at the latter level. Such a cascade effect was observed at the end of 1963 by American [5], French [6], and German [7] investigators simultaneously. The main line of this cascade proceeds from $3p_4$ to $2s_2$ with emission of 2.3951-μ radiation, then to $2p_4$ with the emission of the 1.1523-μ line. Several other branches of such a cascade were also observed [7, 8]. The intensity of a cascade line depends on the intensity of the line preceding it in the cascade. The latter can be controlled by varying the regeneration of the laser in a frequency-dependent manner.

It is very easy to attribute to He a role that it does not entirely deserve, and this was frequently done in the early literature. It should be noted that the strongest He-Ne lines are obtainable in pure neon [9], and many Ne lines can be produced in stimulated emission whose upper level is not connected with an excited state of He. Even some of the so-called He-Ne cascades were eventually observed in pure Ne [10]. Therefore we ought to conclude that the transfer of excitation from He substantially enhances population inversion in certain levels of Ne without being the exclusive cause of such inversion. How important the effect of He can become practically may be judged by the results of Patel [9], who compared stimulated emission in pure Ne with emission in an optimized mixture of He and Ne. In a tube 2 meters long and 1.5 cm in diameter, the maximum output of the 1.1523-μ radiation was 0.2 mW in pure Ne, while in a 10 to 1 He-Ne mixture an output of 10 mW was obtained.

The general appearance of the early He-Ne lasers was shown in Fig. 16, p. 56. These lasers had plane mirrors inside their vacuum envelope. The fabrication of such a system and the adjustment of the mirrors was difficult. Subsequently the plane mirrors were replaced by spherical ones for the reasons discussed in Chapter II, and they were moved to the outside to facilitate fabrication, alignment, and exchange. The passage of radiation out of the vacuum envelope was accomplished with minimal reflections by the use of optical flats as end plates, and by orienting these at the Brewster angle. Figure 79 is the schematic diagram of such a laser; Fig. 80 is a photograph of a laser with external mirrors constructed at the Hughes Research Laboratories in 1962.

The optimal tube diameter seems to be around 6 to 8 mm. Although

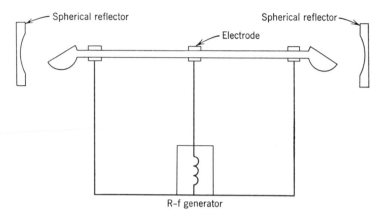

Fig. 79. Diagram of the He-Ne laser with external confocal spherical reflectors. (The curvature of the mirrors in the figure is exaggerated.)

lasers 2 meters long are frequently used in spectroscopic studies, and one 8 meters long has been reported, a 70-cm tube is adequate to excite the lines listed in our table provided that high-quality dielectric mirrors are used, which ensure a reflection coefficient of about 99 per cent for the

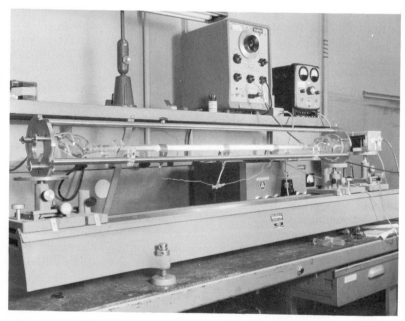

Fig. 80. A He-Ne laser with external reflectors.

weaker lines. The requirements are less stringent for the 1.15-μ line, which has a high gain. Considerably shorter tubes (10 cm) are adequate for the 3.39-μ line, and the reflectivity of the mirrors can also be reduced in this case.

It was shown earlier that the gain, or negative absorption, is proportional to the transition probability and to the factor

$$p = \frac{N_2}{g_2} - \frac{N_1}{g_1}.$$

This factor, which describes the population inversion in the medium, depends on the operating conditions of the discharge and on the geometry as well as the gas composition. It generally varies from the center to the periphery of the discharge, since its value is the result of the balance of processes which include collisions with the walls. Because of the great variability of this factor, experimental values of gain have limited physical meaning; they have practical or engineering significance when applied to situations similar to those in which they were measured, and they serve as measures of comparison for different spectral lines excited simultaneously. The tabulated values of the gain (Table V.2) are those of Faust and McFarlane [11]; the corresponding (not tabulated) values for the other $2s \rightarrow 2p$ lines are of the order of 1 to 2×10^{-4} cm^{-1}. Faust and McFarlane estimated that in an optimized He-Ne discharge with the gain values as stated, the values of p are as follows:

Line	6328 Å	1.15 μ	3.39 μ
p	1.3×10^9 cm^{-3}	1.5×10^8 cm^{-3}	$\geq 9 \times 10^8$ cm^{-3}

Considerable work has been done to determine experimentally the optimal characteristics of various lasers and the radiative outputs obtainable from them. The early results are summarized in the review article of Bennett [12], additional contributions were made by Gordon, White, and others [13, 14, 15]. Only a few outstanding facts are quoted here. The best operation of the 6328-Å and the 3.39-μ lasers is attained for a 5-to-1 He-to-Ne ratio. The product of the total pressure and the tube diameter should lie between 2.9 and 3.6 torr-mm. For the $2s \rightarrow 2p$ transitions the optimal composition is 1 torr He and 0.1 torr Ne with the tube diameter around 7 mm.

The discharge may be excited by means of an rf oscillator using external electrodes. A matching transformer of 10 to 15 turns is convenient for the adjustment of the discharge for optimal operation. Radio frequencies from 23 Mc to 40 Mc have been used with equal success; the 27- to 30-Mc region is preferred. The large fields under the external electrodes tend to drive He out of the tubes. This is no serious detriment when the tubes can be readily refilled. Sealed-off tubes driven by rf excitation get exhausted after a few hundred hours or sooner. Sealed-off tubes of more permanent type have internal electrodes, usually with a heated cathode for d-c operation. Discharge currents between 25 and 100 mA are usually required.

The minimum tube length L_t which produces oscillations is determined by the gain of the line and by the losses at the terminations. For each operating condition one may find an L_t. The power output of the laser of length L is a nearly linear function of L/L_t [14]. Experimental results pertaining to a 6328-Å laser with spherical mirrors and a 6-mm discharge tube are shown in Fig. 81. The minimum tube lengths varied from 61 to 88 cm, depending on the discharge current as shown in the insert. Thus an output of 3 to 8 mW can be obtained from visible He-Ne lasers of

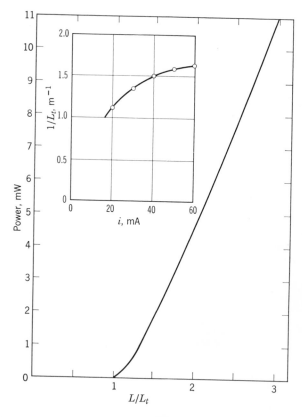

Fig. 81. Output power of a visible neon laser as a function of the length of the discharge. (L_t is the minimum length for oscillations; i is the discharge current. After White, Gordon, and Rigden [14].)

convenient length. Similar results were found for short 1.15-μ lasers. The minimum length could be made as short as 10 cm, and an output of 12 mW was obtainable from discharges 33 cm long [15].

The radiation pattern of the He-Ne laser depends on its construction, particularly on the mirrors and on the limiting aperture.

Precision measurements of Herriott [16] show that the far-field pattern of the original Bell Laboratories laser (with internal reflectors) consists of a beam whose width is 1 min of arc when the reflectors are adjusted to parallelism. The beam obtained from a laser with confocal external reflectors without a limiting aperture is somewhat fuzzy at the edges; the far-field pattern measured between half-power points is about 30 min [17]. With a circular iris of 2-mm diameter placed 3 cm in front of the exit mirror of the confocal laser, both the near and the far fields become sharply limited, the power density increases, and the far field narrows to about 3 min of arc measured between half-power points. The beamwidth is determined by the angular beamwidth of the cavity mode, which is given by the Boyd-Gordon formula: equation (3.21) of Chapter II. This formula is valid whenever the aperture introduced is not so small that its diffraction pattern further limits the definition of the beam.

At low levels of excitation the output of the external reflector He-Ne laser is plane polarized as a consequence of the discriminatory action of the windows, which by their orientation favor one polarization. When the gain in the laser is considerably above the oscillation threshold, the other polarization will also appear. Similarly, a number of cavity modes may be excited simultaneously, and beat frequencies between these oscillations may be observed [18].

Oscillations occur at or near the peaks of those interferometer or cavity resonances that fall within the linewidth of the atomic resonance where appreciable gain is present. This is illustrated in Fig. 82, which shows the "natural" atomic linewidth, the actual linewidth as it appears in the gas due to Doppler broadening, and finally the fine comblike structure of the cavity resonances.

The most relevant modes of the confocal system are similar to those of the plane parallel system. (Section II.3.) In the simplest case of the axial modes, or TEM_{00n} modes of Fox and Li, for each interferometer resonance appearing at frequency ν_n, another resonance exists at the frequency $\nu_{n+1} = \nu_n + \Delta\nu$, where $\Delta\nu = c/2L$. Here L is the separation of the reflectors, and the index n refers to the number of modes in the standing wave pattern formed between the reflector plates. Thus, for 1 meter separation, $\Delta\nu = 150$ Mc. Since the atomic linewidth (Doppler) is about 900 Mc, several of these modes may be excited simultaneously.* The oscillations do

* See Section VI.1 for further discussion of the modes.

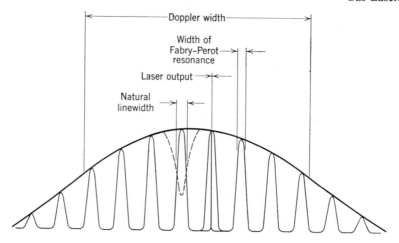

Fig. 82. Spectral linewidth factors in a laser. (Reprinted from *The Journal of the Optical Society of America.*)

not take place exactly at the peaks of the interferometer resonances; they are shifted a small amount toward the center frequency of the atomic resonance.

The beat notes between nearby spectral lines can be detected by means of a multiplier phototube. If it were only for the axial modes, the spectrum would consist of approximately equally spaced lines, 150 Mc apart for a reflector separation of 1 meter. There are off-axis, or unsymmetrical, modes as well, whose excitation depends critically on the adjustment of the reflectors. In the case of $L = 1$ meter, for example, there is an unsymmetric mode separated by 1.3 Mc from the symmetric mode. As a consequence, satellite lines appear in the beat frequency spectrum with 1.3 Mc separation on either side of the main lines. This is shown in Fig. 83, which is adapted from the work of Herriott [16].

The linewidths of the He-Ne laser oscillations are many orders of magnitude narrower than the resolution of the best spectrometers or interferometers; therefore standard optical techniques cannot be used to measure the linewidth. The linewidth may be determined by examining the beat notes between the different interferometer modes. These beat notes are obtained directly from the multiplier phototube on which the laser light is incident; since the phototube is a square law detector, its output contains the beat frequencies. Early measurements of Javan and Herriott [1, 16] indicated linewidths of 10 to 20 kc. Actually, the lines are considerably narrower, but their measurement is difficult because the most minute changes in the distance between the reflectors cause a shift in the lines.

Thus the system responds in the form of frequency modulation to minute thermal fluctuations and mechanical vibrations. Fortunately, two modes subject to similar frequency variations yield a beat frequency that to a large extent is compensated for mechanical variations of length. The degree of this compensation depends critically on the frequency of each of the two interferometer resonances with respect to the center frequency of the atomic resonance. It has been mentioned in Section II.3 that each interferometer mode is pulled toward the center of the atomic resonance line v_c. The extent of pulling is a nonlinear function of the deviation of the frequency of the interferometer mode from v_c; therefore a change in the interferometer length will affect the frequencies of the participating modes in a different way. Consequently, it will also affect the beat frequency unless the participating modes are chosen by tuning in such a manner that these frequency changes of the beat note caused by the pulling are compensated.

Javan and associates [18] produced a 50-kc beat note by mixing two perpendicularly polarized oscillations of a carefully stabilized neon laser operating at 1.15 μ. They obtained a fluctuation of the beat note of only 2 cps over a period of several seconds and from this they concluded that the frequency stability of each oscillation was about 1 cps. Although the experiment was a remarkable one, the final conclusion would have been warranted only if the oscillations had been independent. As a matter of

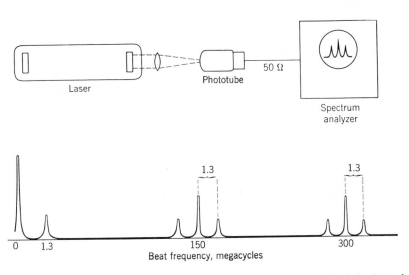

Fig. 83. Beating of optical frequencies. (Reprinted from *The Journal of the Optical Society of America.*)

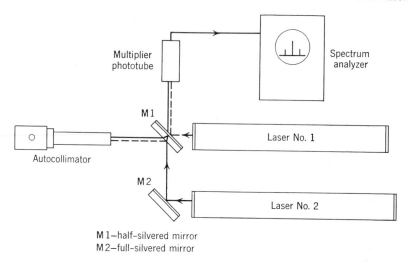

Fig. 84. Mixing of the outputs of two lasers. (Apparatus of Javan, Ballik, and Bond. Reprinted from *The Journal of the Optical Society of America.*)

fact, their fluctuations were correlated because all precautions were taken that fluctuations in laser parameters affect them in the same manner. One might say that after all device fluctuations are compensated, an additional 1 cps independent fluctuation remains.

More meaningful are the results of frequency stability investigations which involve the observation of the beat note obtained by mixing the outputs of two independently oscillating lasers. To observe this signal, it is essential not only that the same area of the photocathode of the multiplier phototube be exposed to the two laser beams but that the wavefronts of the two beams be parallel. This alignment is achieved by a mirror system shown in Fig. 84. In an experiment designed to achieve the greatest freedom from external fluctuations the lasers were supported on a massive shock-mounted table with resonant frequencies of many seconds and located in a cellar room of an isolated building. The difference signals of the two lasers operating at 2.6×10^{14} cps (1.15μ) were observed around 1700 cps. Fluctuations of the beat note indicated a short-term frequency fluctuation of only 20 cps for the individual lasers, or 8 parts in 10^{14} [19].

REFERENCES

1. A. Javan, W. R. Bennett, Jr., and D. R. Herriott, Population inversion and continuous optical maser oscillation in a gas discharge containing a He-Ne mixture, *Phys. Rev. Lett.* **6**, 106–110, 1961.

2. A. D. White and J. D. Rigden, Continuous gas maser operation in the visible, *Proc. IRE* **50**, 1697, 1962.

3. A. D. White and J. D. Rigden, The effect of super-radiance at 3.39 μ on the visible transitions in the He-Ne maser, *Appl. Phys. Lett.* **2**, 211–212, 1963.

4. A. L. Bloom, W. E. Bell, and R. C. Rempel, Laser operation at 3.39 μ in a helium-neon mixture, *Appl. Optics* **2**, 317–318, 1963.

5. H. J. Gerritsen and P. V. Goedertier, A gaseous (He-Ne) cascade laser, *Appl. Phys. Lett.* **4**, 20–21, 1964.

6. R. Grudzinski, M. Paillette, and J. Becrelle, Étude de transitions laser couplées dans un mélange hélium-néon, *Compt. Rend.* **258**, 1452–1454, 1964.

7. D. Rosenberger, Oscillation of three $3p - 2s$ transitions in a He-Ne laser, *Phys. Lett.* **9**, 29–31, 1964.

8. R. der Agobian, R. Cagnard, R. Echard, and J. L. Otto, Nouvelle cascade de transitions stimulées du néon, *Compt. Rend.* **258**, 3661–3663, 1964.

9. C. K. N. Patel, Optical power output in He-Ne and pure Ne maser, *J. Appl. Phys.* **33**, 3194–3195, 1962.

10. R. der Agobian, J. L. Otto, R. Cagnard, and R. Echard, Cascades de transitions stimulées dans le néon pur, *Compt. Rend.* **259**, 323–326, 1964.

11. W. L. Faust and R. A. McFarlane, Line strengths for noble-gas maser transitions; Calculations of gain/inversion at various wavelengths, *J. Appl. Phys.* **35**, 2010–2015, 1964.

12. W. R. Bennett, Jr., Gaseous optical masers, *Appl. Optics Suppl.* **1**, 24–61, 1962.

13. E. I. Gordon and A. D. White, Similarity laws for the effects of pressure and discharge diameter on gain of He-Ne lasers, *Appl. Phys. Lett.* **3**, 199–201, 1963.

14. A. D. White, E. I. Gordon, and J. D. Rigden, Output power of the 6328 Å gas maser, *Appl. Phys. Lett,* **2**, 91–93, 1963.

15. I. M. Belousova, O. B. Danilov, and I. A. Elkina, Optimum operating mode of a He-Ne laser, *Soviet Phys. JETP* **17**, 748–749, 1963 (**44**, 1111–1113, 1963).

16. D. R. Herriott, Optical properties of a continuous He-Ne optical maser, *J. Opt. Soc. Am.* **52**, 31–37, 1962; *Appl. Optics Suppl.* **1**, 118–124, 1962.

17. W. W. Rigrod, H. Kogelnik, D. J. Brangaccio, and D. R. Herriott, Gaseous optical maser with external concave mirrors, *J. Appl. Phys.* **33**, 743–744, 1962.

18. A. Javan, E. A. Ballik, and W. L. Bond, Frequency characteristics of a continuous wave helium-neon optical maser, *J. Opt. Soc. Am.* **52**, 96–98, 1962.

19. T. S. Jaseja, A. Javan, and C. H. Townes, Frequency stability of He-Ne masers and measurements of length, *Phys. Rev. Lett.* **10**, 165–167, 1963.

5. NOBLE GAS LASERS

The observation of stimulated emission in noble gases requires a laser structure described in Section V.4 in connection with the He-Ne laser. Interchangeable mirrors are usually provided, each set peaked for reflection in a narrow spectral region. Such mirrors enable the experimenter to concentrate on a relatively narrow region of the spectrum and avoid the excitation of unwanted oscillations. The spectral selectivity of the apparatus may be further increased by incorporating a dispersive prism between the discharge tube and one of the reflectors, which must then be placed perpendicular to the rays deviated by the prism. The experiments generally require longer tubes than those used for the excitation of the common

He-Ne lines because the gain obtainable is generally lower. Many lines were discovered with tubes 2.25 meters long. The occurrence of stimulated emission is usually inferred from the directional characteristics of the radiation emerging from the ends of the tube and from the effects on the output intensity of the blocking of the mirror opposite the output.

Noble gas lasers have He, Ne, Ar, Kr, and Xe atoms or ions as their working material. We shall discuss the operation of lasers based on radiation emitted from neutral atoms first. For a tabulation of these lines see Appendix A.2.

Helium was observed to emit a 2.0603-μ line in a $7\,^3D \rightarrow 4\,^3P$ transition [1, 2], and a 1.9543-μ line in a $4\,^3P \rightarrow 3\,^3D$ transition [3]. The conditions for the stimulated emission of these two lines are naturally different; in one case the population of the $4\,^3P$ level should be maximized, in the other minimized. The optimal pressure for the excitation of the 2.06-μ line is 8 torr, for that of the 1.95-μ line 0.3 torr.

Neon lines observed in stimulated emission number about 130. Some of these lines were reported to have been observed in He-Ne mixtures only, but generally the Ne lines which are found in these mixtures can be produced in pure Ne also, provided that longer tubes are used and precautions are taken to minimize losses. In principle any spectral line is a potential laser line provided that a practical way is found to create a population inversion for the relevant pair of levels. Consequently the task of making a list of "laser lines" is like the task of making a list of cities with parking problems. All cities can get on the list if drivers can be induced to congregate in them. In the case of neon the creation of population inversion is facilitated by certain near-coincidences between He and Ne levels. Some of these were already introduced in Section V.4. The pertinent numerical data are as follows:

He level		Neon level group	
Symbol	Energy (cm^{-1})	Paschen symbol	Energy (cm^{-1})
$2\,^3S$	159,850	$2s$	158,600–159,540
$2\,^1S$	166,272	$3s$	165,830–166,660
$2\,^1P$	171,129	$6p$	171,010–171,910

Transfer of excitation from He materially aids the operation of lasers with transitions originating at some of the $2s$, $3s$, and $6p$ levels of Ne. The visible 6328-Å laser and the strong 3.39-μ laser belong in this group together with the fourteen near infrared laser lines resulting from $2s \rightarrow 2p$ transitions. In the far infrared region six lines were found between 35.6 and 57.4 μ which result from $6p \rightarrow 6d$ transitions. Stimulated emission in all these lines is aided by the admixture of He. On the other hand the presence of He tends to inhibit lines originating at $5p$ (Paschen) levels [4].

Neon laser lines between 1 and 20 μ are shown graphically in Figs. 85 and 86. The visible lines lie outside the range of the graph, as do numerous lines between 20 and 133 μ. Most of the neon laser lines were observed by Faust, Garrett, McFarlane, and Patel of Bell Telephone Laboratories. Their publications contain a wealth of information about stimulated emission from all noble gases [4, 5, 6, 7].

The laser lines originating from complete atoms of Ar, Kr, and Xe are also shown in Figs. 85 and 86 with the single exception of the 26.944-μ line of Ar. Many laser lines of the heavier gases originate at d levels, while in Ne the lower-lying s and p levels seem to be favored as starting levels.

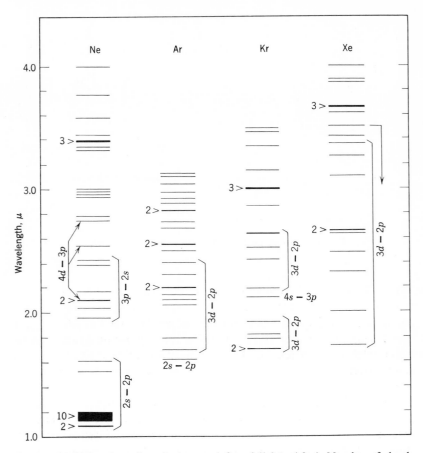

Fig. 85. Noble gas laser lines in the near infrared (1.0 to 4.0 μ). Number of closely spaced lines is indicated when they cannot be shown separately. (For He lasers see ext.)

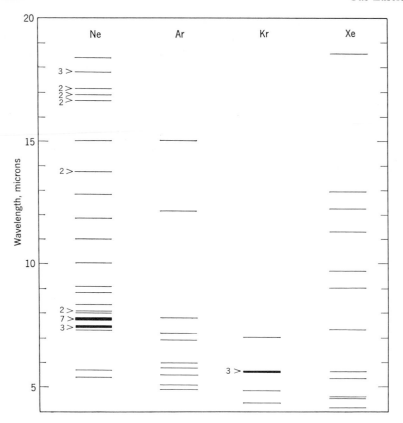

Fig. 86. Noble gas laser lines in the 4-μ to 20-μ range.

Two Xe lasers are worth special notice because of their high gain. In a mixture of Xe (0.02 torr) and He (2 torr) contained in a 5- to 7-mm diameter tube a gain of 1 per cent per cm was obtained at 2.0262 μ [8]. There is no transfer of excitation from He; the improvement caused by He is due solely to an increase in the electron density in the discharge. Under similar operating conditions a gain of 13 per cent per cm is obtained at 3.507 μ [9].

Laser oscillations have been observed on many lines of the *ionized noble gases*. The noble gas ion lasers cover the entire visible spectrum and extend into the near ultraviolet. This copious treasure of visible lasers was discovered almost simultaneously by Bridges at Hughes Research Laboratories [10] and by Gordon and Labuda at Bell Telephone Laboratories. The joint publication of their results represents a notable instance of scientific cooperation among competing laboratories [11]. Additional lines were found by Dana and Laures [12].

Excitation of ionic laser lines requires a discharge with a current density much larger than that necessary for the excitation of the atomic lasers. The higher density is necessary because in singly ionized gas lasers the upper laser level is probably populated by two successive electron collisions; the first produces an unexcited ion from the neutral atom, while the second

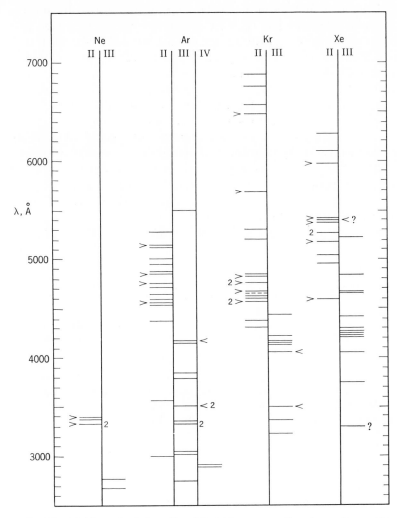

Fig. 87. Noble gas ionic laser lines [12, 14.]   > : strong line. 2: two lines within 10 Å. (A 7993-Å line of Kr II is not shown.)

excites the ion to the upper laser level. This two-step process is deduced from the observed proportionality of the spontaneous emission from the upper level to the square of the discharge current.

The laser configuration is similar to the one used for neutral noble gases. Provision must be made, however, for the passage of very high currents through the discharge tube. This is accomplished by means of a d-c discharge with a heated cathode. Usually the operation is intermittent; the discharge can be powered using a capacitor charged to a potential of 2 to 10 kV. Maximum currents of 40 to 300 amperes were used with tubes around 4 mm in diameter [10, 13, 14]. Continuous operation is possible in many lines with smaller currents passing through narrower tubes [11].

Figure 87 shows the ionic noble gas lasers following the compilation of Bridges and Chester [14], whose paper contains a detailed analysis of the transitions believed responsible for the observed oscillations. The notations of the figure follow the standard spectroscopic practice of designating with Roman numerals II, III, and IV the singly, doubly, and triply ionized spectra, the numeral I being reserved for the spectrum of the neutral atom. The figure is to be taken as an illustration of the state of knowledge near the end of 1964. The rate of discovery of ionic laser lines is rapid and the identification of many lines is subject to revision. It is therefore impractical to print tables of ionic laser lines in a book to be published in 1965. For a tabulation and classification of such lines the reader is referred to the cited paper of Bridges and Chester as well as to their review article [15].

REFERENCES

1. C. K. N. Patel, W. R. Bennett, Jr., W. L. Faust, and R. A. McFarlane, Infrared spectroscopy using stimulated emission techniques, *Phys. Rev. Lett.* **9**, 102–104, 1962.
2. W. R. Bennett, Jr., Gaseous optical masers, *Appl. Optics Suppl.* **1**, 24–61, 1962.
3. R. Cagnard, R. der Agobian, R. Echard, and J. L. Otto, L'émission stimulée de quelques transitions infrarouges de l'helium et du néon, *Compt. Rend.* **257**, 1044–1047, 1963.
4. C. K. N. Patel, W. L. Faust, R. A. McFarlane and C. G. B. Garrett, Laser action up to 57.355 microns in gaseous discharges, *Appl. Phys. Lett.* **4**, 18–19, 1964.
5. W. L. Faust, R. A. McFarlane, C. K. N. Patel, and C. G. B. Garrett, Gas maser spectroscopy in the infrared, *Appl. Phys. Lett.* **1**, 85–88, 1962.
6. W. L. Faust, R. A. McFarlane, C. K. N. Patel, and C. G. B. Garrett, Noble gas optical maser lines at wavelengths between 2 and 35 microns, *Phys. Rev.* **133**, A1477–1486, 1964.
7. C. K. N. Patel, W. L. Faust, R. A. McFarlane, and C. G. B. Garrett, Cw optical maser action up to 133 μ in Ne discharges, *Proc. IEEE* **52**, 713, 1964.
8. C. N. K. Patel, W. L. Faust, and R. A. McFarlane, High gain gaseous (Xe-He) optical masers, *Appl. Phys. Lett.* **1**, 84–85, 1962.
9. R. A. Paananen and D. L. Bobroff, Very high gain gaseous (Xe-He) optical maser at 3.5 μ, *Appl. Phys. Lett.* **2**, 99–100, 1963.

10. W. B. Bridges, Laser oscillation in simply ionized argon in the visible spectrum, *Appl. Phys. Lett.* **4**, 128–130, 1964.
11. E. I. Gordon, E. F. Labuda, and W. B. Bridges, Continuous visible laser action in singly ionized Ar, Kr, and Xe, *Appl. Phys. Lett.* **4**, 178–180, 1964.
12. L. Dana and P. Laures, Stimulated emission in krypton and xenon ions in collision with metastable atoms, *Proc. IEEE* **53**, 78–79, 1965.
13. W. B. Bridges, Laser action in singly ionized krypton and xenon, *Proc. IEEE* **52**, 843, 1964.
14. W. B. Bridges and A. N. Chester, Visible and ultraviolet laser oscillation at 118 wavelengths in ionized Ne, Ar, Kr, Xe, O, and other gases, *Appl. Optics* **4**, 573–580, 1965.
15. W. B. Bridges and A. N. Chester, Spectroscopy of ion lasers, *IEEE J. of Quantum Electronics* **1**, 66–84, 1965.

6. MISCELLANEOUS GAS LASERS

Electric discharges in gases have produced a large variety of laser lines in many substances. The discovery of lasers outside the noble gas group began in 1963; during the year 1964 new materials and lines were reported every month. The knowledge available about these lasers varies over a wide range. At best not only is the line identified but a model is available which explains the occurrence of population inversion on the basis of the physical processes taking place in the discharge, taking into account the rates of the processes involved. In a less favorable situation the transition responsible for the line is identified and general conjectures are available concerning the processes that contribute to the inversion of population of the relevant levels. There are laser lines whose origin is in doubt, most frequently because the measurements of wavelength were not carried out with an accuracy sufficient to distinguish between two transitions of nearly equal energy difference. At worst, there is doubt even concerning the element from which the line originates. Very intensive work is in progress in this field and it seems too early to attempt a systematic organization of this subject in 1964. We shall therefore confine ourselves to a rather sketchy summary of the principal observations.

The material is divided into the following groups:

1. Laser lines in C, N, and O obtained on dissociation of diatomic and polyatomic molecules.
2. Laser lines in atoms and ions of halogens, S, and Hg; lines of ionized atoms. In these substances direct electron impact seems to be the essential factor.
3. Laser lines associated with molecular transitions.

Dissociative Excitation

The principle of dissociative excitation on collision with excited atoms has already been discussed in Section V.1. The best-explored systems in which this process leads to population inversion and laser action are Ne-O_2 and Ar-O_2. The processes are different for the two noble gases; both are illustrated in Fig. 88. The energy levels of oxygen are shown in this figure as reckoned from the lowest bound state of the O_2 molecule, which is 5.080 eV below the ground state of the two O atoms removed from each other. The lowest excited ($1s$) states of Ne and Ar are also shown on the diagram; they are indicated as Ne* and Ar*. Transfer from the Ne* levels leads directly to an unstable molecular level from which the molecule dissociates with one of the oxygen atoms in the starting level ($3p\,^3P_2$) of the laser. In the case of Ar the transfer takes place to two lower-lying levels: $2p\,^1D_2$ and $2p\,^1S_0$. These are metastable; radiative transition from these levels to the triplet ground level is forbidden by the selection rules. Because of their metastable nature, these levels become heavily populated, they become platforms from which the $3p\,^3P_2$ level can be reached by electron impact. The selection rules indicate that population inversion between the

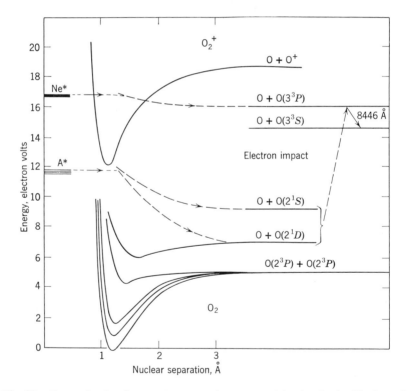

Fig. 88. Energy levels of oxygen, neon, and argon participating in the Ne-O_2 and Ar-O_2 lasers. (Curves represent energies of a common electronic state.)

$3p\,{}^3P_2$ and $3s\,{}^3S_1{}^0$ levels cannot be established by electron collision alone, i.e., without the assistance of a noble gas, because the transition from the ground ${}^3P_2$ level to the $3s\,{}^3S_1{}^0$ level is more likely than a transition to the $3p\,{}^3P_2$ level, the latter being forbidden by the parity rule. The selection rule is directly applicable to the so-called electric dipole transition probabilities only, but it can be shown that electron excitation probabilities are roughly proportional to probabilities of electric dipole transitions.

Bennett, Faust, McFarlane, and Patel [1], who discovered the OI laser and analyzed the processes involved, obtained stimulated emission of the 8446-Å line from an rf discharge in a tube 2 meters long and 7 mm in diameter. The composition of the gas was O_2, 0.014 torr; Ne, 0.35 torr; or alternatively O_2, 0.036 torr; Ar, 1.3 torr. The output power was about 2 mW in each case. The same radiation is also obtainable upon the dissociation of CO, CO_2, NO, and N_2O in the presence of noble gases [2]. Laser radiation of the CI and NI lines may also be obtained from these compounds. The characteristics of the lines observed are as follows [2]:

Spectrum	Wavelength	Transition
CI	$1.0689\ \mu$	$3p\ {}^3D_3 \rightarrow 3s\ {}^3P_2{}^0$
CI	$1.4539\ \mu$	$3p\ {}^1P_1 \rightarrow 3s\ {}^1P_1{}^0$
NI	$1.3583\ \mu$	$3p\ {}^2S_{1/2}{}^0 \rightarrow 3s\ {}^2P_{3/2}$
NI	$1.4544\ \mu$	$4s\ {}^4P_{5/2} \rightarrow 3p\ {}^2D_{5/2}{}^0$

The details of the processes which generate these radiations are not as well explored as those which produce the 8446-Å oxygen line.

Miscellaneous Atomic Lasers

A large number of laser lines have been observed in discharges containing the mixture of an ordinary gas and a noble gas. In some instances an energy transfer from a noble gas to a molecule may be involved, but this is not established with any degree of certainty. It is quite possible that the beneficial effect of the noble gas is more indirect. We confine ourselves to a summary of the experimental results, noting that in most of the cases described the direct electron impact seems to play a major role in the creation of population inversion.

Sulfur. Two lines of SI were obtained from a mixture of SF_6 (0.03 torr) and He (2 torr), or with less efficiency from SF_6 alone [2]:

Wavelength	Transition
$1.0455\ \mu$	$4p\ {}^3P_2 \rightarrow 4s\ {}^3S_1{}^0,$
$1.0628\ \mu$	$4p'\ {}^1F_3 \rightarrow 4s'\ {}^1D_2{}^0.$

Halogens. The structure of the complete halogen atoms is identical to that of the singly ionized noble gases; therefore the discussion of Section

V.2 is applicable to them. We confine the detailed discussion to the laser lines of complete halogen atoms and refer the reader interested in ionic lines to the review article of Bridges and Chester entitled "Spectroscopy of Ion Lasers."[*]

Paananen, Tang, and Horrigan [3] observed two laser lines in an rf-excited discharge in a chlorine-helium mixture. The observations were made in a 1.75-meter-long, 6-mm-diameter tube; the optimal pressures were chlorine 0.1 torr, helium 1.5 torr. Bockasten [4] classified the observed lines as follows:

Wavelength	Transition
1.9755μ	$3d\ ^4D_{7/2} \rightarrow 4p\ ^4P_{5/2}{}^o$,
2.0199μ	$3d\ ^4D_{5/2} \rightarrow 4p\ ^4P_{3/2}{}^o$.

McFarlane [5] obtained nine laser lines of Cl II in a pulsed discharge operating a 1-meter-long tube with a peak current in excess of 500 amperes. The wavelengths extend from 4781 Å to 6095 Å and the radiation is attributed to a series of $4p \rightarrow 4s$ transitions.

The iodine laser lines observed by Rigden and White [6] were classified by Bockasten [4] transitions in I I:

Wavelength	Transition
3.236μ	$5d[2]_{5/2} \rightarrow 6p[1]_{3/2}$,
3.431μ	$5d[4]_{7/2} \rightarrow 6p[3]_{5/2}$.[†]

Fowles and Jensen [7, 8] observed 12 laser lines from a pulsed discharge in an iodine-helium mixture. These lines extend from 4987 Å to 8804 Å and are attributed to I II.

In an rf discharge containing 0.09 torr Br and 1.8 torr Ar, laser action takes place at four very closely placed wavelengths between 8446 Å and 8447 Å. This may arise as a consequence of an excitation transfer from Ar to the Br_2 molecule similar to the process encountered in $O_2[2]$. The laser transition is $5p\,^4D_{3/2}{}^o \rightarrow 5s\,^4P_{3/2}$.

Mercury. A variety of laser oscillations can be obtained from electric discharges containing mercury and a noble gas. The radiation is generated by stimulated transitions in complete mercury atoms and by similar transitions in singly or doubly ionized mercury. The discharges are produced in tubes similar to those described in connection with noble gas lasers; internal electrodes and d-c excitation are recommended, but rf excitation of Hg I lines is possible. The stronger lines can be produced in

---

[*] Ref. 15, Section V.5, p. 207.

[†] The notation for the iodine levels is the one used in the most complete tables of Minnhagen (*Ark. f. Fysik* **21**, 415, 1962).

tubes about 7 mm in diameter and 1 meter long; weaker lines require longer tubes.

The optimum pressure for Hg I lasers is 0.2 to 0.3 torr Hg and about 1 torr noble gas; Hg II and Hg III lasers operate best at about 0.001 torr Hg and 0.5 torr He or other noble gas. The mercury pressure is regulated by heating the tube to the required moderate temperature. The high current (10 to 50 amperes) required for the ionic lasers is usually produced by discharging a condenser through the tube. The different laser lines do not appear simultaneously; their evolution indicates that different processes progressing at different rates are responsible for the population inversions which produce them.

The first Hg lasers were described by Rigden and White [6]; the most accurate spectroscopic work in this field was done by groups of investigators at the Cie Générale de Télégraphie [9, 10], Raytheon Co. [11], and Spectra Physics [12]. The literature contains inaccurate data and erroneous conclusions concerning the transitions that may be involved. A critical examination of the published material and the application of spectroscopic selection and intensity rules leads to the following classification of the Hg I lines observed in stimulated emission [13]:

Wavelength*	Transition
1.1177 μ	$7p\,^1P_1^o \rightarrow 7s\,^3S_1$
1.3674 μ	$7p\,^3P_1^o \rightarrow 7s\,^3S_1$
1.5296 μ	$6p'\,^3P_2^o \rightarrow 7s\,^3S_1$
1.6920 μ	$5f\,^1F_3^o \rightarrow 6d\,^1D_2$
1.6942 μ	$5f\,^3F_2^o \rightarrow 6d\,^3D_1$
1.7073 μ	$5f\,^3F_4^o \rightarrow 6d\,^3D_3$
1.7110 μ	$5f\,^3F_3^o \rightarrow 6d\,^3D_2$
1.7330 μ	$7d\,^1D_2 \rightarrow 7p\,^1P_1^o$
1.8130 μ	$6p'\,^3F_4^o \rightarrow 6d\,^3D_3$
3.93 μ	$\begin{cases} 6d\,^3D_3 \rightarrow 6p'\,^3P_2^o \\ 5g\,G \rightarrow 5f\,F^o \end{cases}$
5.86 μ	$6p'\,^1P_1^o \rightarrow 7d\,^3D_2$
6.49 μ	$\begin{cases} 9s\,^1S_0 \rightarrow 8p\,^1P_1^o \\ 11p\,^3P_1^o \rightarrow 10s\,^3S_1 \end{cases}$

A 3.34-μ line observed in a Hg-Kr mixture and erroneously attributed to Hg I is probably the 3.341-μ Kr I line.

* The values listed are wavelengths in air consistent with energy levels calculated from spontaneous emission spectroscopy. Exceptions are made for the tenth and twelfth lines of Hg. For these lines, whose classifications are uncertain, the best experimental values are listed.

At least ten laser lines were observed in pulsed mercury discharges which are definitely attributable to mercury ions.

Ions of Atmospheric Gases. About thirty laser lines have been obtained in high-current pulsed discharges in various constituents of air [14]. They were identified as O_{II}, O_{III}, C_{III}, C_{IV}, N_{II}, N_{III}, and N_{IV} lines. Their wavelengths cover the entire visible spectrum.

Transitions in Molecular Spectra

Stimulated emission has been observed in the band spectra of N_2, CO, and CO_2. They are excited in high-current, pulsed discharges. The oscillations in N_2 are very strong; they can be excited in tubes only 40 cm long with gas pressure over 1 torr. The N_2 lines are parts of the band spectrum; they fall into six groups in the following wavelength regions: 7580–7620 Å, 7700–7750 Å, 8683–8710 Å, 8844–8910 Å, 10,450–10,505 Å, 12,300–12,350 Å. A peak power output of 100 watts was obtained from the first two groups of oscillations [15, 16].

Four groups of CO radiation were observed in stimulated emission in the following regions: 5186–5198 Å, 5590–5604 Å, 6063–6074 Å, 6595–6614 Å. Peak power output varied from group to group with a maximum of 8 watts in a group, a value which can probably be exceeded by optimizing experimental conditions [16, 17].

Similar laser action at 9.40 μ and 10.41 μ has been obtained from CO_2 [18].

These molecular laser lines seem to have their origin in nonstationary population inversions. Their mechanisms are very actively investigated.

REFERENCES

1. W. R. Bennett, Jr., W. L. Faust, R. A. McFarlane, and C. K. N. Patel, Dissociative excitation transfer and optical maser oscillation in Ne-O_2 and Ar-O_2 rf discharges, *Phys. Rev. Lett.* **8**, 470–473, 1962.
2. C. K. N. Patel, R. A. McFarlane, and W. L. Faust, Optical maser action in C, N, O, S, and Br on dissociation of diatomic and polyatomic molecules, *Phys. Rev.* **133**, A1244–1248, 1964.
3. R. A. Paananen, C. L. Tang, and F. A. Horrigan, Laser action in Cl_2 and He-Cl_2, *Appl. Phys. Lett.* **3**, 154–155, 1963.
4. K. Bockasten, On the classification of laser line in Cl and I, *Appl. Phys. Lett.* **4**, 118–119, 1964.
5. R. A. McFarlane, Optical maser oscillations on iso-electronic transitions in Ar_{III} and Cl_{II}, *Appl. Optics* **3**, 1196, 1964.
6. J. D. Rigden and A. D. White, Optical maser action in I and Hg discharges, *Nature* **198**, 774, 1963.
7. G. R. Fowles and R. C. Jensen, Visible laser transitions in singly ionized iodide, *Appl. Optics* **3**, 1191–1192, 1964.
8. R. C. Jensen and G. R. Fowles, New laser transitions in iodine-inert gas mixture, *Proc. IEEE* **52**, 1350, 1964.

9. M. Armand and P. Martinot-Lagarde, Effet laser sur la vapeur de mercure dans un mélange He-Hg, *Compt. Rend.* **258**, 867–868, 1964.

10. G. Convert, M. Armand, and P. Martinot-Lagarde, Effet laser dans des mélanges mercure-gaz rares, *Compt. Rend.* **258**, 3259–3260, 1964.

11. R. A. Paananen, C. L. Tang, I. A. Horrigan, and H. Statz, Optical maser action in He-Hg r-f discharges, *J. Appl. Phys.* **34**, 3148, 1963.

12. A. L. Bloom, W. E. Bell, and F. O. Lopez, Laser spectroscopy of a pulsed Hg-He discharge, *Phys. Rev.* **135**, A578–579, 1964.

13. K. Bockasten, M. Garavaglia, B. A. Lengyel, and T. Lundholm, Laser lines in Hg I, *J. Opt. Soc. Am.* **55**, 1051–1053, 1965.

14. R. A. McFarlane, Laser oscillation on visible and ultraviolet transitions of ionized O, C, and N, *Appl. Phys. Lett.* **5**, 91–93, 1964.

15. L. E. S. Mathias and J. T. Parker, Stimulated emission in the band spectrum of N_2, *Appl. Phys. Lett.* **3**, 16–18, 1963.

16. P. K. Cheo and H. G. Cooper, Excitation mechanisms of population inversion in CO and N_2 pulsed lasers, *Appl. Phys. Lett.* **5**, 42–44, 1964.

17. L. E. S. Mathias and J. T. Parker, Visible laser oscillations from CO, *Phys. Lett.* **7**, 194–196, 1963.

18. C. K. N. Patel, Interpretation of CO_2 optical maser experiments, *Phys. Rev. Lett.* **12**, 588–590, 1964.

VI

Variation of Laser Oscillations in Space and Time

1. MODE STRUCTURE AND RADIATION PATTERN

The theory of mode structure was outlined in Chapter II, and a number of basic facts concerning mode structure were included in the general description of the ruby (Section III.1) and the helium-neon laser (Section V.4). Here we summarize general experience and supplement the material already presented, with emphasis on discoveries made during the years 1962 to 1964.

Experience concerning the mode structure of solid lasers derives mostly from the ruby. The mode structure of gaseous lasers has been studied on He-Ne lasers at the wavelengths 1.15 μ and 6328 Å. For the modes of the gas laser diffraction effects are significant; for the modes of the ruby laser they are not. This is perhaps the greatest difference in principle. In practice, there are many factors which require entirely different techniques for the study of the modes of ruby and those of neon. The gas laser is more easily studied because we can view the radiation in a steady-state condition. It is easier to vary the mirrors, their alignment, and the distance between them, and it is not particularly difficult to introduce diaphragms between the reflectors. One of the greatest obstacles in studying the modes of the ruby laser is the preparation of a sufficiently perfect crystal with strictly parallel terminal surfaces and a uniform reflecting coating; the greatest frustration occurs when two apparently identically prepared crystals exhibit differing mode structures under identical conditions of excitation.

Observations of mode and pattern structure are made under a variety of conditions, some at high-power levels, some barely above threshold. The measurements pertain to the angular distribution of the beam in the far field, the distribution of intensity at the exit mirror of the laser, the frequency of the emitted radiation, and the power output. For pulse-excited lasers, all these quantities vary in time; we are concerned not only with their time averages but with their correlations as well. The variations of these parameters and their correlations from one situation to another are interpreted in terms of the mode structure of the radiation field present in the laser. The distribution of radiative energy among the different modes within the laser determines the spectral distribution, angular divergence, and power of the laser output. The characteristics that are often desired of a laser, i.e., maximum power output, minimum beam divergence, and narrowest spectral distribution of energy, are generally incompatible requirements. Their incompatibility becomes apparent if one contemplates their relationships to the mode structure. The highest output power is obtained when the process of stimulated emission reduces the population inversion to its minimum level uniformly across the entire useful portion of the spontaneous emission linewidth and the entire body of the laser material. Minimum angular divergence is obtained when only modes having equal transverse configurations are excited. Least spectral width (highest monochromaticity) is obtained when only one mode is excited.

Under uncontrolled conditions many modes are excited either simultaneously or consecutively, with a resulting variation of the output characteristics of the laser. The situation is considerably different in solid lasers typified by ruby and in gaseous lasers typified by He-Ne. It is practical to discuss these types separately.

Mode Structure of Ruby Lasers

One of the most conspicuous properties of the ruby laser is the fluctuation of its output within the duration of a single exciting pulse. The irregular pulsations of intensity which were already mentioned in Chapter III will be discussed in detail in the next section. At present we are primarily interested in the spatial variation of the radiation characteristics. The fluctuations of intensity in time are relevant to the present topic insofar as they may be produced by shifting from one mode to another.

Radiation of the same frequency may be emitted from modes having different transverse configurations. Consider the ruby laser as a Fabry-Perot interferometer. Clearly a whole series of rings in the far-field pattern corresponds to radiation of the same wavelength; each ring corresponds to a path difference greater by one wavelength than the preceding ring. The question arises: Do modes of common frequency radiate coherently? The interference experiments of Abella and Townes [1] answer this question in the affirmative. Interference patterns can be obtained from apertures transmitting radiation from different rings.

For one and the same transverse mode configuration oscillations may occur at different frequencies corresponding to various numbers of half-wavelengths between reflecting terminals. All frequencies must lie within the spectral range for which the threshold is exceeded. We calculated in Chapter II that the frequency difference of adjacent modes (of the same transverse configuration) is $c/2L$, where c is the velocity of light in the material and L the distance of the reflectors. The index of refraction of ruby is 1.76, so that for a 5-cm ruby rod Δv is 1700 Mc/sec. Such frequency differences were observed by mixing experiments (Chapter III). For rubies of this size several difference frequencies are observed in the 7- to 70-Mc range as well [2]. The difference frequencies in the 20- to 70-Mc range correspond to two modes with a common number of axial nodes but different transverse configurations. The difference frequencies around 10 Mc/sec and below seem to result from the splitting of modes, which in an ideal material would produce radiation of a common frequency. The beats can be eliminated by reducing the reflecting surface on one end of the ruby to a very small circle, so that the transverse modes disappear. Other evidence for the identification of the low-frequency beats comes from the observation of confocal ruby resonator rods. A characteristic of a confocal resonator is that its modes are degenerate in frequency; i.e., they can occur only with frequency separations of $c/4L$. For a 5-cm ruby rod the value of $c/4L$ is 854 Mc/sec; therefore no beats should be detected in the 7- to 70-Mc range, and none were found for the confocal rod.

The number of modes excited increases as the excitation is increased above threshold. This has been demonstrated by spectroscopic measurements [3] as well as by observations of the luminous spots at the terminal mirrors [4]. It does not follow, however, that a single-mode operation can always be achieved by exciting a laser barely to threshold, nor does it follow that multimoding necessarily occurs when the threshold is exceeded by a few per cent [3]. The excitation of the modes is influenced to a large extent by minor irregularities and asymmetries present in the laser. A general characteristic of mode and pulsation experiments is that only the most homogeneous, uniform crystals produce results which are regular enough for a sensible theoretical analysis. It has already been noted in Chapter III that the mode structure of a ruby undergoing pulsation shifts from one spike to the next.

Many ramifications of the mode structure of ruby are reviewed in an excellent paper of Stickley [2], which is also recommended for further references. The far-field radiation pattern of a high quality ruby laser looks like the pattern of an ordinary Fabry-Perot interferometer illustrated in Fig. 3. The central bright circle is surrounded by rings at angular distances calculable by means of elementary physical optics. For crystals with imperfections or for improperly adjusted mirrors, the symmetry of the pattern is destroyed [5].

Mode Structure of Gas Lasers

Gas lasers are usually provided with circular mirrors having equal spherical curvatures, or with one plane and one spherical mirror. The latter system is reducible to the former, since the plane mirror forms an image of the spherical one. The mirrors are most frequently used in a nearly confocal configuration; the radius of curvature b is nearly equal to the distance L separating the centers of the spherical mirrors. According to the calculations of Boyd and Kogelnik [6] the electric field distribution across the mirrors has the form

$$E(\rho, \theta) = E_0 r^q L_p{}^q(r^2) \exp(-r^2) \cos q\theta, \tag{1.1}$$

where $\rho = (x^2 + y^2)^{1/2}$ is the polar coordinate in the transverse plane, and $r = \rho/w_s$ is the reduced polar coordinate defined in terms of the constant w_s, whose physical meaning is the spot size of the axially symmetric mode

$$w_s = \left(\frac{\lambda b}{\pi}\right)^{1/2} \left(\frac{L}{2b - L}\right)^{1/4}. \tag{1.2}$$

The numbers p and q are integers; $L_p{}^q$ denotes a Laguerre polynomial of order p and index q. The mode with a transverse electric field distribution (1.1) and $n - 1$ nodal planes between the mirrors is called a TEM$_{pqn}$ mode.

A change in the mirror distance affects only the constant w_s. In the special case of a confocal system, $L = b$ and (1.2) reduces to $w_s = (\lambda b/\pi)^{1/2}$, an expression already encountered in Section II.3. The discussion in that chapter was confined to the TEM$_{00n}$ mode of a confocal resonator.

The frequency differences of oscillations in two modes characterized by indices p, q, n and p', q', n' are

$$\Delta\nu = \frac{c}{2L}[\Delta n + (2\Delta p + \Delta q)\pi^{-1} \cos(1 - L/b)].^{\star} \tag{1.3}$$

In the confocal case this reduces to

$$\Delta\nu = \frac{c}{2L}[\Delta n + \Delta p + \Delta q/2], \tag{1.4}$$

where $\Delta n = n - n'$, $\Delta p = p - p'$, and $\Delta q = q - q'$.

The last equation is a generalization of equation (3.18) of Chapter II. It shows the multiple degeneracy of the confocal resonator modes; all frequencies are separated by integral multiples of $c/4L$. The frequency depends only on the sum of $2n + 2p + q$. An additional degeneracy not

---

$\star$ The equation is valid for small $|b - L|/b$.

apparent from (1.3) and (1.4) is due to the fact that one may replace $\cos q\theta$ in (1.1) with $\sin q\theta$. When q is an odd integer a new geometrical configuration results whose frequency is the same as that of the original mode. When the distance of the mirrors is changed from the confocal position,

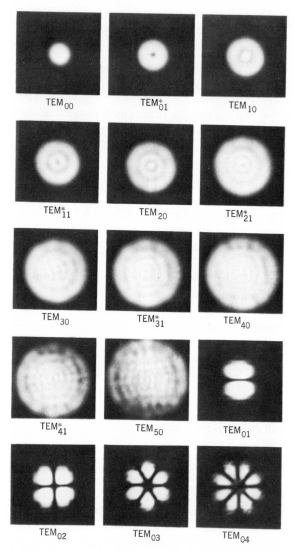

Fig. 89. Axi-symmetrical modes of a concave mirror interferometer. Asterisk designates two degenerate modes combining in space and phase quadrature to form a circularly symmetric mode [7]. (Courtesy Bell Telephone Laboratories.)

and $b \neq L$, the mode degeneracy is partly lifted. In this case all modes with a common n and a common value of $2p + q$ still have the same frequency.

Figure 89 is the photograph of radiation patterns obtained from a He-Ne laser (1.15) operating in 15 axi-symmetric modes. They were obtained by Rigrod [7] with a semiconcave resonator. The reader accustomed to seeing similar pictures showing the lines of electric and magnetic fields in circular transmission lines is warned that the photographs represent the intensity distribution in the far field obtained with light of horizontal polarization.

The circularly symmetric modes ($q = 0$) were isolated by adjusting the diameter of a circular aperture on the optical axis; the modes with azimuthal periodicity ($q = 1, 2, 3$, and 4) were isolated by means of two straight wires crossing the optic axis at appropriate angles, and suitable adjustment of the diameter of the circular aperture. When the circular aperture is accurately centered on the optic axis at either mirror, a small opening admits the fundamental TEM_{00} mode first. As the aperture size is increased, this mode becomes distorted and is replaced by the next higher mode in a smooth transition. This process is repeated for each of the circularly symmetric modes; all lower-order modes are replaced by the highest-order mode permitted by the diffraction losses of the aperture and the available laser gain, despite the fact that diffraction losses are lower for lower-order modes.

Rigrod suggests that a possible explanation of this unexpected dominance of the highest-order axi-symmetric mode may lie in the ability of the highest mode to utilize the available population inversion over a larger volume of the laser than is possible for lower-order modes.

The patterns of Fig. 89 are obtained only when utmost care is taken to maintain axial symmetry. This is difficult to do because of the presence of the exit windows oriented at the Brewster angle. It is easier to obtain the radiation patterns of modes that correspond to rectangular symmetry. These are shown in Fig. 90. They were obtained by Kogelnik and Rigrod [8] with a nearly spherical cavity $L \approx 2b = 130$ cm. The indexing of the modes here follows rectangular coordinates.

In general the radiation pattern of a laser will not be as regular as the pictures in Figs. 89 and 90 because many modes will oscillate simultaneously. The presence of different modes can be detected by beat frequency and spectroscopic measurements. The beat frequencies of gas lasers are in a more convenient region for detection than those of ruby lasers. In the laser used to produce the patterns of Fig. 90, for example, the lowest frequency of axial modes is 115 Mc/sec, and lower beat frequencies are obtained by mixing axial and nonaxial modes. The observed frequencies are in good agreement with the values calculated [9]. The purity of a mode can be tested by the analysis of the beat frequencies. When modes with a

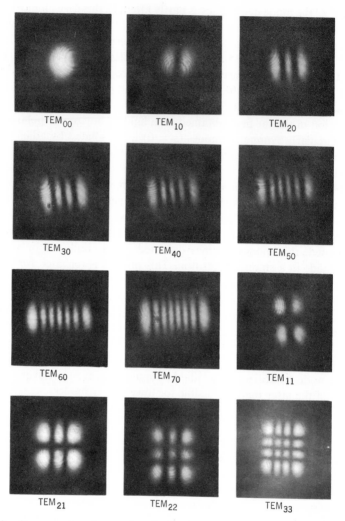

Fig. 90. Some modes of a nearly spherical cavity. All beams are polarized horizontally [8]. (Courtesy Bell Telephone Laboratories.)

common transverse configuration are excited, only the beat notes of frequency $f = c/2L$ and its multiples should be formed. The test is not an absolute one, especially not in the case of the highly degenerate confocal cavity. Spectroscopic measurements provide a more complete picture than beat frequency measurements but they require extremely high resolution. They can be performed with Fabry-Perot interferometers of long spacing.

Such interferometers have a very short spectral range because rings of different orders overlap. In a situation requiring both extreme resolution and an adequately large spectral range compatible with the linewidth of the spontaneous radiation it may be necessary to employ a shorter and a longer interferometer in series. The combination preserves the spectral range of the shorter Fabry-Perot interferometer and the resolution of the longer. Using such techniques, Polanyi and Watson [10, 11] explored the mode spectrum of eight He-Ne lasers operating at 6328 Å, some with plane mirrors, others in confocal or nearer-than-confocal configurations. In a nearly confocal laser 28 simultaneously oscillating modes were detected. Excellent agreement was found between the observed frequencies and those predicted from the theory. The power distribution among the axial modes follows a Gaussian curve centered around the peak of the spontaneous emission line.

REFERENCES

1. I. D. Abella and C. H. Townes, Mode characteristics and coherence in optical masers, *Nature* **192**, 957, 1961.
2. C. M. Stickley, A study of transverse modes of ruby lasers using beat frequency detection and fast photography, *Appl. Optics* **3**, 967–979, 1964.
3. M. Ciftan, A. Krutchkoff, and S. Koozekanani, On the resonant frequency modes of ruby optical masers, *Proc. IRE* **50**, 84–85, 1962.
4. V. Evtuhov and J. K. Neeland, Observations relating to the transverse and longitudinal modes of a ruby laser, *Appl. Optics* **1**, 517–520, 1962.
5. C. M. Stickley, Optical quality and radiation patterns of ruby lasers, *Appl. Optics* **2**, 855–860, 1963.
6. G. D. Boyd and H. Kogelnik, Generalized confocal resonator theory, *Bell Syst. Tech. J.* **41**, 1347–1369, 1962.
7. W. W. Rigrod, Isolation of axi-symmetrical optical resonator modes, *Appl. Phys. Lett.* **2**, 51–53, 1963.
8. H. Kogelnik and W. W. Rigrod, Visual display of isolated optical-resonator modes, *Proc. IRE* **50**, 220, 1962.
9. D. R. Herriott, Optical properties of a continuous He-Ne optical maser, *J. Opt. Soc. Am.* **52**, 31–37, 1962; *Appl. Optics Suppl.* **1**, 118–124, 1962.
10. T. G. Polanyi and W. R. Watson, Gaseous optical maser with external mirrors, *J. Appl. Phys.* **34**, 553–560, 1963.
11. T. G. Polanyi and W. R. Watson, Interferometric investigation of modes in optical gas masers, *J. Opt. Soc. Am.* **54**, 449–454, 1964.

2. PULSATIONS OF THE OUTPUT OF SOLID LASERS

The irregular variation of the ruby laser output has already been noted in Chapter III. The spikes or pulsations of intensity shown in Figs. 26 and 27 (page 92) observed on flash-excited rubies were noted in many four-level solid lasers and in cw ruby lasers as well [1, 2, 3].

The fact that oscillations in the intensity of the output should occur is easily explained qualitatively by the fact that the photon density builds up very rapidly in the laser and that in the presence of a high photon density stimulated transitions will occur at a much faster rate than excitations are supplied. Consequently the population of the upper laser level is depleted below a point where oscillations can be sustained, or at least to a point where the population inversion is replenished faster than it is depleted by the emission of radiation. The resulting fluctuation of intensity had been noticed in connection with masers before the advent of lasers. To explain such intensity fluctuations Statz and De Mars [4] derived a pair of non-linear differential equations linking photon density P (light intensity) with the inversion density N in the material. The inversion density for an idealized maser or laser having two levels with population densities N_1 and N_2 is defined as $N = N_2 - N_1$. Let photons leak out of the material at the constant rate C; then

$$\frac{dP}{dt} = BNP - C. \qquad (2.1)$$

The first term represents the number of photons created per unit volume as a result of stimulated emission. It is proportional to the inversion and to the number of photons already present; B is a constant. If population inversion is created by pumping at the rate A, and it decays in the absence of stimulated emission at the rate $1/\tau$, the rate of change of N is given by

$$\frac{dN}{dt} = A - \frac{N}{\tau} - 2BNP, \qquad (2.2)$$

because the creation of each photon decreases the inversion by 2. Equations (2.1) and (2.2) are the *Statz-De Mars equations* valid for the special case under consideration.

Many attempts were made to obtain solutions of the Statz-De Mars equations which can be correlated with experimental findings. A solution may take the form illustrated in Fig. 91, where P and N are plotted as functions of time. The variable N is renormalized so that the value $N = 1$ corresponds to the threshold of oscillations. When the excitation begins, the value of P is 0 and N has a negative value. Then N begins to increase at a rate determined by the intensity of pumping. As N exceeds 1, the laser becomes unstable and the photon density P builds up until it stimulates the emission of radiation so fast that N starts to decrease. When N reaches 1 again, the electromagnetic energy in the laser cavity reaches its maximum, and it continues to stimulate transitions in the laser material, whose population inversion now sinks below the threshold level. Now P decreases and eventually the population inversion builds up again.

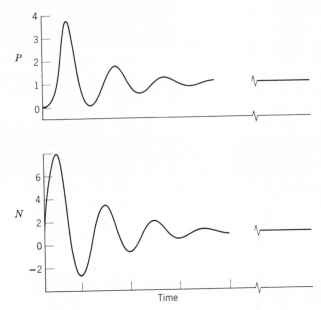

Fig. 91. Time dependence of photon density P and inversion N in a damped oscillation according to the Statz-De Mars equation.

Although the differential equations are not solvable in a closed form, numerical and approximate solutions have been obtained for a variety of values of the parameters. It is relatively simple to obtain "small signal" solutions which are valid for small deviations of N from 1. The calculations quickly lead to rapidly damped oscillations which do not describe the observed phenomena. The main conclusion, based mostly on the theoretical analysis of Makhov [5] and Sinnett [6], is that the differential equations in their simplest form do not admit periodic solutions, but only damped oscillatory ones. Actually, damped as well as undamped oscillations have been observed in some solid lasers. To obtain strictly periodic solutions it is necessary to add to the equations further terms that may be interpreted physically as interactions of various types for which there is little other physical evidence. Another possible way out of the difficulty is to permit each spike to die out and the next one to start from the noise, thus eliminating the requirement for the continuity of the solution. New analytical methods were recently proposed by Korobkin and Uspensky [7], and by Kleinman [8], which lead to approximately periodic solutions.

The appearance of the pulsations as they are observed on ordinary ruby and other solid-state lasers is very irregular and does not seem to resemble the regular curves calculated by Statz and De Mars. We must keep in mind, however, that the mathematical solutions are obtained for a homogeneous and essentially isotropic medium, uniformly excited, oscillating in a simple mode which assures essentially uniform photon density throughout the material. In practice this is never the case. The nonuniformity of radiation density apparent at the end surfaces of the ruby is alone sufficient to invalidate some of the assumptions.

It seems that the relaxation oscillations are very sensitive to small variations of the parameters, and the irregular spikes are formed as a result of the interaction of many oscillations whose amplitude and phase are greatly influenced by the inhomogeneities of the material, the irregularities of the exciting radiation, temperature variations over the solids, and the like. In very homogeneous crystals and under carefully controlled experimental conditions regular pulsations are observed. Figure 92 shows the output of an extremely high quality ruby crystal with multilayer dielectric reflectors. At room temperature the pulse amplitude was about 50 kW and the repetition rate was 200 kc. At reduced temperatures the pulse amplitude approached 100 kW and the repetition rate 500 kc. The record of Fig. 92 was made with a ruby 6.35 cm long and 1 cm in diameter with 80 per cent reflective coating on one end. Similar observations were made on other materials [9].

We can calculate that the time elapsing between successive spikes of regular oscillations is proportional to the square root of the linewidth. This relationship is established by making use of the dependence of gain on linewidth. It is then possible to relate the variation of the repetition rate of the pulsation to the variation of the linewidth with temperature [10].

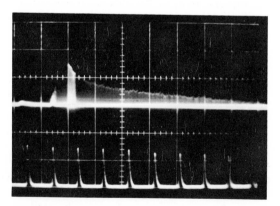

Fig. 92. Regular pulsations in ruby laser output. Time scale: upper—200 μsec/cm; lower—5 μsec/cm. Power scale 5 kw/cm. (Hughes Research Laboratories.)

Although random deviations from perfect uniformity in the laser greatly influence the appearance of the pulsations, they should not be regarded as the cause of pulsations. There are regular and controllable factors of pulsations which will now be examined more closely. Ordinarily oscillations take place in several modes simultaneously and the distribution of energy among the different oscillatory modes varies over time. The exhaustion of population inversion in different parts of the laser is the principal cause of the shift from one oscillatory mode to another, because different oscillatory modes feed on different parts of the laser structure. It has been stated in Chapter I that the probability of stimulated transition is proportional to the density of the radiation field at the site of the atom. This statement is correct in a radiation field consisting of a single plane wave, or in a chaotic field consisting of an *uncorrelated* ensemble of plane waves. When the radiation field consists of a standing wave pattern, the situation must be analyzed more carefully. The interaction of electromagnetic radiation with matter is comprehended microscopically in terms of a perturbation calculation. The major term in this calculation arises from the interaction of the electric field with the electric dipole moment of the atomic system. When the atom is located in a node of the electric field in a standing wave pattern, the stimulated electric dipole radiation is absent. Once radiation is present in a laser, stimulated emission burns holes in the population inversion. The term *hole burning* is frequently used to indicate nonuniform depletion in spatial or frequency distribution. Since the fluorescent linewidth is generally much broader than the linewidth of a laser oscillation in a single mode, the problem of hole burning is often discussed in the frequency domain. It has meaning insofar as atoms capable of emitting in a narrow frequency domain can be identified and distinguished from other atoms capable of emitting in another frequency range of the fluorescent line. Even if atoms can be so identified, there are usually energy exchange processes operating among them, and if these processes act quickly compared with the rate of stimulated transitions, it is not possible to burn a hole in the frequency distribution of population inversion. Whether a hole can be burned in the spatial distribution of population inversion depends on the rate at which the spatial redistribution of energy is accomplished over distances of the order of $\lambda/2$.

Tang, Statz, and De Mars [11] estimated the cross relaxation times in ruby. Their calculations indicate that the holes in the frequency distribution would be filled with a time constant of about 10^{-12} sec, while it would take about 10^{-4} sec for the diffusion of excitation from one Cr ion to the next. From the duration of the spikes in ruby we know that it takes of the order of 10^{-7} sec or less to deplete significantly the population inversion. Thus on theoretical grounds it is not readily possible to burn a hole in the frequency distribution, but it is possible to do so in the spatial distribution because the spatial cross relaxation is too slow a process to smooth out the density of the excited states.

Consider now the oscillation of a ruby laser in a single axial mode. We have then nodal planes of the electric field in planes parallel to the mirrors one-half wavelength apart. The induced emission produced by this standing wave structure is zero in these nodal planes and maximum halfway between them. Consequently the population inversion will develop maxima at the electric field nodes and minima in between. This distribution of the inverted population is most unfavorable for the mode that produced it. Consider now the next axial mode, which has one more half-wavelength between the mirrors, and investigate whether the amplitude of a small oscillation in this mode can grow in the environment determined by the first mode of oscillation. It is readily recognized that the spatial distribution of population inversion is more favorable for the second mode. In the middle of the crystal the maxima of the electric field of this mode and the maxima of population inversion will coincide. The second mode therefore will have a greater gain than the one already excited to a large amplitude; it will go into oscillation and it will overtake the first mode. Similar argument is applicable to the third, fourth, etc. axial mode as long as all the frequencies of these modes lie close together near the peak of the fluorescent line. Tang, Statz, and De Mars [11] have shown that the number of axial modes excited depends on the following parameters:

1. the excess pump power α, defined as

$$\alpha = \frac{p - p_0}{p_1 - p_0},$$

where p is the pumping rate applied and p_0 and p_1 are, respectively, the pumping rates which produce equal population of the two levels ($N = 0$), and the population inversion required for threshold ($N = 1$);

2. the relative mode separation, $\beta = \delta v / \Delta v$, where δv is the frequency separation of adjacent longitudinal modes and Δv is the half-width of the fluorescent line.

Figure 93 shows the number of excited axial modes as a function of α for several values of β. It is practically impossible in an ordinary situation to avoid the excitation of more than one longitudinal mode, and once several modes are excited, energy is fed back and forth between them producing a very irregular composite pattern. It is therefore very interesting to construct a special laser capable of oscillating only in one mode. To achieve this one should avoid the formation of a standing wave pattern. Tang and associates [12, 13] performed interesting experiments with a

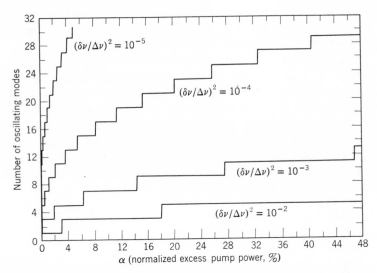

Fig. 93. Number of oscillating modes in a laser for various values of excess pump power; $\delta\nu$ is the separation in frequency between successive longitudinal modes and $2\Delta\nu$ is the emission linewidth. (Reprinted from the *Journal of Applied Physics.*)

traveling wave laser illustrated in Fig. 94. Light originating in the laser is not reversed and sent through the same path in the opposite direction, but is led around the ruby through the 45-degree quartz prisms. It passes through the ruby always in the same direction. If the apparatus consisted only of the ruby and the quartz prisms, light could travel in either direction. To assure the excitation of waves traveling in one direction only, and at the

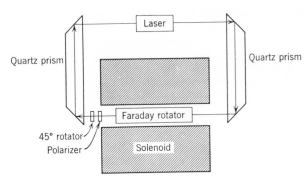

Fig. 94. Solid-state laser with optical isolator for suppression of unwanted multimode oscillations and standing waves. The laser is provided with antireflection coatings on both ends.

same time to assure a single-plane polarization, an optical isolator consisting of a polarizer, a Faraday rotator, and a quartz plate is incorporated in the optical circuit. The quartz plate rotates the plane of polarization by 45 degrees always in the same direction, the Faraday rotator rotates the polarization by plus or minus 45 degrees, depending on the direction of propagation with respect to the magnetic field. With such an apparatus it is possible to achieve single-mode operation of the laser as the regularity of oscillations and the single ring obtainable in a high-resolution Fabry-Perot interferometer show. When the same ruby crystal is used without the optical isolator the pulsations lose their regularity and the Fabry-Perot analysis of the laser output shows the presence of a number of closely and equally spaced frequencies [13].

REFERENCES

1. P. P. Sorokin and M. J. Stevenson, Stimulated infrared emission of trivalent uranium, *Phys. Rev. Lett.* **5**, 557–559, 1960.
2. H. Statz, C. Luck, C. Shafer, and M. Ciftan, Observations on oscillation spikes in multimode lasers, *Advances in Quantum Electronics*, Columbia Univ. Press, New York, 1961, pp. 342–347.
3. D. F. Nelson and W. S. Boyle, A continuously operating ruby optical maser, *Appl. Optics* **1**, 181–183, 1962. (Also *Appl. Optics Suppl.* **1**, 99–101, 1962.)
4. H. Statz and G. de Mars, Transients and oscillation pulses in masers, *Quantum Electronics*, Columbia Univ. Press, New York, 1960, pp. 530–537.
5. G. Makhov, On the problem of pulsed oscillations in ruby maser, *J. Appl. Phys.* **33**, 202–204, 1962.
6. D. M. Sinnett, An analysis of the maser oscillator equations, *J. Appl. Phys.* **33**, 1578–1581, 1962.
7. V. V. Korobkin and A. Uspensky, On the theory of the pulsations in the output of the ruby laser, *Soviet Phys. JETP* **18**, 693–697, 1964 (**45**, 1003–1008, 1963).
8. D. A. Kleinman, The maser rate equations and spiking, *Bell Syst. Tech. J.* **43**, 1505–1532, 1964.
9. E. Bernal, J. F. Ready, and D. Chen, Oscillatory character of $CaWO_4:Nd^{3+}$ laser output, *Proc. IEEE* **52**, 710–711, 1964.
10. H. Weber, Temperaturabhängigkeit der Spikefolgezeit eines Rubin Laser, *Phys. Lett.* **11**, 288, 1964.
11. C. L. Tang, H. Statz, and G. de Mars, Spectral output and spiking behavior of solid-state lasers, *J. Appl. Phys.* **34**, 2289–2295, 1963.
12. C. L. Tang, H. Statz, and G. de Mars, Regular spiking and single-mode operation of ruby laser, *Appl. Phys. Lett.* **2**, 222–224, 1963.
13. C. L. Tang, H. Statz, G. A. de Mars, and D. T. Wilson, Spectral properties of a single-mode ruby laser, *Phys. Rev.* **136**, A1–8, 1964.

3. GIANT PULSE TECHNIQUES

The irregular pulsations of the laser are greatly disturbing for almost any application, especially communications, where the timing and the control of the intensity envelope are particularly important. Fortunately, it is possible to remove these irregularities and at the same time greatly increase the peak intensity by regulating the regeneration in the laser. This method of control was first proposed by Hellwarth [1]. It is accomplished by detaching the reflectors from the ruby and inserting a fast shutter between the ruby and one of the reflectors. With the shutter closed, excitation in the ruby can be built up far above the level of threshold with the shutter open. The shutter is kept closed until a high excitation is reached; when it is opened, the radiation builds up rapidly and all the excess excitation is discharged in an extremely short time. The intensity of the resulting short pulse exceeds that obtainable from an ordinary laser flash by several orders of magnitude. Because of its extremely high power the flash so produced is called the *giant pulse*.

The principle of giant pulse production is readily comprehended with the aid of Fig. 95, which illustrates the essential features of the experimental apparatus of Collins and Kisliuk [2]. The rotating chopper wheel initiates

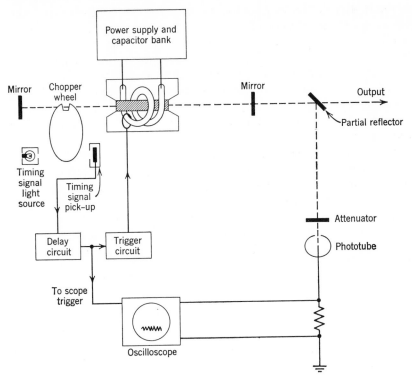

Fig. 95. Generation of a giant pulse with a mechanical chopper.

the firing of the flashlamps and after a suitable time delay, of the order of 1 msec, it opens the optical path between the mirrors. The output of the laser as a function of time is then measured by means of a photocell to which a fraction of the output is diverted.

The various techniques that involve an artificial impairment of the optical path in a laser with the purpose of delaying the onset of laser oscillations are usually referred to as *Q-spoiling*, or *Q-switching*, techniques. The term originates from the theory of resonators in radio engineering; the reason for its use becomes apparent if one contemplates the laser as a cavity resonator.

For reasons of speed and convenience Hellwarth and McClung [3] accomplished *Q*-switching by electro-optical means. In their original experiments they employed a shutter which, in its closed state, greatly diminished regeneration in the laser instead of cutting it off entirely. Their switching scheme exploits the natural polarization of the stimulated emission of ruby which is observed when the optic axis of the ruby does not coincide with the cylinder axis. (See Section III.1.) A schematic diagram of the Hellwarth-McClung laser is shown in Fig. 96. A nitrobenzene Kerr cell is placed between one of the detached reflectors and the ruby rod so that its electric field is applied at 45 degrees to the plane of the ruby *c*-axis. When the electric field of the Kerr cell is turned on to its quarter-wave value, the polarization of the laser light which passes through the cell twice is rotated 90 degrees from the favored plane of polarization. In this situation regeneration is insufficient for oscillations until a much higher level of excitation is reached than is required for oscillations with the Kerr cell absent.

To produce a single giant pulse, the Kerr cell is activated, the exciting flashlamp is fired, and after about 500 μsec the Kerr cell is suddenly turned off in a time less than 0.02 μsec. The resulting pulse shape and timing are reproducible. An oscilloscope trace is shown in Fig. 97. A total peak intensity of 600 kW was reported in the early experiments of Hellwarth and McClung with a ruby cylinder 3 cm long and 0.9 cm in diameter. This figure

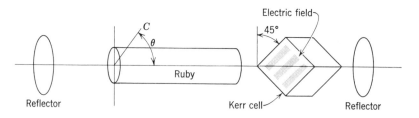

Fig. 96.   Diagram of a giant pulse laser with a Kerr cell.

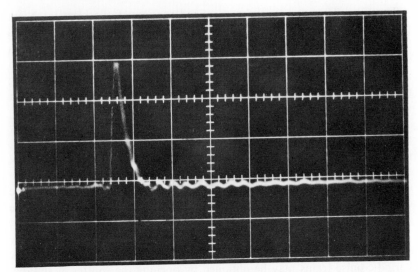

Fig. 97. Oscilloscope trace of a giant pulse laser. Vertical scale: Power output (relative). Horizontal scale: Time (0.1 μsec per cm).

contrasts with a maximum of 6 kW obtainable without the pulsed reflector on cylinders of about the same size. The name "giant pulse" is justified by the surprising increase in power obtainable by this technique. During the year 1962 several investigators obtained peak power outputs from larger lasers in excess of 15 MW, and 100 MW was exceeded by the end of 1963.

Operation of the Kerr cell requires a d-c voltage supply of about 10 kV but almost no current drain. In the interest of fast switching the shutter is kept closed with the voltage applied to the cell, and the shutter is opened by short-circuiting the plates of the cell. In this manner switching may be accomplished in 5 nsec, a time interval much shorter than that required for the evolution of the pulse.

We repeat that the shutter described here is not an "absolute" one which prevents laser action no matter how high the excitation. It only increases the threshold at which oscillations may set in, because at sufficiently high levels of excitation amplification will take place in all polarizations. However, the onset of oscillations is delayed until a higher level of excitation is built up than is possible without the shutter, and when the shutter is opened all the excess is unloaded at once. An absolute electro-optical shutter may be constructed by incorporating a Glan-Thomson prism between the laser rod and the Kerr cell. With this shutter, or with a mechanical one, the level of excitation can be built up higher than with a shutter based on the preferred polarization in the ruby.

The Glan-Thomson prism is a refined version of the classical Nicol polarizer. It permits light of one polarization to pass through and diverts light polarized 90 degrees from the preferred orientation to another path where it can be absorbed. The polarizer is usually cemented together from two prisms and the cement is frequently damaged by the high output; therefore specially constructed polarizers must be used for high-power work.

Note that if the shutter is left open and the exciting flash persists after the giant pulse for a period long enough to reach the threshold condition, then the laser will break into the ordinary pulsations that take place in the absence of the shutter. Therefore, if it is essential that only one pulse be emitted, the shutter must be closed again. Fortunately, this need not be done very fast because the recovery time of the laser after the giant pulse is at least 10 μsec, which is ample time to close an electro-optical shutter. The time of recovery to the initial state after a pulse depends on the energy of the pulse. Low-energy pulses require proportionately less recovery time. Periodic pulse trains may be obtained by opening the shutter at suitably chosen intervals.

A number of ingenious methods are available for Q-switching in addition to the ones already mentioned. Each has its particular merit; some excel in speed, while others are employed because of their simplicity and low cost.

The principal disadvantage of the mechanical switch illustrated in Fig. 95 is its slowness. With the wheel revolving at 10,000 rpm, tens of microseconds elapse from the time the slot first begins to expose the ruby until the ruby face is fully exposed. Faster mechanical switching can be achieved by focusing the rays of the laser and by placing the shutter in the focal plane [4]. This arrangement is recommended only for low power levels because the air will break down at the focal point.

Fast mechanical switching may also be accomplished by rotating one of the mirrors or by replacing one of the mirrors with a rotating totally reflecting prism. The giant pulse laser marketed by Trion Instruments, Inc. (Ann Arbor, Mich.) is based on the last principle. The rotating prism method is the most favored mechanical method for the generation of giant pulses. The firing of the flashtube is synchronized with the rotation of the prism so that firing occurs at a predetermined time before the prism reaches the reflecting position.

An interesting Q-spoiling method depends on the deflection of light waves in an ultrasonic field. Such a field can be produced in a fluid cell placed between the mirrors of a laser. The ultrasonic waves travel perpendicular to the path of the light; the deflection of the light beam results from the alternating compressions and rarefactions, which alter the density

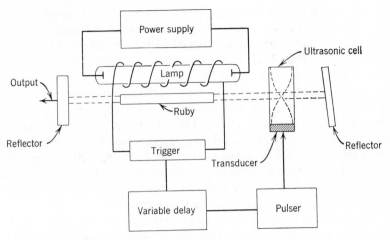

Fig. 98. Laser controlled by ultrasonic cell. (The offset angle of the right reflector is exaggerated.)

and the index of refraction of the liquid. Figure 98 shows the experimental apparatus of De Maria and co-workers [5]. The reflectors are not positioned parallel, one of the reflectors being offset from its "true" Fabry-Perot orientation by a small angle of the order of 1 mrad. This deviation from parallelism is such that laser oscillations do not occur with the available optical pumping. When the overpopulation of the upper level reaches its desired value the ultrasonic cell is shock-excited with a pulse of short duration. As the spontaneous radiation from the ruby rod passes through the ultrasonic field the beam is refracted and for a short period of time radiation will be directed perpendicular to the offset reflector. At this time the light path is open and the giant pulse is formed.

The ultrasonic shutter can be used not only for the generation of a single giant pulse but also for the synchronization of the random output spikes of a laser to a suitable external signal frequency. It may be used internally, i.e., with the laser crystal serving as the ultrasonic cell, but ordinarily the coupling of these functions is not very practical [6].

A Q-switch of extreme simplicity can be constructed by incorporating proper bleachable absorbers in the laser. These are materials which are initially highly absorbent, but which become transparent upon strong illumination. Bret and Gires [7] used colored glasses containing compounds of Se and Cd which have an initial transmission coefficient of about 10^{-6} for a radiation of 6943 Å and whose "high-level" transmission coefficient is 30 per cent. The variation of the transmission coefficient upon irradiation is very fast (1 nsec), and it is reversible. Giant pulses of the same quality were produced with these passive switches as are obtainable with the more complicated and expensive electro-optical and mechanical shutters. Similar results were achieved with solutions of the bleachable dye kryptocyanine [8, 9] used with a ruby laser and a polymethine dye used with a neodymium laser [10].

The reflectivity of semiconductor surfaces increases upon strong irradiation. This effect may also be used for the production of a giant pulse. One of the laser mirrors is replaced by an appropriate polished semiconductor surface (Si, Ge, InP, InSb, for ruby), whose initial low reflectivity holds off oscillations until the gain in the laser material reaches a high value; then pulse and reflectivity rise together [11, 12]. The limited experience with this type of Q-switch indicates that the mirror surface rapidly deteriorates as a result of laser operation.

Giant pulse technique is by no means restricted to ruby lasers; considerable experience has been obtained with Q-switching Nd-glass lasers, and in principle the method is applicable to any laser material.

The calculation of the dynamics of the giant pulse, including its energy balance and power capability, requires an elaborate mathematical analysis. This is the subject of the next section. For the benefit of the reader who does not wish to concern himself with the mathematical theory, we emphasize now that the purpose of Q-switching is not energy economy. In fact, the total coherent radiation obtainable with a given flash of excitation is substantially decreased by the incorporation of the shutter. However, the maximum power level can be increased by three orders of magnitude, and the timing and shape of the pulse become well defined.

The alternating electric fields produced in the giant pulse are considerable. In front of a ruby laser 1 cm in diameter radiating with a peak power of 20 MW the peak radiative flux density is 2.55×10^{11} W/meter^2. This flux density corresponds to a peak electric field $E = 1.39 \times 10^7$ V/meter. The above calculation applies outside of the partial reflector. In the region between the reflectors the radiation density is naturally even higher.

REFERENCES

1. R. W. Hellwarth, Control of fluorescent pulsations, *Advances in Quantum Electronics*, Columbia Univ. Press, New York, 1961, pp. 334–341.
2. R. J. Collins and P. Kisliuk, Control of population inversion in pulsed optical masers by feedback modulation, *J. Appl. Phys.* 33, 2009–2011, 1962.
3. F. J. McClung and R. W. Hellwarth, Giant optical pulsations from ruby, *J. Appl. Phys.* 33, 828–829, 1962.
4. N. G. Basov, V. S. Zuev, and P. G. Kriukov, Augmentation of the power output of a ruby laser by Q-switching, *Appl. Optics* 1, 767–768, 1962.
5. A. J. De Maria, R. Gagosz, and G. Barnard, Ultrasonic-refraction shutter for optical maser oscillators, *J. Appl. Phys.* 34, 453–456, 1963.

6. G. E. Danielson and A. J. De Maria, Internal gating of optically pumped, high-gain, solid state lasers, *Appl. Phys. Lett.* **5**, 123–125, 1964.
7. G. Bret and G. Gires, Giant-pulse laser and light amplifier using variable transmission coefficient glasses as light switches, *Appl. Phys. Lett.* **4**, 175–176, 1964.
8. P. Kafalas, J. I. Masters, and E. M. E. Murray, Photosensitive liquid used as a nondestructive passive Q-switch in a ruby laser, *J. Appl. Phys.* **35**, 2349–2350, 1964.
9. B. H. Soffer, Giant pulse laser operation by a passive reversibly bleachable absorber, *J. Appl. Phys.* **35**, 2551, 1964.
10. B. H. Soffer and R. H. Hoskins, Generation of giant pulses from a Nd-laser by a reversible bleachable absorber, *Nature*, **204**, 276, 1964.
11. C. H. Carmichael and G. N. Simpson, Generation of giant optical maser pulses using a semiconductor mirror, *Nature* **202**, 787, 1964.
12. W. R. Sooy, M. Geller, and D. P. Bortfeld, Switching of semiconductor reflectivity by a giant pulse laser, *Appl. Phys. Lett.* **5**, 54–56, 1964.

4. GIANT PULSE THEORY

Formulation of the Problem

The problem of giant pulse dynamics is to deduce the evolution of the giant pulse in time from a model representing the laser. This model consists of a material with at least two energy levels among which radiative transitions can take place, and in which a population inversion can be created by means of an external agent, the pump. The material is confined between mirrors and provision is made for switching, i.e., for the variation of the loss of radiation from the structure.

The following quantities are of principal interest in connection with the giant pulse:

    a. the total energy radiated,
    b. the peak power radiated,
    c. the time of formation of the giant pulse from switching to peak,
    d. the rates of rise and fall.

Hellwarth [1, 2] published several estimates for these quantities in terms of the parameters of the laser and the variables that determine its physical state, as well as the rate of switching. Here we shall solve the dynamic problems completely under certain limiting assumptions, the most important of which is that of *fast switching*. This means that the shutter is switched in time so short that no significant change in population inversion takes place during the switching process. The fast-switching calculations are certainly applicable when the giant pulse is produced with a Kerr cell switch or a fast-acting mechanical switch. For the sake of mathematical simplicity we assume, contrary to fact, that the laser material is homogeneous, isotropic, and uniformly excited. With such assumptions the best we can hope for is a rough agreement with results obtained on real materials.

In formulating the equations that govern the process of stimulated emission in the period following the switching, we shall neglect the effects of processes which are slow in comparison with the formation of the giant pulse. In particular, we shall neglect the effects of continued pumping and of spontaneous emission on the population inversion.

The essential physical variables of the problem are photon density and population inversion per unit volume. At the start of the process the inversion is high and the photon density is low. As the laser is switched on, the photon density rises, slowly at first, then more and more rapidly, since the rate of photon production is proportional to the photon density already present. Photons are produced at the expense of the stored inversion, which decreases ever more rapidly until the inversion remaining is no longer sufficient to maintain the rate of photon creation at the level of the photon loss rate. At this time the photon density begins to decline and the giant pulse dies out at a rate determined by the rate of escape of photons from the laser.

The *laser material* is characterized by the following parameters:

1. N_0, the number of active ions per unit volume,
2. α_0, the absorption coefficient of the unexcited laser material. The parameter α_0 is a function of the frequency; we shall use its peak value at the center of the fluorescent line.

The *laser geometry* is characterized by the following variables:

1. V, the volume of the laser material,
2. l, the length of the laser material,
3. L, the optical distance between the reflectors calculated with due regard for the refractive indices of the materials situated between reflectors.

The *physical state of the laser* is characterized by the following variables:

1. Φ, the number of photons between the reflectors, divided by V.
2. $N = N_2 - N_1$, the population inversion per unit volume.*

The reflectivities r_1 and r_2 of the reflectors are relevant device parameters of the laser. The loss coefficient γ is the fractional loss of photons in a single passage. When only reflection losses are significant $\gamma = -\frac{1}{2}\log r_1 r_2$, but in general other losses will be present in a laser equipped for Q-switching and consequently its loss coefficient will be larger than that calculated from reflection losses alone.

Both photon density and inversion are functions of position as well as time. There are two reasons for the spatial variation. First, the initial

---

* For the sake of simplicity we assume that $g_1 = g_2$; otherwise the definition of inversion has to be modified as was done in Section I.6.

excitation varies with the radial distance from the geometrical axis of the laser. Second, the relevant photon density is the sum of two densities: that of a wave increasing exponentially to the right, and that of a wave increasing similarly to the left. The total photon density is then a convex function of the displacement along the laser axis; hence its largest values are assumed at the ends with a dip located near the middle. This variation of the photon density creates a corresponding and opposite variation of the inversion along the axial direction. Nevertheless an approximate solution of the problem may be obtained by neglecting the spatial variation of N and introducing the fictitious photon density $\Phi(t)$ in place of a true photon density which varies from point to point. The approximation will be good for short lasers and bad for long ones. We shall re-examine the validity of the solution at the conclusion of calculations.

A useful auxiliary laser parameter in this problem is the *lifetime T of a photon*. This is related to the time of a single passage $t_1 = L/c$, and to the fractional loss γ in a single passage as follows: $T = t_1/\gamma$. It is a fundamental unit of time characteristic of the laser.

The initial state for the formation of the pulse is achieved by pumping the laser with an optical source and keeping the loss coefficient at a value much higher than γ. During this period of excitation the population inversion rises from $-N_0$ to a positive value N_i; the photon density also rises to a value Φ_i. The subscript i indicates that the values are "initial" values for the giant pulse. At time $t = 0$ the loss coefficient is reduced to γ and the formation of the pulse begins.

It was shown in Chapter I that α, the coefficient of amplification, is proportional to the population inversion N. We may write

$$\alpha = \alpha_0 N/N_0, \tag{4.1}$$

where α_0 is the absorption in the unexcited material. To simplify matters we neglect the spectral distribution of energy and calculate as if the entire phenomenon took place at the frequency that corresponds to the peak of the line. Then α and α_0 denote coefficients measured at the center of the line.

The intensity of a photon packet traveling along the x-axis varies as $e^{\alpha x}$; therefore starting with ΦV photons the increase in the number of photons from amplification in the laser of active length l is approximately $\alpha l \Phi V$ and this increase takes place in time t_1.* Photons are lost at the rate of $\Phi V/T$; therefore, neglecting photons created by spontaneous emission, the variation of Φ with time is described by the equation:

$$\frac{d\Phi}{dt} = \left(\frac{\alpha l}{t_1} - \frac{1}{T}\right)\Phi. \tag{4.2}$$

* It is understood that $\alpha l \ll 1$.

Actually one has to proceed carefully because the photon density is not uniform throughout the laser, and because equation (4.2) is only an approximation valid when $\alpha l - \gamma \ll 1$. Consider the true photon density $\Phi(x, t)$ at the point x as a function of time.* After the elapse of the time $2t_1$ each photon in a given volume element returns to the same volume element after passing through the laser twice and after it suffers reflection losses at both ends. Thus at time $t + 2t_1$ the photon density in the neighborhood of x will be given by

$$\Phi(x, t + 2t_1) = \Phi(x, t)r_1r_2e^{2\alpha l},$$

where α is the average amplification coefficient in the ruby at time t. Then, with the notation $-\gamma = \frac{1}{2} \log r_1r_2$, we get

$$\Phi(x, t + 2t_1) - \Phi(x, t) = \Phi(x, t)(e^{2\alpha l - 2\gamma} - 1).$$

Hence, when $\alpha l - \gamma \ll 1$, we can write

$$\frac{\Phi(x, t + 2t_1) - \Phi(x, t)}{2t_1} \approx \left(\frac{\alpha l}{t_1} - \frac{\gamma}{t_1}\right)\Phi(x, t).$$

This is already of the form of equation (4.2), provided that $2t_1$ may be regarded as an infinitesimal increment of time. The interest in this problem centers around phenomena that occur in a time interval of the order of T to $10T$; therefore the approximation is good when $t_1/T = \gamma \ll 1$. This condition and $\alpha l - \gamma \ll 1$ must be satisfied. Together they imply that αl must also be small.

If the contribution of continued pumping is neglected, the density of population inversion varies at the rate

$$\frac{dN}{dt} = -\frac{2\alpha l}{t_1}\Phi \tag{4.3}$$

because the stimulated emission of a photon causes N to decrease by 2. Equations (4.2) and (4.3) are special cases of the Statz-De Mars equations (2.1) and (2.2).

We eliminate α by means of (4.1), introduce the normalized variables

---

* The function $\Phi(x, t)$ is related to the function $\Phi(t)$ introduced earlier by the equation $\int\Phi(x, t)Adx = \Phi(t)V$. Here A is the cross sectional area of the laser and integration is extended over the full length of the laser. Since $\Phi(t)$ is referred to the volume of the active material and not that of the entire laser, it is not a true photon density. Failure of Wagner and Lengyel to clarify this point in their original publication [3] led to erroneous conclusions [4]. At interfaces, where the index of refraction η changes, the quantity $\Phi(x, t)/\eta$ is continuous.

$n = N/N_0$, $\varphi = \Phi/N_0$, and change the timescale to make $T = t_1/\gamma$ the unit of time. Then

$$\frac{d\varphi}{dt} = \left(\frac{\alpha_0 l}{\gamma} n - 1\right)\varphi; \qquad \frac{dn}{dt} = -\frac{2\alpha_0 l}{\gamma} n\varphi. \qquad (4.4)$$

We shall now introduce the constant n_p defined by the equation $\alpha_0 l n_p = \gamma$. The final form of the differential equations is [3]:

$$\frac{d\varphi}{dt} = \left(\frac{n}{n_p} - 1\right)\varphi; \qquad \frac{dn}{dt} = -\frac{2n\varphi}{n_p}. \qquad (4.5)$$

Once the timescale has been adapted to the laser by making $T = 1$, there remains only a single parameter characteristic of the laser, namely n_p, the inversion at the instant of the peak photon density.

At the time of switching the photon density φ is very low. It rises from φ_i, reaches a peak φ_p generally many orders of magnitude higher than φ_i, and then declines to zero. The population inversion n is a monotone-decreasing function of time starting at n_i and ending at n_f. Figure 99 illustrates the typical curves traced out by these variables. The initial rise

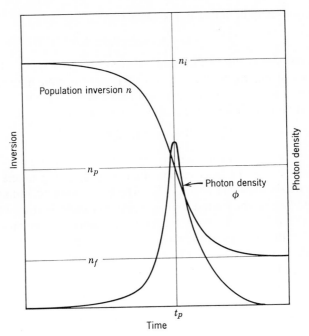

Fig. 99. Inversion and photon density in the giant pulse.

of φ is exponential; it proceeds with a time constant $\tau = n_p T/(n_i - n_p) = t_1/(\alpha_i l - \gamma)$ in accordance with the calculations of Hellwarth [1].

First Integrals

We obtain a solution of the basic differential equation (4.5) in two steps. The first integration gives information concerning the physical quantities characteristic of the giant pulse as a whole. These are the *total energy converted to radiation* and the *peak photon density attained*. They are obtained by eliminating the time from (4.5). It follows then that

$$\frac{d\varphi}{dn} = \frac{n_p}{2n} - \frac{1}{2}.$$ (4.6)

Therefore

$$\varphi = \varphi_i + \frac{1}{2}\left[n_p \log \frac{n}{n_i} - (n - n_i)\right].$$ (4.7)

We can determine the final population inversion from (4.7) by substituting $n = n_f$ and noting that φ_i and φ_f are negligibly small. Then

$$n_p \log (n_f/n_i) = n_f - n_i.$$ (4.8)

Equation (4.8) may be stated in the form

$$n_f/n_i = \exp\{(n_i/n_p)[n_f/n_i - 1]\}.$$ (4.9)

Figure 100 shows the relationship between n_f/n_i and n_i/n_p. The graph enables one to determine the fraction of inversion remaining from the initial conditions. The energy utilization factor is $(n_i - n_f)/n_i$.

The total radiative energy generated in the laser is

$$E = \tfrac{1}{2}(n_i - n_f)VN_0h\nu.$$ (4.10)

Not all this energy represents useful output, however. There are radiation loss mechanisms in the laser cavity other than coupling to the output. Therefore we should write $\gamma = \gamma_c + \gamma_i$, where γ_c represents radiation loss due to coupling to the output and γ_i represents incidental losses due to other causes, such as diffraction, scattering, absorption at the mirrors, etc. The useful output energy of the pulse is $E_0 = E\gamma_c/\gamma$.

The peak power is calculated from (4.7); note that the peak is reached when $n = n_p$. Therefore, neglecting φ_i, we have

$$\varphi_p = \tfrac{1}{2}[n_p \log (n_p/n_i) - (n_p - n_i)].$$ (4.11)

Figure 101 shows φ_p/n_p as a function of the variable n_i/n_p. It is a condensation of the numerical data published elsewhere [3].

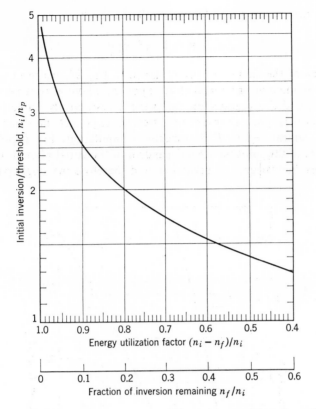

Fig. 100. Energy utilization factor and inversion remaining after pulse.

The peak number of photons in the laser is $\varphi_p N_0 V$. The photons carry an energy $h\nu$; they decay with a lifetime $T = t_1/\gamma$. Again only the fraction γ_c/γ of the power dissipation represents useful output. Taking all these factors into consideration, we find for the peak power radiated by the laser

$$P = \frac{\varphi_p N_0 V h\nu\gamma_c}{t_1}. \tag{4.12}$$

The Evolution of the Pulse in Time

Having obtained φ as a function of n, we turn to the more tedious task of relating φ and n to t. The main physical purpose of this analysis is to obtain the time delay involved in the evolution of the pulse, and the approximate duration of the pulse. We substitute $\varphi(n)$ from (4.7) into (4.5), which is readily integrated formally with the result

$$t = -\int_{n_i}^{n} \frac{n_p \, dn'}{2n'\varphi(n')}. \tag{4.13}$$

In view of the shape of $\varphi(n)$ as shown in Fig. 99, we recognize three regions of integration: the central region B, where φ is large, and the regions A and C preceding and following it, respectively. In handling the integral (4.13) it proves convenient to treat the regions A and C analytically, and the central region B by machine computation. For region B the properties of the solution are independent of the initial photon density φ_i (to a very high degree of accuracy), and therefore the single parameter

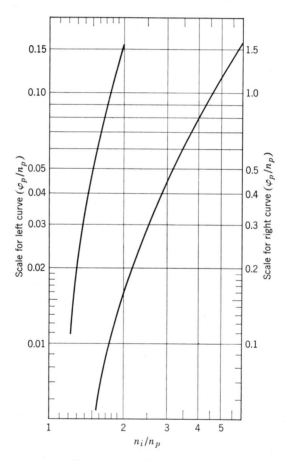

Fig. 101. The function φ_p/n_p.

n_i/n_p characterizes the giant pulse. The substitution $z = -\log n/n_p$ places the origin of the new variable at the peak of the pulse. To separate the three regions let us introduce the quantities $z_1 = z_i + 0.01 < 0$, and $z_2 = z_f - 0.01 > 0$. The regions A, B, and C are then characterized by $z_i < z < z_1$, $z_1 < z < z_2$, and $z_2 < z < z_f$, respectively. The expression for time becomes

$$t = \int_{z_i}^{z} \frac{dz'}{F(z')}, \qquad (4.14)$$

where

$$F(z) = 2\varphi(n)/n_p = (2\varphi_i/n_p) + z_i - z + e^{-z_i} - e^{-z}. \qquad (4.15)$$

It is convenient to arrange calculations so that the instants of passage from region A to B and from region B to C serve as reference points in regions A and C, respectively. We introduce

$$T_1 = \int_{z_i}^{z_1} \frac{dz'}{F(z')} \quad \text{and} \quad T_2 = \int_{z_i}^{z_2} \frac{dz'}{F(z')}.$$

In interval A the function $F(z)$ may be approximated by

$$(2\varphi_i/n_p) + (e^{-z_i} - 1)(z - z_i),$$

because $z_i \leqq z \leqq z_i + 0.01$. We note that

$$e^{-z_i} - 1 = (n_i - n_p)/n_p.$$

Hence in evaluating integrals of the type (4.14) in the region A the integrand may be written

$$n_p[2\varphi_i + (n_i - n_p)(z - z_i)]^{-1}.$$

Therefore, noting that $z_1 = z_i + 0.01$, we obtain

$$T_1 = \frac{n_p}{n_i - n_p} \log \left(1 + \frac{n_i - n_p}{200\varphi_i} \right), \qquad (4.16)$$

and

$$t - T_1 = \frac{n_p}{n_i - n_p} \log \left[\frac{2\varphi_i + (z - z_i)(n_i - n_p)}{2\varphi_i + 0.01(n_i - n_p)} \right]. \qquad (4.17)$$

In the central region the first term on the right side of (4.15) may be neglected in comparison with the other terms. Consequently the integral (4.14) may be evaluated as a function of a single parameter z_i. Thus t is obtained as a function of n/n_p and the parameter n_i/n_p. It is then possible to calculate n/n_p and φ/n_p as functions of t and the parameter n_i/n_p [3]. Four curves obtained by machine calculations for relevant values of the

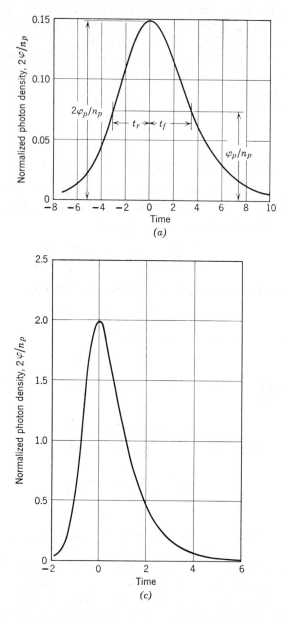

Fig. 102. Photon density versus time in the central region of a giant pulse. (Time is measured in units of photon lifetime T in the Fabry-Perot interferometer. Origin at peak.) (a) $\log n_i/n_p = 0.5$, $n_i/n_p = 1.649$; (b) $\log n_i/n_p = 1.0$, $n_i/n_p = 2.718$; (c) $\log n_i/n_p = 1.5$, $n_i/n_p = 4.482$; (d) $\log n_i/n_p = 2.0$, $n_i/n_p = 7.389$.

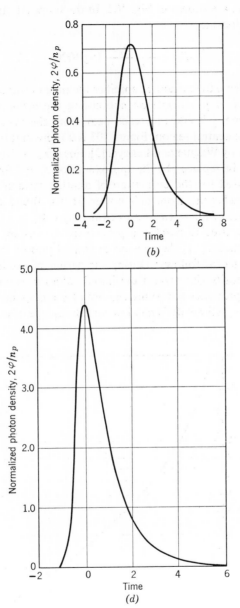

(b)

(d)

parameter n_i/n_p are shown in Fig. 102. In the terminal phase of the giant pulse the relationship

$$t - T_2 = -\frac{n_p}{n_p - n_f} \log 100(z_f - z) \qquad (4.18)$$

is applicable. Here the instant T_2 specifies the time of transit into region C.

The quantity of prime interest concerning the evolution of the giant pulse is the time t'_p it takes to reach peak from the instant T_1 when the pulse enters the central region. Figure 103 is a representation of the values of t'_p calculated by Wagner and Lengyel [3]. For $n_i/n_p > 5$, $(\log n_i/n_p > 1.6)$, the graph may be replaced by the approximation $t'_p = 7.9 n_p/n_t$. Figure 103 may also be used for the estimation of another parameter, t_r, the time required to reach peak from half power. It was found empirically that within the range of interest t_r is approximately $0.4 t'_p$.

The time required to reach the peak from the instant of switching is $t_p + T_1$. The quantity T_1 depends on the initial photon density φ_i, which may be estimated as follows: During the period of excitation, inversion and photon density rise toward the initial values n_i and φ_i, respectively. The principal processes governing the rise of φ are spontaneous emission with a lifetime τ_L, stimulated emission, and the escape of photons from the

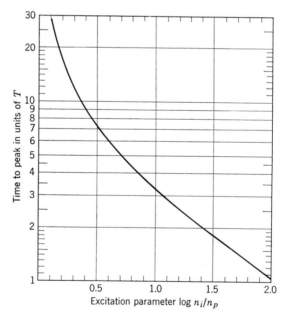

Fig. 103. Time to peak from the instant of entry into central region.

laser at the rate corresponding to the preswitching value of γ. We will count only those photons which propagate in the proper direction, i.e., which are included in the laser beam. It is immaterial what happens to photons that are spontaneously emitted in a lateral direction. Then, assuming N_2 ions in the excited state, the number of photons per second emitted spontaneously in the proper direction is $N_2 \Omega / 4\pi \tau_L$, where Ω is the solid angle of the laser beam. We note that

$$2N_2 = N_2 - N_1 + N_2 + N_1 = N_0(1 + n);$$

therefore the differential equation which takes the place of (4.4) during the excitation period is

$$\frac{d\varphi}{dt} = \frac{\Omega}{4\pi} \frac{1 + n}{2\tau_L} + \left(\frac{\alpha_0 ln}{t_1} - \frac{\gamma'}{\gamma} \frac{1}{T}\right)\varphi, \tag{4.19}$$

where $\gamma' > \gamma$ is the loss rate prior to switching. Again introducing T as the unit time we get

$$\frac{d\varphi}{dt} = \frac{\Omega(1 + n)T}{8\pi\tau_L} + \left(\frac{n}{n_p} - \frac{\gamma'}{\gamma}\right)\varphi > 0. \tag{4.20}$$

Only a small error is introduced by replacing the "greater than" sign in (4.20) by the "equals" sign, because on the scale of T the rise of φ is slow. The factor of φ in (4.20) is negative during the excitation period, because if n/n_p were to exceed γ'/γ, the laser would fire. How close n/n_p is permitted to get to the limit γ'/γ depends on experimental conditions. The assumption that it rises to one-half this limit may be approximately true in a typical situation. This means that

$$\frac{n_i}{n_p} \approx \frac{1}{2} \frac{\gamma'}{\gamma}. \tag{4.21}$$

Then

$$\varphi_i \approx \frac{n_p}{n_i} \frac{\Omega(1 + n_i)T}{8\pi\tau_L}. \tag{4.22}$$

Admittedly the estimate of φ_i is a rough one. However, because of the logarithmic character of (4.17) a change in φ_i by a factor of 10 would change T_1 only by 1.1.

The foregoing calculations were based on the assumption that the switching takes place instantaneously at $t = 0$. Wang [5] showed that the method can be generalized for the case of moderately fast switching. In this case the loss represented by the second term on the right side of (4.2) decreases linearly from a high value to $1/T$. Wang's solution correlates well with the solution of the simpler case discussed here, and it permits a more direct determination of the half-width of the giant pulse than the calculations of W.agner and Lengyel.

Optimization of the Output

Adjustment of the coupling γ_c provides a method of varying the power and the energy output of a giant pulse laser. The question arises what choice of γ_c maximizes the peak output power, assuming that all other parameters of the laser including the initial excitation n_i remain constant. The total loss rate $\gamma = \gamma_i + \gamma_c$ determines the threshold inversion n_p according to the equation

$$\alpha_0 l n_p = \gamma_i + \gamma_c; \tag{4.23}$$

therefore with γ_i fixed, either n_p or γ_c is to be regarded as the independent variable of the problem. Equation (4.12) may be reformulated by eliminating γ_c using (4.23) and by writing t_1 in the form

$$t_1 = l\eta(1 + \epsilon)/c, \tag{4.24}$$

where $l\eta/c$ is the time of passage through the active material. Then

$$P = \frac{N_0 h\nu\alpha_0 c}{\eta} \frac{V}{1 + \epsilon} \varphi_p(n_p - \gamma_i/\alpha_0 l). \tag{4.25}$$

The first fraction in (4.25) is a material constant. For ruby it is 4.17×10^{10} joules/cm³ sec. The last, variable part of (4.25) can be put in simple form by introducing the *reduced threshold population* $p = n_p/n_i$ and the loss factor $q = \gamma_i/\alpha_0 l n_i$. Then it follows from (4.11) that

$$\varphi_p(n_p - \gamma_i/\alpha_0 l) = \tfrac{1}{2} n_i^2 [(1 - p + p \log p)(p - q)]. \tag{4.26}$$

Adjustment of coupling for maximum power requires that the value of p which maximizes (4.26) be found for given q. This is obtainable from Fig. 104, which represents in graphic form the results of Menat [4], who obtained equations (4.25) and (4.26). Once the maximizing p is found, n_p and γ_c can be calculated, provided that n_i and γ_i are known. Unfortunately n_i and γ_i are seldom known with the required accuracy.

The preceding discussion was based on the assumption that γ_c is constant in time. Vuylsteke [6] examined the giant pulse problem under more general circumstances than assumed here. Although his argument involves assumptions that are not particularly applicable to a giant pulse laser, his general conclusion is valid: To obtain the maximum power output from a giant pulse laser one should start with a small γ_c, then suddenly increase γ_c to its maximum value near 1 at the time when radiation density within the laser reaches its maximum. To accomplish this increase one must perform a second switching operation, which must be timed with respect to the first

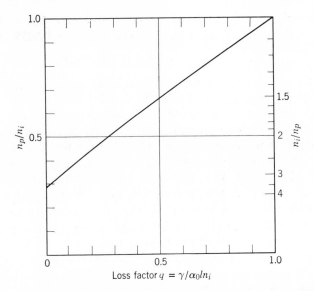

Fig. 104. Optimization of the giant pulse for peak output. (After Menat [4].)

switching operation. This mode of operation is called the *pulse transmission mode*. It is applicable in a situation where the possibility exists of controlling the reflectivity of one of the mirrors as a function of time or when the optical path can be switched between mirrors of different reflectivities.

A Numerical Example

The theory of the giant pulse laser may be illustrated by the examination of the numerical values of the physical variables.

For pink ruby, $N_0 h = 4.65$ joules/cm^3 and $\alpha_0 = 0.4$ cm^{-1} at room temperature. In a typical situation the loss coefficient γ with the shutter open varies between 0.05 and 0.20, the optical length is around 30 cm, and the initial inversion is between 0.1 and 0.3.

We now choose the following specific design values to illustrate the application of the theory developed: $l = 5$ cm, $t_1 = 10^{-9}$ sec (for an optical path of 30 cm), $\gamma = 0.1$, and $\gamma_i = 0$. From the assumed data it follows that $n_p = \gamma/\alpha_0 l = 0.05$; $T = 10^{-8}$ sec. The initial excitation n_i must exceed n_p. We choose for illustration $n_i = 0.15 = 3n_p$. The conditions required for the application of the theory are fulfilled, since with the above choice of the parameters we get $\alpha l = n_i \alpha_0 l = 0.3$ at the start of the pulse, and αl decreases as the pulse evolves. Thus we have $\alpha l - \gamma \leqq 0.2$ for the entire pulse. It follows from the graph of Fig. 100 that the energy utilization factor is 0.94 and n_f/n_i is 0.06. The energy of the pulse is calculated from

(4.10) as 0.321 joules for each cubic centimeter of ruby. The peak power output is calculated by means of (4.11), which gives $\varphi_p = 0.0225$; therefore

$$W_p = \varphi_p N_0 h\nu/T = 10.5 \times 10^6 \text{ W/cm}^3.$$

The general shape of the pulse will be similar to that shown in Fig. 102b, which is strictly applicable to the case $n_i/n_p = 2.718$.

To calculate the time of evolution of the pulse during the starting period (Region A) it is necessary to estimate the density of the useful photons present at the start. Assuming the value of 10^{-6} for $\Omega/4\pi$ and using $\tau_L = 3 \times 10^{-3}$ sec for the fluorescent lifetime of the ruby, we obtain from (4.22) the value $\varphi_i = \Phi_i/N_0 = 0.65 \times 10^{-12}$. This corresponds to 4×10^6 photons per cm³ traveling in the correct direction. With the assumed data substituted into (4.16), we obtain $T_1 = 10.2$ for the starting time (in units of T) of the central region. From the graph of Fig. 103 it appears that $t'_p = 2.8$ for $n_i/n_p = 3$; therefore the total time for the evolution of the pulse from the instant of switching to the attainment of the peak is $13T$ or 13×10^{-8} sec.

Note that a decrease of the initial excitation causes a decrease in the energy utilization factor, and therefore the total energy output is reduced drastically.

The theoretical calculations assume homogeneous and isotropic crystals uniformly excited. Since such conditions do not prevail in practice, the peak power output of an actual laser will remain far below the theoretical limit calculated under these extreme simplifying assumptions.

Critical Comments and Generalizations

The giant pulse theory presented suffers from assumptions which are necessary to assure a relatively simple mathematical form but which limit the applicability of the theory. As has already been stated, the spatial variation of the photon density within the active material was neglected, and the theory, therefore, applies to short giant pulse lasers only. For the present purpose a laser is short when $1 + \alpha l$ is a good approximation of $e^{\alpha l}$.

In the general case, one must consider the density of the photons traveling to the right and left separately. Let these be given by the functions $\Phi^+(x, t)$ and $\Phi^-(x, t)$. They satisfy the partial differential equations

$$\frac{1}{v}\frac{\partial \Phi^+}{\partial t} + \frac{\partial \Phi^+}{\partial x} = \alpha\Phi^+$$

and

$$\frac{1}{v}\frac{\partial \Phi^-}{\partial t} - \frac{\partial \Phi^-}{\partial x} = \alpha\Phi^-,$$

where v is the velocity of light in the medium.

The variation of the inversion is governed by the equation

$$\frac{\partial N}{\partial t} = -2\alpha v(\Phi^+ + \Phi^-),$$

and the loss at the mirrors is taken into account by relating the boundary values of Φ^+ and Φ^-. These equations do not lead to simple solutions such as we discussed earlier, but when certain reasonable approximations are made, the average value of $\Phi^+ + \Phi^-$ satisfies the ordinary differential equation we have used.

Another fundamental limitation of the approach presented is that it neglects the spectral distribution of the fluorescent line and the selective properties of the Fabry-Perot interferometer with regard to frequency. When a laser is excited barely above threshold, the operation in a single mode is possible. This is not the case, however, in giant pulse operation. Here we must deal with the simultaneous evolution of a large number of modes over a range of frequencies. An adequate treatment of the giant pulse phenomenon should take into account the interaction of a number of oscillations all feeding from the same reservoir of excited ions.

REFERENCES

1. R. W. Hellwarth, Control of fluorescent pulsations, *Advances in Quantum Electronics*, Columbia Univ. Press, New York, 1961, pp. 334–341.
2. F. J. McClung and R. W. Hellwarth, Giant optical pulsations from ruby, *J. Appl. Phys.* **33**, 828–829, 1962.
3. W. G. Wagner and B. A. Lengyel, Evolution of the giant pulse in a laser, *J. Appl. Phys.* **34**, 2040–2046, 1963.
4. M. Menat, Giant pulses from a laser: Optimum conditions, *J. Appl. Phys.* **36**, 73–76, 1965.
5. C. C. Wang, Optical giant pulses from a *Q*-switched laser, *Proc. IEEE* **51**, 1767, 1963.
6. A. A. Vuylsteke, Theory of laser regeneration switching, *J. Appl. Phys.* **34**, 1615–1622, 1963.

VII

Nonlinear Phenomena

1. THEORY OF NONLINEAR PHENOMENA IN LIGHT PROPAGATION

The propagation of electromagnetic radiation in a material can be examined from several points of view. First one might take a purely macroscopic look at matter, forgetting that it is composed of discrete particles. The incident electromagnetic field produces a polarization in the matter; for the sake of simplicity let us be concerned only with the electric polarization $\mathbf{P}$. In the classical, linear theory of wave propagation, this polarization is generally assumed to be proportional to the electric field $\mathbf{E}$. For isotropic materials $\mathbf{P}$ is parallel to $\mathbf{E}$, and when the material is an ideal insulator a sinusoidally varying $\mathbf{E}$ produces a sinusoidally varying $\mathbf{P}$ in the same phase. Under such circumstances the vector $\mathbf{D} = \epsilon_0 \mathbf{E} + \mathbf{P}^\star$ is also proportional to $\mathbf{E}$; one writes $\mathbf{D} = \epsilon \mathbf{E}$ and deduces from Maxwell's equations the dependence of the velocity of propagation in the medium on the scalar dielectric constant ϵ. The laws of reflection and refraction then follow in a known manner. In a lossy medium, i.e., in a medium with a finite conductivity, the phase of $\mathbf{P}$ differs from that of $\mathbf{E}$. The dielectric constant ϵ is then complex, and the attenuation of the wave is related to the imaginary part of ϵ, or, what is the same, to the out-of-phase component of $\mathbf{P}$. In an anisotropic material $\mathbf{P}$ is not always parallel to $\mathbf{E}$, and the scalar relationship between $\mathbf{D}$ and $\mathbf{E}$ is replaced by a tensor relationship. Still, linearity is assumed and we write

$$
\begin{aligned}
D_1 &= \epsilon_{11}E_1 + \epsilon_{12}E_2 + \epsilon_{13}E_3, \\
D_2 &= \epsilon_{21}E_1 + \epsilon_{22}E_2 + \epsilon_{23}E_3, \\
D_3 &= \epsilon_{31}E_1 + \epsilon_{32}E_2 + \epsilon_{33}E_3.
\end{aligned}
\tag{1.1}
$$

These equations may also be written in the shorthand form $D_i = \epsilon_{ik}E_k$, where summation over the repeated indices is understood but not indicated. The ϵ's are components of a tensor; they transform with the transformation

---

$\star$ This form is appropriate for the rationalized MKS system, which is preferred in the discussion of wave propagation.

of the coordinate system. Using equation (1.1) together with Maxwell's equations, one can proceed to derive the laws of crystal optics as this is done in classical texts [1].

In principle one could follow through with the laws of wave propagation in vacuum, calculate the polarization **P** created in the dielectric and then the electromagnetic wave launched by the variation of **P**, and finally add the new wave to the original wave. In practice this second approach is more complicated than the first, but it leads to the same result. As long as **P** and **E** are strictly proportional, the original wave and the wave created by the polarization of the dielectric vary at the same rate and remain in the same phase relationship; therefore the two waves propagate together.

The linear dependence of **P** on **E** is essential in all these calculations, and we must examine the relationship of these quantities more closely. In order to learn what **P** is and how it depends on **E**, it is best to adopt a microscopic point of view, taking into account that apparently continuous matter consists of particles whose charge distribution is affected by electric and magnetic fields. Polarization is a purely empirical quantity in the macroscopic theory. In the microscopic theory its existence is deduced from the interaction of the electromagnetic field with the motion of charged particles of which matter is composed. To arrive at a theory of polarization, two steps must be taken: First, the action of the field on a single isolated particle of the proper type must be calculated. Then the macroscopic polarization is calculated, taking into account the mutual interactions of particles as they are distributed in the medium under consideration.

As light propagates through matter, the rapidly varying electromagnetic field exerts forces on all charged particles, but the nuclei, because of their inertia, respond with much less displacement than the electrons. The inner electrons of an atom are tightly bound to the nucleus, so that the primary polarizing effect of the radiation is exerted through the valence electrons. These are displaced from their normal orbits. Since the radiation fields derived from ordinary light sources are much weaker than the atomic electric and magnetic fields that bind the electrons to the nucleus, the effect of the incident light will be a perturbation similar to that produced by a small harmonic force acting on an oscillator. The perturbation creates electric dipoles and multipoles whose macroscopic manifestation is the polarization. As long as the perturbation is small, the resulting polarization is proportional to the electric field of the incident wave. The actual calculation of the perturbation is a complicated task in quantum theory and is outside the scope of this book.

It is instructive to calculate the motion of a *free* electron subjected to a simple electromagnetic wave. The result of this classical calculation is that the motion of the electron is neither parallel to the **E** field nor proportional to it, since one must consider the force resulting from the $e(\mathbf{v} \times \mathbf{B})$ term as well as the term $e\mathbf{E}$. This conclusion points up the role of the binding forces in determining polarization. The linear theory of polarization is applicable only when $E \ll E_a$, where E_a is the binding field acting on the electron.

When dealing with the propagation of light of the intensity obtainable from lasers, the limits of validity of the linear theory may be exceeded. Nonlinear optics is not tied to lasers entirely, however. The various electro-optic and magneto-optic phenomena are all manifestations of a nonlinear response of matter to an impressed electric and magnetic field. The calculations pertaining to these effects always include second-order mixed terms consisting of products of components of a large static field $\mathbf{E}_0$ or $\mathbf{B}_0$ and components $\mathbf{E}$ or $\mathbf{B}$ of a rapidly oscillating field. When experimenting with laser light we can create situations where the terms of higher than the first order in the time variable fields are not negligible. Such situations may lead to frequency multiplication, production of combination frequencies, and other interesting phenomena.

The basic relationship between frequency conversion and nonlinearity can be understood most easily if one considers a scalar, or one-dimensional, problem first. In one dimension the polarization P which vanishes for $E = 0$ may be written in the following form:

$$P = XE(1 + a_2E + a_3E^2 + \cdots). \qquad (1.2)$$

Here X is the linear polarizability, the a's are the nonlinear coefficients. They are generally much smaller than 1. Consider now the polarization created by an applied field of the form $E = E_0 \sin \omega t$. As long as the a's are neglected, the variation of P will be of the form $P_0 \sin \omega t$, but this will no longer be the case when $a_2 = 0$. The second term in (1.2) contributes a polarization

$$P_2 = a_2XE_0{}^2 \sin^2 \omega t = \tfrac{1}{2}a_2XE_0{}^2(1 - \cos 2\omega t). \qquad (1.3)$$

The first term in the parentheses is a d-c polarization which arises from the quadratic nonlinearity in the same way as d-c currents are produced in a square-law detector. The part of the polarization with the $\cos 2\omega t$ dependence results in the generation of the *second harmonic*. It is worth noting that if the material is of such nature that reversal of the sign of E simply reverses the sign of P, then the even-order terms are absent in (1.2) and a second harmonic described above is not produced. Higher harmonics arise from the higher-order terms in (1.2); they generally decrease rapidly in intensity because the terms of the sequence 1, a_2, a_3, etc. decrease rapidly.

The mixing of frequencies is deduced by substituting $E = E_1 \sin \omega_1 t + E_2 \sin \omega_2 t$ in (1.2). The expression that corresponds to (1.3) is

$$P_2 = a_2 X(E_1{}^2 \sin^2 \omega_1 t + E_2{}^2 \sin^2 \omega_2 t + 2E_1 E_2 \sin \omega_1 t \sin \omega_2 t). \quad (1.4)$$

It is readily resolved into a constant term plus terms of frequencies $2\omega_1, 2\omega_2, \omega_1 + \omega_2,$ and $\omega_1 - \omega_2$.

In the general physical situation as encountered in crystals, the direction of **P** does not coincide with that of **E**. Every component of **P** may in principle depend on every component of **E**. As long as the relationship is linear, it is expressible in terms of a tensor of rank 2:

$$\mathbf{P} = \mathbf{X} \cdot \mathbf{E}, \quad (1.5)$$

whose detailed form is

$$P_i = \sum_{k=1}^{3} X_{ik} E_k, \quad i = 1, 2, 3. \quad (1.6)$$

When **P** is given by (1.6) an electric vector **E** whose components vary harmonically at the angular frequency ω produces a harmonic polarization varying at the same rate.

When the relationship between E and P involves higher powers of **E**, the polarization will contain components varying at the rate $0, 2\omega, 3\omega,$ $4\omega,$ etc. These terms arise in anisotropic crystals in the same manner as they arise in the one-dimensional model which led to equations (1.3) and (1.4). The expression of the nonlinear polarization in anisotropic materials is rather complicated, for the induced polarization depends not only on the magnitude of the electric vector but on the magnitude and direction of all vectors that characterize the electromagnetic field. Let a harmonic plane wave be specified as follows:

$$\mathbf{E} = \mathbf{E}_\omega \sin (\omega t - \mathbf{k} \cdot \mathbf{r}). \quad (1.7)$$

Here the vector **k** is the phase normal; $k = 2\pi/\lambda$. The magnetic induction **B** is calculable from (1.7) by means of Maxwell's equations. The polarization **P** is a function of the vectors $\mathbf{E}_\omega$ and **k**. When a static electric or magnetic field is also present, the expression of **P** may contain terms dependent on $\mathbf{E}_0, \mathbf{B}_0,$ and $\mathbf{E}_\omega$ as well. The mixed terms linear in $\mathbf{E}_\omega$ but involving $\mathbf{E}_0$ or $\mathbf{B}_0$ as well are responsible for the ordinary electro- and magneto-optic effects.

A general discussion of the dependence of polarization on the field is to be found in the review article of Franken and Ward [2]. Here we concentrate on the lowest-degree term which provides frequency mixing or conversion. It is called the second-harmonic term $\mathbf{P}_{2\omega}$, whose components are related to the electric vector by means of the equations

$$P_i = X_{ijk}E_jE_k, \qquad i = 1, 2, 3, \qquad (1.8)$$

where summation over the repeated indices is understood.

The tensor $\mathbf{X}$ is of rank 3; it has 27 elements.* Since the order of writing of E_j and E_k is immaterial, $X_{ijk} = X_{ikj}$ for all combination of indices. The number of independent elements is further reduced by symmetry considerations. The reduction depends on the symmetry elements of the crystal class in question. A tensor of rank 3 vanishes for any crystal with an inversion center. In such a crystal all coordinate directions may be reversed simultaneously and the relations between all physical quantities remain unchanged. Thus, replacing E_j and E_k by $-E_j$ and $-E_k$, respectively, one should obtain $-P_i$. Then from $-P_i = X_{ijk}(-E_j)(-E_k)$ and (1.8), it follows that $X_{ijk} = 0$. Eleven of the 32 crystal classes have a center of inversion. The third-rank tensors also vanish in the crystal class O, leaving 20 crystal classes in which second-harmonic generation may take place [3].

In a crystal whose symmetry does not cause $\mathbf{X}$ to vanish, a polarization varying at twice the applied frequency may be induced. This polarization is capable of launching a wave of the double frequency. We wish now to examine the restriction imposed on the radiation of this second harmonic by the optical dispersion of the crystal. If the refractive indices for the fundamental and the second-harmonic radiation were identical, appreciable conversion could be achieved by irradiating a thick crystal at the fundamental frequency. The variation of the refractive index imposes a limitation on the production of second-harmonic radiation.

Let us consider a plane wave of angular frequency ω passing through a sheet of material of thickness l. We seek an expression for the intensity of the second-harmonic radiation at the exit surface of the sheet. For the sake of simplicity the attenuation of the fundamental wave through the crystal is neglected. The electric field at the fundamental frequency varies as $\sin(k_1x - \omega t)$; *the second-harmonic polarization* varies as $\sin(2k_1x - 2\omega t)$, because the spatial variation of this polarization is anchored to the spatial variation of the fundamental wave. The *second-harmonic radiation*, on the other hand, has the spatial variation $\sin(k_2x - 2\omega t)$, where $k_2 = 2\omega/v_2$, v_2 being the phase velocity for radiation of angular frequency 2ω. The second-harmonic electric field at the exit surface arises through the superposition of the radiation generated throughout the crystal, each contribution added in the proper phase relationships. The contribution from the

---

* $\mathbf{X}$ may depend on the frequency.

slab between x and $x + dx$ to the electric field at the terminal surface is proportional to

$$\sin [2k_1x - 2\omega(t - t')] \, dx,$$

where $t' = (l - x)/v_2$ is the time it takes the radiation of angular frequency 2ω to reach the terminal surface. Since $2\omega t' = k_2(l - x)$, the second-harmonic electric field generated is proportional to

$$\int_0^l \sin [(2k_1 - k_2)x - 2\omega t + k_2l] \, dx.$$

This integral when evaluated yields a time-varying function of the form $\sin (\varphi - 2\omega t)$ multiplied by an amplitude

$$A = \frac{\sin (k_1 - \frac{1}{2}k_2)l}{k_1 - \frac{1}{2}k_2}. \tag{1.9}$$

On introducing the refractive indices n_1 and n_2 for the angular frequencies ω and 2ω, respectively, we have

$$k_1 = \frac{2\pi n_1}{\lambda_0} \quad \text{and} \quad k_2 = \frac{4\pi n_2}{\lambda_0},$$

where λ_0 is the wavelength of the fundamental frequency in vacuum. Then the intensity of the second harmonic at the exit surface is proportional to

$$I = \frac{\sin^2 \frac{2\pi}{\lambda_0} (n_1 - n_2)l}{(n_1 - n_2)^2}. \tag{1.10}$$

In the absence of dispersion ($n_1 = n_2$) the intensity of the second harmonic at the exit face increases as the square of the crystal thickness. However, if there is dispersion, the maximum possible intensity is that which can be obtained with a crystal of characteristic thickness

$$l' = \frac{1}{4} \frac{\lambda_0}{|n_1 - n_2|}. \tag{1.11}$$

This thickness is often referred to as a "coherence length" and is of the order $20\lambda_0$ for the typical crystals used for second-harmonic generation.

The periodic variation of the intensity of the second harmonic with plate thickness was verified in the experiment of Maker, Terhune, Nisenoff, and Savage [4]. A thin (0.78 mm) quartz plate was placed in the path of ruby laser radiation as shown in Fig. 105. Rotation of the crystal plate varied its effective thickness for the radiation passing through in a fixed direction. The experimental results shown in Fig. 106 demonstrate the

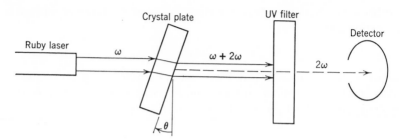

Fig. 105. Experiment showing the effect of dispersion on second-harmonic generation.

periodic variation required by (1.10). Excellent numerical agreement was achieved between the calculated and the observed variation in effective thickness.

Efficient production of a second harmonic in a crystal of appreciable thickness thus requires the matching of the refractive indices applicable to the fundamental and the second-harmonic frequencies. In certain bire-fringent crystals it is possible to choose a direction of propagation such that the ordinary refractive index at one frequency is equal to the extra-ordinary refractive index for the other. Figure 107 shows sections of four refractive index surfaces of two uniaxial crystals, quartz and KDP. The

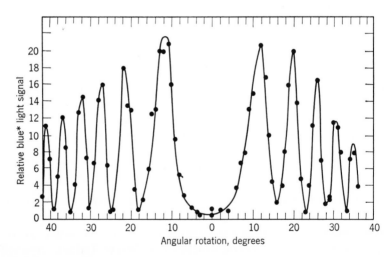

Fig. 106. Second-harmonic generation as a function of the angle of rotation of a 0.78-mm quartz slab. (After Maker *et al.* [4].)

* As 3472-Å radiation appeared to Maker and associates.

subscripts 1 and 2 refer to the ruby laser fundamental and second-harmonic frequencies, respectively, the superscripts o and e refer to the ordinary and the extraordinary rays. Since the crystals are uniaxial, the complete refractive index surfaces are generated by rotating the given sections about the z-axis.

It is seen from Fig. 107 that for quartz neither the n_1^o nor the n_1^e surface intersects either the n_2^o or the n_2^e surface, whereas for KDP the matching condition can be satisfied for rays deviating from the z-axis by the angle θ_0, because $n_1^o = n_2^e(\theta_0)$. The ordinary refractive index n^o is independent of the direction of the ray, but the extraordinary refractive index $n^e(\theta)$ is a function of the angle included between the optic axis and the wave normal. According to one of the basic propositions of crystal optics, the ordinary and the extraordinary rays in a uniaxial crystal propagate with identical speeds along the optic axis, while at an angle θ to the optic axis the velocity of the extraordinary ray is

$$v_e(\theta) = [v_o^2 \cos^2 \theta + v_e^2 \sin^2 \theta]^{1/2}, \qquad (1.12)$$

where $v_e = v_e(90°)$ is the velocity of this ray in the plane perpendicular to the optic axis. Therefore $n^e(\theta) = c/v_e(\theta)$ satisfies the equation

$$\frac{1}{[n^e(\theta)]^2} = \frac{\cos^2 \theta}{[n^o]^2} + \frac{\sin^2 \theta}{[n^e(90°)]^2}. \qquad (1.13)$$

The n's appearing in (1.13) are all functions of the frequency. For the frequency 2ω we write

$$\frac{1}{[n_2^e(\theta)]^2} = \frac{\cos^2 \theta}{[n_2^o]^2} + \frac{\sin^2 \theta}{[n_2^e(90°)]^2}. \qquad (1.14)$$

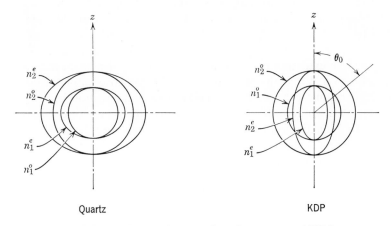

Quartz   KDP

Fig. 107.   Refractive index surfaces for quartz and KDP.

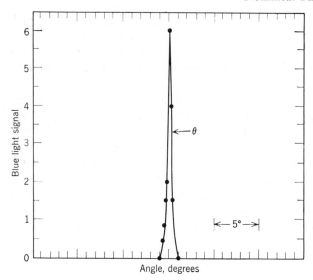

Fig. 108. Second-harmonic intensity as a function of crystal orientation for KDP. Maximum output occurs at $\theta_0 = 55° \pm 2°$. Incident beam from ruby laser. (After Maker *et al.* [4].)

The matching angle θ_0 of Fig. 107 can be calculated by equating $n_2^e(\theta)$ with the known n_1^o and solving (1.14) for θ. Figure 108 shows the observed variation of second-harmonic intensity with the angle θ in the neighborhood of θ_0 [4].

The generation of a second harmonic is a special case of a mixing experiment in nonlinear optics. It is easily seen from the examination of equations (1.4) and (1.8) that the simultaneous application of two fields with frequencies ω_1 and ω_2 produces a polarization at the sum and difference frequencies, $\omega_1 + \omega_2$ and $\omega_1 - \omega_2$. Therefore it is possible to convert energy into radiation at the sum and difference frequencies. This is simply the extension of the principle of *parametric amplification* to the optical region. From the point of view of parametric amplification, the second-harmonic generation is a special case of interaction between two waves with a common frequency. In practice, the generation of sum and difference frequencies is a more difficult matter because at least three waves have to be kept in step, in contrast to the two waves in the case of harmonic generation. The condition for these waves to remain in step is that the vector equation

$$\mathbf{k}_3 = \mathbf{k}_1 \pm \mathbf{k}_2 \tag{1.15}$$

must be satisfied in addition to the scalar equation

$$\omega_3 = \omega_1 \pm \omega_2.$$

The magnitudes of the **k** vectors in a crystal depend, of course, on the direction of the wave normal and on the polarization because $k = \omega/v$, where v is a function of direction and polarization.

So far we have been concerned with harmonic generation within a nonlinear medium upon incidence of a strong light signal. Bloembergen and Pershan [5] have shown that the electromagnetic boundary conditions at the surface of a nonlinear medium require the appearance of a reflected signal at the second-harmonic frequency. In fact, the incorporation of nonlinear polarization in the theory of dielectric media leads to a generalization of the laws of reflection and refraction. The angular relations and the intensities of the refracted and reflected harmonic waves have been calculated [5].

Third-harmonic generation occurs as a consequence of the cubic term in the polarization. In the anisotropic case such a term is replaced by a tensor of fourth rank with $3^4 = 81$ components. The expression is of the form

$$P_i = X_{ijkl}E_jE_kE_l. \qquad (1.16)$$

This tensor component does not change with the permutation of the last three indices, and the tensor does not need to vanish for materials with a center of symmetry. In particular, *third-harmonic generation is possible in isotropic materials*, but the matching of the refractive indices presents a serious practical problem. As we noted in the case of second harmonics, the effect of nonlinear polarization is the mixing of three waves. The third-order term (1.15) accomplishes the mixing of four waves for which $\omega_1 \pm \omega_2 \pm \omega_3 \pm \omega_4 = 0$. Again a similar relationship must hold among the wave vectors.

The experimental material pertaining to harmonic generation and mixing is the subject of the next section.

REFERENCES

1. M. Born and E. Wolf, *Principles of Optics*, Pergamon Press, New York, 1957.
2. P. A. Franken and J. F. Ward, Optical harmonics and nonlinear phenomena, *Rev. Mod. Phys.* **35**, 23–39, 1963.
3. *American Institute of Physics Handbook*, McGraw-Hill, New York, 1957, p. 9-17.
4. P. D. Maker, R. W. Terhune, M. Nisenoff, and C. M. Savage, Effects of dispersion and focusing on the production of optical harmonics, *Phys. Rev. Lett.* **8**, 21–22, 1962.
5. N. Bloembergen and P. S. Pershan, Light waves at the boundary of nonlinear media, *Phys. Rev.* **128**, 606–622, 1962.

2. FREQUENCY CONVERSION EXPERIMENTS

When radiation from a ruby laser is brought to a focus in a quartz crystal, the emission of light at twice the original frequency may be observed. Franken and associates made the first such observation in 1961 [1].

Shortly after the initial discovery it was demonstrated that an efficient conversion of energy from fundamental to second-harmonic radiation takes place only when the two kinds of waves are kept in step in accordance with equation (1.15). The index-matching method of Giordmaine [2] and Maker [3] already mentioned in Section VII.1 provides a means of obtaining efficient conversion from an *unfocused* laser beam propagating in a uniaxial crystal in a preferred direction. (See Fig. 108.) The efficiency of conversion depends on the intensity of the incident radiation. At low intensities, such as those obtainable from an ordinary ruby, the conversion efficiency increases linearly with the incident intensity. According to the experience of Terhune, Maker, and C. M. Savage [4], the conversion efficiency in ADP and KDP crystals saturates just under 20 per cent. This saturation is obtained with focused giant pulse radiation which provides sufficient energy concentration to damage the crystals. A second-harmonic peak power of 200 kW has been obtained with 6mJ energy in a single pulse.

A. Savage and Miller [5, 6] performed a series of experiments to compare the second-harmonic-generating capabilities of crystals for ruby (6943 Å) and for neodymium (1.06 μ) radiation. The same crystals may not be useful for both radiations because the material must be transparent for both the fundamental and the second harmonic. The relative values of the second-harmonic output for ruby are tabulated in Table VII.1. The tabulated values are for orientation only; they have no intrinsic physical significance. More significant are components of the second harmonic polarization tensor X determined for Nd radiation. These are in Table VII.2.*

Miller [6] made the remarkable discovery that the element X_{ijk} for all these materials can be obtained from a fixed matrix by multiplication with the products of the *linear optical susceptibilities*. Let the linear part of the polarization be given by

$$P_i^L = X_{ij}E_j, \tag{2.1}$$

and the quadratic part by

$$P_i^Q = X_{ijk}E_jE_k. \tag{2.2}$$

Here all coefficients are functions of the frequency ω. Miller's theorem asserts that

$$X_{ijk} = X_{ii}^{(2\omega)}X_{jj}^{(\omega)}X_{kk}^{(\omega)}\,\delta_{ijk}.\dagger \tag{2.3}$$

Here δ_{ijk} is a matrix that is the same for all materials within the same crystal symmetry class. The important consequence of Miller's theorem is

* Note that the best harmonic generators for Nd are opaque to the second harmonic of ruby.

† Repetition of indices does not mean summation in (2.3).

that those crystals exhibit large nonlinear effects which have large linear susceptibilities at the frequencies considered.

We have seen in Section VII.1 that the quadratic term in P should lead not only to frequency doubling but to the appearance of a d-c term and to the mixing of two frequencies impressed upon the material simultaneously. Both of these effects were observed. A d-c pulse of about 200 μV was obtained from a KDP crystal through which a 1MW radiation from ruby was passing [7]. The mixing experiments reported include the production of the sum frequencies of radiations from two ruby lasers held at different temperatures [8], the addition of the frequencies of a ruby and a neodymium laser [9], and even the mixing of the incoherent light of a mercury source with the ruby laser light [10]. In each case the second harmonic of the laser radiations is also generated and the output of the desired frequency is maximized by satisfying the vector wave number equation through adjustment of the direction of propagation.

In semiconductor injection lasers one can generate second-harmonic and combination frequencies between the different cavity modes within the laser itself [11]. This effect is expected because of the large nonlinear polarizability of GaAs and similar materials.

Optical second-harmonic generation has been observed in calcite as a function of an applied d-c electric field. This crystal possesses a center of inversion, but the electric-field-induced harmonic generation can be explained because the imposition of the electric field removes the symmetry,

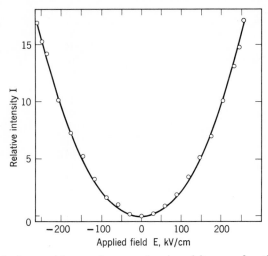

Fig. 109. Optical second-harmonic generation in calcite as a function of applied d-c field. (After Terhune *et al.* [12].)

which demands the vanishing of the quadratic polarization tensor. Examination of the variation of the second-harmonic output as a function of the applied field shows a small but definite second-harmonic output for 0 d-c field. The pertinent observations of Terhune, Maker, and Savage [12] are reproduced in Fig. 109. These observations suggest that the second harmonic in this case is generated either by an induced quadrupole moment which depends quadratically on the electric field components, or by an electric polarization that is bilinear in E and its spatial derivatives.

The production of third harmonics generally requires higher incident fields than second-harmonic productions. Such experiments were performed by Maker and Terhune [13]. They require giant pulse lasers and are very difficult to perform. Their interpretation leads to considerable complexities which one begins to appreciate when contemplating the form of the tensor that is responsible for the third-degree term of polarization.

It is of interest to know whether or not the harmonics generated are *exact* harmonics. High-precision measurements of wavelengths of the fundamental and the second harmonic have not disclosed any detectable

TABLE VII.1.   RELATIVE VALUES OF SECOND-HARMONIC
OUTPUT FOR 6943-Å RADIATION [5]

Power level 200 watts at the focusing lens, except for crystals marked with an asterisk, which were explored with low laser power. Outputs are normalized for KDP output = 1000.

Material	Number of Samples	Crystal Face Normal to Beam	Harmonic Output
KDP	2	(110)	1000
ADP	2	(110)	720
K-doped $NaNbO_3^*$	2	(101)	230
Quartz	3	(001)	34.0
$NaClO_3^*$	2	(110)	11.0
$NaClO_3^*$	2	(111)	8.0
Tourmaline	1	(001)	10.0
TGS[a]	2	(101)	3.2
TGS	2	(100)	1.3
TGS	2	(001)	1.0
Rochelle salt	3	(110)	1.2
$NaBrO_3$	2	(111)	0.54
GASeH[b]	1	(001)	2.0
GGSH	1	(001)	0.82
GASH	3	(001)	0.39
GGSeH	1	(001)	0.21

[a] Triglycine sulfate.
[b] Guanidine aluminium selenate hexahydrate.

difference from the 2-to-1 frequency ratio [14, 15]. These careful examinations of the frequency ratio are motivated by the conjecture that phonon processes might be significant in the second-harmonic production. These could provide shifts in the frequency of the second-harmonic radiation, but no experimental evidence for shifts has been found.

TABLE VII.2. SECOND-ORDER POLARIZATION COEFFICIENTS
FOR 1.06-μ RADIATION [6]

The coefficients are normalized for KDP = 1. To convert to electrostatic units multiply by 3×10^{-9}.

Crystal	X_{312}	X_{123}	Crystal	X_{333}	X_{311}	X_{133}
KDP	1.00	1.01 ± 0.05	ZnO	14.3 ± 0.4	4.3 ± 0.4	4.7 ± 0.4
ADP	0.99 ± 0.06	0.98 ± 0.05	CdS	63 ± 4	32 ± 2	35 ± 3
KH$_2$AsO$_4$	1.06 ± 0.06	1.12 ± 0.05	BaTiO$_3$	14 ± 1	37 ± 3	35 ± 3
Gap	—	175 ± 30		X_{111}		
GaAs	—	560 ± 140	Quartz	0.82 ± 0.04		

REFERENCES

1. P. A. Franken, A. E. Hill, C. W. Peters, and G. Weinreich, Generation of optical harmonics, *Phys. Rev. Lett.* **7**, 118–119, 1961.
2. J. A. Giordmaine, Mixing of light beams in crystals, *Phys. Rev. Lett.* **8**, 19–20, 1962.
3. P. D. Maker, R. W. Terhune, M. Nisenoff, and C. M. Savage, Effects of dispersion and focusing on the production of optical harmonics, *Phys. Rev. Lett.* **8**, 21–22, 1962.
4. R. W. Terhune, P. D. Maker, and C. M. Savage, Observation of saturation effects in optical harmonic generation, *Appl. Phys. Lett.* **2**, 54–55, 1963.
5. A. Savage and R. C. Miller, Measurements of second harmonic generation of the ruby laser line in piezoelectric crystals, *Appl. Optics* **1**, 661–663, 1962.
6. R. C. Miller, Optical second harmonic generation in piezoelectric crystals, *Appl. Phys. Lett.* **5**, 17–19, 1964.
7. M. Bass, P. A. Franken, J. F. Ward, and G. Weinreich, Optical rectification, *Phys. Rev. Lett.* **9**, 446–448, 1962.
8. M. Bass, P. A. Franken, A. E. Hill, C. W. Peters, and G. Weinreich, Optical mixing, *Phys. Rev. Lett.* **8**, 18, 1962.
9. R. C. Miller and A. Savage, Harmonic generation and mixing of CaWO$_4$:Nd^{3+} and ruby pulsed laser beams in piezoelectric crystals, *Phys. Rev.* **128**, 2175–2179, 1962.
10. A. W. Smith and N. Braslau, Optical mixing of coherent and incoherent light, *IBM J. Res. Dev.* **6**, 361–362, 1962.
11. A. W. Smith, M. I. Nathan, *et al.*, Harmonic generation in injection lasers, *J. Appl. Phys.* **35**, 733–734, 1964.
12. R. W. Terhune, P. D. Maker, and C. M. Savage, Optical harmonic generation in calcite, *Phys. Rev. Lett.* **8**, 404–406, 1962.
13. P. D. Maker and R. W. Terhune, Study of optical effects due to an induced polarization third order in the electric field strength, *Phys. Rev.* **137**, A801–818, 1965.

14. H. S. Boyne and W. C. Martin, Experimental determination of the frequency ratio of optical harmonics, *J. Opt. Soc. Am.* **52**, 880–884, 1962.
15. I. D. Abella, Optical harmonic frequency ratio measurements, *Proc. IRE* **50**, 1824–1825, 1962.

3. RAMAN EFFECT

The Classical Raman Effect

Scattering is the change in directional distribution that radiation suffers when passing through matter. It is usually observed with radiation from a practically monochromatic source. Most of the scattered radiation is observed to have the same frequency as the incident beam. This directional redistribution of radiation without a change of frequency is referred to as *Rayleigh scattering*. A small fraction of the energy may, however, be scattered at a number of discrete frequencies, some higher and some lower than that of the incident radiation. The lines found at lower frequencies, which are called Stokes lines, are more intense than the lines found at higher frequencies, the anti-Stokes lines. The occurrence of these discrete lines in the spectrum of the scattered light in addition to the line of the incident light is called the *Raman effect*. A repetition of the experiment, using the same scattering substance but changing the frequency of the incident light, will always yield the same pattern: the number of Raman lines and their frequency shifts from the Rayleigh line remain constant. The frequency shifts of the Raman lines, their intensity, and their polarization are characteristic for the scattering substance.

An apparatus for the measurement of Raman scattered light consists essentially of a sample cell illuminated by one or several very intense light sources, and a high-speed spectrometer with photographic or photoelectric recording, collecting the light scattered at right angles to the direction of

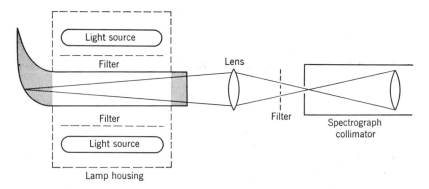

Fig. 110. Experimental arrangement for Raman spectroscopy.

the incident light. Figure 110 shows the schematic of a typical apparatus for Raman spectroscopy.

In classical physics the occurrence of the Raman effect is explained as a result of the interaction of the polarization induced by the incident light with the internal motions of the molecule. Both rotational and vibrational motions should be considered. In the case of rotation, the polarizability of the molecule may be dependent on the orientation of the molecule with respect to the incident wave; in the case of vibration, the polarizability may be a function of the intermolecular distance. These molecular motions are slow compared with the variation of the electromagnetic vectors in the optical region. The modulation of the polarization P at the rate ν_i of the molecular motions causes the generation of radiation at the frequencies $\nu_p \pm \nu_i$, where ν_p is the frequency of the incident radiation. It is easy to see that a molecular vibration produces a Raman line only when it changes the polarizability of the molecule. According to the classical theory, Stokes and anti-Stokes lines should appear with equal intensity. Experimental evidence shows that the Stokes lines are far more intense. Only quantum theory gives a satisfactory quantitative description of the Raman effect.

The following semiclassical argument provides some insight into the situation: The scattering process is an interaction between the molecule, which has its discrete energy levels W_k, and the incoming photon with the energy $h\nu_p$. During the interaction between molecule and photon, the molecule undergoes a double transition by first absorbing and then emitting a photon. The absorption of the photon will raise the energy of the molecule to $W_k + h\nu_p = W'$. In general this will not correspond to a stationary state of the system (Fig. 111). The molecule will therefore make a virtual

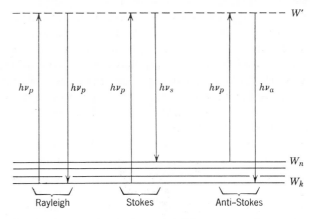

Fig. 111.   Energy-level schemes of different types of scattering.

transition to an intermediate state W', but since energy is not preserved by this transition, it will return within an extremely short time to a stationary state under emission of a photon. If this is the initial state, W_k, the frequencies of incident and emitted photon are the same (Rayleigh line). If the transition is made to an excited state of energy W_n, the emitted photon has a lower frequency $h\nu_p - W_n = h\nu_s$ (Stokes line). Similarly, if the incoming photon interacted with a molecule in the excited state of energy W_n, the molecule may either return to the same state, under emission of a photon of the same frequency, or return to the ground state under emission of a photon of higher frequency, $h\nu_p + W_n = h\nu_a$ (anti-Stokes line). The two processes, which result in a net energy transfer between molecule and photons, constitute the Raman effect. This consideration explains why the Stokes lines are more intense than the anti-Stokes lines: Only molecules in an excited energy state can produce the anti-Stokes lines, and since in thermal equilibrium the number of molecules in the various energy states is governed by the Boltzmann distribution law, the population of the ground state exceeds that of the excited states. The calculation of the selection rules and line intensities requires the application of perturbation theory in quantum mechanics. The principal difference between fluorescence and Raman effect is that in fluorescence there is a transition to a stationary upper level, whereas for Raman effect there is no such stationary state.

The usefulness of the Raman effect is based on the fact that it is easier to make spectroscopic observations in the visible and in the near ultraviolet region than in the far infrared. By using the Raman effect it is possible to shift molecular spectra from the region of 100 to 3000 cm^{-1} to a convenient region by observing the differences between the molecular frequencies and that of a mercury arc (2536.5 Å) or another similar source.

Raman spectroscopy was an important tool for the exploration of molecular structure when detectors in the far infrared were very crude. With the development of good infrared detectors, Raman spectroscopy has lost some of its significance. Only an infinitesimal fraction of the source energy is converted into a Raman spectrum; therefore powerful sources and long exposure times are required. Since lasers provide a high-power monochromatic source, it is logical to try them out as Raman sources. The direct use of an ordinary ruby laser as an irradiator is possible, but does not seem to offer great advantages [1]. The desirable properties of the ruby laser are offset by its relatively low duty cycle, and most of all by the low frequency of its output. The Raman scattering is proportional to ν^4, thus giving the mercury source a great intrinsic advantage. In addition, detection is again easier in the 2500- to 3000-Å region than in the 7000- to 9500-Å region. With powerful gas lasers available in the blue and green region of the spectrum, the laser may yet be employed as a Raman source in the classical manner. Nevertheless, the ruby laser is an important tool of Raman spectroscopy, since it can be used to excite *stimulated Raman emission*, provided that the material to be examined is included in the laser configuration.

Stimulated Raman Effect

In the classical Raman effect the particles of matter scatter in random phase, and the resulting radiation is distributed uniformly in all directions. In the case of the stimulated Raman effect to be described the radiators are kept in phase, with a resulting sharp directionality of the emitted radiation. Such a phenomenon can occur only when the material is put in the condition of negative absorption for the Raman radiation. When this condition is achieved and mirrors are provided for feedback, the spontaneous or ordinary Raman effect will start the wave, which is then amplified and produces a Raman laser radiation.

The possibility of producing such a condition evolved before the advent of lasers. Javan [2] and Yajima [3] examined the conditions for amplification in two- and three-level masers excited by irradiation (optical pumping). They arrived at generalizations of the condition for negative absorption (equation (6.11) of Chapter I) valid for the case of very intense pumping radiation.

It is clear from Fig. 112 that negative absorption can be produced for the frequency ν_{s0} by the application of a strong pump signal of frequency

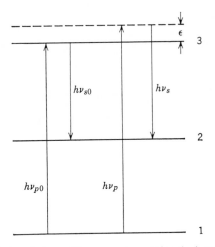

Fig. 112. Stimulated emission with resonant pumping (ν_{p0}) and with nonresonant pumping (ν_p).

ν_{p0}, which will cause saturation of level 3 and hence inversion of population for levels 2 and 3. Beyond this, quantum-mechanical calculations show that negative absorption can be achieved with a signal of frequency ν_p, which leads to the virtual level above level 3 provided that

$$\nu_p - \nu_{p0} = \nu_s - \nu_{s0} = \epsilon/h. \tag{3.1}$$

The mechanism is the same as that discussed in connection with the ordinary Raman scattering: A photon of energy $h\nu_p$ is absorbed, one of energy $h\nu_s$ is emitted, and the molecule changes its energy by the amount $h(\nu_p - \nu_s) = h(\nu_{p0} - \nu_{s0})$, a quantity equal to the energy difference between levels 2 and 1. The calculations of Yajima show that the coefficient of absorption, α_s, can be made negative by suitable choice of the pump power, and moreover that $|\alpha_s|$ increases with pump power and decreases with deviation of the pump frequency from ν_{p0}. It appears, therefore, that under proper circumstances one should be able to obtain *amplification at the Raman frequency* ν_s.

The calculations sketched above did not lead directly to the Raman laser, which was discovered accidentally. While experimenting with a giant pulse laser provided with a nitrobenzene-filled Kerr cell as a shutter, Woodbury and Ng [4] observed the emission of radiation at 7670 Å. The energy emitted at this wavelength was about one-fifth the energy emitted at 6943 Å; the collimation of the beams appeared about equal. A group of investigators led by Eckhardt and Hellwarth identified the 7670-Å radiation as a line of the Raman spectrum of nitrobenzene. In an experimental arrangement sketched in Fig. 113 they produced a host of similar lines in organic fluids contained in a cell within the mirrors of the giant pulse laser [5]. These lines were identified by comparing the wave number difference between ruby (14,402 cm^{-1}) and the observed lines with the known Raman shifts of the substance investigated. The first results of Eckhardt and associates are reproduced in Table VII.3. They show excellent agreement with Raman shifts measured by classical methods.

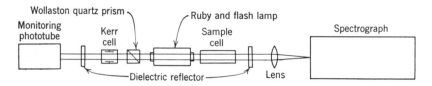

Fig. 113. Experimental arrangement for measurements of stimulated Raman scattering.

TABLE VII.3. STIMULATED RAMAN EMISSION OF SEVERAL LIQUIDS

Observed wave number deviations from ruby (14,402 cm^{-1}) are listed against most intense Raman shifts in prior literature. (After Eckhardt, Hellwarth, et al. [5].)

Liquid	Ruby Wave Number Minus Liquid Wave Number (cm^{-1})	Strongest Raman Shifts (cm^{-1})
Benzene	3064 ± 4	3064
	990 ± 2	991.6
	2 × (992 ± 2)	
Nitrobenzene	1344 ± 2	1345
	2 × (1346 ± 2)	1004
	3 × (1340 ± 5)	
Toluene	1004 ± 4	785
		1002
1 Bromonaphthalene	1368 ± 4	1363
		3060
Pyridine	992 ± 2	991
	2 × (992 ± 5)	3054
Cyclohexane	2852 ± 1	801
		2853
Deuterated benzene C_6D_6	944.3 ± 1	944.7
	2 × (944 ± 1)	2292

Three observations indicate that the phenomenon described is *stimulated emission*, that is, the manifestation of an amplification in the material that overcomes cavity losses. First, the beam collimation is the same as that of the ruby radiation. Second, spectral narrowing is observed when the input intensity is increased. Third, a marked threshold exists both for the pump intensity and for the length of the liquid column for the production of this Raman radiation.

Stimulated Raman spectra of many solids, liquids, and gases have been produced. Both Stokes and anti-Stokes lines were observed and the measured frequency shifts are in excellent agreement with those expected from theory [6–10].

REFERENCES

1. S. P. S. Porto and D. L. Wood, Ruby optical maser as a Raman source, *J. Opt. Soc. Am.* **52**, 251–252, 1962.
2. A. Javan, Transitions à plusieurs quanta et amplification maser dans les systèmes à deux niveaux, *J. Phys. Radium* **19**, 806–808, 1958.
3. T. Yajima, Three-level maser action in gas, *J. Phys. Soc. Jap.* **16**, 1594–1604, 1961.
4. E. J. Woodbury and W. K. Ng, Ruby laser operation in the near IR, *Proc. IRE* **50**, 2367, 1962.

5. G. Eckhardt, R. W. Hellwarth, F. J. McClung, *et al.*, Stimulated Raman scattering from organic liquids, *Phys. Rev. Lett.* **9**, 455–457, 1962.
6. M. Geller, D. P. Bortfeld, and W. R. Sooy, New Woodbury-Raman laser materials, *Appl. Phys. Lett.* **3**, 36–40, 1963.
7. G. Eckhardt, D. P. Bortfeld, and M. Geller, Stimulated emission of Stokes and anti-Stokes Raman lines from diamond, calcite, and α-sulfur single crystals, *Appl. Phys. Lett.* **3**, 137–138, 1963.
8. R. W. Minck, R. W. Terhune, and W. G. Rado, Laser-stimulated Raman effect and resonant four-photon interactions in gases H_2, D_2, and CH_4, *Appl. Phys. Lett.* **3**, 181–184, 1963.
9. B. P. Stoicheff, Characteristics of stimulated Raman radiation generated by coherent light, *Phys. Lett.* **7**, 186–188, 1963.
10. D. P. Bortfeld, M. Geller, and G. Eckhardt, Combination lines in the stimulated Raman spectrum of styrene, *J. Chem. Phys.* **40**, 1770–1771, 1964.

4. CLASSICAL THEORY OF AMPLIFICATION AND RAMAN EFFECT

Certain important aspects of the nonlinear interaction of light and matter can be comprehended in the framework of classical physics. In what follows, we shall illustrate on a greatly simplified model the type of calculations that can be carried out. It was stated in Section VII.1 that the nonlinear propagation effects can be calculated by relating the variation of **P** with **E**. We shall examine this matter further.

In a nonmagnetic insulator Maxwell's equations lead to the relation

$$\nabla \times \nabla \times \mathbf{E} + \epsilon_0\mu_0 \frac{\partial^2 \mathbf{E}}{\partial t^2} = \mu_0 \frac{\partial^2 \mathbf{P}}{\partial t^2}, \tag{4.1}$$

where ϵ_0 and μ_0 are the inductive capacities of vacuum. They are related to the velocity of light by the equation $c = (\epsilon_0\mu_0)^{-1/2}$. We can separate **P** into a part which depends linearly on **E**, and a nonlinear part

$$\mathbf{P} = \mathbf{P}_L + \mathbf{P}_{NL}, \tag{4.2}$$

where $\mathbf{P}_L = \epsilon_0\chi\mathbf{E}$. For the sake of simplicity we assume a scalar suscepti-bility χ, but the calculation proceeds in a like manner in the anisotropic case. We write $\epsilon = \epsilon_0(1 + \chi)$, and obtain in place of (4.1)

$$\nabla \times \nabla \times \mathbf{E} + \epsilon\mu_0 \frac{\partial^2 \mathbf{E}}{\partial t^2} = \mu_0 \frac{\partial^2 \mathbf{P}_{NL}}{\partial t^2}. \tag{4.3}$$

Thus the linear part of the polarization is taken into account by the use of the parameter ϵ in place of ϵ_0. As a consequence, the velocity of waves in the medium becomes $v = (\epsilon\mu_0)^{-1/2}$ in place of c. We shall assume that the linear part of **P** has been so disposed of, and we shall drop the subscripts from $\mathbf{P}_{NL}$ in further discussion of wave propagation.

In the general situation one must consider **E** and **P** in three dimensions and not assume that these vectors are always parallel. Nevertheless for the sake of illustrating the mathematical technique involved, it may be instructive to consider a scalar problem.

We assume that all electric fields are parallel to the x-axis and we examine the growth of the amplitude of a plane wave:

$$E_x = A(z) \cos (kz - \omega t) \tag{4.4}$$

as a consequence of a polarization P_x varying in time at the same angular frequency. The variation of P_x in space need not be the same as that of E_x, and the phases of these two quantities need not coincide at $z = 0$ and $t = 0$. Therefore we write

$$P_x = P_0 \cos (k'z - \omega t + \varphi). \tag{4.5}$$

We assume that the variation of A with z is slow compared with k, and we seek to determine the rate of this variation. The first term in (4.3) is

$$-\frac{\partial^2 E_x}{\partial x^2} \approx 2A'k \sin (kz - \omega t) + k^2 A \cos (kz - \omega t). \tag{4.6}$$

The second term is

$$\epsilon\mu_0 \frac{\partial^2 E_x}{\partial t^2} = -\epsilon\mu_0\omega^2 E_x = -k^2 E_x. \tag{4.7}$$

Therefore

$$2A'k \sin (kz - \omega t) = -\mu_0\omega^2 P_0 \cos (k'z - \omega t + \varphi), \tag{4.8}$$

or, after trigonometric simplifications,

$$2A'k \sin kz = \mu_0\omega^2 P_0 \sin (k'z + \varphi - 90°). \tag{4.9}$$

Amplification of the electric field takes place at a maximum rate at $z = 0$ when $\varphi = 90°$. When, on the other hand, $\varphi = -90°$, maximum deamplification will take place there. When $k' = k$, the phase relationship between E and P is preserved over the medium. Maximum amplification takes place everywhere when the polarization leads the field by $90°$. The equation (4.8) may be put in a complex form,

$$2A'k \operatorname{Re} e^{i(kz - \omega t + \pi/2)} = \mu_0\omega^2 P_0 \operatorname{Re} e^{i(k'z - \omega t + \varphi)}, \tag{4.10}$$

from which it follows that

$$\frac{dA}{dt} = k\epsilon^{-1} \operatorname{Re} e^{i[(k' - k)z + \varphi - \pi/2]}. \tag{4.11}$$

The foregoing analysis is a simplified version of the calculation necessary in the three-dimensional case. Not only must we permit a tensor relationship between $\mathbf{P}$ and $\mathbf{E}$, but these vectors may have a different spatial distribution, that is, k and k' must be replaced by vectors which are not necessarily collinear. Finally, the time variation of **P** and **E** may not take place at a single frequency. In the general case equation (4.8) describes only the relation valid for the Fourier components of angular frequency ω.

To discuss the one-dimensional model of frequency mixing, we consider the medium to be subject to the influence of an electric field which is the sum of two plane waves with angular frequencies ω_1 and ω_2. Their velocities may be different because ϵ is a function of the frequency. Thus

$$E_x = E_1 \cos (\omega_1 t - k_1 z) + E_2 \cos (\omega_2 t - k_2 z). \qquad (4.12)$$

Assuming a quadratic polarization of the form (1.8), we obtain in the one-dimensional case $P = XE^2$. The full expression of P is

$$P = X[E_1{}^2 \cos^2 (\omega_1 t - k_1 z) + E_2{}^2 \cos^2 (\omega_2 t - k_2 z)$$
$$+ 2E_1 E_2 \cos (\omega_1 t - k_1 z) \cos (\omega_2 t - k_2 z)]. \qquad (4.13)$$

The first two terms play a role in frequency doubling. Mixing is accomplished by the last term, which may be written in the form

$$XE_1 E_2\{\cos [(\omega_1 + \omega_2)t - (k_1 + k_2)z] + \cos [(\omega_1 - \omega_2)t - (k_1 - k_2)z]\}. \qquad (4.14)$$

The polarization is now resolved into its Fourier components with the components at frequencies $\omega_1 + \omega_2$ and $\omega_1 - \omega_2$ written out in (4.14).

Given a wave at the frequency $\omega_3 = \omega_1 + \omega_2$, we have

$$E_3 = A_3(z) \cos (k_3 z - \omega_3 t); \qquad (4.15)$$

its growth is determined by the polarization

$$P_3 = XE_1 E_2 \cos [(k_1 + k_2)z - \omega_3 t + \varphi_3]. \qquad (4.16)$$

Using (4.11) with obvious modifications, we have

$$\frac{dA(z)}{dz} = \frac{k_3 X E_1 E_2}{\epsilon_3} \cos [(k_1 + k_2 - k_3)z + \varphi_3 + 90°]. \qquad (4.17)$$

Amplification or attenuation at different depths will remain in phase when the value of $k_1 + k_2 - k_3$ is 0. A similar relationship can be written for the growth (or attenuation) of the wave of frequency $\omega_4 = \omega_1 - \omega_2$.

When waves are present at the three frequencies ω_1, ω_2, and $\omega_3 = \omega_1 + \omega_2$, three equations similar to (4.17) describe the growth of their amplitudes A_1, A_2, and A_3. Energy may be transferred from one oscillation to the others. This is the phenomenon of parametric amplification based on the quadratic response of the material in which the waves propagate. More general discussion of this problem is found in the literature [1].

In order to analyze the stimulated Raman effect quantitatively, one must first assess the effect of the impressed electric oscillations on a molecular system and calculate the time-variable polarization. Then the amplifying or attenuating properties of a medium with such polarization are calculated in the manner already illustrated. Again we simplify the problem by making a one-dimensional model and by regarding the molecule as also one-dimensional with one degree of freedom.

Let x denote the vibrational coordinate of the molecule with $x = 0$ chosen as the equilibrium value. The damped oscillations of the molecule are described by

$$\ddot{x} + \Delta_0\dot{x} + \omega_0^2 x = F(t), \tag{4.18}$$

an equation formerly encountered in Chapter II (4.1). The term $F(t)$ is the impressed force, Δ_0 is a small damping term, and ω_0 is the angular frequency of the free undamped oscillation. It is assumed that an external electric field E exerts a force on the molecule proportional to E^2, and that the change in polarizability induced by the molecular deformation x is proportional to x. Then the nonlinear polarizability to be calculated is of the form

$$P = \alpha x E, \tag{4.19}$$

where α is constant; x depends on E and on the parameters of the molecule. It is to be calculated from (4.18). The calculation has to be carried out for the different frequencies at which oscillations may arise when the molecule is subjected to an electric field consisting of a large "pump" field at angular frequency ω_p and a small signal field at the angular frequency ω_s. Hence

$$E = E_p \cos \omega_p t + E_s \cos \omega_s t. \tag{4.20}$$

The driving force $F(t) = \beta E^2$ has components at the frequencies $2\omega_p$, $\omega_p + \omega_s$, $\omega_p - \omega_s$, and $2\omega_s$. Since the molecular oscillator has very low loss, it will respond significantly only to a narrow band of frequencies around its resonant frequency ω_0. Of the frequencies listed above only $\omega_p - \omega_s$ can lie in this range because the molecular oscillations proceed at much lower rates than the optical oscillations. Without a loss of generality we can assume $\omega_p > \omega_s$.* We set $\omega_p - \omega_s$ equal to ω_0; then the molecule is subjected to a force at this frequency:

$$F(\omega_0, t) = \beta E_p E_s \cos \omega_0 t. \tag{4.21}$$

This force produces a displacement which lags 90 degrees behind the driving force. It is

$$x = \beta E_p E_s \omega_0^{-1} \Delta_0^{-1} \cos (\omega_0 t - \pi/2). \tag{4.22}$$

* We have not used the relation $E_p > E_s$; this is a practical consideration which enters later.

The polarization is obtained by substituting the expression of E from (4.20) and that of x from (4.22) into (4.19). Again a combination of frequencies takes place. The first term in (4.20) generates

$$\frac{\alpha\beta}{\omega_0 \Delta_0} E_p{}^2 E_s \{\cos [(\omega_p + \omega_0)t - \pi/2] + \cos [(\omega_p - \omega_0)t + \pi/2]\}. \quad (4.23)$$

The second term generates

$$\frac{\alpha\beta}{\omega_0 \Delta_0} E_p E_s{}^2 \{\cos [(\omega_s + \omega_0)t - \pi/2] + \cos [(\omega_s - \omega_0)t + \pi/2]\}. \quad (4.24)$$

The second term in (4.23) is of the frequency ω_s. It leads the signal E_s by 90 degrees, and therefore will cause the amplification of that signal. The first term in (4.24) is of frequency ω_p. It lags behind the signal E_p by 90 degrees, and therefore will cause its attenuation. In this manner energy fed into the system at the higher pump frequency ω_p can be transformed into energy at the signal frequency $\omega_s = \omega_p - \omega_0$. So far we have shown that amplification at the frequency ω_s is possible. Then with the addition of mirrors feedback is provided and radiation at this frequency is built up starting from the noise level to a high intensity whenever the amplification is large enough to overcome all losses in the system. To ensure adequate amplification, the pump amplitude E_p is chosen as large as practically possible. The need for doing this is apparent from (4.23).

The first term in (4.23) indicates that a signal with a frequency $\omega_p + \omega_0$ may also be amplified provided that a signal at the Stokes frequency $\omega_s = \omega_p - \omega_0$ is already present. Therefore under favorable circumstances an anti-Stokes radiation at the frequency $\omega_p + \omega_0$ may also be generated. When all these signals are already present in sufficient intensity, further combinations at frequencies $\omega_p \pm 2\omega_0$, $\omega_p \pm 3\omega_0$, and so forth may also arise.

It is seen from the formulas (4.23) and (4.24) that the Raman effect is a third-order effect. Therefore it may occur in media with a center of symmetry, particularly in isotropic materials.

The above discussion of the stimulated Raman effect is over-simplified largely because we have used a one-dimensional model. A correct treatment of this subject takes into account the vector character of the electric field, and the spatial and directional distribution of the oscillations, as well as the finite nature of linewidths. Concerning these matters, and the still controversial directional and intensity distribution of Raman radiation, the reader is referred to the literature [2–5].

REFERENCES

1. J. A. Armstrong, N. Bloembergen, J. Ducuing, and P. S. Pershan, Interactions between light waves in a non-linear dielectric, *Phys. Rev.* **127**, 1918–1939, 1962.

2. E. Garmire, F. Pandarese, and C. H. Townes, Coherently driven molecular vibrations and light modulation, *Phys. Rev. Lett.* **11**, 160–163, 1963.
3. N. Bloembergen and Y. R. Shen, Coupling between vibrations and light waves in Raman laser media, *Phys. Rev. Lett.* **12**, 504–507, 1964.
4. V. T. Platonenko and R. V. Khokhlov, On the mechanism of operation of a Raman laser, *Soviet Phys. JETP* **19**, 378–381, 1964 (**46**, 555–559, 1964).
5. V. M. Fain and E. G. Yashchin, Theory of stimulated Raman radiation, *Soviet Phys. JETP* **19**, 474–483, 1964 (**46**, 695–709, 1964).

5. MULTIPLE-PHOTON ABSORPTION

The simultaneous absorption of more than one photon by an atom that is not capable of absorbing a single photon of the energy employed in the experiment is a phenomenon closely related to the nonlinear processes discussed in this chapter. The theoretical possibility of such a process was demonstrated by Göppert-Mayer in 1931, but experimental realization came only with the advent of lasers because the experiments require a monochromatic source of very high intensity.

Kaiser and Garrett demonstrated double-photon absorption in CaF_2 crystals doped with Eu in 1961 [1]. Such absorption was observed later in Cs vapor [2] and in a number of aromatic organic compounds, such as naphthalene, anthracene, phenanthrene, and others [3, 4, 5], The simultaneous absorption of three photons was demonstrated by Singh and Bradley in 1964 [6].

The chief experimental problem in these studies is to measure the absorption, which is infinitesimal in comparison with the radiation present at the laser frequency. The occurrence of a multiple-quantum absorption must be inferred from the state of the absorbing material. The materials chosen for the experiment must have an energy level at twice the single-photon energy above their ground state, and they must return to the ground state by means of a fluorescent or phosphorescent process which serves as an indicator that atoms have been raised to the level in question. The situation in the case of a two-quantum absorption is favorable because the direct return from the double-quantum level to the ground level in a single transition is forbidden, so that the atom is forced to return over a detour with the emission of radiation of lower frequency.

The multiple-quantum-absorption experiments were done with ruby; the absorption of two quanta of this radiation produces an energy change equivalent to 28,800 cm^{-1}. In all cases fluorescence or phosphorescence was observed in the blue and green regions corresponding to energies between 17,000 and 25,000 cm^{-1}. Excitation of the material by ultraviolet light from the flashtube of the laser is ruled out by careful filtering and by demonstrating that the fluorescent output is proportional to the square of the laser output, which is monitored separately. Harmonic generation is eliminated as a cause of the observed phenomenon by carrying out the experiments in materials which, because of their symmetry, do not generate a second harmonic.

The theory of double-quantum absorption indicates that the cross section of the process is proportional to the rate at which quanta are incident and to the factor $g(2\nu_i - \nu_c)$, where ν_c is the center of the absorption band, $g(\nu - \nu_c)$ is the line shape of the absorption, and ν_i is the frequency of the incident photon. It is also shown that the double-photon process preserves the parity of the state; therefore it will always occur between states among which a transition with single-photon emission is forbidden [7]. Triple-photon absorption, on the other hand, results in the change of parity and in the generation of fluorescence proportional to the third power of the incident intensity.

REFERENCES

1. W. Kaiser and C. G. B. Garrett, Two photon excitation in $CaF_2:Eu^{2+}$, *Phys. Rev. Lett.* **7**, 229–231, 1961.
2. I. D. Abella, Optical double-photon absorption in cesium vapor, *Phys. Rev. Lett.* **9**, 453–455, 1962.
3. W. L. Peticolas, J. P. Goldsborough, and K. E. Rieckhoff, Double photon excitation in organic crystals, *Phys. Rev. Lett.* **10**, 43–45, 1963.
4. S. Singh and B. P. Stoicheff, Double-photon excitation of fluorescence in anthracene single crystals, *J. Chem. Phys.* **38**, 2032–2033, 1963.
5. A. H. Adelman and C. M. Verber, Two-photon excitation of phosphorescence and fluorescence, *J. Chem. Phys.* **39**, 931–933, 1963.
6. S. Singh and L. T. Bradley, Three-photon absorption in naphthalene crystals by laser excitation, *Phys. Rev. Lett.* **12**, 612–614, 1964.
7. D. A. Kleinman, Laser and two-photon processes, *Phys. Rev.* **125**, 87–88, 1962.

VIII

Laser Applications

Laser applications are so diverse and so numerous that their adequate discussion would require an entire book. All we can do here is to make a quick survey of this field and select a few examples for detailed discussion.

Three basic properties distinguish the laser light from light obtainable from other sources: high intensity, monochromaticity and the related coherence in time domain, coherence of radiation emanating from different parts of the laser and the resulting collimation. In all these attributes laser light exceeds ordinary light by several orders of magnitude. The availability of lasers makes it possible to accomplish previously impossible scientific and technological tasks, and in some cases it makes the performance of otherwise difficult tasks easier.

Some of the applications are in the field of pure science, as is the exploration of the laws of interaction of atoms and molecules with electromagnetic fields of high intensity. These are special situations about which very little can be said in general. The multiple-quantum-absorption experiments described in Section VII.5 belong in this category.

Many of the promising laser applications lie in the field of measurement and instrumentation. These and the communications applications depend primarily on the precision properties of the laser light. Technological, military, and biological applications depend mostly on the ability of laser light to concentrate large power in a small volume over a short period of time.

1. APPLICATIONS TO MEASUREMENT AND INSTRUMENTATION

Measurement of Distance and Motion

The coherence of the light obtainable from a gas laser makes it possible to extend the range and precision of measurements based on interferometry, while the high monochromaticity leads to an improvement of the precision of measurements based on a frequency change. We are dealing with improvements by a factor of at least 1000, and the results are quite spectacular.

Interferometry with ordinary light sources is possible only when the path difference does not exceed a few centimeters. With a He-Ne laser as a source, the permissible path difference exceeds any convenient laboratory distance. Such a laser was used to determine the length of a meter bar by an automatic fringe counting method [1].* In many laboratories He-Ne lasers are used with interferometric measuring equipment to evaluate the quality of optical components such as lenses, prisms, and laser rods. When such measurements are made with ordinary light sources, it is necessary to insert a high-quality compensating plate in the reference leg of the interferometer. For large optical components the production of compensating plates of the required quality is prohibitively difficult. No such compensation is necessary for a laser light.

The great sensitivity of the laser frequency to a minute displacement of one of its mirrors may be used as a detector of extremely small motion, such as that which must be observed on the suspended mass of a seismograph. The velocity of a moving object can be measured by comparing the frequency of the signal reflected from the object with the emitted frequency. The frequency shift is given by the formula $\Delta f = 2fv/c$, where v is the radial velocity of the target. For a near infrared laser f is about 10^{14} cps; therefore one obtains Doppler shifts of about 10 kc per centimeter per second of target velocity. Thus it is possible to measure very low velocities and to measure high velocities with great precision.

Townes and his collaborators performed an improved version of the Michelson-Morley experiment whose object is to test the isotropy of space with respect to light propagation [2]. In the new experiment two He-Ne lasers were mounted at right angles on a rotatable table and their frequency difference was observed as a function of orientation with respect to the motion of the Earth. The experiment confirmed with three times the precision of the classical experiments that there is no anisotropy in the velocity of light associated with the motion of the Earth.

Macek and Davis [3] designed an ingenious rotation sensor based on the classical experiments of Michelson and Gale, who produced interference fringes between two parts of a split beam which were led around a closed loop in opposite directions. The diagram of the laser rotation sensor is shown in Fig. 114. Four He-Ne lasers, operating at 1.15 μ, are arranged on the sides of a square, and four external reflectors complete a closed ring path through the lasers.† Instead of the standing wave oscillations which are obtained with the light reflected back on the same path, traveling wave oscillations are obtained by directing the waves around the optical

---

* The purpose of the experiment was to compare the meter with the wavelength of the 4358-Å line of Hg^{198}.

† Actually one laser is sufficient.

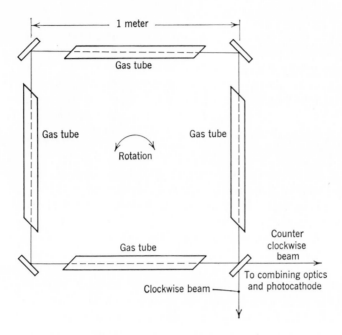

Fig. 114.   Laser rotation sensor.

ring. The resonance condition which determines the frequency of oscillation of the ring laser requires that the ring path consist of an integral
number of wavelengths. Light can travel around the ring in either direction,
so that the system has two similar independent modes. If the instrument
has no rotational motion, the optical lengths in both directions are equal.
If there is a rotation, the optical path is reduced in one direction and
extended in the other, so that the frequencies of the two modes will be
shifted up and down, respectively. The frequency difference of the two
modes is $\Delta f = 4\omega A/p\lambda$, where ω is the rotation rate in radians per second,
A is the area enclosed by the ring, and p is the perimeter of the ring. By
extracting a fraction of both beams and combining these with suitable
optics on a photocathode, Macek and Davis succeeded in obtaining beat
notes as low as 40 cps, corresponding to a rotation rate of 4 degrees per
hour. Such a performance is not competitive with that of conventional
gyroscopes, but the experiment has its intrinsic interest.

The cruder measurements of large distances involved in surveying and
ranging are performed with pulsed lasers. These are discussed under
ranging applications.

Measurement of Optical Quantities

Laser methods have been devised to determine electron densities and temperatures of plasmas by measuring either the index of refraction, i.e., a change of optical length, or the spectral linewidth. The refractive index of a plasma is related to the electron density because $n^2 = 1 - (\omega_p/\omega)^2$, where ω is the angular frequency of the radiation for which the refractive index is determined, and ω_p, the plasma angular frequency, is a function of the electron density n_e according to the formula

$$\omega_p{}^2 = 4\pi e^2 n_e/m, \tag{1.1}$$

where m is the mass of the electron. Clearly, a better resolution can be obtained when ω is chosen not very much larger than the plasma frequency ω_p. Ashby and Jephcott [4] determined the index of refraction of a plasma by incorporating the plasma in a resonant cavity coupled to the original He-Ne laser in the manner shown in Fig. 115. Interference occurs within the laser when radiation is reflected back into it from the external cavity. If the external optical path length is altered either by moving the mirror on the extreme right or by changing the index of refraction, the laser output is modulated at the Doppler frequency corresponding to the velocity of the motion. The He-Ne laser is particularly interesting from the point of view of this application, because it can operate simultaneously at 0.63 μ and 3.39 μ. Since both radiations are produced by electron transitions from the same initial level, any modulation of the infrared radiation produces a complementary modulation of the red light, which can be detected easily with a photomultiplier. Thus the plasma interferometer operates at 3.39 μ for improved sensitivity to electron density, while the output is observed at 0.63 μ for the convenience of detection. A filter prevents the 0.63 μ radiation from reaching the plasma. The change in the index of refraction can be calculated by observing the number of interference fringes on an oscilloscope trace when the plasma discharge is initiated. With this

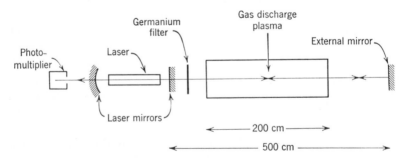

Fig. 115.   Measurement of electron density in a plasma.

method Ashby and Jephcott measured electron densities of the order of 10^{15} per cm^3.

The spectral distribution of the light scattered by electrons is related to the electron velocity distribution. Hence it is possible to obtain information about electron temperature in a plasma by spectral analysis of monochromatic laser light scattered from the plasma [5].

Cummins, Knable, and Yeh devised a method for observing the spectral broadening associated with Rayleigh scattering from macromolecules [6]. The measurement employs a He-Ne laser whose output is split with one beam passing through a sample before being combined with the other beam. With an elaborate modulation scheme, changes in the linewidth of a few cycles per second can be detected. The significance of this experiment lies in the fact that it opens up a new method of attack on molecular properties. Although angular scattering intensity and polarization measurements have been employed in the study of polymers for many years, the additional information carried by the spectral distribution of the scattered light could not be utilized because of the limited monochromaticity of the source and the limited resolution of the spectroscopic apparatus.

Spectroscopic Analysis

Quite different from the truly spectroscopic use of stimulated emission discussed in earlier parts of this book is the use of the laser pulse as a carrier of heat to vaporize substances for spectrochemical analysis. Minute samples can be vaporized by focusing the laser beam on a small spot. After vaporization, the material may be raised to the temperature required by emission spectroscopy by a condenser discharge initiated following the laser pulse. Such spectrochemical equipment is now commercially available. (Jarrell-Ash Co., Waltham, Mass.) It is particularly adapted to the analysis of biological materials. Sample sizes of 10^{-7} g are analyzed, and the process takes only 0.01 sec [7].

Illumination

Lasers have been used as light sources for telephoto pictures, for microscope illuminators, and for high-speed photographic systems. These applications make use of the high brightness and the beam collimation of lasers. Multiply pulsed, Q-switched lasers are suitable for technical motion-picture photography. Ellis and Fourney [8] obtained pictures of bubble formation at the rate of 200,000 frames per second with a ruby laser controlled by a Kerr cell as a light source.

A comprehensive article by Smith [9] contains many other interesting instrumentation applications of lasers together with further references to the literature.

REFERENCES

1. K. D. Mielenz, H. D. Cook, L. E. Gillilland, and R. B. Stephens, Accurate length measurement of meter bar with He-Ne laser, *Science* **146**, 1672–1673, 1964.
2. T. S. Jaseja, A. Javan, J. Murray, and C. H. Townes, Test of special relativity or of the isotropy of space by use of infrared masers, *Phys. Rev.* **133**, A1221–1225, 1964.
3. W. M. Macek and D. T. M. Davis, Jr., Rotation rate sensing with traveling-wave ring lasers, *Appl. Phys. Lett.* **2**, 67–68, 1963.
4. D. E. T. F. Ashby and D. F. Jephcott, Measurement of plasma density using a gas laser as an infrared spectrometer, *Appl. Phys. Lett.* **3**, 13–16, 1963.
5. S. E. Schwarz, Scattering of optical pulses from a non-equilibrium plasma, *Proc. IEEE* **51**, 1362, 1963.
6. H. Z. Cummins, N. Knable, and Y. Yeh, Observation of diffusion broadening of Rayleigh-scattered light, *Phys. Rev. Lett.* **12**, 150–153, 1964.
7. R. C. Rosan, M. K. Healy, and W. F. McNary, Spectroscopic ultra-microanalysis with a laser, *Science* **142**, 236–237, 1963.
8. A. T. Ellis and M. E. Fourney, Application of a ruby laser to high-speed photography, *Proc. IEEE* **51**, 942, 1963.
9. G. F. Smith, Applications of lasers to instrumentation, *Instr. Soc. Amer. Trans.* **3**, 353–365, 1964.

2. COMMUNICATIONS AND RANGING APPLICATIONS

In the field of communications lasers offer two unusual advantages. The first of these pertains to the bandwidth. It is known that the rate at which information can be transmitted is proportional to the bandwidth of the information carrier. The step from microwaves to the optical region expands the available band width by a factor of 10,000 or more. Therefore, if proper methods of modulation and demodulation were found for the laser light, an extremely potent information carrier could be achieved. A single laser could replace all the present information-carrying systems between the east and west coasts of the United States, if its bandwidth could be used as effectively as one now uses carrier bandwidth at radio frequencies.

The second immediate consideration in connection with information transmission is the ability to aim it in the proper direction. A point-to-point communication requires the concentration of the information carrier into a narrow beam. The narrowness of a microwave beam is limited by diffraction. Antennas of considerable size are required to produce a beam only a few degrees wide in the centimeter region. For laser light the dimensions of the radiator required for the same gain are decreased by a factor of 10,000. In fact, with radiation of wavelength 1 μ or less, the practical beamwidth is limited by secondary considerations, and not by the size of the radiator. It is not at all difficult to obtain beamwidths of a few microradians. These narrow beams seem especially interesting from the point of view of point-to-point communications in space, where atmospheric attenuation does not interfere with the propagation of radiation. Atmospheric scattering is one of the limiting factors in the application of lasers to terrestrial communications. This limitation can be mastered, however, by building fixed long-distance pipelines analogous to long-distance telephone cables.

The basic question is: Can the problems of modulation, demodulation, and multiplexing be solved in such a manner that a significant fraction (say 0.1 per cent) of the theoretically possible channel capacity is utilized? Clearly one must use a laser whose output can be stabilized in frequency and in amplitude. The amplitude or frequency modulation of a gas laser at a few megacycles is not a difficult problem in itself, but the multiplexing of a system capable of carrying many messages has not been accomplished yet. There is a vast literature dealing with modulation of lasers using electric and magnetic fields as well as ultrasonic fields in a cell incorporated within the laser cavity. Lack of space prevents us from discussing these interesting technical problems. Equally difficult is the problem of demodulation of the signal in the presence of many other signals of nearly equal frequency. Filtering or separation of a really narrow spectral region, say 1 Mc at 10^{14} cps, is still more a possibility than an accomplishment in 1964.

In any case, the use of the laser as an information carrier is a field of great potential application and a large-scale effort is being made to make this application a reality.

One aspect of communications is the determination of the position of a distant object—in short, ranging. The first application of the laser actually demonstrated was in this field. The ranging experiment performed at the Hughes Research Laboratories almost immediately after the discovery of the ruby laser led to the development of the giant pulse laser. The application of Q-switching techniques provides timed pulses of several megawatts peak power and a few nanoseconds duration. In a rangefinder a sample of such a signal switches on a counting circuit and the signal returned from the target terminates the count. The result is a digital count that can be calibrated directly in distance. The short duration of the Q-switched laser makes it possible to perform ranging to accuracies of a few meters. In a rangefinding system the output beam of a laser is processed through a collimating telescope, providing it with a collimation sharper than that directly available from the laser. The light reflected from the target is gathered through a telescope of larger aperture and is filtered to reduce the effect of scattered light from the environment. The filtered signal is then detected with a photomultiplier. In principle the discrimination against noise could be increased by narrowing the optical filter to a band width barely wider than the transmitted linewidth, but in practice the construction of such narrow filters of proper size and stability has not been accomplished. Therefore the monochromaticity of the laser light is not fully exploited in a laser rangefinder of this type. A typical rangefinder, the Hughes Colidar (Acronym for Coherent Light Detection And Ranging), is shown in Fig. 116. It has a range of about 16 km in fairly good weather against non-cooperative targets of moderate size (tanks, jeeps, cars) with an accuracy of ±5 meters [1, 2]. Similar instruments are made by several other companies and by American military laboratories. Greater range, reliability, and accuracy may be obtained against cooperative targets such as those which may be used in surveying.

High-power laser equipment has been employed for ranging on the moon and for the study of the upper atmosphere. Fiocco and Smullin [3, 4] obtained reflections from atmospheric constituents at heights of 60 to 140 km, and several meteorological research stations have started to employ pulsed laser rangefinders for the study of cloud formation.

Theoretically one can improve the sensitivity of the optical laser rangefinder considerably by making use of the time coherence of the laser signal. In principle it is possible to employ coherent detection in the following manner: A weak signal is generated in a cw laser and is fed to a pulse-

Fig. 116.   Colidar Rangefinder. (Courtesy Hughes Aircraft Company.)

modulated laser amplifier, which provides the high-power pulse. The return signal is mixed with a sample of the signal obtained from the signal generator. Such a ranging system was proposed by Biernson and Lucy [5]. If the problem of signal amplification is successfully solved, such a system should provide considerably improved sensitivity. Amplification of a laser pulse by means of a second laser is, of course, possible, but the question is whether a relatively low-level laser output can be amplified without the introduction of excessive noise.

REFERENCES

1. M. L. Stitch, E. J. Woodbury, and J. H. Morse, Optical ranging system uses laser transmitters, *Electronics* **34**, (April 21) 51–53, 1961.
2. G. F. Smith, Lasers for communications and optical ranging, *Light and Heat Sensing*, edited by H. J. Merrill, Pergamon Press, New York, 1963 (pp. 221–234).
3. L. D. Smullin and G. Fiocco, Project Luna See, *Proc. IRE* **50**, 1703–1704, 1962.
4. G. Fiocco and L. D. Smullin, Detection of scattering layers in the upper atmosphere (60–140 km) by optical radar, *Nature* **199**, 1275, 1963.
5. G. Biernson and R. F. Lucy, Requirements of a coherent laser pulse-doppler radar, *Proc. IEEE* **51**, 202–213, 1963.

3. APPLICATIONS TO SHAPING AND WELDING

The ability of the laser beam to carry a high concentration of energy to a predetermined spot is easily utilized for the drilling of small holes and for the welding of small metal parts. From the point of view of these applications the refined properties of the laser beam are irrelevant; only the total energy delivered in the pulse and the focusing of the beam are of any consequence. Ordinarily ruby lasers are employed without Q-switching.

What can be done with focused laser beams is illustrated in Figs. 117 and 118. Drilling and welding operations are usually accomplished with radiation focused by means of a 3- to 5-cm lens. Drilling is most practical in the case of fine components, such as those found in electron tubes. Reasonably accurate circular holes can be punched in thin sheets with a single pulse. Several pulses are required to perforate thicker sheets. In a series of experiments on metal sheets it was found that 12 pulses from a 4-joule ruby laser perforated a 0.16-cm cold-rolled steel sheet [1]. The holes were nearly circular in cross section but they were definitely tapered in depth, the entrance diameter being about twice the exit diameter. Holes can be drilled in other metals and ceramic materials as well, but they are equally irregular.

The laser beam is particularly suited for the welding of fine wires, contacts in miniature assemblies, electron tubes, etc. When welding with conventional sources, there is always the problem of applying the heat rapidly enough to a confined region, because there is a tendency for metals of high conductivity to conduct the heat away almost as fast as it can be supplied. In the case of a laser beam, there is no question about the adequacy of the rate at which heat is supplied. In fact, it is often necessary to control that rate in order to avoid excessive vaporization of the material and the formation of a hole which freezes in the material between the repeated pulses in an operation that requires many pulses such as the welding of a seam. Titanium and tungsten have been welded successfully with pulses from ruby lasers repeated from 1 to 30 times per second. Special metal-working laser equipment is commercially available, e.g., from Maser Optics, Boston, Mass.

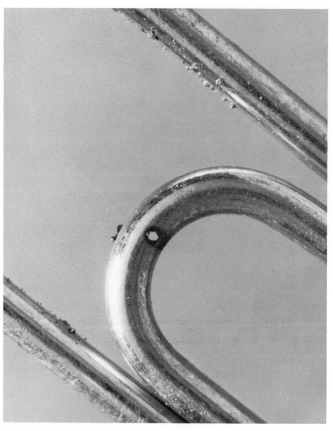

Fig. 117. Hole drilled with laser beam. Diameter of hole in paperclip about 0.18 mm. (Courtesy Hughes Aircraft Company.)

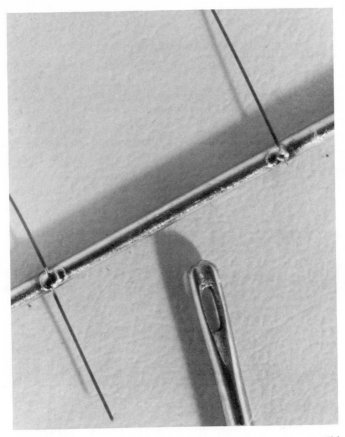

Fig. 118. Wires welded by laser beam. Heavy wire Ni, 0.5-mm diameter. Thin wires W, 0.08-mm diameter. (Courtesy Hughes Aircraft Company.)

REFERENCE

1. D. L. Williams, The laser as a machine tool, *Proc. Nat. Electronics Conf.* Chicago, October 1963, 574–587.

4. BIOLOGICAL AND MEDICAL APPLICATIONS, DISCUSSION OF HEALTH HAZARDS

The unique capability of the laser as an instrument for delivering energy into precisely determined regions of space has been applied to many problems in biological research. The monochromatic nature of the radiation which produces a different response in different organic materials is also a useful property. Biological application of lasers began in 1961 and expanded enormously in 1963. Because of the unavailability of other lasers of sufficient power output, early biological work was limited to radiations of 6943 Å and 10,600 Å in wavelength.

The effect of laser irradiation of blood group substances and enzymes has been studied. Changes were observed in the inhibitory action of antibodies. Some studies on blood group substances indicate that laser irradiation may enhance the biological reactivity of a molecule. The earliest work published in this field was that of a group of French investigators [1] who exposed human blood cells to ruby laser radiation focused to a spot about 2.5 μ in diameter. With pulse energies of about 0.5 joule red blood cells were destroyed, but white blood cells, which are transparent to the radiation used, escaped damage for the most part. The way is thus opened to the selective destruction of certain cells which are intermixed with other cells in the living organism. Selective destruction of cancer cells with laser beams is being actively investigated, and there have been some preliminary indications of success.

In addition to the effect of laser radiation on individual cells, including plant cells, the effect of this radiation on intact animals is being studied. Fine, Klein, and Scott [2] prepared a review of this subject with many references to work in progress in 1963.

In another biological application highly localized lesions are produced in the nervous system of an experimental animal so that the effect of such lesions on the organism may be studied. An example of this work is the study of the effect of lesions in spiders on their web-constructing ability. Lesions were produced by irradiation with a focused laser beam to avoid making a cut in the exoskeleton of the spiders [3].

The most successful therapeutic application of the laser has been in eye surgery, where a laser beam was used to reattach a detached retina. During the 1940's a technique was developed for the therapeutic coagulation of a spot on the retina by means of a very intense light source. Light from a continuously operating high-pressure xenon lamp was led into the eye through optical components which permitted simultaneous observation and aiming. The lesion which effects the reattachment is produced in 0.25 to 1.5 sec. The same thermal energy can now be delivered with a ruby or neodymium laser in a fraction of a millisecond. The lesion produced by the laser may be more confined in spatial extent because heat is not conducted away in the shorter time interval. Also, since the lesion is caused in such a short time, the normal reaction of the eye to a bright light does not occur and the burn is not smeared over the retina. The patient need not be anesthetized because the operation is completed in an extremely short time. Several apparently successful eye operations were performed with lasers in 1963. Optical systems specifically designed for such operations are designed and marketed by a number of firms [4]. The effect of the laser on the eye is a subject of very active study [4, 5, 6].

It seems appropriate to mention at this point some appraisal of the hazards of experimenting with lasers. Severe local burns can be caused when the laser beam is focused on any part of the body, and burns of lesser consequence may be caused even by unfocused beams from very powerful lasers. The primary danger is, of course, to the eye because it automatically focuses the incident radiation on the retina. Obviously one must under all circumstances avoid looking directly into the laser when there is a possibility that it may be fired. The pulsed laser is most dangerous because all its energy is delivered in a much shorter time than it takes to close the eyelid.

Experiments on rabbits have shown that the threshold of retinal damage by light depends both on the total energy of the light pulse and on its peak intensity. Ham and co-workers [7] found that an energy density of 0.7 to 0.8 joule/cm^2 at the retina produces minimal damage when either a xenon flashlamp or a ruby laser is used for irradiation, provided that the energy is delivered in about 0.2 msec. For a giant pulse of 30 nsec duration the threshold of damage is lower by a factor of 10. The quoted figures were obtained with a retinal spot of 0.8 mm diameter (area 5×10^{-3} cm^2); therefore the optical energy entering the eye was only about 3.5×10^{-3} joule in the case of the ordinary pulse and 3.5×10^{-4} joule in the case of the giant pulse. Since a minute fraction of the normal pulse energy is sufficient to damage the eye, one should avoid the possibility that specular reflection from a metal or glass surface reaches an observer's eye. The beam may be observed on a matte white screen. The primary danger with a continuously operating laser is from the infrared coherent radiation and from the incoherent ultraviolet radiation which may be emitted by the discharge used for excitation. The experimenter may not be immediately aware of the presence of these radiations. In any case, the laser beam is not the only hazard. A careless experimenter may be electrocuted by the power supply before he becomes blinded by the beam.

Since the energy output of pulsed lasers varies from about 0.1 joule to 1000 joules and the collimation of the output beams is also highly variable it is not practical to state quantitative safety rules applicable in every case. The precautions must be appropriate to the total energy concentration available under given circumstances.

REFERENCES

1. M. Bessis, F. Gires, G. Mayer, G. Nomarski, Irradiation des organites cellulaires à l'aide d'un laser à rubis, *Compt. Rend.* **255**, 1010–1012, 1962.
2. S. Fine, E. Klein, and R. E. Scott, Laser irradiation of biological systems, *IEEE Spectrum* **1**, 81–95, 1964.

3. P. N. Witt, C. F. Reed, and F. K. Tittel, Laser lesions and spider web constructions, *Nature* **201**, 150, 1964.
4. N. S. Kappany, N. Silbertrust, and N. A. Peppers, Laser retinal photocoagulator, *Appl. Optics* **4**, 517–522, 1965.
5. M. M. Zaret, G. M. Breinin, *et al.*, Ocular lesions produced by an optical maser, *Science* **134**, 1525–1526, 1961.
6. R. A. Malt and C. H. Townes, Optical masers in biology and medicine, *New England J. Medicine* **269**, 1417–1421, 1963.
7. W. T. Ham, R. C. Williams, *et al.*, Optical Masers, *Acta Ophthalmologica Suppl.* **76**, 60–78, 1963 (Supplemented by private communication).

Appendix

TABLE A.1. CORRECTION OF WAVELENGTHS FOR MEASUREMENTS IN AIR, $\Delta\lambda = \lambda_0 - \lambda$

The wavelength in vacuum, λ_0, is the reciprocal of the wave number σ

3000 Å to 14,900 Å

Corrections in Ångströms

λ_0 Ångströms	000	100	200	300	400	500	600	700	800	900
3000	0.87	0.90	0.92	0.95	0.98	1.00	1.03	1.05	1.08	1.10
4000	1.13	1.16	1.18	1.21	1.24	1.26	1.29	1.32	1.34	1.37
5000	1.39	1.42	1.45⁻	1.47	1.50	1.53	1.55	1.58	1.61	1.64
6000	1.66	1.69	1.72	1.74	1.77	1.80	1.83	1.85⁻	1.88	1.90
7000	1.93	1.96	1.98	2.01	2.04	2.07	2.09	2.12	2.15⁻	2.17
8000	2.20	2.23	2.25	2.28	2.31	2.34	2.36	2.39	2.42	2.44
9000	2.47	2.50⁻	2.52	2.55	2.58	2.61	2.63	2.66	2.69	2.71
10,000	2.74	2.77	2.80	2.82	2.85⁻	2.88	2.90	2.93	2.96	2.99
11,000	3.01	3.04	3.07	3.09	3.12	3.15⁻	3.18	3.20	3.23	3.26
12,000	3.28	3.31	3.34	3.37	3.39	3.42	3.45⁻	3.47	3.50	3.53
13,000	3.56	3.58	3.61	3.64	3.66	3.69	3.72	3.75⁻	3.77	3.80
14,000	3.83	3.85	3.88	3.91	3.94	3.96	3.99	4.02	4.04	4.07

$1.0\ \mu$ to $9.9\ \mu$

Corrections in Ångströms

λ_0 Microns	0.0	0.1	0.2	0.3	0.4	0.5	0.6	0.7	0.8	0.9
1	2.7	3.1	3.3	3.6	3.8	4.1	4.4	4.6	4.9	5.2
2	5.5⁻	5.7	6.0	6.3	6.5	6.8	7.1	7.4	7.6	7.9
3	8.2	8.5	8.7	9.0	9.3	9.5	9.8	10.1	10.4	10.6
4	10.9	11.2	11.5⁻	11.7	12.0	12.3	12.5	12.8	13.1	13.4
5	13.6	13.9	14.2	14.4	14.7	15.0	15.3	15.5	15.8	16.1
6	16.3	16.6	16.9	17.2	17.4	17.7	18.0	18.3	18.5	18.8
7	19.1	19.4	19.6	19.9	20.2	20.4	20.7	21.0	21.3	21.5
8	21.8	22.1	22.4	22.6	22.9	23.2	23.4	23.7	24.0	24.3
9	24.5	24.8	25.1	25.3	25.6	25.9	26.2	26.4	26.7	27.0

Beyond the range of this table: $\Delta\lambda = 2.725 \times 10^{-4}\lambda_0$.

293

TABLE A.2. NOBLE GAS SPECTRAL LINES OBSERVED IN STIMULATED EMISSION

The table contains the wavelengths, wave numbers, and transitions for the complete atoms of helium, neon, argon, krypton, and xenon observed in stimulated emission. Generally the measurements of wavelength in the infrared are not carried out with the accuracy reflected by the tables, but the experimental accuracy in most instances is adequate to identify the line with a transition among levels known from measurements in a more accessible spectral region. The tabulated values of λ_{air} and σ are the ones consistent with the identified energy levels as listed in Moore's tables. In the case of the $4f$ levels of neon, Moore's tables have been corrected to take into account the more recent measurements of Johansson.* Where no definite identification could be made, the measured value is listed in the column for λ_{air} if the measurement was reported in air. These items are starred. Where λ_0 was reported in the original publication, a correction was made so that all values of λ in the table are consistently wavelengths in air. The accuracy of these starred wavelengths is variable, the uniform appearance of the tables notwithstanding. Their last digits should not be relied on; they serve only as indications. While the lower excited energy levels are known to a high accuracy, this is not the case for the higher levels which are involved in the generation of radiation in the far infrared. Consequently one must question the accuracy of the last digit in the wavelength of most of the neon lines above 35 μ.

The consistent system for designating noble gas levels is the Racah notation (except for helium). Nevertheless in the case of the lower levels of neon the Paschen symbols are so generally used as common names that it seemed desirable to include these in the tabulation. They are listed for all s-p transitions.

Although many lines of the ionized noble gases were observed in stimulated emission during the nine months preceding the compilation of these tables, it is impractical to incorporate these. At the time this book is written the stimulated-emission spectroscopy of noble gas ions is in such a fluid state that a compilation of its results is not likely to be of lasting value.

Lines of He I observed in stimulated emission

λ_{air} microns	σ cm^{-1}	Transition	Reference
1.9543	5115.5	$4\,^3P$–$3\,^3D$	g
2.0603	4852.3	$7\,^3D$–$4\,^3P$	l

Lines of Ne I observed in stimulated emission

λ_{air} microns	σ cm^{-1}	Transition Racah Notation	Paschen Symbols	References	Notes
0.5852	17,082.0	$3p'[\frac{1}{2}]_0$–$3s'[\frac{1}{2}]_1^\circ$	$2p_1$–$1s_2$	a	Requires a trace of Ar.
0.5939	16,832.3	$5s'[\frac{1}{2}]_1^\circ$–$3p[\frac{5}{2}]_2$	$3s_2$–$2p_8$	b	
0.6046	16,534.9	$5s'[\frac{1}{2}]_1^\circ$–$3p[\frac{3}{2}]_1$	$3s_2$–$2p_7$	b	
0.6118	16,340.7	$5s'[\frac{1}{2}]_1^\circ$–$3p[\frac{3}{2}]_2$	$3s_2$–$2p_6$	c	
0.6294	15,884.4	$5s'[\frac{1}{2}]_1^\circ$–$3p'[\frac{3}{2}]_1$	$3s_2$–$2p_5$	c	

* Ark. f. Fys. **25**, 381, 1963.

Lines of Neɪ (continued)

λ_{air} microns	σ cm^{-1}	Transition Racah Notation	Paschen Symbols	References	Notes
0.6328	15,798.0	$5s'[\tfrac{1}{2}]_1{}^o-3p'[\tfrac{3}{2}]_2$	$3s_2-2p_4$	d	Strongest line.
0.6352	15,739.1	$5s'[\tfrac{1}{2}]_1{}^o-3p[\tfrac{1}{2}]_0$	$3s_2-2p_3$	b	
0.6401	15,618.1	$5s'[\tfrac{1}{2}]_1{}^o-3p'[\tfrac{1}{2}]_1$	$3s_2-2p_2$	c	
0.7305	13,685.8	$5s'[\tfrac{1}{2}]_1{}^o-3p'[\tfrac{1}{2}]_0$	$3s_2-2p_1$	b	
0.8865	11,276.8	$4s'[\tfrac{1}{2}]_1{}^o-3p[\tfrac{1}{2}]_1$	$2s_2-2p_{10}$	D	
0.8989	11,122.2	$4s'[\tfrac{1}{2}]_0{}^o-3p[\tfrac{1}{2}]_1$	$2s_3-2p_{10}$	D	
1.0295	9710.4	$4s'[\tfrac{1}{2}]_1{}^o-3p[\tfrac{5}{2}]_2$	$2s_2-2p_8$	D	
1.0621	9413.0	$4s'[\tfrac{1}{2}]_1{}^o-3p[\tfrac{3}{2}]_1$	$2s_2-2p_7$	D	
1.0798	9258.4	$4s'[\tfrac{1}{2}]_0{}^o-3p[\tfrac{3}{2}]_1$	$2s_3-2p_7$	e	
1.0844	9218.8	$4s'[\tfrac{1}{2}]_1{}^o-3p[\tfrac{3}{2}]_2$	$2s_2-2p_6$	e	
1.1143	8971.8	$4s[\tfrac{3}{2}]_1{}^o-3p[\tfrac{5}{2}]_2$	$2s_4-2p_8$	e	
1.1178	8944.1	$4s[\tfrac{3}{2}]_2{}^o-3p[\tfrac{5}{2}]_3$	$2s_5-2p_9$	e, f	
1.1390	8776.9	$4s[\tfrac{3}{2}]_2{}^o-3p[\tfrac{5}{2}]_2$	$2s_5-2p_8$	e	
1.1409	8762.5	$4s'[\tfrac{1}{2}]_1{}^o-3p'[\tfrac{3}{2}]_1$	$2s_2-2p_5$	e	
1.1523	8676.1	$4s'[\tfrac{1}{2}]_1{}^o-3p'[\tfrac{3}{2}]_2$	$2s_2-2p_4$	e, f, x	Strongest line.
1.1525	8674.4	$4s[\tfrac{3}{2}]_1{}^o-3p[\tfrac{3}{2}]_1$	$2s_4-2p_7$	t, x, C	
1.1602	8617.2	$4s'[\tfrac{1}{2}]_1{}^o-3p[\tfrac{1}{2}]_0$	$2s_2-2p_3$	e	
1.1614	8607.9	$4s'[\tfrac{1}{2}]_0{}^o-3p'[\tfrac{3}{2}]_1$	$2s_3-2p_5$	e, f	
1.1767	8496.2	$4s'[\tfrac{1}{2}]_1{}^o-3p'[\tfrac{1}{2}]_1$	$2s_2-2p_2$	e	
1.1789	8480.1	$4s[\tfrac{3}{2}]_1{}^o-3p[\tfrac{1}{2}]_2$	$2s_4-2p_6$	D	
1.1985	8341.5	$4s'[\tfrac{1}{2}]_0{}^o-3p'[\tfrac{1}{2}]_1$	$2s_3-2p_2$	e, f	
1.2066	8285.3	$4s[\tfrac{3}{2}]_2{}^o-3p[\tfrac{3}{2}]_2$	$2s_5-2p_6$	e, f	
1.2689	7878.6	$4s[\tfrac{3}{2}]_1{}^o-3p[\tfrac{1}{2}]_0$	$2s_4-2p_3$	g, h, C	
1.2912	7742.6	$4s[\tfrac{3}{2}]_2{}^o-3p'[\tfrac{3}{2}]_2$	$2s_5-2p_4$	h, C	
1.5231	6563.9	$4s'[\tfrac{1}{2}]_1{}^o-3p'[\tfrac{1}{2}]_0$	$2s_2-2p_1$	e	Strong line.
1.7162	5825.3	$4s[\tfrac{3}{2}]_1{}^o-3p'[\tfrac{1}{2}]_0$	$2s_4-2p_1$	D	
1.8210	5489.9	$4p'[\tfrac{1}{2}]_0-4s[\tfrac{3}{2}]_1{}^o$	$3p_1-2s_4$	D	
1.8277	5470.0	$4f[\tfrac{9}{2}]_{4,5}-3d[\tfrac{7}{2}]_4{}^o$		i	J of initial level uncert.
1.8283	5468.2	$4f[\tfrac{9}{2}]_4-3d[\tfrac{7}{2}]_3{}^o$		i, j	
1.8304	5461.8	$4f[\tfrac{5}{2}]_{2,3}-3d[\tfrac{3}{2}]_2{}^o$		i	J of initial level uncert.
1.8403	5432.5	$4f[\tfrac{5}{2}]_2-3d[\tfrac{3}{2}]_1{}^o$		i	
1.8592	5377.3	$4f[\tfrac{7}{2}]_3-3d[\tfrac{5}{2}]_2{}^o$		i	
1.8598	5375.5	$4f[\tfrac{7}{2}]_{3,4}-3d[\tfrac{5}{2}]_3{}^o$		i	J of initial level uncert.
1.9574	5107.5	$4p'[\tfrac{3}{2}]_2-4s'[\tfrac{3}{2}]_1{}^o$	$3p_4-2s_5$	h	
1.9577	5106.6	$4p'[\tfrac{1}{2}]_1-4s[\tfrac{3}{2}]_1{}^o$	$3p_2-2s_5$	C	
2.0350	4912.6	$4p'[\tfrac{3}{2}]_2-4s[\tfrac{3}{2}]_1{}^o$	$3p_4-2s_4$	k, C	
2.1019	4756.6	$4d'[\tfrac{5}{2}]_2{}^o-4p[\tfrac{3}{2}]_2$		e, l	Strong line.
2.1041	4751.3	$4p'[\tfrac{1}{2}]_0-4s'[\tfrac{1}{2}]_1{}^o$	$3p_1-2s_2$	h, k, t, C	Strong line.
2.1708	4605.3	$4p[\tfrac{1}{2}]_0-4s[\tfrac{3}{2}]_1{}^o$	$3p_3-2s_4$	h, t, C	Strong line.
2.3260	4298.0	$4p[\tfrac{5}{2}]_2-4s[\tfrac{3}{2}]_2{}^o$	$3p_8-2s_5$	D	
2.3951	4174.0	$4p'[\tfrac{3}{2}]_2-4s'[\tfrac{1}{2}]_1{}^o$	$3p_4-2s_2$	j, m, n, C	
2.4219	4127.9	$4d[\tfrac{3}{2}]_1{}^o-4p[\tfrac{5}{2}]_2$		u	
2.4250	4122.7	$4p'[\tfrac{3}{2}]_1-4s'[\tfrac{1}{2}]_1{}^o$	$3p_5-2s_2$	o, C	

Lines of Ne I (continued)

λ_{air} microns	σ cm^{-1}	Transition Racah Notation	Paschen Symbols	References	Notes
2.5393	3937.0	$4d[\frac{1}{2}]_1{}^o\!-\!4p[\frac{3}{2}]_2$		p	
2.5524	3916.8	$4p[\frac{1}{2}]_1\!-\!4s[\frac{3}{2}]_2{}^o$	$3p_{10}\!-\!2s_5$	D	
2.7573	3625.7	$4d[\frac{3}{2}]_1{}^o\!-\!4p[\frac{1}{2}]_0$		p	
2.7819	3593.7	$5s'[\frac{1}{2}]_0{}^o\!-\!4p[\frac{3}{2}]_1$	$3s_3\!-\!3p_7$	p	
2.9448	3394.9	$5s[\frac{3}{2}]_1{}^o\!-\!4p[\frac{1}{2}]_1$	$3s_4\!-\!3p_{10}$	p	
2.9668	3369.7	$4d[\frac{3}{2}]_1{}^o\!-\!4p'[\frac{3}{2}]_1$		p	
2.9804	3354.3	$4d[\frac{3}{2}]_2{}^o\!-\!4p'[\frac{3}{2}]_1$		p	
3.027*	3303*	$4d[\frac{3}{2}]_2{}^o\!-\!4p'[\frac{1}{2}]_1$?		p	Term level may be $4p'[\frac{3}{2}]_2$.
3.0712	3255.2	$5s'[\frac{1}{2}]_1{}^o\!-\!4p[\frac{1}{2}]_0$	$3s_2\!-\!3p_3$	w	
3.3173	3013.7	$5s[\frac{3}{2}]_1{}^o\!-\!4p[\frac{5}{2}]_2$	$3s_4\!-\!3p_8$	p	
3.3333	2999.2	$5s'[\frac{1}{2}]_1{}^o\!-\!4p'[\frac{3}{2}]_1$	$3s_2\!-\!3p_5$	o, p	
3.3352	2997.5	$5s[\frac{3}{2}]_2{}^o\!-\!4p[\frac{5}{2}]_3$	$3s_5\!-\!3p_9$	u	
3.379*	2959*	$7s'[\frac{1}{2}]_0{}^o\!-\!5p'[\frac{3}{2}]_1$	$5s_3\!-\!4p_5$ or p_2	p	Term level may be $5p'[\frac{1}{2}]_1$.
3.3902	2948.8	$5s'[\frac{1}{2}]_1{}^o\!-\!4p'[\frac{1}{2}]_1$	$3s_2\!-\!3p_2$	p	
3.3913	2947.9	$5s'[\frac{1}{2}]_1{}^o\!-\!4p'[\frac{3}{2}]_2$	$3s_2\!-\!3p_4$	m, p, q	Strongest line.
3.4471	2900.2	$5s[\frac{3}{2}]_1{}^o\!-\!4p[\frac{3}{2}]_1$	$3s_4\!-\!3p_7$	p	
3.5835	2789.8	$5s[\frac{3}{2}]_2{}^o\!-\!4p[\frac{3}{2}]_2$	$3s_5\!-\!3p_6$	p	
3.7736	2649.3	$4p'[\frac{1}{2}]_0\!-\!3d[\frac{3}{2}]_1{}^o$		p	
3.9806	2511.5	$5s[\frac{3}{2}]_1{}^o\!-\!4p[\frac{1}{2}]_0$	$3s_4\!-\!3p_3$	p	
4.2172	2370.6	$5s'[\frac{1}{2}]_1{}^o\!-\!4p'[\frac{1}{2}]_0$	$3s_2\!-\!3p_1$	w	Strong line.
5.4033	1850.2	$4p'[\frac{1}{2}]_0\!-\!3d'[\frac{3}{2}]_1{}^o$		p	
5.6651	1764.7	$4p[\frac{1}{2}]_0\!-\!3d[\frac{3}{2}]_1{}^o$		p	
7.3208	1365.6	$6s[\frac{3}{2}]_2{}^o\!-\!5p[\frac{5}{2}]_3$	$4s_5\!-\!4p_9$	p	
7.425*	1346*	Uncertain		p	
7.4779	1336.9	$4p[\frac{3}{2}]_2\!-\!3d[\frac{5}{2}]_3{}^o$		p	
7.4973	1333.4	$6s[\frac{3}{2}]_2{}^o\!-\!5p[\frac{5}{2}]_2$	$4s_5\!-\!4p_8$	p	
7.5292	1327.8	$6s[\frac{3}{2}]_1{}^o\!-\!5p[\frac{3}{2}]_1$	$4s_4\!-\!4p_7$	u	
7.6141	1313.0	$4p[\frac{5}{2}]_1\!-\!3d[\frac{5}{2}]_2{}^o$		p	
7.6490	1307.0	$4p[\frac{5}{2}]_2\!-\!3d[\frac{7}{2}]_3{}^o$		p	
7.6994	1298.4	$4p'[\frac{3}{2}]_2\!-\!3d'[\frac{5}{2}]_3{}^o$		p	
7.7386	1291.9	$4p[\frac{5}{2}]_2\!-\!3d[\frac{3}{2}]_2{}^o$		p	
7.7634	1287.8	$4p'[\frac{1}{2}]_1\!-\!3d'[\frac{3}{2}]_2{}^o$		p	
7.7794	1285.1	$6s[\frac{3}{2}]_2{}^o\!-\!5p[\frac{3}{2}]_1$	$4s_5\!-\!4p_7$	p	
7.8347	1276.0	$6s[\frac{3}{2}]_2{}^o\!-\!5p[\frac{3}{2}]_2$	$4s_5\!-\!4p_6$	p	
8.0066	1248.6	$4p'[\frac{3}{2}]_1\!-\!3d'[\frac{5}{2}]_2{}^o$		p	
8.0599	1240.4	$4p[\frac{5}{2}]_3\!-\!3d[\frac{7}{2}]_4{}^o$		p	
8.3345	1199.5	$4p[\frac{5}{2}]_2\!-\!3d[\frac{5}{2}]_2{}^o$		p	
8.844*	1130*	$4p[\frac{5}{2}]_3\!-\!3d[\frac{5}{2}]_3{}^o$?		p	Term level may be $3d[\frac{5}{2}]_2{}^o$.
9.0871	1100.2	$6s[\frac{3}{2}]_1{}^o\!-\!5p[\frac{1}{2}]_0$	$4s_4\!-\!4p_3$	p	
10.060	993.7	$4p[\frac{1}{2}]_1\!-\!3d[\frac{1}{2}]_1{}^o$		p	
10.978	910.6	$4p[\frac{1}{2}]_1\!-\!3d[\frac{3}{2}]_2{}^o$		p	
11.857	843.1	$5p[\frac{1}{2}]_1\!-\!5s'[\frac{1}{2}]_0{}^o$	$4p_{10}\!-\!3s_3$	p	
12.832	779.1	$5p'[\frac{1}{2}]_0\!-\!4d[\frac{3}{2}]_1{}^o$		p	

Lines of NeI (continued)

λ_{air} microns	σ cm^{-1}	Transition Racah Notation	Paschen Symbols	References	Notes
13.75*	727*	Uncertain		p	
14.93*	670*	Uncertain		p	
16.634	601.0	$5p[\frac{3}{2}]_2-4d[\frac{5}{2}]_2^o$		p	
16.663	600.0	$5p[\frac{3}{2}]_2-4d[\frac{5}{2}]_3^o$		p	
16.889	591.9	$5p[\frac{3}{2}]_1-4d[\frac{5}{2}]_2^o$		p	
16.942	590.1	$5p[\frac{3}{2}]_2-4d[\frac{7}{2}]_3^o$		p	
17.153	528.8	$5p'[\frac{3}{2}]_2-4d'[\frac{5}{2}]_3^o$		p	
17.184	581.8	$5p'[\frac{3}{2}]_2-4d'[\frac{3}{2}]_2^o$		p	
17.800	561.7	$5p'[\frac{1}{2}]_1-4d'[\frac{3}{2}]_2^o$		p	
17.836	560.5	$5p'[\frac{3}{2}]_1-4d'[\frac{3}{2}]_2^o$		p	
17.884	559.0	$5p[\frac{5}{2}]_3-4d[\frac{7}{2}]_4^o$		p	
18.391	543.6	$5p[\frac{5}{2}]_2-4d[\frac{5}{2}]_2^o$		p	
20.474	488.3	$6p[\frac{1}{2}]_0-5d[\frac{1}{2}]_1^o$		p	
21.746	459.7	$6p[\frac{1}{2}]_0-5d[\frac{3}{2}]_1^o$		p	
22.830	437.9	$5p[\frac{1}{2}]_1-4d[\frac{3}{2}]_2^o$		p	
25.416	393.3	$6p'[\frac{1}{2}]_0-5d'[\frac{3}{2}]_1^o$		p	
28.045	356.5	$6p[\frac{3}{2}]_1-5d[\frac{1}{2}]_0^o$		p	
31.544	316.9	$6p[\frac{3}{2}]_2-5d[\frac{5}{2}]_3^o$		p	
31.919	313.2	$6p[\frac{3}{2}]_1-5d[\frac{5}{2}]_2^o$		r	
32.008	312.3	$6p[\frac{5}{2}]_2-5d[\frac{7}{2}]_3^o$		p	
32.507	307.5	$6p'[\frac{3}{2}]_2-5d'[\frac{5}{2}]_3^o$		p	
33.83*	296*	Uncertain		p	A 6p–5d transition.
34.542	289.4	$6p'[\frac{1}{2}]_1-5d'[\frac{3}{2}]_2^o$		p	
34.670	288.4	$6p[\frac{5}{2}]_2-5d[\frac{5}{2}]_2^o$		r	
35.593	280.9	$7p[\frac{1}{2}]_0-6d[\frac{3}{2}]_1^o$		r	
37.22	268.6	$7p'[\frac{1}{2}]_0-6d'[\frac{3}{2}]_1^o$		r	
41.73	239.6	$6p[\frac{3}{2}]_1-5d[\frac{3}{2}]_2^o$		r	
50.69	197.2	$7p[\frac{1}{2}]_2-6d[\frac{3}{2}]_2^o$		s	
52.40	190.8	$7p'[\frac{1}{2}]_1-6d'[\frac{3}{2}]_2^o$		s	
53.47	187.0	$7p[\frac{3}{2}]_2-6d[\frac{5}{2}]_3^o$		r	
54.00	185.1	$7p[\frac{3}{2}]_1-6d[\frac{5}{2}]_2^o$		r	
54.10	184.8	$7p[\frac{5}{2}]_2-6d[\frac{7}{2}]_3^o$		r	
55.51	180.1	$7p'[\frac{3}{2}]_1-6d'[\frac{5}{2}]_2^o$		s	
57.34	174.3	$7p[\frac{5}{2}]_3-6d[\frac{7}{2}]_4^o$		r	
68.31	146.3	$7p[\frac{1}{2}]_1-6d[\frac{3}{2}]_2^o$		v	
72.08	138.7	$8p'[\frac{1}{2}]_0-7d'[\frac{3}{2}]_1^o$		s	
85.01	117.6	$8p[\frac{3}{2}]_2-7d[\frac{5}{2}]_3^o$		v	
86.93	115.0	$8p'[\frac{3}{2}]_2-7d'[\frac{5}{2}]_2^o$		s	
88.47	113.0	$8p[\frac{3}{2}]_1-7d[\frac{5}{2}]_2^o$		s	
89.82	111.3	$8p[\frac{5}{2}]_3-7d[\frac{7}{2}]_3^o$		s	
93.02*		Undetermined		s	
106.0	94.3	$10p[\frac{1}{2}]_0-9d[\frac{3}{2}]_1^o$		s	
124.4*		$\begin{cases} 9p[\frac{3}{2}]_1-8d[\frac{5}{2}]_2^o, \\ \text{or } 9p[\frac{3}{2}]_2-8d[\frac{5}{2}]_3^o \end{cases}$		s	
126.1*		Undetermined		s	
132.8*		Undetermined		s	

Lines of Ar I observed in stimulated emission

λ_{air} microns	σ cm^{-1}	Transition Racah Notation	References	Notes
1.6180	6178.8	$5s[\frac{3}{2}]_2{}^o-4p'[\frac{3}{2}]_2$	e, l	
1.6941	5901.4	$3d[\frac{3}{2}]_2{}^o-4p[\frac{3}{2}]_2$	e, l	Strong line.
1.7915	5580.5	$3d[\frac{1}{2}]_1{}^o-4p[\frac{3}{2}]_2$	e, l	Possibly J = 0 to J = 1.
2.0616	4849.2	$3d[\frac{3}{2}]_2{}^o-4p'[\frac{3}{2}]_2$	e, l	Strong line.
2.0986	4763.8	$3d[\frac{1}{2}]_1{}^o-4p[\frac{1}{2}]_0$	n, C	
2.1534	4642.5	$3d[\frac{3}{2}]_2{}^o-4p'[\frac{1}{2}]_1$	n, C	
2.204*	4536*	$3d[\frac{1}{2}]_{0(1)}^o-4p'[\frac{3}{2}]_{1(2)}$	p	Possibly J = 1 to J = 2.
2.3133	4321.6	$3d[\frac{1}{2}]_1{}^o-4p'[\frac{1}{2}]_1$	p	
2.3966	4171.4	$3d[\frac{1}{2}]_0{}^o-4p'[\frac{1}{2}]_1$	p	
2.5008	3997.7	$6d'[\frac{3}{2}]_2{}^o-6p[\frac{1}{2}]_1$	p	
2.548*	3920*	Uncertain	p	
2.5661	3895.9	$5p'[\frac{1}{2}]_0-5s'[\frac{1}{2}]_1{}^o$	p	
2.6836	3725.3	$5p[\frac{3}{2}]_1-3d[\frac{5}{2}]_2{}^o$	p	
2.7356	3654.5	$5p'[\frac{1}{2}]_1-3d'[\frac{3}{2}]_2{}^o$	p	
2.822*	3542*	Uncertain	p	A 5p–5s transition.
2.881*	3470*	Uncertain	p	
2.9272	3415.3	$5p[\frac{1}{2}]_0-3d[\frac{3}{2}]_1{}^o$	p	
2.9788	3356.1	$5p[\frac{5}{2}]_2-5s[\frac{3}{2}]_1{}^o$	p	
3.0453	3282.8	$5p[\frac{5}{2}]_2-5d[\frac{5}{2}]_3{}^o$	p	
3.0988	3226.2	$5p[\frac{5}{2}]_3-3d[\frac{5}{2}]_3{}^o$	p	
3.1325	3191.5	$5p[\frac{1}{2}]_1-5s[\frac{3}{2}]_2{}^o$	p	
4.915*	2034*	Uncertain	p	
5.119*	1952*	Uncertain	p	
5.4666	1828.8	$5d[\frac{7}{2}]_4-4f[\frac{9}{2}]_{5(4)}$	p	J of term. level uncertain.
5.8460	1710.1	$6p[\frac{1}{2}]_0-6s[\frac{3}{2}]_1{}^o$	p	
6.0515	1652.1	$4d[\frac{1}{2}]_1{}^o-5p[\frac{5}{2}]_2$	p	
6.938*	1441*	Uncertain	p	
7.2146	1385.7	$6p[\frac{1}{2}]_1-6s[\frac{3}{2}]_2{}^o$	p	
7.798*	1282*	$4f[\frac{3}{2}]_{1(2)}-4d[\frac{3}{2}]_2$	p	J of initial level uncertain.
12.137*	824*	$4d'[\frac{3}{2}]_1{}^o-4f[\frac{3}{2}]_{1(2)}$	p	J of term. level uncertain.
15.035*	665*	$5d'[\frac{3}{2}]_2{}^o-5f[\frac{5}{2}]_{2(3)}$	p	J of term. level uncertain.
26.937	371.1	$4d'[\frac{3}{2}]_2{}^o-4f[\frac{5}{2}]_3$	p	

Lines of Kr I observed in stimulated emission

λ_{air} microns	σ cm^{-1}	Transition Racah Notation	References	Notes
1.6897	5916.7	$4d[\frac{1}{2}]_1{}^o-5p[\frac{1}{2}]_1$	e, l	
1.6936	5903.0	$4d[\frac{5}{2}]_2{}^o-5p[\frac{3}{2}]_1$	e, l	
1.7843	5603.0	$4d[\frac{1}{2}]_0{}^o-5p[\frac{1}{2}]_1$	e, l	
1.8167	5503.0	$4d[\frac{7}{2}]_4{}^o-5p[\frac{5}{2}]_3$	C	
1.8185	5497.5	$4d'[\frac{5}{2}]_2{}^o-5p'[\frac{3}{2}]_2$	e, l	
1.9211	5203.9	$8s[\frac{3}{2}]_1{}^o-6p[\frac{5}{2}]_2$	e, l	
2.1165	4723.4	$4d[\frac{3}{2}]_2{}^o-5p[\frac{3}{2}]_1$	e, l, u	Strong line.

Lines of Kr I (continued)

λ_{air} microns	σ cm^{-1}	Transition Racah Notation	References	Notes
2.1902	4564.4	$4d[\tfrac{3}{2}]_2^o-5p[\tfrac{3}{2}]_2$	e, l, u	Strong line.
2.4260	4120.8	$4d[\tfrac{1}{2}]_1^o-5p[\tfrac{3}{2}]_1$	n	
2.5234	3961.9	$4d[\tfrac{1}{2}]_1^o-5p[\tfrac{3}{2}]_2$	u, y	
2.626*	3808*	Uncertain	p	
2.8655	3488.8	$6p[\tfrac{5}{2}]_3-6s[\tfrac{3}{2}]_2^o$	p	Other alternative possible.
2.9870	3346.9	$6p'[\tfrac{3}{2}]_1-6s'[\tfrac{1}{2}]_0^o$	p	Other alternative possible.
3.0528	3274.8	$6p'[\tfrac{3}{2}]_1-5d[\tfrac{5}{2}]_2^o$	p	
3.0664	3260.3	$6p[\tfrac{1}{2}]_1-6s[\tfrac{3}{2}]_2^o$	p, u	
3.1506	3173.1	$6p'[\tfrac{1}{2}]_0-5d[\tfrac{3}{2}]_1^o$	p	
3.3410	2992.3	$4d[\tfrac{1}{2}]_1^o-5p[\tfrac{1}{2}]_0$	p, u	
3.4671	2883.5	$7s[\tfrac{3}{2}]_1^o-6p[\tfrac{1}{2}]_1$	p	
3.4874	2866.7	$6p'[\tfrac{1}{2}]_1-7s[\tfrac{3}{2}]_2^o$	p	Term. level possibly $5d[\tfrac{3}{2}]_1^o$.
4.3736	2285.8	$5d[\tfrac{3}{2}]_1^o-6p[\tfrac{3}{2}]_2$	p, u	
4.8820	2047.8	$5d[\tfrac{5}{2}]_2^o-6p[\tfrac{5}{2}]_3$	p	Other alternative possible.
5.2985	1886.8	$5d[\tfrac{3}{2}]_1^o-6p[\tfrac{1}{2}]_0$	p	Other alternative possible.
5.5686	1795.3	$5d[\tfrac{7}{2}]_3^o-6p[\tfrac{5}{2}]_2$	p	
5.5848	1790.1	$6d[\tfrac{7}{2}]_4^o-4f[\tfrac{9}{2}]_5$	p, u	
5.6291	1776.0	$6d[\tfrac{3}{2}]_2^o-4f[\tfrac{5}{2}]_3$	p, u	
7.0561	1416.8	$4f[\tfrac{7}{2}]_{3(4)}-5d[\tfrac{7}{2}]_4^o$	p	

Lines of Xe I observed in stimulated emission

λ_{air} microns	σ cm^{-1}	Transition Racah Notation	References	Notes
1.7326	5770.2	$5d[\tfrac{3}{2}]_1^o-6p[\tfrac{5}{2}]_2$	z	
2.0262	4933.9	$5d[\tfrac{3}{2}]_1^o-6p[\tfrac{3}{2}]_1$	l, y, A	Strong line.
2.3193	4310.4	$5d[\tfrac{5}{2}]_3^o-6p[\tfrac{5}{2}]_2$	e, y	
2.4825	4027.2	$5d[\tfrac{5}{2}]_3^o-6p[\tfrac{5}{2}]_3$	z	
2.6269	3805.8	$5d[\tfrac{5}{2}]_2^o-6p[\tfrac{5}{2}]_2$	e, y, A	Strong line.
2.6511	3771.0	$5d[\tfrac{3}{2}]_1^o-6p[\tfrac{1}{2}]_0$	e, y, A	Strong line.
2.6601	3758.2	$5d'[\tfrac{3}{2}]_1^o-6p'[\tfrac{1}{2}]_0$	B	
3.1069	3217.8	$5d[\tfrac{5}{2}]_3^o-6p[\tfrac{3}{2}]_2$	e, y, A	Strong line.
3.2739	3053.6	$5d[\tfrac{3}{2}]_2^o-6p[\tfrac{1}{2}]_1$	n, A	Strong line.
3.3667	2969.5	$5d[\tfrac{5}{2}]_2^o-6p[\tfrac{3}{2}]_1$	e, y, A	Strong line.
3.4335	2911.7	$7p[\tfrac{5}{2}]_2-7s[\tfrac{3}{2}]_1^o$	p	
3.5070	2850.7	$5d[\tfrac{7}{2}]_3^o-6p[\tfrac{5}{2}]_2$	e, y, A	Strongest line.
3.6209	2761.0	$5d'[\tfrac{3}{2}]_2^o-7p[\tfrac{3}{2}]_2$	B	
3.6509	2738.3	$7p[\tfrac{1}{2}]_1-7s[\tfrac{3}{2}]_2^o$	p	
3.6788	2717.5	$5d[\tfrac{1}{2}]_1^o-6p[\tfrac{1}{2}]_1$	e, y	
3.6848	2713.1	$5d[\tfrac{5}{2}]_2^o-6p[\tfrac{3}{2}]_2$	e, y	
3.8686	2584.2	$5d'[\tfrac{5}{2}]_3^o-6p'[\tfrac{3}{2}]_2$	B	
3.8939	2567.4	$5d[\tfrac{7}{2}]_3^o-6p[\tfrac{5}{2}]_3$	e, y	
3.9956	2502.1	$5d[\tfrac{1}{2}]_0^o-6p[\tfrac{1}{2}]_1$	e, y	

Lines of Xe I (continued)

λ_{air} microns	σ cm^{-1}	Transition Racah Notation	References	Notes
4.1516	2408.1	$5d'[\tfrac{5}{2}]_2{}^o-7p[\tfrac{3}{2}]_1$	B	
4.5381	2203.0	$5d[\tfrac{3}{2}]_2{}^o-6p[\tfrac{5}{2}]_2$	w	Strong line.
4.6097	2168.8	$5d'[\tfrac{3}{2}]_2{}^o-6p'[\tfrac{1}{2}]_1$	B	
5.3551	1866.9	$5d[\tfrac{1}{2}]_1{}^o-6p[\tfrac{5}{2}]_2$?	w	$\Delta k = 2$!
5.5739	1793.6	$5d[\tfrac{7}{2}]_4{}^o-6p[\tfrac{5}{2}]_3$	e, y	Strongest line.
7.3147	1366.7	$5d[\tfrac{3}{2}]_2{}^o-6p[\tfrac{3}{2}]_1$	e, y	
9.0040	1110.3	$5d[\tfrac{3}{2}]_2{}^o-6p[\tfrac{3}{2}]_2$	e, y	
9.700	1030.6	$5d[\tfrac{1}{2}]_1{}^o-6p[\tfrac{3}{2}]_1$	y	
11.296	885.04	$5d'[\tfrac{5}{2}]_3{}^o-4f[\tfrac{9}{2}]_4$?	p	
12.263	815.26	$5d[\tfrac{1}{2}]_0{}^o-6p[\tfrac{3}{2}]_1$	y	
12.913	774.18	$5d[\tfrac{1}{2}]_1{}^o-6p[\tfrac{3}{2}]_2$	y	
18.500	540.38	$5d'[\tfrac{3}{2}]_2{}^o-4f[\tfrac{5}{2}]_3$	p	

REFERENCES TO TABLE A.2

a. Bridges and Chester, *Appl. Optics* **4**, 573–580, 1965.
b. White and Rigden, *Appl. Phys. Lett.* **2**, 211, 1963.
c. Bloom, *Appl. Phys. Lett.* **2**, 101, 1963.
d. White and Rigden, *Proc. IRE* **50**, 1697, 1962.
e. Bennett, *Appl. Optics Suppl.* **1**, 24, 1962.
f. Javan et al., *Phys. Rev. Lett.* **6**, 106, 1961.
g. Cagnard et al., *Compt. Rend.* **257**, 1044, 1963.
h. Agobian et al., *Compt. Rend.* **257**, 3844, 1963.
i. McFarlane et al., *Proc. IEEE* **51**, 468, 1963.
j. Rosenberger, *Phys. Lett.* **9**, 29, 1964.
k. Smiley, *Appl. Phys. Lett.* **4**, 123, 1964.
l. Patel et al., *Phys. Rev. Lett.* **9**, 102, 1962.
m. Gerritsen and Goedertier, *Appl. Phys. Lett.* **4**, 20, 1964.
n. Otto et al., *Compt. Rend.* **258**, 2779, 1964.
o. Agobian et al., *Compt. Rend.* **258**, 3661, 1964.
p. Faust et al., *Phys. Rev.* **133**, A1477. 1964.
q. Bloom et al., *Appl. Optics* **2**, 317, 1963.
r. Patel et al., *Appl. Phys. Lett.* **4**, 18, 1964.
s. Patel et al., *Proc. IEEE* **52**, 713, 1964.
t. Agobian, *Compt. Rend.* **259**, 323, 1964.
u. McMullin, *Appl. Optics* **3**, 641, 1964.
v. McFarlane et al., *Proc. IEEE* **52**, 318, 1964.
w. Brunet and Laures, *Phys. Lett.* **12**, 106, 1964.
x. Bennett and Knudson, *Proc. IEEE* **52**, 861, 1964.
y. Faust et al., *Appl. Phys. Lett.* **1**, 85, 1962.
z. Courville et al., *J. Appl. Phys.* **35**, 2547, 1964.
A. Walter and Jarrett, *Appl. Optics* **3**, 789, 1964.
B. McFarlane et al., *Quantum Electronics III*, 584, 1964.
C. Agobian et al., *J. Phys. Radium* **25**, 887, 1964.
D. Zitter, *J. Appl. Phys.* **35**, 3070, 1964.

Author Index

Aagard, R. L., 105, 109
Abella, I. D., 97, 177, 215, 221, 266, 278
Ackerman, J. A., 23
Adelman, A. H., 278
der Agobian, R., 177, 201, 206, 300
Ainsley, N., 158
Alire, R. M., 166
Armand, M., 213
Armstrong, J. A., 276
Arnold, C. B., 23
Asawa, C. K., 67, 101
Ashburn, E. V., 7
Ashby, D. E. T. F., 282, 283, 284
Axe, J. D., 145, 157

Ballik, E. A., 200, 201
Ballman, A. A., 134
Bardeen, J., 153
Barnard, G., 234
Basov, N. G., 1, 2, 136, 141, 153, 156, 157, 158, 188, 190, 191, 234
Bass, M., 265
Becrelle, J., 201
Bell, W. E., 192, 201, 213
Belousova, I. M., 201
Bennett, Jr., W. R., 55, 57, 177, 180, 183, 191, 195, 200, 201, 206, 209, 212, 300
Beran, M. J., 29
Bergstein, L., 76, 83
Berkley, D. A., 93, 97
Bernal, E., 228
Bernard, M., 141, 157
Bertolotti, M., 96
Bessis, M., 291
Bevacqua, S. F., 157
Bhaumik, M. L., 167
Biernson, G., 287
Birnbaum, G., 48, 82, 83, 88, 89
Bloembergen, N., 6, 261, 276, 277

Bloom, A. L., 192, 201, 213, 300
Bobroff, D. L., 207
Bockasten, K., 210, 212, 213
Boeckner, C., 169
Bogdankevich, O. V., 158
Bonch-Bruevich, A. M., 134
Bond, W. L., 129, 135, 200, 201
Born, M., 12, 23, 29, 261
Bortfeld, D. P., 235, 272
Bowen, D. E., 135
Bowness, C., 109
Boyd, G. D., 78, 79, 80, 83, 135, 136, 217, 221
Boyle, W. S., 57, 110, 112, 228
Boyne, H. S., 266
Bozeman, W. R., 14
Bradley, L. T., 277, 278
Brangaccio, D. J., 201
Braslau, N., 265
Brecher, C., 166, 167
Breinin, G. M., 292
Bret, G., 233, 235
Bridges, W. B., 204, 206, 207, 210, 300
Brophy, V. A., 167
Brunet, H., 300
Burns, G., 6, 144, 145, 150, 157, 158
Butayeva, F. A., 169, 177

Cagnard, R., 177, 201, 206, 300
Carlson, J. P., 83
Carlson, R. O., 144
Carmichael, C. H., 235
Chang, N. C., 129, 135
Chasmar, R. P., 23
Chen, D., 228
Cheo, P. K., 213
Cheroff, G., 157
Chester, A. N., 206, 207, 210, 300
Chizhikova, Z. A., 95, 97

Ciftan, M., 23, 97, 103, 109, 221, 228
Coleman, C. D., 14
Collins, R. J., 94, 95, 97, 229, 234
Connes, P., 77, 83
Convert, G., 213
Cook, H. D., 284
Cook, J. J., 23
Cooper, H. G., 213
Courville, G. E., 300
Crosby, G. A., 163, 164, 166
Crosswhite, H. M., 115, 116, 134
Cummins, H. Z., 97, 177, 283, 284

Damon, E. K., 16, 23
Dana, L., 205, 207
Danielson, Jr., G. E., 235
Danilov, O. B., 201
Davis, Jr., D. T. M., 281, 284
Debever, J. M., 157, 158
Debye, P. P., 23
De Kinder, Jr., R. E., 135
De Maria, A. J., 233, 234, 235
De Mars, G., 222, 223, 224, 225, 226, 228, 238
Devlin, G. E., 102, 103, 106, 108, 109
D'Haenens, I. J., 67, 101
Di Domenico, M., 97, 109
Dieke, G. H., 115, 116, 134
Dietz, R. E., 160
Dousmanis, G. C., 158
Ducuing, J., 276
Dumke, W. P., 142, 157
Duncan, R. C., 130, 135, 136
Dunlap, A. K., 6
Duraffourg, G., 141, 157

Echard, R., 177, 201, 206
Eckhardt, G., 270, 271, 272
Elkina, I. A., 201
Ellis, A. T., 283, 284
Eltgroth, P., 109
Engeler, W. E., 147, 148, 149, 157
Engstrom, R. W., 23
Etzel, H. W., 130, 131, 135
Evtuhov, V., 11, 67, 95, 97, 101, 111, 112, 221

Fabrikant, V. A., 169, 170, 177
Fain, V. M., 277

Faust, W. L., 177, 183, 195, 201, 203, 206, 209, 212, 300
Fenner, G. E., 144, 151, 157
Feofilov, P. P., 125, 134, 135
Fergason, J. L., 23
Fine, S., 290, 291
Fiocco, G., 287
Flowers, W. L., 23
Flynn, J. T., 16, 23
Fourney, M. E., 283, 284
Fowles, G. R., 210, 212
Fox, A. G., 72, 73, 77, 80, 83, 197
Franken, P. A., 6, 255, 261, 265
Fried, D. L., 109

Gagosz, R., 234
Galanin, M. D., 95, 97
Gallagher, C. C., 157
Gandy, H. W., 129, 130, 131, 135
Garavaglia, M., 213
Garfinkel, M., 147, 148, 149, 157
Garmire, E., 277
Garrett, C. G. B., 127, 128, 129, 135, 203, 206, 277, 278
Geller, M., 235, 272
Gerritsen, H. J., 201, 300
Gillilland, L. E., 284
Ginther, R. J., 129, 130, 131, 135
Giordmaine, J. A., 262, 265
Gires, F., 233, 235, 291
Goedertier, P. V., 201, 300
Goldsborough, J. P., 278
Goldstein, B. S., 157, 158
Gordon, E. I., 195, 196, 201, 204, 206, 207
Gordon, J. P., 5, 6, 78, 79, 83
Goryushko, A. G., 167
Gould, G., 170, 177
Grivet, P., 6
Grudzinski, R., 201
Guggenheim, H. J., 160
a la Guillaume, C. B., 157, 158
Göppert-Mayer, M., 277

Hall, R. N., 144, 145, 157
Ham, W. T., 291, 292
Hanes, G. R., 97
Hansen, J. R., 23
Hardwick, D. L., 96, 109
Healy, M. K., 284
Heavens, O. S., 177

Hellwarth, R. W., 83, 229, 230, 234, 235, 240, 251, 270, 271, 272
Herriott, D. R., 55, 57, 191, 197, 198, 200, 201, 221
Herzberg, G., 38
Hill, A. E., 265
Holonyak, N., 157
Horrigan, F. A., 210, 212, 213
Hoskins, R. H., 67, 101, 122, 134, 235
Hughes, T. P., 97
Hurwitz, C. E., 157, 158

Isaenko, V. I., 134

Jacobs, S., 170, 177
Jarrett, S. M., 300
Jaseja, T. S., 201, 284
Javan, A., 1, 2, 55, 56, 57, 191, 198, 199, 200, 201, 269, 271, 284, 300
Jensen, R. C., 210, 212
Jephcott, D. F., 282, 283, 284
Johansson, I., 294
Johnson, L. F., 6, 119, 121, 125, 127, 134, 135, 136, 159, 160
Jones, F. E., 23

Kafalas, P., 235
Kaiser, W., 127, 128, 129, 135, 277, 278
Kamal, A. K., 7
Kappany, N. S., 292
Kariss, Ya. E., 125, 134, 135
Keck, P. H., 135
Kemble, E. C., 38
Keyes, R. J., 157, 158
Khokhlov, R. V., 277
Kingsley, J. D., 144, 151, 157
Kisliuk, P. P., 57, 83, 229, 234
Kiss, Z. J., 130, 135, 136
Kittel, C., 137
Klein, E., 290, 291
Kleinman, D. A., 83, 223, 228, 278
Knable, N., 177, 283, 284
Knudson, J. W., 300
Kogelnik, H., 80, 83, 201, 217, 219, 221
Koozekanani, S., 23, 97, 221
Korobkin, V. V., 223, 228
Koster, G. F., 183
Kotik, J., 75, 83
Kriukov, P. G., 234

Krokhin, O. N., 141, 156, 157, 158, 188, 190, 191
Kruse, P. W., 18, 23
Krutchkoff, A., 23, 97, 221
Kulchintskii, V. A., 167

Labuda, E. F., 204, 206, 207
Lankard, J. R., 135, 145, 157
Laures, P., 205, 207, 300
Lax, B., 2, 136, 153, 158
Lempicki, A., 165, 166, 167
Lengyel, B. A., 7, 213, 246, 248, 251
Leontovich, A. M., 95, 97
Levitt, R. S., 158
Lewis, H. R., 135
Li, T., 23, 72, 73, 77, 80, 83, 109, 197
Lopez, F. O., 213
Luck, C. F., 109, 228
Lucy, R. F., 287
Lundholm, T., 213
Lyons, H., 167
Lyubimov, V. V., 134

Macek, W. M., 281, 284
Maiman, T. H., 1, 4, 49, 57, 61, 64, 66, 67, 90, 99, 101
Maker, P. D., 257, 258, 260, 261, 262, 264, 265
Makhov, G., 223, 228
Malt, R. A., 292
Marsh, O. J., 167
Martin, W. C., 266
Martinot-Lagarde, P., 213
Masters, J. I., 235
Mathias, L. E. S., 213
Mauer, P. B., 135
Maurer, R. D., 135
May, A. D., 106, 109
Mayer, G., 291
McClung, F. J., 101, 102, 230, 234, 251, 272
McClure, D. S., 38
McCormick, J. J., 136
McCumber, D. E., 159, 160
McFarlane, R. A., 177, 183, 195, 201, 203, 206, 209, 210, 212, 213, 300
McGlauchlin, L. D., 18, 23
McGowan, J. W., 177
McKenna, J., 106, 109
McMullin, P. G., 300

McMurtry, B. J., 93, 97
McNary, W. F., 284
McQuistan, R. B., 18, 23
Mead, S. P., 83
Meggers, W. F., 14
Melngailis, I., 158
Menat, M., 248, 249, 251
Merrill, H. J., 287
Merry, R. W., 7
Meyers, F. J., 101, 102
Mielenz, K. D., 284
Miller, R. C., 262, 265
Minck, R. W., 272
Minnhagen, L., 210
Missio, D., 109
Mitchell, A. C. G., 40, 48
Moore, C. E., 14, 179, 180, 182, 183, 294
Morantz, D. J., 167
Morse, J. H., 287
Mueller, C. W., 158
Mueller, L., 134
Murray, E. M. E., 235
Murray, J., 284
Muzii, L., 96

Nasledov, D. N., 157
Nassau, K., 134, 135, 136
Nathan, M. I., 6, 144, 145, 150, 157, 158, 265
Neeland, J. K., 95, 97, 111, 112, 221
Nelson, D. F., 94, 97, 110, 112, 228
Nelson, H., 158
Neumann, J. von, 153
Newstein, M. C., 75, 83
Ng, W. K., 270, 271
Nisenoff, M., 257, 261, 265
Nomarski, G., 291

Okaya, A., 23
Otto, J. L., 177, 201, 206, 300

Paananen, R. A., 207, 210, 212, 213
Paillette, M., 201
Pandarese, F., 277
Pantell, R. H., 97
Parker, J. T., 213
Parrent, G. B., 29
Patel, C. K. N., 177, 193, 201, 203, 206, 209, 212, 213, 300

Peppers, N. A., 292
Pershan, P. S., 261, 276
Peters, C. W., 265
Peticolas, W. L., 278
Pettit, G. D., 135
Phelan, R. J., 158
Pilkuhn, M., 158
Platonenko, V. T., 277
Polanyi, T. G., 221
Pollack, S. A., 135
Popov, Yu. M., 141, 156, 157, 158
Porto, S. P. S., 133, 134, 136, 271
Prather, J. L., 38
Pressley, R. J., 165, 167
Price, J. F., 6
Prokhorov, A. M., 1

Quist, T. M., 157

Rabinowitz, P., 170, 177
Rado, W. G., 272
Ready, J. F., 96, 109, 228
Rediker, R. H., 158
Redmann, J. J., 135
Reed, C. F., 292
Rempel, R. C., 192, 201
Rieckhoff, K. E., 278
Rigden, J. D., 191, 196, 201, 210, 211, 212, 300
Rigrod, W. W., 201, 219, 221
Rogachev, A. A., 157
Rogala, T., 109
Rosan, R. C., 284
Rosenberger, D., 201, 300
Rupprecht, H., 158
Ryvkin, S. M., 157

Samelson, H., 165, 166, 167
Sanders, J. H., 1
Sarles, L. R., 102
Savage, A., 262, 265
Savage, C. M., 257, 261, 262, 264, 265
Schachter, H., 76, 83
Schawlow, A. L., 1, 5, 55, 57, 84, 88, 89, 97, 100, 101, 102, 103, 106, 109
Schelkunoff, S. A., 83
Schimitschek, E. J., 165, 167
Schuldt, S. B., 105, 109
Schwarz, S. E., 101, 102, 284

Scott, R. E., 290, 291
Sette, D., 96
Shafer, C. G., 109, 228
Shen, Y. R., 277
Shitova, E. I., 7
Silbertrust, N., 292
Silver, S., 83
Simms, S. D., 23, 109
Simpson, G. N., 235
Singer, J. R., 6
Singh, S., 277, 278
Sinnett, D. M., 223, 228
Smiley, V. N., 300
Smith, A. W., 265
Smith, G. F., 283, 284, 287
Smith, R. A., 23
Smullin, L. D., 287
Snitzer, E., 123, 124, 134
Soden, R. R., 135, 136
Soffer, B. H., 122, 134, 235
Solomon, R., 134
Soltys, T. J., 144
Sooy, W. R., 235, 272
Sorokin, P. P., 2, 53, 57, 113, 127, 131, 134, 135, 145, 157, 228
Spencer, K. J., 6
Statz, H., 109, 183, 213, 222, 223, 224, 225, 226, 228, 238
Stebbings, R. F., 177
Stephens, R. B., 284
Stern, F., 157
Stevenson, M. J., 2, 53, 57, 113, 127, 131, 134, 135, 228
Stickley, C. M., 216, 221
Stitch, M. L., 287
Stoicheff, B. P., 97, 272, 278
Sturge, M. D., 146, 157
Summer, W., 23
Suzuki, C. K., 167
Svelto, O., 97, 109

Tandy, P. C., 157
Tang, C. L., 75, 83, 210, 212, 213, 225, 226, 228
Telk, C. L., 167
Teller, E., 153
Terhune, R. W., 257, 261, 262, 263, 264, 265, 272
Thomas, R. A., 134

Title, R. S., 136
Tittel, F. K., 292
Townes, C. H., 1, 5, 6, 84, 88, 89, 97, 170, 177, 201, 215, 221, 277, 281, 284, 292
Triebwasser, S., 157
Tsarenkov, B. V., 157

Uspensky, A., 223, 228

Van Vleck, J. H., 46, 48
Vanyukov, M. P., 134
Verber, C. M., 278
Volfson, N. S., 7
Voloshin, V. A., 167
Vuylsteke, A. A., 248, 251

Wagner, W. G., 82, 83, 88, 89, 246, 248, 251
Walter, W. T., 300
Wang, C. C., 247, 251
Ward, J. F., 6, 255, 261, 265
Watson, W. R., 221
Weaver, J. N., 97
Weber, H., 228
Weber, J., 1
Weinreich, G., 265
Weiser, K., 158
Weisskopf, V. F., 46, 48
Welch, J. D., 157, 158
Wentz, J. L., 109
Whan, R. E., 163, 164, 166
White, A. D., 191, 195, 196, 200, 201, 210, 211, 212, 300
White, B. G., 167
White, C. E., 135
Wieder, I., 102
Williams, D. L., 289
Williams, R. C., 292
Wilson, D. T., 228
Winston, H., 167
Witt, P. N., 292
Wittke, J. P., 101, 136
Wolf, E., 12, 23, 29, 261
Wolff, N. E., 165, 167
Wolga, G. J., 93, 97
Wood, D. L., 127, 128, 135, 271
Woodbury, E. J., 270, 271, 287
Wright, A. J. C., 167

Yajima, T., 269, 270, 271
Yariv, A., 6, 133, 134, 135, 136
Yashchin, E. G., 277
Yeh, Y., 283, 284
Young, C. G., 135
Young, K. M., 97

Zaret, M. M., 292
Zeiger, H. J., 5
Zemansky, M. W., 40, 48
Zitter, R. N., 300
Zuev, V. S., 234

Subject Index

Absorption, 29, 40
  coefficient, 57
  cross section, 43
  in neodymium ions, 125
  in rare earth ions, 117
  in ruby, 99
  in semiconductors, 151
  line, 40
  negative, 43, 140
  spectrum of ruby, 99
Amplification of radiation, 43, 47
Amplifier, laser, 57, 287
Anti-Stokes lines, 266, 276
Applications of lasers, 279–292
Argon, energy levels, 179
  lasers, 203, 298
Atomic constants, 13
Atomic energy levels, 29
  see also specific materials, e.g., Neon energy levels
Axial modes, 69

Basov-Krokhin diagram, 190
Beamwidth of radiation pattern, 79, 94
Beating of optical frequencies, 198, 216, 219
Benzophenone-naphthalene system, 166
Benzoylacetonate, 162
Bibliography of lasers, 4
Biological applications, 289–292
Black-body radiation, 9, 51, 63
Bleachable-absorber switch, 233
Bohr's frequency relation, 29
Boltzmann's law, 38, 65

Calibration of detectors, 19
Calorimeters, 16
Carbon lasers, 209
Cavity modes, 69

Cells, destruction by laser light, 290
Cesium, excitation with He light, 169
  laser, 170
Charge compensation in ionic crystals, 121
Chelate, 162
  laser, 165
Chlorine lasers, 210
Chromium concentration in ruby, 90, 102
Chromium ion spectrum, 97
Cobalt laser, 159
Coherence, 23–29
  length, 27, 257, 280
  of laser output, 93, 95, 215, 295
Colidar rangefinder, 286
Collision broadening, 45
Communications applications, 284
Competition of modes, 80, 221
Composite lasers, 106–109
Confocal interferometer, 77, 216
Corrections for wavelength measurements in air, 293
Crystal field effects in spectroscopy, 34, 98, 158
Cw ruby lasers, 109
Cyclotron resonance scheme, 153
Cylindrical resonator modes, 70

Degeneracy of atomic energy levels, 29
Degenerate distribution of carriers, 143
De Maria's Q-switch, 232
Destruction of cells, 290
Detached retina operation, 290
Detailed balance principle, 184
Detectors, radiation, 15
Dibenzoylmethide, 162
Diffraction loss of Fabry-Perot modes, 74, 82
Direct transitions in semiconductors, 141
Dissociative excitation, 176, 207

Doppler broadening, 44
Drilling with lasers, 287
Dysprosium laser, 129

Efficiency, of excitation, 105
of neodymium laser, 124
of ruby lasers, 96, 112
of semiconductor lasers, 149
Einstein's relations, 31
Electric dipole radiation, 35
Electric field and power, 13, 234
Electric impulse scheme, 155
Electro-optical Q-switch, 230
Electron density measurements, 282
Elliptic cylinders as reflectors, 103
Emission of radiation, spontaneous, 30
stimulated, 30
Energy levels of atoms, Ar, 179
Cs, 170
He, 37, 192
Ne, 172, 178, 182, 192
Energy levels of ions, Cr^{3+}, 52, 98
Eu^{3+}, 165
Pr^{3+}, 119
Sm^{2+}, 128
trivalent rare earths, 116
U^{3+}, 132, 133
Energy levels of semiconductors, 137, 141
Energy output of lasers, 96, 124
see also individual lasers
Energy utilization in giant pulse, 241
Erbium laser, 130
Eu^{3+} energy levels, 165
Europium chelate laser, 165
Europium lasers, chelate, 165
crystalline, 129
Excess pump power, 226
Excitation of lasers, gas lasers, 168–177
ruby laser, 90, 103–109
semiconductor lasers, 143, 153–157
see also specific lasers
Eye surgery, 290

Fabry-Perot interferometer, 20, 71, 221
Fast switching, 235
Fermi-Dirac distribution, 137
Fermi level, 137
Field distribution in laser modes, 72, 77, 217–221
Flashlamps for laser excitation, 90

Fluctuations of laser output, 91, 123, 215, 221–226
Fluid-state lasers, 161–167
Forbidden transitions, 36
Four-level solid lasers, 53, 112–136
Free carrier absorption, 151
Frequency conversion, 261–265
Frequency pulling, 81
Frequency stability of a He-Ne laser, 199
Fresnel number, 73
Füchtbauer-Ladenburg formula, 42

Gadolinium laser, 129
Gallium arsenide laser, 142
Gas lasers, 54, 168–213
Gaussian lineshape, 46, 61
Giant pulse, 228–251
applications, 285
techniques, 228–234
theory, 235–251

Halogen lasers, 209
Harmonic generation, 254–265
Health hazards, 291
Helium lasers, 202, 294
Helium-neon lasers, 172–175, 191–201
Hellwarth-McClung pulsing scheme, 230
History of discoveries, 1, 4, 153
Hole burning, 225
Holmium laser, 130
Homogeneous broadening, 44

Illumination by lasers, 283
Index of refraction measurements, 282
Indirect transitions in semiconductors, 141
Indium phosphide laser, 152
Inhomogeneous broadening, 46
Integrated absorption cross section, 43
Interference of light, 24
Interferometer, confocal, spherical, 77
Fabry-Perot, 20
Interferometer modes, see Modes
Interferometry, 280
Iodine lasers, 210
Ionic lasers, 205
Irradiation of body tissue, 290

Javan's gas laser, 55
j-j coupling, 34

Kerr-cell shutter, 230
Krypton lasers, 203, 298

Lambert's law, 9
Laser, definition of, 3
  history of, 1, 4, 153
Laser amplifier, 57, 287
Laser applications, see Applications, also
  specific types
Lasers, see specific types, e.g., Ruby
Lifetime of atomic level, 31
Lifetime of a photon in a laser, 237
Lineshape, 44–47
Linewidth formula, 88
Linewidth theory, 44, 83–89
Liquid crystal viewer, 15
Longitudinal modes, 69
Lorentz lineshape, 45, 60
L-S coupling, 33

Maser, 1
  optical, 2
Mechanical Q-switch, 229, 232
Medical applications, 289
Mercury lasers, 210
Metastable state, 38
Michelson interferometer, 25
Michelson-Morley experiment, 281
Mixing of frequencies, 198, 216, 219, 255,
  260, 263
Mode, density, 71
  excitation, 226
  interaction, 80
  separation, 68, 216
  theory, 67–71
Modes, of a gas laser, 197, 217
  of a ruby laser, 216
  of a semiconductor laser, 146
  of oscillation, 67, 214
Modulation of laser light, 285
Molecular lasers, 212
Monochromatic radiation, 23
Moon, ranging on, 286
Multiple photon absorption, 277
Multiplicity of atomic levels, 29

Negative absorption, 43, 140, 168–177
Negative temperature, 43
Neodymium laser, 119–127
Neon energy levels, 172, 178, 182, 192

Neon lasers, 56, 172, 191–206, 294
Nickel laser, 159
Nitrogen lasers, 209, 212
Noble gas ions, 181
Noble gas lasers, 201–207, 294
Noble gases, laser lines, 294–300
  spectroscopy, 177–183
Nonlinear phenomena, 252–278
Nonlinear polarization of dielectric, 254
N-type semiconductor, 138

Optical excitation, 63, 90, 103, 161, 170
Optical maser, 2
Optical ranging, 285
Oxygen lasers, 176, 208

Pair coupling, 178
Parametric amplification, 260, 272
Parity of atomic state, 36
Parity rule, 36, 278
Partial coherence, 27
Paschen symbols, 179, 294
Passive Q-switch, 233
Phonon-terminated lasers, 158
Photocathodes, spectral response of, 17
Photoconductive sensors, 17
Photoelectric effects, 16
Photographic applications, 283
Photomultiplier, 16
Photovoltaic effect, 18
Piezoelectric crystals, 264
Planck's law of radiation, 9
Plasma physics applications, 282
P-n junction, 138
P-n junction lasers, 142
Polarization, electric, 252
  nonlinear, 254, 272
  tensor, 255, 262
Polarization of laser output, 94, 151, 197
Population inversion, 40, 47, 140, 168–177
Power output of lasers, see specific lasers
  and Giant pulse
Praseodymium laser, 119
Principle of detailed balance, 184
P-type semiconductor, 138
Pulsations of laser output, 91, 221–224
Pulse, giant, see Giant pulse
Pulse transmission mode, 249
Pumping, see Excitation

Q-switching, 230, 236, 248
Quantum efficiency of photodetector, 16
Quantum numbers, 32
Quasi-Fermi levels, 140
Quasi-monochromatic radiation, 23

Racah's symbols, 178, 294
Radiation detectors, 14–19
Radiation pattern, of gas laser, 197, 218
    of ruby laser, 94, 216
Radiative flux, 9
Raman effect, 266–272
    stimulated, 269
Raman laser, 270
Rangefinder, optical, 286
Rare earth, elements, 113
    ions, 115
    lasers, 117–131
Rate equations, four-level laser, 66
    three-level laser, 61
Rayleigh scattering, 266, 283
Refraction in uniaxial crystals, 259
Refractive index of air, 13
Regular pulsations, 224
Relativity, test of, 281
Resonant transfer of energy, 171, 202
Retina, reattachment of, 290
Retinal damage, 291
Rotation sensor, 281
Ruby, absorption spectrum of, 99
    composition of, 90
    fluorescence of, 99
    spectroscopy of, 97
Ruby laser, 49–52, 90–96, 101, 109, 230,
    249
    cw operation, 109
    efficiency, 96
    giant pulse, 230
    in satellite lines, 102
    output, 95
    polarization, 94
    radiation pattern, 94
    spectrum, 92, 101
Russell-Saunders coupling, 33

Safety problems, 291
Samarium laser, 127
Schawlow-Townes linewidth formula, 88

Second harmonic generation, 254
    at an interface, 261
    in applied electric field, 263
    in crystals, 256
Selection rules, spectroscopic, 36
Self-reproducing configurations, 72
Semiconductor lasers, 54, 136–158
Semiconductor-mirror switch, 234
Semiconductor physics, 137
Single-mode laser, 227
Space communications applications, 284
Spectroscopic applications, 283
Spectroscopic nomenclature, 32, 179
Spectroscopy of noble gases, 177–183
Spectroscopy of ruby, 97–101
Spherical reflectors, 77
Spontaneous emission, 30, 36
Spontaneous transition probability, 30
Stability of the gas laser, 199
Standing waves in lasers, 67, 222
Statz-De Mars equations, 222, 238
Stefan-Boltzmann law, 10
Stimulated emission 30, 225
Stimulated Raman effect, 269
Stokes lines in Raman spectroscopy, 266,
    276
Sulfur lasers, 209

Temperature dependence of laser spec-
    trum, 101, 122, 132, 148
Terms (spectroscopic), 33
Test of relativity, 281
Third harmonic generation, 261, 264
Three-level laser, 52, 61
Three-photon absorption, 277
Threshold condition, 57–60, 102, 183
Threshold current in semiconductors, 150
Threshold excitation energies, 49, 96, 103,
    109
    see also individual lasers
Thulium laser, 130
Transition probabilities (rates), 30
Transition rates in ruby, 64
Transmission of information by lasers, 284
Transverse modes, 69
Traveling wave laser, 227
Trumpet-shaped laser, 110
Two-photon absorption, 277

Ultrasonic Q-switch, 232
Units, spectroscopic, 12
Uranium laser, 131

Van Cittert-Zernike theorem, 28
Velocity measurements, 281
Visibility of interference fringes, 27

Wavelength corrections for air, 293
Wavelength tables, common neon lasers, 191
    miscellaneous gases, 209–212
    noble gas atoms, 294–300
    rare earth and actinide materials, 117

Wavelength variation with temperature, *see* Temperature
Wavelengths of lasers, *see* specific materials
Wavenumber, 12
Welding with lasers, 287
Wien's displacement law, 10

Xenon lasers, 203, 299

Ytterbium laser, 130